THE SECRET

HISTORY OF THE SWORD

Adventures in Ancient Martial Arts

J. CHRISTOPH AMBERGER

DISCLAIMER

Please note that the author and publisher of this book are NOT RESPONSIBLE in any manner whatsoever for any injury that may result from practicing the techniques and/or following the instructions given within. Since the physical activities described herein may be too strenuous in nature for some readers to engage in safely, it is essential that a physician be consulted prior to training.

First published in 1996 by Hammerterz Forum

Revised and expanded edition published in 1999 by Multi-Media Books, Inc., a division of Multi-Media Communications Network, Inc.

Library of Congress Cataloging Number: 98-68617

ISBN: 1-892515-04-0

Distributed by:
Unique Publications
4201 Vanowen Place
Burbank, CA 91505
(800) 332-3330

First edition
05 04 03 02 01 00 99 98 97 1 3 5 7 9 10 8 6 4 2

Printed in the United States of America

"(The fight in hot blood) appertains to all ages, and will no doubt endure until at least man has been civilized out of all manhood."

Ted Huber

There's only one reason why people sit down to write a book. And don't let anyone tell you anything else. All we want to do is see our name in print—to claim our own little bit of immortality.

I'd like to dedicate this book especially to those people in my little world who I care most about being remembered by: My wife Joanna, and my sons Max and Sebastian. All others will have to wait for my next magnum opus.

I thank some fellow fencers and fighters for their input, inspiration, and guidance:

Dr. Pit Pieper.
The late Prof. Dr. Herbert Lüthy.
Rainer Köbelin.
S. Matthew Galas.
Nick Evangelista.
Dr. William Gaugler.

Daniel Frisch.
Dr. Martin Knof.
Malcolm Fare.
Kim Roether.
Stephen Hand.
Didier Pallanca.

TABLE OF CONTENTS

Hans Baldung Grien, "Fencing Landsknechte" (1516)

"Lernt fechten in den Wehren,
Im Spieß, Degen und Schwert,
Kommt eim zu Nutz und Ehren
Wer solche Künste lehrt."

anonymous German
Landsknecht, 1545

(Learn how to fence with all weapons,
with pike, rapier, and sword.
It will be of benefit and honor to
him who teaches these arts.)

PRELUDE

COMBAT FOR SURVIVAL
Early Duel without Peer Supervision

Sutor (1612)

Duel between Sir Edward Sackville and Lord Bruce, A.D. 1610[1]

We met at Tergosa in Zealand, it being the place allotted for rendezvous, where he, accompanied with one Mr. Crawford, an English gentleman, for his second, a surgeon, and a man, arrived with all the speed he could. And there having rendered himself, I addressed my second, Sir John Heidon, to let him understand, that now all following should be done by consent, as concerning the terms whereon we should fight, as also the place.

To our seconds we gave power for their appointments, who agreed we should go to Antwerp, from thence to Bergen-op-Zoom, where in the midway, but a village divides the States territories from the Archduke's. And there was the destined stage, to the end, that, having ended, he that could, might presently exempt himself from the justice of the country, by retiring into the dominion not offended.

It was farther concluded, that in case any should fall or slip, that then the combat should cease, and he whose ill-fortune had so subjected him, was to acknowledge his life to have been in the other's hands. But in case one party's sword should break, because that could only chance by hazard, it was agreed that the other should take no advantage, but either then be made friends, or else upon even terms go to it again.

Thus these conclusions being each of them related to his party, was by us both approved, and assented to. Accordingly, we embarked for Antwerp. And by reason my Lord, as I conceive, because he could not handsomely, without danger of discovery, had not paired the sword I sent him to Paris, bringing one of the same length, but twice as broad, my second excepted against it, and advised me

[1] from Anonymus. ***Reflections on Duelling and on the Most Effectual Means for Preventing It***, Edinburgh: W. Creech, 1790; p. 52f.

xi

to match my own, and send him the choice, which I obeyed, it being, you know, the challenger's privilege to elect his weapon.

At the delivery of the sword, which was performed by Sir John Heidon, it pleased the Lord Bruce to choose my own, and then, past expectation, he told him, that he found himself so far behind-hand, as a little of my sword would not serve his turn; and therefore he was now resolved to have me alone, because he knew (for I will use his own words) "that so worthy a gentleman, and my friend, could not endure to stand by and see him do that which he must, to satisfy himself and his honour."

Hereto Sir John Heidon replied, that such intentions were bloody and butcherly, far unfitting a noble personage, who should desire to bleed for reputation, not for life; withal adding, he thought himself injured, being come thus far, now to be prohibited from executing those honourable offices he came for. The Lord, for answer, only reiterated his former resolutions; whereupon Sir John, leaving him the sword he had elected, delivered me the other, with his determinations. The which, not for matter, but manner, so moved me, as though, to my remembrance, I had not of a long while eaten more liberally than at dinner, and therefore unfit for such an action (seeing the surgeons hold a wound upon a full stomach much more dangerous than otherwise), I requested my second to certify him, I would presently decide the difference, and therefore he should meet me on horseback, only waited on by our surgeons, they being unarmed.

Together, we rode, but one before the other some twelve score, about two English miles; and then Passion, having so weak an enemy to assail as my direction, easily became victor, and, using his power, made me obedient to his commands.

I being verily mad with anger the Lord Bruce should thirst after my life with a kind of assuredness, seeing I had come so far, and needlessly, to give him leave to regain his lost reputation, I bade him alight, which, with all willingness, he quickly granted, and there in a meadow, ankle-deep in water at the least, bidding farewell to our doublets, in our shirts began to charge each other, having afore commanded our surgeons to withdraw themselves a pretty distance from us, conjuring them besides, as they respected our favours, or their own safeties, not to stir, but suffer us to execute our pleasures: we being fully resolved (God forgive us!) to dispatch each other by what means we could.

I made a thrust at my enemy, but was short, and in drawing back my arm I received a great wound thereon, which I interpreted as a reward for my short shooting; but in revenge I pressed in to him, though I then missed him also, and then receiving a wound in my right pap, which past level through my body, and almost to my back.

And there we wrestled for the two greatest and dearest prices we could ever expect trial for, honour and life; in which struggling my hand, having but an ordinary glove on it, lost one of her servants, though the meanest; which hung by a skin, and to fight yet remaineth as before, and I am put in hope one day to recover the use of it again.

But at last, breathless, yet keeping our holds, there passed on both sides propositions of quitting each other's sword. But when amity was dead, confidence could not live; and who should quit first was the question, which, on neither part, either would perform; and, restriving again afresh, with a kick and a wrench together, I freed my long captived weapon: which incontinently leveling at his throat, being master still of his, I demanded if he would ask his life, or yield his sword; both which, though in that imminent danger, he bravely denied to do.

Myself being wounded, and feeling loss of blood—having three conduits running on me—which began to make me faint, and he courageously persisting not to accord to either of my propositions, remembrance of his former bloody desire, and feeling of my present estate, I struck at his heart, but with his avoiding missed my aim, yet passed through the body, and drawing out my sword repassed it through again, through another place; when he cried, "Oh! I am slain!" seconding his speech with all the force he had, to cast me.

But being too weak, after I had defended his assault, I easily became master of him, laying him on his back; when being upon him, I redemanded if he would request his life, but it seemed he prized it not at so dear a rate to beholden for it; bravely replying he scorned it. Which answer of his was so noble and worthy, as I protest I could not find in my heart to offer him any more violence, only keeping him down, till at length his surgeon, afar off, cried out he would immediately die if his wounds were not stopped. Whereupon I asked if he desired his surgeon should come, which he accepted of; and so being drawn away, I never offered to take his sword, accounting it inhuman to rob a dead man, for so I held him to be.

This thus ended, I retired to my surgeon, in whose arms after I had remained for want of blood, I lost my sight, and withal, as I then thought, my life also. But strong water and his diligence quickly recovered me, when I escaped a great danger. For my Lord's surgeon, when nobody dreamt of it, came full at me with his Lord's sword; and had not mine, with my sword, interposed himself, I had been slain by those base hands: although my Lord Bruce, weltering in his blood, and past all expectation of life, conformable to all his former carriage, cry'd out: "Rascal! Hold thy hand!"

So may I prosper as I have dealt sincerely with you in this relation; which I pray you, with the inclosed letter, deliver to my Lord Chamberlain. And so &c.

Yours,
Edward Sackville
Louvain, the 8th of Sept., 1610

SALUT

Writers of modern fencing books hardly ever concern themselves with more than a few paragraphs on fencing's history, juggling Vikings and duellists and knights and dungeons and dragons with merry abandon. And as modern coaches and instructors are becoming experts in physiology, sports medicine, nutrition, electrics, and electronics, they are only too happy to pass on to their students the ready-to-go, prepackaged factoids that have settled like dust on the records of fencing history.

Some of these myths cropped up through the sheer obstinacy of writers and the credulity of a reverent audience. Aldo Nadi, fencing genius and author of the admirable *On Fencing*, proudly proclaimed *"I have never read more than one sentence in each of the various books on fencing, which have been put, unsolicited, into my hands."*[2] Had he read more, he might not have credited Giacomo di Grassi with "developing" the *"single sword, a cutting and thrusting rapier with a basket hilt"*[3] — whose predecessors can be traced back decades before di Grassi ever set quill to paper.

Most fencing writers' sections on their sport's history are well-intentioned and far less patronizing than that of Nadi.[4] But they, too, tend to be riddled with inconsistencies and errors—errors that are quoted as solid truths by later writers in a game of telephone spanning decades and centuries: a game of taking the master's practical credentials and infering an equally well-rounded state of information into his knowledge of history.

Even the first-hand transmission of content through the primary sources rarely occurs without glitches. Some titles are just so rare that authors throughout the centuries had to rely mainly on second opinion (sometimes their own prejudice) to represent their main tenets. Not even the best fencing historians are immune to this. Take the great Aylward, for example. He claims that in Roworth's *Art of Defence on Foot*, *"the ancient taboo of the point is retained."*[5]

Oddly, even if you only thumb through Roworth's work, you can't help but notice that Roworth indeed devotes an entire chapter to the thrust, and, of course, the proper defense against the opponent's thrusts.[6]

Back in the last decades of the 19th century, a German professor was one of the first to look at the manuals of the old fighters with more than an art historian's eye. Combining the skills of the philologist, the historian, and the hands-on fighter, Dr. Karl Wassmannsdorff's analytical work has been unmatched in 125 years.

Few of his contemporaries escaped without being taken to task for being a tad too carefree and uncritical with using and passing on information. And with names like Vigéant, Castle, and Hergsell finding themselves among those whose works, bibliographies, and chronologies Wassmannsdorff found fault with[7], I don't even want to think about the truckloads of rock salt necessary to make the sloppy compilations of Arthur Wise and George Cameron Stone digestible…

[2]Nadi, Aldo. *On Fencing*, New York: Putnam, 1943; p. 39.

[3]ibid., p. 17.

[4]Nadi's devoted student Dr. William Gaugler wrote to me: *"You may be interested to know that Maestro Nadi once admitted to me that he knew very little about the history of fencing. He was an honest man, and he knew his limitations. His statement, of course, confirms your observations concerning the ignorance of fencers in general. Indeed, they know little about the history of their art."* (Fax to the author of Sept. 26, 1997)

[5]Aylward, J.D. *The English Master of Arms*, London: Routledge & Kegan Paul, 1956; p. 219.

[6][Roworth,C.] *The Art of Defence on Foot with the Broad Sword and Sabre Uniting the Scotch and Austrian Methods into one Regular System, to which is added Remarks on the Spadroon*, London: Printed for T. Egerton at the Military Library near Whitehall, 1798; pp. 67-80.

[7]Wassmannsdorff, Karl. *Aufschlüsse über Fechthand-schriften und gedruckte Fechtbücher des 16. und 17. Jahrhunderts*, Berlin: R. Gaertners Verlagsbuchhand-lung, 1888; p. 19f.

Darn that Darwin

I myself blame Darwin for a hefty chunk of fencing mythology—
or at least that populist school of Linear Evolutionism that tries to squeeze
each and every subject into the straitjacket of pseudo-Darwinian criteria.

Few modern fencers and amateur fencing historians—there are no true
professionals in this game—can resist the temptation to put current fencing
phenomena into a simplistic evolutionary context in which the present is
considered a superior product of "weedin' out the weak." This approach equates
evolution with a linear process toward perfection—whose apex usually can be
found about 50 nostalgic years before the sorry state of the present.

(This approach has recently been put into so many words by a German
instructor of stage fencing. Ch. Walther, evidently a retrospective devolutionist,
stipulated *"sportive cut and thrust fencing, with its specific technique and tactics, is
the last living form of a long European evolutionary history of the artful use of bladed
and staff weapons. In this regard, stage fencing has to accept sports fencing as a point
of origin."*[8])

There is really no shame in that. After all, everyone's doing it. But that
doesn't do much to put aside this inherent contradiction: Linear Evolutionists
(or Devolutionists, take your pick) operate from a naively condescending vantage
point—from a position of assumed superiority that uses the past as an oddity or
curiosity item to contrast the athletic achievements of the modern sport against.
Ironically, this approximates a fundamentally creationist attitude, according to which
the present is considered the "crown of creation"—unassailable and indisputable in
all its glory and radiance. You can picture Darwin spinning in his grave!

Evolution is rarely a linear development toward a final state of perfection, but
rather a constant process of adaptation and spontaneous mutation in unsuspected
directions depending on a changing environment. Dozens of extraneous factors
bodychecked, manhandled, and slam-dunked the development of swordplay until
it mutated from a quick and dirty way of spilling your adversary's guts in the dust
into the protracted Olympian phraseology of the art of fencing.

Men behaving badly

Sir Richard Burton began his famous *Book of the Sword* with the observation
that *"the history of the sword is the history of mankind."* Most scholars have been so
impressed with this that they felt obliged to include it in their own works.

I think Burton was only half right. In my opinion, the history of the sword
is the history of the Y chromosome.

A few years ago, I was invited to give a speech in Dresden, Germany.
Back then, before children, I used to like to travel, and used every opportunity to
reconcile the formal obligations toward my host with lengthy expeditions through
a city's armories and used book stores.

That November, I strolled through the Moritzburg, a palace built by the
Saxon king August the Strong, on a small island located smack dab in the
middle of an artificial lake. August and his wild oats used it as a hunting lodge.
(Accordingly, the edged weapons exhibits are somewhat sparse.)

[8]Walther, Ch. —"Fechten,"
from *Schauspielen*, Berlin,
1981. Quoted from Kamm,
Walther. *Fechten in der
darstellenden Kunst,* Aachen:
Meyer & Meyer, 1994; p. 16.

In one dark, cold corridor, however, I saw a painting that brought home the chromosomal link between cold steel and adolescent males. It is the painting of a boy who was to become Elector Christian II.

At the time, he may have been 13, maybe younger, dressed in the frilly garb of a courtier. At his side, a swept-hilt rapier, its gracefully serpentine quillons worked in blued steel and gold, encrusted with gems and precious stones. In front of him, a hand-and-a-half sword—simple and unadorned: a horrific implement of war, unfashionable already at the time the painting was made.

But it was not the weapons that drew my attention. It was the expression on the boy's face: a mixture of elated curiosity and confidence radiating from within as he touches the weapon of the warrior he is about to become. At that very moment, the ornamental rapier fades into the background as he enters the single most powerful transitional period in his life.

Testosterone high

In Finland, spanking new Ph.D.s receive a smallsword along with the usual handshake/diploma combo—symbolizing their induction into what used to be considered the intellectual upper crust.

Apart from its official symbolism as the emblem of secular power, justice, and nobility, the sword also signifies a period of transition in male life. If you believe the French historian Jacques LeGoff,[9] the demographics of the knights errant correspond closely to those of the rambunctious rapier-wielding students who terrorized peaceful German burghers in the 16th and 17th centuries. Its symbolism still figures prominently in the German Mensur, a transitional combative ritual aimed at reducing the fighter to the core of his character... and allowing him to build on what he discovers as he approaches full manhood.

Mark Wiley, in his *Filipino Martial Culture*, provides a glimpse into the psycho-mechanics of martial male initiation rites:

> *"The transmission of sacred knowledge in sacred time and space effects physical and psychological changes in the martial arts practitioner. The student at once 'finds' himself while persevering through hard and demanding practice and sparring sessions and by passing through various rites of passage and initiation. The 'real' unveils itself in the applied skills of the student as he perfects them in training and through sparring. As the student progresses in rank along the martial social structure, he becomes oriented to the world in which he lives. (...) He is no longer a layman but a martial arts practitioner on his way to become a* mandirigma, *a warrior."*[10]

(In regard to knightly tournaments, fight not only included the element of spritual advancement. Because young knights not only fought for vainglory and love. They also fought for money, and to lay a foundation for a reputation that would help them to gain power and influence as adult men. Family fortunes were made or lost in the lists. The fight was about capturing men, horses, weapons... and ransom money. In fact, the transfer of wealth among the active participants of the knightly tournament exceeded even that of the merchants, jugglers, and bookies at the plebeian periphery.)[11]

[9] see LeGoff, Jacques. *The Medieval Imagination*, Chicago and London: The University of Chicago Press, 1988.

[10] Wiley, Mark V. *Filipino Martial Culture,* Rutland, VT and Tokyo: Charles E. Tuttle Company, 1998; p. 89.

[11] The exchange of goods and ransom involved a complex system of loans, pledges, debts, and promises—and competed with the Church's own cash cows, alms and charitable donations. Worse, they opened up the concept of material gain in an ideology that renounced worldly gain as long as it didn't affect Church revenues.

The sentiment of the sword

Swordfighting is a game of short-term tactics and long-term strategies, of weighing scenarios, controlling and directing the opponent's actions—a mutual effort of snaring and entrapping.

At the core of the fighter's state of mind is the willingness to take risks. Taking risks is the privilege of the free spirit. (In *Beowulf*, this attitude is called *collen-ferth*, bold in spirit.[12])

It is not so much a measure of guts as it is one of intellect: it requires the capability to assess a situation from all angles, to calculate different outcomes based on independet interpretation and evaluation of past experience, present situation, and reasonable expectation of future results—and to put both into a perspective that is immediately relevant to the present.

It is about developing scenarios and arriving at a risk/reward assessment by virtue of your own, responsible spirit—about weighing rewards and freely accepting all consequences of the outcome, no matter if they are positive or negative.

My two cents worth

I started fencing in 1984, when I was an exchange student at the University of Aberdeen in Scotland. I was 21 back then, way beyond hope to ever amounting to anything competitively.

(Not that I hadn't wanted to start fencing earlier—in fact, as a child, I was turning any stick, dowel, even long strips of linoleum remnants into swords— just that I grew up in the Old World mindset that you have to be born into an art, have a long family background in it, or at least start really, really young to get anywhere. Or you might just as well not try.)

Despite my Old World upbringing, I was a quick learner. But I quickly ran into a problem that I've encountered with every other non-essential activity in my life. To actually be able to make progress, you have to have time and leisure. No, let's be honest: *You have to be consequent enough to make your pursuit an absolute priority.*

Blood, sweat, and beer

There was only one narrowly defined period in my life that I had the time and discipline to pursue the art of the sword in a system that today is much maligned by the moralist mainstream, and little understood even by those few who still practice it.

Even in its current, somewhat degenerated form, the system of the Schläger still comprises the essence of a very primal, basic, and fundamentally human approach to the art of the sword.

Its influence on the mind is latent, and many of those who faced off against another man in a Mensur never become fully aware of its effects. Only years of reflection, rumination, and re-evaluation of those few minutes you actually spent fighting an opponent with your wit, your conditioning, and a yard-long piece of sharp steel in your hand, can make you realize the complex shift in your personality that is triggered the moment your second measures the distance by jamming his blade in between you and your opponent.

[12]See Nicholson, Lewis E. — "Hunlafing and the Point of the Sword," in Nicholson, Lewis E. and Frese, Dolores Warwick. *Anglo-Saxon Poetry: Essays in Appreciation*, Notre Dame, IN and London: University of Notre Dame Press, 1975; p. 51.

Matters of consequence

If the art of fencing is about calculating scenarios and gaining competitive control over your opponent, the Mensur is all about consequences. There is something disturbing about facing the possibility of being permanently scarred or mutilated by a hideously sharp-looking blade. Feeling the fencing goggles tighten around your skull, you enter a twilight zone—and you are uncertain how you will be emerging from it: a smooth-skinned, clean-shaven young man with all his boyish good looks intact. Or some patched-up, sewn-up Frankenstein with sutures across your mug.

Oddly enough, once you've been hit, you don't really care any more. The scar becomes part of you, as much as the nose in your face. It is a mark of you breaking all dictates of what society passes as common sense, to see your place in the world as an individual, a solitary animal rather than part of a nodding herd.

In his *The Art and Science of Fencing*, Nick Evangelista observes:

"I believe [fencing] is based on something real—universal principles dealing with the way human beings think and move. By mastering the application of these concepts, through long, hard study, and practice, a fencing student is led logically to personal control—first over himself, and then over his opponents." [13]

The Mensur adds a third dimension—the realization that, if push comes to shove in un-friendly confrontation, skill and mastery in a human art may be no match for dumb luck.

But by readily accepting the reality and consequences of your actions as a free man, you can liberate yourself of many of the misconceptions you've had about accepted and unquestioned notions of civilization and human nature. If you care to recognize the complex animal instincts deep within yourself— a rather stultefying mix of fear, panic, aggression, blood-lust—the Mensur invites you to find out about your core fundamentals.

And as pitiful as these may turn out to be, you can build up on what you've found, becoming stronger in the process.

Rewriting fencing history

Ever since Herodotus and Thucydides, the works of historians have straddled a precarious position between chronicling events and creating mythology. Histories are, after all, written by the winners. And the very time-line observed in the chronicle often provides the skeleton for the myth, by artificially ordering and weighing events retrospectively. It is the task of the historian to identify these myths and discover the factual reality obscured by them.

This, of course, is tedious and sometimes inconvenient work. After all, *"myths create an orderly past and give us a sense of a future in which we are greater than we can ever be today."* [14] Historical truth, however, is elusive, disorderly— and often downright uncomfortable.

Paradoxically, the Information Age appears to be spawning its own breed of orderly myth, perpetuated and reinforced by the sheer power of repetition. As the

[13] Evangelista, Nick. *The Art and Science of Fencing*, Indianapolis, IN: Masters Press, 1997; p. 40.

[14] Tegner, Bruce. *Self-Defense Nerve Centers and Pressure Points for Karate, Jujitsu and Atemi-Waza*, Ventura, California: Thor Publishing Co., (1968) 1990; p. 21.

journalist John Lawton put it a few years ago: *"The irony of the Information Age is that it has given new respectability to uninformed opinion."*

Striving to establish an ordered past, structuring events from the vantage point of eclectic retrospective has dominated the writing of fencing history in the post-Darwinian age. To obtain a more balanced idea of the intrinsic values of long-forgotten fighting systems, I decided to abandon the concept of progress and linear evolution that willy-nilly permeates social and other pseudo-sciences today. After all, the present is not an improvement on the past, but merely a product of randomly changing environments.

Fencing history can never really be considered out of its social context. Weapons and the skills necessary to handle them have never been exclusively a function of pure utility. The men wielding them were and are products of their respective environments, its moral and legal systems, its fashions and status symbolism. And each combative situation puts the fighters into a dramatically different environment, in which a ray of sunlight, the personal level of stress, even the contents of one's stomach or lower intestine could be as lethal to a fighter as the opponent's mastery of a closed system of fighting skills.

The fencing historian has to take all these factors into consideration before passing a conclusive judgment about the quality and effectiveness of a particular school or system.

E pluribus unum?

Since I began to publish *Hammerterz Forum* in 1994, I have found myself being considered a close accomplice to fundamentally divergent views on sword-play. My research has been interpreted as exclusively supportive of traditional sports fencing, the art of fencing, Schläger fencing, saber fencing, cut-and-thrust fencing, theatric fencing, modern Renaissance fencing. (In fact, only top-level competitive sports fencing really doesn't care much for historical research.)

But the purpose of my work is not to be divisive. Let's be honest. Does it really matter if a closed system of swordplay is theoretically superior or inferior to another? If one system is "more lethal"? Discussions like this are about as fruitful as arguments between modern polo players and the nomadic forefathers of the sport about the "softening" of the modern sport because it is no longer played with the heads of your slain enemies...

The purpose of this book and *Hammerterz Forum* (where many of the essays enclosed here first appeared) is to obtain a clearer understanding of what swordplay was and meant in its changing historical environments, not to declare any one system the evolutionary winner to the exclusion of all others.

Twenty-twenty hindsight—for generations to come!

It's easy to flex the pumped-up biceps of late historic insight at our predecessors. But after all, the people who cared enough about fencing to try and piece together what scattered facts and anecdotes had made it through the ages were mostly fighters—men of action concerned primarily with transmitting the theoretic abstract of their practical experience.

In this volume, I will introduce you to my own findings about the history of the sword. Findings that contradict most of what you may have read about swordfighting in the past. And I want you to join me on the far more interesting and challenging adventure—of trying to create a new, fresh mythology, derived from speculations about the roots of long-forgotten European martial arts that were ancient when an ambitious Frankish chieftain by the name of Karl crowned himself Roman Emperor.

Of course, chances are that a few years from now, my own attempts will be challenged by future generations of fencers and fencing historians—each armed with a handful of new insights, and the fiercely independent self-assertiveness that characterizes anyone who lives and thinks by the sword.

One more thing

While I try to give chapter and verse for every argument I present, as the formal standards of academia dictate, I categorically reject academic structure and jargon. I believe that the academic style has the same effect on the transmission of ideas that formaldehyde has on living tissue: it turns the most spirited discussion, the most brilliant ideas into limp, gray blobs of dead matter that make your scalp itch just looking at them.

The lore of the sword derives its perennial appeal from the action of the individual fighter—and the glorious (and often glorified) word-of-mouth accounts of the survivors, retainers, and admirers. It is their accounts that we owe our present knowledge to—and this is why I include them as interludes in the upcoming analysis.

The examples presented in this book are intended to provide a sympathetic platform for a deeper and more thorough critical approach to the evaluation of the sword's heritage and the study of ancient fighting systems.

So buckle up and enter a world of cunning and strength, of violence and calculated risks, of the crimson killing instincts and the ice-cold clarity of the martial mind. Enter a world you will never be able to fully reconstruct or fully understand:

Welcome to The Secret History of the Sword!

J. Christoph Amberger
Baltimore, August 1998

PART ONE

STUDIES IN MYTHOLOGY

Fencers practicing with the two-handed sword. Joachim Meyer, 1570.

STUDIES IN MYTHOLOGY

CASE IN POINT 1

An Assault at Arms: Sword vs. Bayonet, in *Harper's Weekly*, May 16, 1874.

"The question whether the bayonet or the sword is the better weapon in the hands of a soldier is one which still remains undecided, although military authorities are inclined to award the palm to the latter.

To non-military persons it would seem to be the more handy weapon, and, wielded by a skillful swordsman, would probably, as a rule, be at least a match for the heavier bayonet, although the latter, by reason of its length and weight, forms a very formidable weapon in hands accustomed to its use.

The illustration on this page shows an animated trial of skill between two proficients in the use of these weapons, witnessed by a throng of interested spectators."

Moving Target:
On the Varied Backgounds of the Saber Target

Ah, tradition—the true driving force of history! It makes royalty out of rogues, elevates gibberish into cherished ritual. Tradition has the depth of an eggshell—while appearing as impenetrable and unquestionable as the polar ice cap.

Modern fencing, of course, has its share of silly traditions. The most complex—and one of my all-time favorites—is the explanation of why the target of the modern sports saber is restricted to above the waistline.

Most fencers today have been told that this is because there supposedly was a gentlemen's agreement between fighting horse soldiers not to hit each other's legs and horses. And I've even heard the explanation that this supposed saber taboo goes straight back to the knightly tournaments. (After all, the guys in the tin cans wanted to claim their vanquished opponent's horse as booty—as undamaged as possible.)

"Makes sense to me"

All this sounds very logical. But historically speaking, it is irrelevant if an explanation makes sense. (Most rationalizations do indeed just that.) The questions that need to be asked are:

Has there been a universally accepted definition of the competitive saber target? And:

How old is the tradition?

I have tried to make sense of this in the past.[15] But this cursory review of the sources will convince even the most curmudgeonly sceptic that the history of the saber target is indeed far from clear-cut. And depending on cultural and chronological context, the theory of a unified taboo zone below the belt evaporates like a shot of tequila on a Weber kettle grill.

Analysing the target area of the saber throughout the past 200 years not only reinforces the usefulness of a critical approach toward fencing mythology. It also provides valuable insight into the systematic transformation that turned the saber from a weapon of war into the implement of competitive sports.

Cut and thrust

Let's save the matter of horseflesh for later and concentrate on the pedestrian predecessors of the modern saber for a moment. There is ample evidence that the leg remained a valid target well into the second decade of the 20th century. (Of course, the native English and Central European backsword and broadsword traditions of the Middle Ages and the Renaissance also include cuts at the thigh, knee, and foot. For the sake of argument, however, let's just focus on the more recent past.)

From the 18th century up until the 1870s, the curved-bladed saber was a sub-category of cut-and-thrust broadsword, thus part of antagonistic combat systems. As such, the leg and thigh remained preferred targets in both equestrian and pedestrian combat drills with broadsword, spadroon, backsword, and saber.

Most 18th- and 19th-century manuals indeed treat the cut to the leg as a matter of course.[16] Roworth includes a chapter on the Cut at the Advanced Leg or Thigh, which *"can seldom be made without considerable danger to the person who attempts it against a swordsman, as it must be always attended with an inclination of the body, and the head being thus brought forward, becomes exposed, even when the leg or thigh at which the stroke is directed, is removed out of distance."*[17]

The broadsword tradition is evident in the French approach to saber fencing, as well as in the related English and American systems.

Toward the latter third of the 19th-century, Central Europe presents a slightly different picture. Here, the use of the saber particularly among the university students had created a more regulated agonistic and competitive environment with the *"Comment"*—a set of rules and agreements regulating cut-and-thrust fencing far more and far earlier than in the mainly antagonistic context of the cut-and-thrust broadsword in England, America, or France.

The Austrian master Gustav Hergsell points out that hits below the waist are prohibited by the dictates of polite manners (*"der Anstand"*),[18] although he mentions that below-the-waist was considered fair game by many fencing schools.

[15]Amberger, J. Christoph. — "Below the Belt—A Brief History of Sabre Taboos," in *The Sword*, New Series #41, January 1995; p. 28f.

[16]The following titles provide an excellent sample: Lonnergan, A. *The Fencer's Guide*, London: Self-published, 1771; p. 185f; Angelo, Henry and Rowlandson, Thomas. *Hungarian and Highland Broadsword*, London: H. Angelo, 1799; Taylor, John. *The Art of Defence on Foot with the Broad Sword and Sabre: adapted also to the Spadroon, or Cut-and-Thrust Sword*, London: T. Egerton, 1804; p. 88f; Mathewson, Thomas. *Fencing Familiarized; or, a New Treatise on the Art of the Scotch Broad Sword*, Edinburgh?: W. Cowdroy, 1805; p. 11f.

[17]Roworth, p. 86.

[18]Hergsell, Gustav. *Die Fechtkunst*, Wien, Pest, Leipzig: A. Hartleben's Verlag, 1881; p. 259.

The great Barbasetti echoes this dictate of polite manners when he calls for an exclusion of cuts below the waistline in *"chivalrous and honourable combat."*[19]

Hergsell and Barbasetti are representatives of the two competing saber schools of the late 19th century. Neither makes reference to horseflesh, but both point out that conventions and implicit agreements, dictated by chivalrous and polite manners, determined what was considered fair play on the planche and the duelling ground.

H. Angelo (1799)

Leg o'lamb

Even though he did not include the leg or thigh cut as a category in his offensive repertoire, the fencing instructor of the U.S. Naval Academy in Annapolis, Antoine J. Corbesier, wrote in his broadsword manual:

"Generally the cut at the flank is made at the lower part of the leg instead of the flank (...)"[20]

The continuum is maintained by O'Rourke:

"Cut 4—Leg: —Cut from No. 4 to No. 1; allow the sword to continue the sweep until it touches the right shoulder; edge to the right, arm slightly bent, and nails up."[21]

In 1880, J. M. Waite recommends:

"Feint a thrust at your adversary's breast over his blade, and as he raises his guard, pass your point to your right, and without touching his blade, clear his point and deliver a cut inside his leg above the knee with a longe."

Or, alternatively,

"Beat your adversary's sword to your right, then suddenly straighten your arm, and turning the edge inwards, longe, and deliver a cut on the inside of his leg."

And as a Guard for the Inside Leg:

"The same as for outside the leg, except that you move your hand to the left until it hangs over the right knee."[22]

[19]Barbasetti, Cav. Luigi. **Das Säbelfechten,** Wien: Verlag der Allgemeinen Sportzeitung (Victor Silberer), 1899; p. 35.

[20]Corbesier, Antoine J. **Principles of Squad Instruction for the Broadsword**, Philadelphia: J.B. Lippincott, 1869; p. 43.

[21]O'Rourke, Matthew J. **A New System of Sword Exercise, with a Manual of the Sword for Officers, Mounted and Dismounted**, New York: Geo. R. Lockwood, 1873; p. 53.

To the historically inclined, O'Rourke's work is endorsed by one Brevet Brig.-Gen. G. A. Custer: *"I most heartily commend him to the favorable consideration of the War Department, sincerely hoping that some action may be had by which this system of Sword Exercise may be introduced into the permanent organization of the army."*

It was... and little good it did him.

[22]Waite, J.M.. **Lessons in Sabre, Singlestick, Sabre & Bayonet, and Sword Feats; or, How to use a cut-and-thust sword**, London: Weldon & Co., 1880; p. 45.

Rondelle (1892)

In 1892, the French Maitre d'Armes Louis Rondelle incorporates the thigh cut in his repertoire of basic saber cuts:

"Thigh Cut.—Lower the point, extend the arm, lunge with opposition, give the saber cut across the thigh, drawing the sword backward; recover on guard quickly, being well covered."[23]

And in 1894, Edward Breck recommends the Thigh Cut, to be executed like the flank cut, *"only the object is the adversary's thigh."*[24]

Risk and reward

O'Rourke recommends Guard Three to ward off an attack against the leg: *"Lower the hand, and bring it across the body until it comes a little below, and in front of, the left hip; nails up; edge of the sword to the left, with the point in front of the right leg."*

and Guard Four: *"Turn the hand, nails down and carry it across until it clears the right hip; edge of the sword to the right, and the point in front of the right leg."*[25]

Obviously, even a layman can see in the illustration below that the point of the parrying soldier is dangerously far removed from the more worthwhile target areas:

[23]Rondelle, Louis. **Foil and Sabre**, Boston: Dana Estes & Co., 1892; p. 204.

[24]Breck, Edward. **Fencing**, New York: American Sports Publishing Co., [1894] 1902; p. 41.

[25]O'Rourke; p. 57 and 58.

O'Rourke (1873)

At the beginning of the 19th-century, Taylor had stressed that the leg and thigh cut always must be preceded by a feint at the upper body or head, which *"brings the antagonist to a St. George's Guard, in which case you must advance considerably to effect your cut."*

However, he cautions the attacker that the leg cut *"will always be extremely hazardous with the sword in real contest, unless your antagonist advances his right foot by standing much too wide upon guard. Otherwise, in striking at his leg, your head and sword arm must become exposed even to a person wholly ignorant of the science; and his attention not being occupied by endeavouring to parry, his blow at the head would probably prove fatal, even though he received a cut on the leg at the same instant."*[26] (This advice also appears verbatim a few years earlier in Roworth. Fancy, both had the same printer-publisher.)[27]

In Germany, W. Roux is no stranger to the dangers posed by the leg cut: *"The low tierce, or rather seconde [aims at] the right flank or underneath the arm, but also at the right thigh or knee, provided that the opponent has put his foot not sideways but into the line, and keeps the right leg bent. But since it is to be expected that the opponent will withdraw his leg—particularly when your cut is executed with a slightly lowered fist—and hit a high tierce a tempo at your arm, this cut for the right thigh cannot be recommended."*[28]

Henry Angelo recounts the reason why Lord Pembroke stopped taking fencing lessons:
"Desiring him (Lord Pembroke) in one of his lessons, to make a full stroke at his legs, at the same time prepared to guard them, Lord Pembroke made a full blow on his head, and laid him flat on the floor, leaving on it a purple memento of his mistake. The enraged master called out, 'I said the legs!' when his lordship replied, 'I thought you said the head; I see I shall never make anything of this exercise, so I had better pay you for your lessons, and leave off.'"[29]

The Master's misfortune illustrates the primary weakness of the leg cut: The defence against it turns the entire upper body into an opening.

Broadswordsmen and sabreurs of the 18th- and 19th-century practiced a technique called "slipping the leg" to defend against an opponent's thigh cut.

Angelo, for example, arranged his 1799 *Guards and Lessons of the Highland Broadsword*[30] around the attack/defence sequence of head and leg cuts:

"Lesson 1: Cut at Antagonist's Head. Guard your own. Cut at Antagonist's Leg. Guard your Head.
Lesson 2: Cut at Antagonist's Head. Guard your own. Feint at Antagonist's Leg. Guard Your Head. Cut at Antagonist's Leg. Guard your Head.
Lesson 3: The same as the second, after which cut at Antagonist's Ribs.
Lesson 4: Cut at Antagonist's Head. Guard your own. Cut at Antagonist's Leg. Shift your own. Cut at Antagonist's Head. Guard your own.
Lesson 5: Disengage from an outside Guard and drop your point falling square to the right. Antagonist cuts at your face. Receive him upon an inside guard, and cut at his thigh. Guard your Head. Cut at Antagonist's Head."[31]

[26] Taylor; p. 88-89.

[27] Roworth; p. 87.

[28] Roux, W. *Anweisung zum Hiebfechten mit geraden und krummen Klingen,* Jena: Mauke, 1840; p. 11.

[29] Angelo, Henry. *Reminiscences of Henry Angelo,* London: Kegan Paul, Trench, Trübner & Co., 1904; p. 322.

[30] Angelo, Henry and Rowlandson, Thomas (illustrator). *The Guards and Lessons of the Highland Broadsword,* London: Angelo, 1799. Single sheet reprinted by Hammerterz Verlag, Baltimore, in 1996.

[31] The younger Angelo brother mentions that Henry's Naval Cutlass Exercise was based on the one for Highland Broadsword: *"During the blockade of the Scheld and Dutch ports, in the summer of 1812, my brother was on a visit to his friend, Captain Rainier, of the 'Norge' frigate, and whilst on board that ship, thinking it might be beneficial, and an amusement, to the sailors, he drilled the crew in an appropriate use of their cutlasses, and it met with such approbation and practice in other ships, that it ultimately became a portion of the instruction for the Navy, on board the 'Excellent' in Portsmouth."* See Angelo, Edward Anthony. *Observations on Angelo's Military Exercises formed by (the late) Henry Angelo, Esq., Superintendent of Sword Exercise to the Army,* London: Parker, Furnivall, and Parker, 1853; p. 9.

Much like his English forebears, Corbesier recommends that in the case of an attack against one's leg *"the best parry is to draw back the right foot quickly against the left, at the same time stretching the arm, bringing the sword in line (edge down) and cutting at the head, without defending one's self otherwise."*[32]

Waite's recommendation is strikingly similar:
"As your adversary cuts at your leg, draw it quickly back and assume the first position (...), and at the same time deliver a diagonal cut on his head or arm, with good opposition, so that should your adversary feint at your leg and cut at the head, the opposition will guard his attack."[33]

Rondelle has little to add:
"Parry of the Thigh Cut.—This cut is parried by an escape to the rear. Quickly carry the right leg, which is attacked, twelve inches behind to the rear of the left leg, the foot flat upon the floor."[34]

Only West Point's Wayne is more imaginative:
"To slip a cut at the right leg is very common, and undoubtedly its best defence; for a cut at the leg can seldom be made without considerable danger to the person who attempts it, as it must always be attended with an inclination of the body. (...) On an intimation of a cut at the leg, quickly withdraw the right foot ten or twelve inches to the rear of the left, resting upon its toe, and simultaneously, if on the guard of tierce, cut 4 at the sword arm, or 2 at the head or arm. Cut 7 at either head or arm can be delivered from either engagement."[35]

While Rondelle's counter attack is a stop-cut to the upper arm of the opponent (see page 14), Corbesier's recommendation of attacking the head of the opponent while slipping the leg echoes the late 18th- and early 19th-century broadsword practice manuals which recommend to cut at the head of the attacker while removing one's leg, as well as immediately guard one's own head immediately after the execution of a leg cut.

Breck still includes avoiding the thigh cut in his defensive repertoire. But he already points out that *"this is well to practice, although, as a matter of fact, no cuts are counted below the hip by the rules of the A.F.L.A."*[36]

Mano a mano

[32]Corbesier; ibid.

[33]Waite; p. 47.

[34]Rondelle; p. 206.

[35]Wayne, H.C. **Exercise for the Broad Sword, Sabre, Cut and Thrust, and Stick,** Washington: Gideon & Co., 1849; p. 24.

[36]Breck; p. 43.

Barbasetti, founder of the Vienna Neustadt school, already represents the new Radaelli method of the *sciabola di terreno*. This is the duelling weapon of choice for Italian officers and gentlemen—and as such reflects a stronger influence of duelling reglementation than the contemporary broadsword school of, say, Rondelle or even Hergsell.

Characteristic for the Italian and Italian-influenced school is the exclusion of the lower body, as well as explicit regulations about what areas of the sword arm are taboo.

While Barbasetti again adduces "chivalrous behavior" for his call not to aim at the opponent's sword hand,[37] Pavese in Baltimore stipulates that the proper target includes the *"right forearm (but not on wrist or elbow)"* [38] without further comment.

(In the saber duel, wrist and elbow could be protected by bandages. The forearm, however, was a popular target for stop cuts that could terminate a first-blood duel with calculable risk to both parties involved.)

The inclusion of elbow and wrist in the taboo zones clearly illustrates that there is no connection between antagonistic combat and the regulations of competitive, agonistic saber: Cavalrymen were explicitly instructed to hit at both swordarm and bridle hand of the opponent. In fact, Rondelle wants to focus exclusively on these targets in cavalry drill.[39] And as Barbassetti points out in an earlier chapter, saber duels in which the thrust was allowed usually were terminated by an injury to the lower arm.[40]

Manschette Guard after Fehn (late 19th century)

Off the cuff

In Austria and Germany, stop-cut practice against the hand and lower arm had spawned the sub-system of *Manschette* (lit.: "cuff").

Hergsell[41] calls this fencing variety a *Spielerei mit dem Säbel*, horsing around with the saber. This technique seems to have developed from stop-cut practice. The target was restricted to the hand and the cuff of the fencing glove. The fencers usually observed a firmly fixed stance, lunges and advances were prohibited.

While Hergsell considers this system as detrimental to the overall quality of saber fencing, he concedes that it *"sharpens the eye and softens the wrist for quickly executed cutting."* The lightning speed with which *Manschette* fencers were able to execute stop cuts against the opponent's sword arm from seemingly impossible angles made them mean opponents in saber bouts. But the technical advantage of their one specialty usually wore thin soon.

Typically, a trained saber fencer was able to defeat them rather quickly, as the *Manschette* fencer's offensive repertoire was restricted to the medium range, and his defensive relied mainly of quickly moving hands and arms out of harm's way. They also were not used to the regular parries and had a tendency not to guard the head and upper body.

Nonetheless, Hergsell spells out in his *Duell-Codex* that a *Manschett-Duell*, i.e., a duel with the only allowable target being the sword hand and arm of the opponent, is not an acceptable option. For one, it's limited target area and frivolous character made it incompatible with the serious life-and-death affair the duel

[37]Barbasetti. *Säbelfechten*, p. 79.

[38]Pavese, Generoso. **Foil and Sabre Fencing**, Baltimore: Kings Bros., 1905; p. 135.

[39]Rondelle; p. 214.

[40]Barbasetti, *Säbelfechten*; p. 60: *"Es ist ein Vorurtheil, zu glauben, dass die Zulassung des Stosses im Duell zugleich den tödlichen Ausgang desselben bedingt. Nichts ist falscher als diese Ansicht, wenn auch ein Stich tödlich sein kann. Aber gerade deshalb wird keiner der beiden Duellanten besondere Lust verspüren, ihn zu erhalten. (...) In der That werden fast alle Duelle, bei welchen der Stich gestattet ist, durch Verwundung des Unterarms erledigt."*

[41]Hergsell. **Fechtkunst**, p.294.

was supposed to be. And second:

> *"Without taking into consideration that in certain circumstances a cut against the hand or arm can be far more dangerous than a light cut against the body, seconds must not consent to any such submitted condition under any circumstance."*[42]

Bastardized forms

In the first years of the 20th century, the broadsword schools were gradually taken over by the Italian system and its Hungarian and French offshoots.

Under the French influence of the FIE and the Military Academy of Joinville le Port, the leg and thigh remained valid target area for competitive saber at least until the end of World War I.[43] In the 1920s, the leg and thigh were gradually abandoned as target area even in practice. The groin area, however, remained valid at least until 1939,[44] even though the modern target definitions are quoted explicitly as early as 1930,[45] and implicitly practiced since before WWI.[46]

In the case of the saber duel, however, low cuts remained at least permissible, even though not recommended due to the risk they posed to the fencer. Hergsell notes:

> *"In the saber duel, cuts ought to be executed according to the custom of the art (schulgerecht) only against the head or upper body above the belt. Lower aimed cuts, however, executed by an unpracticed fencer or a naturalist, cannot be admonished by the seconds."*[47]

[42]Hergsell, Gustav. **Duell-Codex**, Wien, Pest, Leipzig: A. Hartleben's Verlag, 1891; p. 80.

[43]Tilmont, R.L., Breed, Geoffrey H., O'Connor, W. Scott (edd. and transl.). **Fencing: Foil, Epee, Sabre, Theory, Methods, and Regulations practiced at the Military School of Joinville le Pont**, New York: The Amateur Fencers League of America, 1915; p. 46.

[44]Castello, Julio Martinez. **The Theory and Practice of Fencing**, New York and London: Charles Scribner's Sons, 1933; p. 150 (fig. 3) and Huber (below).

[45]Cass, Eleanor. **The Book of Fencing**, Lothrop, Lee, and Shepard Co., 1930; p. 236.

[46]Cf. Meienreis, Walther. **Säbelfechten**, Leipzig: Grethlein, c. 1913.

[47]Hergsell. **Duell-Codex**, p. 79.

[48]Huber, Ted. **Fundamental Swordsmanship**, Ann Arbor, MI: Edwards Brothers' Inc., 1939; p. 73.

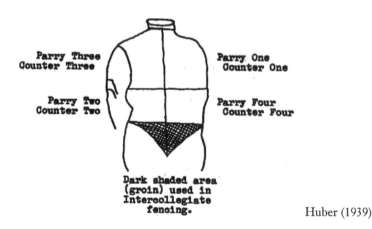

Huber (1939)

Living fossil

An interesting phenomenon is mentioned in the booklet published by the American Ted Huber, Captain of the Temple University fencing team in 1939. According to him, U.S. *"intercollegiate fencing includes the groin and forearm. In gym fencing the legs and forearm are inviolate."*[48]

Target definitions, in particular the exclusion of perfectly good and effective zones such as legs and groin, typically indicate that a system is not aimed at raw survival or gaining absolute dominion over the opponent.

Crosnier—who never loses a word about the history of the saber—probably says it best when he links the sports saber to the foil:

> *"The saber (…) has a mental approach similar to the foil. It has its conventions and technical preparation. (…) like the foil, its exchanges are generally longer and faster."* [49]

The origins for the rules of the modern sports saber, therefore, are to be found in the conventions of the later competitive sport, rather than in the principles governing the saber as a weapon of war. Tegner points out the different approaches when he compares the sport of boxing with the requirements for self-defence, which interestingly match with those of the saber:

> *"The terms 'low blow' and 'hitting below the belt' derive from the sport of boxing and they imply unfair and unsporting tactics. For self-defense, which is not a sport and in which there are no rules, low blows and hitting below the belt—kicking into the knee or shin, for example—are efficient, practical and appropriate tactics (…)"* [50]

[49]Crosnier, Roger. *Fencing with the Saber*, London: Faber & Faber, (1954) 1965 (2nd ed.); p. 14.

[50]Tegner; p. 98.

INTERLUDE

ANTAGONISTIC COMBAT:
Mounted Mêlée

Mounted sword practice
after Heck (1851)

Battle Scenes from Balaclava[51]

It so happened that Captain Morris, the officer in command of the 17th
Lancers, was advancing in front of his left squadron, and thence it resulted
that the portion of the regiment which outflanked the battery fell under his
personal leadership.

In the direct front of the ranks, thus awaiting the charge of our horsemen,
there was sitting in his saddle a Russian who seemed to be the squadron leader.
Morris drove his horse full at this officer, and in the instant which followed the
contact, the sword of the assailant had transfixed the trunk of the Russian, passing
through with such force that its hilt pressed against the man's body.

For a moment, there was nothing to hinder the enemy from capturing many
of the English who here remained wounded and disabled. Of these, Morris himself
was one; and his misfortune was a consequence of the determination which
induced him to 'give point' to his adversary. 'I don't know,' he would afterwards
say, 'I don't know how I came to use the point of my sword, but it's the last time I
ever do.'

When his sword, driving home to the hilt, ran through the Russian squadron
leader whom he had singled out for his first adversary, the Russian tumbled over

[51] quoted after Kingslake,
A.W. *The Invasion of the
Crimea*, in O'Rourke;
p. 93f *note*.

on the off-side of his horse, drawing down with him in his fall the sword which had slain him; and since Morris, with all his strength, was unable to withdraw the blade, and yet did not choose to let go his grasp of the handle, or to disengage himself from the wrist-knot, it resulted that, though still in his saddle, he was tethered to the ground by his own sword arm.

Whilst thus disabled, Morris received a saber-cut on the left side of the head, which carried away a large piece of bone above the ear, and a deep, clean cut passing through the acorn of his forage cap, which penetrated both plates of the skull."

Later that day, General Scarlett, "found himself nearing a front of the column at a point very near its center, and the spot at which Scarlett thus rode was marked by the presence of a Russian officer who sat erect in his saddle some few paces in front of his people, and confronting the English intruder.

Moved perhaps by such indication of rank as was to be gathered in one fleeting moment from the sight of a staff officer's hat, the Russian officer chose Eliott [an officer on General Scarlett's staff] for his adversary.

He faced him as he approached and endeavored to cut him down. Evading or parrying the cut, Eliott drove his sword through the body of his assailant, and the swiftness with which he was galloping up, whilst delivering his thrust, was so great that the blade darted in to the very hilt; but until the next moment, when Eliott's charger had rushed past, the weapon, though held fast by its owner, still could not be withdrawn. Thus it resulted that the Russian officer was turned round in his saddle by the leverage of the sword which transfixed him. Before he could withdraw the blade, he was carried forward into the ranks of the enemy."

CASE IN POINT 2

French cavalry, c. 1865

A Horse is a Horse, of Course, of Course:
(And no-one would hit at a horse, of course.)

W̲e have so far established that cut-and-thrust fencers didn't think twice about slicing and dicing up their opponents' legs as long as they could do it with impunity. Was there at least an ounce of humane concern for their mounts, as modern tradition has it?

Historical battle lore shows horses injured or killed by sword cuts more or less accidentally—usually as a consequence of a powerful stroke that took out their rider. Hewitt summarizes Malmesbury's vignette of Geoffrey, Duke of Normandy:

> *"At the siege of Antioch, Godfrey of Bouillon, with a Lorrainian sword, cut asunder a Turk who had demanded single combat, so that one half of the man lay panting on the ground, while the other half was carried off by the horse at full speed; so firmly did the unbeliever keep his seat. Another also, who attacked him, he clove asunder from the neck to the groin; nor did the dreadful stroke stop here, but cut entirely through the saddle and the backbone of the horse."*[52]

But horses were not only accidental targets of sword cuts. Facing mounted opponents armed with pistols and saber, a horseman's weakest spot was his mount. And military strategists of all eras were experts in pinpointing and exploiting opponents' weaknesses. It is no coincidence that the tactical role of cavalry began its eclipse with the invention of the socket bayonet:

[52]Hewitt, John. *Ancient Armor and Weapons in Europe*, [Oxford: John Henry & James Parker, 1855] London: Random House, 1996; p. 163.

H. Angelo (1799)

As early as 1730, a Spanish general exhorted the effectiveness of poles to stop an attacking horseman. By *"pointing at the horse's eyes or tapping its head with [a pole], the horse will shy and refuse to advance. (...) If a horse will not ride down a man armed with only a pole, how much less will cavalry prosper against formed battalions, whose bayonets, bullets and din of arms (...) are even more capable of scaring the horses."*[53]

The horse was an ideal target: large, defenseless, and protected only by the blade and prowess of its master. Hit it, hurt it, frighten it, and chances are it will rear and throw off its rider—who then is an under-armed pedestrian at the mercy of his enemy, his *"pistols outclassed by muskets and [his] saber ineffective against a wall of bayonets."*[54]

It was not only possible, therefore, for saber-wielding troopers to aim at the opponent's horse, but absolutely prudent and desirable to do just that. But did it really happen? We don't have to look far to prove that it did.

Like a horse and carriage

In 1687, Sir William Hope advises his gentle readers considering the use of the shearing sword from horseback to *"lean your body a little forwards that so you may the better defend your horse's head. (...) You must also endeavour as much as possible to defend your horse's face, and his bridle reins, because when once a horse getteth a smart blow in the face, it maketh him afterward instead of advancing, to retire, which will be a great disadvantage to you, also if your bridle reins should be cutt, you would be put in a bad condition."*[55] To Hope, the *"only pursuit upon horseback is a plain stroke either at your adversary or his horse."*[56]

H. Angelo (1799)

Napoleonic nags

So much for the crude civilian attitudes of the 17th-century. Surely, the dashing horse soldiers of the Napoleonic age would have been much more attached to their equine buddies?

In the saber (or "Hungarian broadsword") part of Henry Angelo's *Hungarian and Highland Broadswords*, written in the heyday of cavalry battles, we find that

[53]Chandler, David. *The Art of War in the Age of Marlborough*, New York, 1976; p. 82.

[54]Jones, Archer. *The Art of War in the Western World*, Urbana, IL & Chicago: University of Illinois Press, 1987; p. 268.

[55]H[ope], Sir W[illiam]. *The Scots Fencing Master*, Edinburgh: John Reid, 1687; p. 127f.

[56]Hope; p. 19.

troopers had to be able to defend their horses against saber cuts. Parries to protect the horse's head and rear, as well as the rider's upper legs, in fact make up most of the defensive repertoire of the mounted trooper.

Cut and thrust remained integral parts of saber exercise. The most important technique on the battlefield, however, continued to be the outmanoeuvering of the opponent:

"The chief object of the cavalry soldier must be to gain, by turnings, wheelings, and vaultings, &c., the left side of his opponent and never expose his own."[57]

To achieve this tactical advantage, troopers were advised to direct attacks against the opponent's horse:

H. Angelo (1799)

"The weakest point [of a mounted trooper] is the left rear; an enemy in this position should be attacked at once. (. . .) In pursuit endeavor to gain the enemy's left rear; cut at the hocks, if necessary. When pursued keep the enemy to the right rear, and prevent him from closing by rear cuts or thrusts, or by striking his horse's head, the reins, or the bridle hand."[58]

Gericault (1812)

A guard of the horse's hocks is illustrated in Theodore Géricault's painting *Portrait of an Officer of the Chasseurs Commanding a Charge*—offered to the Salon in 1812.

Of course, this in itself could be interpreted as a martial pose struck for the benefit of a painter eager to glorify his subject. Luckily, a contemporary printed source corroborates the iconographic source: Craig's 1812 *Rules and Regulations for the Sword Exercise of the Cavalry* are appallingly unconcerned with animal rights:

[57] Heck, Johann Georg. *Iconographic Encyclopedia of Science, Literature, and Art,* vol. III, New York: Rudolph Garrigue, 1851; p. 552.

[58] *Provisional Regulations for Saber Exercise, United States Army,* Washington: Government Printing Office, 1907; p.48-9.

[59]Craig, Robert H. *Rules and Regulations for the Sword Exercise of the Cavalry to which is added The Rules for Drill and the Evoluions of the Light Cavalry,* Baltimore: self-published, 1812; p. 9. It might be argued that the American Craig would not have been qualified by first-hand experience to advise on cavalry sword combat. The book, however, cannot be considered an original work. In fact, the only difference between Craig's sword treatise and that of his compatriot Robert Hewes (1751-1830), a glassmaker and "teacher of the sword exercise of cavalry," are a few words at the beginning of chapters, the initial recommendation (Hewes recommends the work for the New England and Massachusetts cavalry, Craig to the U.S. Cavalry), and a few minor details in the costumes of the depicted troopers.

Since Hewes 1802 edition (Hewes, Robert. *Rules and Regulations for the Sword Exercise for the Cavalry, to which is added the Review Exercise,* Boston: William Norman, 1802. — Another edition was published two years later (1804) under the title *An Elucidation of Regulations for the Formations and Movements of Cavalry* at Salem. This version has 84 pages and 32 folding plates!) is called the "the first American, from the London edition," and he only lays claim to have "revised and corrected" it, Craig and Hewes are simply putting their names on an earlier English work, Faucitt's *Rules and Regulations for the Sword Exercise of Cavalry,* London: T. Egerton, 1796. Thus, Craig has the collective weight of Whitehall behind his opinions.

[60]Craig; p. 35.

[61]Alessandri, A. and André, Émile. *L'Escrime du Sabre a Cheval,* Paris: Ernest Flammarion, n.y. (c. 1880); p. 34: *"La prime haute sert aussi a parer la tete du cheval en certain cas. (Note: Pour la parade de la tete du cheval par la prime haute comme c'est seulement l'extrémité de l'arme qui se trouve opposée a l'ennemi (meme en se dressant sur les étriers) a cause de la distance, le sabre du pareur risque de heurter par contre-coup, la tete de son cheval.)"*

[62]Craig; ibid.

Craig (1812)

Alessandri (1880)

"Of the eight Guards against cavalry, five are for the protection of the rider and his horse in front, and three for the purpose of covering them, when under the necessity of retiring."[59]

The following guard ("guard horse, near-side protect") protects the horse's head, as well as that of the rider:

"Direct the point of the blade to the left of the horse's head, and in a diagonal line from the hand, which is not to droop, but to be carried a little forward."[60]

(This technique is still traceable in French manuals after their roaring defeat in the Franco-German War of 1870–71.)[61]

To switch into the "off-side protect," the soldier is to *"raise the blade till it becomes perpendicular, carrying it at the same instant in a brisk motion forwards to the off ear of the horse, and in the exact position of right protect."*[62]

The drill Craig and all his predecessors include also leaves little doubt as to how horses were regarded in hand-to-hand combat:

"Offensive: *Cut I at the horse's head on the nearside.*

Defensive: *The defence is, nearside protect.*

O: *Cut II at the horse's head on the off side*

D: *Horse, off side protect.*

O: *Cut I at the adversary's face off side. Parry cut III by sinking the guard.*

D: *Left protect, and return cut III at the antagonist's wrist.*

O: *Cut I at the the thigh or body on the off side.*

D: *Right protect, resting the hilt of the sword on the knee, when return cut IV at the adversary's neck.*

O: *Make cut I at the sword arm.*

D: *Come to the sword arm protect.*

O: *Cut II at the bridle arm from the rear.*

D: *Bridle arm protect.*

> **O:** *Give point at the back, near side.*
> **D:** *Left parry.*
> **O:** *Cut I at the back of the head, nearside.*
> **D:** *Left protect.*
> **O:** *Cut II at the face, nearside.*
> **D:** *Right protect.*
> **O:** *Cut I at the horse's head, on the nearside.*
> **D:** *Horse near side protect, and as the adversary moves forward,*
> *return cut VI at his sword arm, at the same time press your*
> *horse up to his near side and give him the point, by which*
> *the attack is changed, and he in his turn becomes on the defensive."*[63]

Post-Napoleonic Romanticism also did little to put knackers out of business. U.S. Brevet Major H.C. Wayne, late director of the sword exercise in the U.S. Military Academy at West Point, admonishes his students when opposing cavalry, *"after parrying, endeavor to return a cut or thrust (a thrust is preferable) at the rider; but if he continues his course without checking, and the pace is too rapid to admit a return thrust or cut at him, give a swinging cut at the horse, to ham-string him if possible."*[64]

Patton (1914)

Patton's greatly reduced repertoire—which eliminates parries and cuts completely—has no place for attacks against the opponent's horse. But even he still manages to think far enough ahead to realize that the occasional enemy might indeed respond in an old-fashioned way, by cutting at the horse instead of obligingly falling over pierced and dead:

"Guard to the right rear: The right hand, nails down, is rested on the cantle near the center, or may be held in the air near this position. (...) This guard will only be taken in cases of emergency. It is always preferable to circle and receive the attack on the right or right front."[65]

Mythmakers

Given the historical evidence, the modern rationalization of the saber target becomes untenable. Indeed, even the "tradition" of this explanation is elusive.

[63]Craig; p. 86 f.

[64]Wayne; p. 43.

[65][Patton, George S. jr.] ***Saber Exercise***, Washington: Government Printing Office, 1914; p. 27.

Considering the inclusive saber target of the 19th-century, it comes as no surprise that no 18th- or 19th-century manual mentions considerations for horseflesh at all in regard to the saber or cut-and-thrust sword as a weapon of antagonistic combat. Nor do the masters of the Italian, Vienna Neustadt, or the post-WWII Polish-Hungarian schools.

There is one single precedent for restricted target area in mounted combat with sabers: James E. Sullivan, in his 1909 *Official Supporting Rules*,[66] lists "Mounted Broadsword Rules" along with "Rules for Skittles", "Obstacle Races," "Revolver Shooting" and other marginal sports of the day. Since one page is enough for Sullivan to sum up the rules, I will include them here in their entirety:

> *"Contestants shall be required to furnish their own horses, weapons, and equipments, and no allowance will be made to continue the contest for want of same.*
>
> *"All contests must be fought with regulation broadswords.*
>
> *"Contestant will toss for choice of position before the attack. When the trumpeter sounds the signal for the attack, the contestants shall gallop their horses to the center and meet right hand to right hand and continue the attack on the other for a space of two minutes, which shall be considered the length of each round; referee to decide the winner of each round at the expiration of it; nine two-minute rounds shall constitute the battle; the referee and judges shall give their decision to the contestant gaining the largest number of rounds at the conclusion of the battle.*
>
> *"Should both contestants strike at the same time, the referee shall award the point to the contestant who, in his estimation, has delivered the most effective cut.*
>
> *"Both contestants shall show fair and equal play.*
>
> *"Should either keep out of the reach of the other for more than two minutes, the usual one-minute rest will be taken, and then the judges shall draw four lines each four feet apart and on the signal of attack, each swordsman shall be required to bring his horse (within thirty seconds) to his opponent or forfeit a point.*
>
> *"**Immediate disqualification shall follow the deliberate striking of an opponent's horse by an opponent.** One minute shall be allowed to expire between each round.*
>
> *"Should the contestant be disabled and the judges do not consider his injuries as serious, he shall be allowed five minutes to renew the battle, if he chooses to.*
>
> *"**A point can only be scored by a blow on the armor; no cut on head or arms shall count.** It is fair to strike an opponent anywhere above the lower part of the armor; any cut delivered below the armor shall be considered a foul, and cause the loss of a point.*
>
> *"Should the swordsman be unhorsed during the attack, he shall be allowed to continue on foot until round is ended, then he shall be remounted and continue until contest is decided."*

[66]See Sullivan, James E. ***Official Sporting Rules Containing the Official Rules for Miscellaneous Games and Contests Not Scheduled in Other Numbers of Spalding's Athletic Library***, New York: American Sports Publishing Co. (A.G. Spalding), 1909; p. 69.

Unfortunately, there is no description of the prescribed "armor," no details if the padded fencing vests of heavy saber and bayonet practice are considered armor, or if actual breastplates as worn by cuirassiers were involved. Still, the conditions under which the contest took place allow a few conclusions about the background of the fighters.

Horses, weapons, and armor have to be supplied by the combatants, a not inconsiderable expense even in 1909. The nature of this pastime would suggest that the horses had to be animals especially trained not only to be easily manoeuvered by thigh pressure but also to remain responsive as steel clashed about their ears. The presence of a trumpeter, the use of regulation broadswords, and the skills of the swordsmen further suggest that this is exclusively a cavalry affair—and since the fighters are at liberty to determine if they want to continue a fight after receiving an injury, the contestants may have been exclusively members of the officer corps.

Rules of the game

Low cuts are penalized by point deductions, and—for safety reasons—intentional hits against the horses are punished by immediate disqualification. But hits against the head and arms—traditional targets of cut-and-thrust fencing in both agonistic and antagonistic scenarios—are considered off-target, much like in foil competition

The rules and regulations suggest that this is a purely agonistic, Olympian contest in which a winner is determined by scoring a higher number of points hitting the prescribed target while adhering to the rules.

The quoted rules are one of the few and scarce sources documenting the very existence of this obscure and extinct sport. The origins plausibly could be sought in friendly, agonistic competition among horse soldiers. Armor and rules provide protection not afforded by the conditions of antagonistic combat.

This indeed would establish a pecedent for a cavalry code that protected the thighs and horse of the swordsman. And indeed, it may be these very rules that spawned the mythology of the saber target.

Some points, however, speak against a direct influence of the competitive military mounted broadsword on the establishment of civilian cut-and-thrust targets.

The first argument is the scarcity of the sources, as well as the social background of the fighters: This is a marginal sport whose implied skills are of too rarified for use in military combat, and too limited to translate into the broader base of civilian systems.

Civilian cut-and-thrust fencing on foot as well as military equestrian systems designed for combat include the thigh and leg as a target consistently throughout their histories. In fact, Breck's *Fencing*—also published under the imprint of Spalding's Athletic Library—still includes the leg as target only seven years earlier in the second (1902) edition.

Indeed, it seems that the very translation of what by then must have been anecdotal tradition does not gather steam until the 1960s—generations after cavalry had discarded both saber and horse for tank, helicopter, and automatic rifles, and the officers who engaged in mounted broadsword competitions had switched to less costly pastimes – do we find first tentative speculations:

"It may be that [the sports saber's] restricted target area is somehow related to the fact that when fighting on horseback men kept their blows directed above the hips of their opponents to avoid hitting the horses."[67]

[67]Vebell, Edward. *Sports Illustrated's Book of Fencing.* Philadelphia and New York: J.B. Lippincott Co., 1962; p. 64.

The metamorphosis to official historic tradition then takes place quite rapidly. By the early 1990s, Vebell's historicizing rationalization has crystallized from salle braggadocio into fencing gospel. On the occasion of the 1992 World Cup Sabre in Washington, D.C., the program of the organizers trumpeted:

> *"Since it was considered taboo to injure another man's horse, attacks focused on the enemy's upper body."*[68]

[68]Ferguson, Diane. *USFA Program Book 1992 World Cup Sabre*, Denver, CO: USFA, 1992.

Not that there's anything wrong with this.

After all, there's no harm in modern sabreurs' desire to identify with the dashing horse soldiers of the Napoleonic Wars. But in this case, the myth has created a past that appears impoverished compared to the actual historic background. And if nothing else, this essay may add a variety of choices to fencers in search of a more exciting identity than reality can supply.

INTERLUDE

ANTAGONISTIC COMBAT:
Fight for survival

Teutonic warriors (after Pollington, Stephen. *The English Warrior.*)

Troublesome Teutons[69]

Because Lord Ekke saw that Didrik wanted to fight, he became quite merry and drew his sword, and he hit into the rocks that fire flew from it.[70] They had no other light than the fire that came from the rocks. They faced off and fought so valiantly that no-one since has heard of two men who battled as ferociously. And wherever they hit, one on the weapon of the other, it looked as if sparkling fire emanated from the spot. And the blows resounded like the roar of Thor's thunder.

They cut the armor off each other's bodies—yet none received a wound. Then Lord Ekke hit on Didrik's helmet that Didrik fell to the ground and his senses faded. Then Lord Ekke threw himself on him, grasped his arms, held him hard and said: "I will bind you or you shall not live any longer. Surrender your arms, quickly. I will lead you to my stronghold and let the royal children, who armed me today, look at you."

Didrik applied: "I'd rather die now than have the nine regal daughters and their mother see me fettered. I would be scorned by all women and girls as long as I live."

[69]after Hyltén-Cavallius, Gunnar Olof (ed.). *Sagan om Didrik af Bern*, Stockholm, 1850 (Svava 100-104); contained in Ritter-Schaumburg, Heinz. *Dietrich von Bern, König zu Bonn*, München and Berli: Herbig, 1982; pp. 336f.

[70]Unless there was a special technique involved in generating festive illumination by smashing that expensive pattern-welded blade into granite, this seems to be a highly unlikely action. However, we find the same activity attributed to rowdy German students in the 17th and 18th centuries.

31

At this, Didrik wrestled his arms free, grasped Lord Ekke by the throat, and they fought for a long time. Didrik's stallion Falcon saw that his master was in dire need. He tore his tether, ran to Lord Ekke, reared on his hind legs, and with his front hooves hit onto Lord Ekke's back that he nearly broke it.

Thus Didrik gained the upper hand and immediately cut into Lord Ekke's throat that the head came off. Then he removed his armor, put on Lord Ekke's gear, and tied the sword Ekkisax to his side. (. . .) He rode out of the forest. There he met a man who was well armed.

This was Fasholt the Proud. Fasholt hailed Didrik, thinking it was Lord Ekke, his brother, because he recognized the weapons.

Didrik replied: "My name is not Ekke." There Fasholt replied: "You rotten dog and murderer. You sneaked up on my sleeping brother and killed him. Had he been awake, your lot would have been different. Because he was the best of all fighters."

Didrik replied: "You are wrong. He was awake when I fought with him, and he forced me to kill him. He challenged me for gold and silver and for the sake of the nine regal daughters and their mother, and according to warrior's custom. That's why I dismounted and beat him to Hel.[71] Had I known that he was such a valiant fighter, I would not have dared to fight him. And know this for certain, I did not take his weapons till he was dead."

Lord Fasholt drew his sword and dealt a blow onto Didrik's helmet that he toppled off his horse and was nearly unconscious.

Lord Fasholt never had to deal more than one blow against the man who fell before him, and he never took anybody's weapons. This is why he rode off quickly.

When Didrik came to his senses again, he rose hastily and gallopped after Fasholt, hailed him, and asked to square off with him: "If you're as good a fighter as people say, then don't run from a single man! If you don't want to square off with me, then you'll be disgraced wherever you go, because you did not dare to avenge your brother."

Fasholt turned his horse. He would rather fight than be disgraced. Both dismounted, faced each other, and began the battle.

Each gave the other shattering hits. Didrik received three wounds; Fasholt had five, all heavy, and he bled liberally. Now he worried for his life. Thus, he surrendered to Didrik and offered his service, although he was a faultless warrior.

Didrik replied: "You are an excellent man and a noble warrior. Your life I am glad to spare. Your service I want not, because I shall not trust you until you have avenged your brother's death. If you want my amends, then I will do you the honor to swear an oath onto you, and you to me, that we help each other, no matter what need we may get into, as if we were brothers by birth, and each shall call the other comrade."

[71] Not a typo: Hel is the Germanic goddess of the dead.

This appeased Fasholt. They swore oaths as Didrik had proposed, then mounted their horses and rode off as fast as they could.

STUDIES IN MYTHOLOGY

CASE IN POINT 3

Scene from the American Civil War

The Seduction of Art:
Cut vs. Thrust in Military Swordplay

"Poets—and hussar lieutenants—are after all nothing more to humanity than highly superfluous luxury pets, and it is surprising indeed that the wise men in Berlin have not slapped special taxes on their existence."

Hanns Heinz Ewers [72]

"I do wish that the Yankees would capture all the cavalry (. . .) They will never fight. So I think it is useless to have them in the Army Eating rations."

anonymous Confederate infantry soldier [73]

The romantic image of cavalry battles centers around the charge of gallant troopers, who, saber in hand, gallop against overwhelming odds, defying death and foe. But by the time the surviving horses returned to camp after the Light Brigade had charged Russian artillery at Balaclava, cavalry had outlived itself even as a tactical weapons system. On the battlefields of Europe, sword or saber, celebrated and cherished weapons of the mounted trooper, had become anachronisms, much as the longbow had three hundred years earlier.

[72]Ewers, Hanns Heinz. from – "Armer Freddy", in *Ameisen* München: Georg Müeller. Verlag; p. 8.

[73]Quoted from Ward, Geoffrey C., Burns, Ric and Ken. *The Civil War, An Illustrated History*, New York: Alfred A Knopf, 1990; p. 227.

In fact, as early as the 1680s cavalry could rarely force battle on cavalry. It could fight infantry only at the cost of facing the defensive superiority of the foot soldiers. Confronted with a wall of men armed even with inferior pike substitutes, saber-wielding cavalrists stood no chance of breaking through the ranks.[74] And even if they did, contemporary historians did not hold the effects of the sword in particularly high esteem:

> *"It were to be wish'd that if Horsemen be obliged by their capitulation to furnish themselves with swords, that their Officers would see them provided of better than ordinarily most of them carry, which are such as may be well enough resisted by either a good Felt, or a Buff-coat."*[75]

In the Napoleonic era, the role of mounted shock troops diminished even further. Cavalry had become the inferior weapon system, *"its pistols dominated by muskets and its charge with sabers overmatched by a line of musketeers with bayonets."*[76]

Only its greater mobility assured it a continued, if greatly decreased, tactical place in armies. Nowhere can a more qualified personal account of this phenomenon be found than in the diaries of Nadezhda Durova, a female Russian cavalry officer during the Napoleonic Wars:

> *"Although I love the cavalry madly, although I am a horse soldier from my cradle, every time I watch the infantry advancing at a sure, firm pace, with fixed bayonets and menacing drum-roll, I feel an emotion which has something of both reverence and dread, I don't know how to express it. All that comes to mind at the sight of a formation of hussars or uhlans flying past is the thought of what gallant lads they are, how well they ride, how dashingly they cross sabers! Woe to the enemy, and this woe usually consists of more or less dangerous wounds or captivity, and nothing more.*
>
> *But when columns of infantry rush toward the enemy with their rapid, smooth, disciplined motion, there are no more gallant lads, that's all over: these are heroes who bear inevitable death or go to inevitable death themselves—there is no middle ground. The cavalryman gallops up, gallops away, wounds, rushes past, turns back again, and sometimes kills, but his every motion is eloquent of mercy for the enemy: all this is merely the harbinger of death. But the infantry formation is death itself, dreadful, inevitable death."*[77]

Kegan's appreciation of cavalry action is less flattering:

> *"Indeed, unless cavalry action resolved itself into a complex of single combats, it was pretty harmless to the participants. Mercer recalls watching two lines of French and British light cavalry skirmishing with each other on ground between the armies, on the evening of 17 June [1815, the night before Waterloo].*
>
> *'The foremost of each line were within a few yards of each other—constantly in motion, riding backwards and forwards, firing their carbines or pistols, then reloading, still on the move. I did not see a man fall on either side; the thing appeared quite ridiculous; and but for hearing the bullets*

[74]Jones; p. 267.

[75]Turner, Sir James. *Pallas Armata. Military Essayes of the Ancient Grecian, Roman, and Modern Art of War*, (London: Richard Chiswell, 1683) New York: Greenwood Press, 1968; p. 171.

[76]Jones; p. 401.

[77]Durova, Nadezhda. *The Cavalry Maiden—Journals of a female Russian Officer in the Napoleonic Wars* (transl. by Zirin, Mary Fleming), London, Glasgow, Toronto, Sydney, Auckland: Paladin Grafton Books, 1988; p. 201.

whizzing overhead, one might have fancied it no more than a sham fight.' He has an equally dismissive account of cavalry's occasional mutual harmlessness even in the performance of its true shock role. (...) Cavalry could, it must be emphasized, suffer very grievously at the hands of other cavalry when nerves failed, horses were blown, or weapons markedly unequal."[78]

Disuse of the sword

In 1853, Edward Anthony Angelo felt compelled to defend his brother Henry's works on military sword exercise in a small booklet. He states:

"It has been much the fashion for old officers to say, they never saw the sword or bayonet used during their long period of service, and that in fact they were useless both to the Officer and Soldier, and only a burden to them; and these remarks generally emanating from individuals speaking of the 'Peninsula,' (as if there were no other fields of action, (...) leave an impression upon the minds of young soldiers of the present day, that the hostile parties never come into collision, and that it is only boring and useless tiring them by either a Sword or a Bayonet Exercise!"[79]

Still, supporters of the sword frequently told the anecdote of the French Marshal Ney who, at the battle of Neuwied, was unhorsed and thrown to the ground—then saw himself attacked by six Dragoons:

"But he sprang to his feet and laid about him so furiously with his sword, that they were unable to capture him until an additional force came to their aid, and not even then until after his sword had broken off short in his hand."[80]

Eight years after Angelo's note, Berriman in the United States confirms that the sword was indeed very popular – as a symbol of the gentleman and officer:

"Too true it is that the great majority of officers merely carry it as the badge of their authority, without any sufficing or even proximate knowledge of its practical values and resources; they point with it, flourish it, salute with it, —but of its real excellence and utility as an instrument in the hands of a soldier, it is to be feared that the majority know little or nothing at all."[81]

Last gasp

By the time the uniting German states steamrolled Napoleon III in the Franco-German War (1870-71), the odds had changed even further in favor of infantry: German horsemen prudently stayed off the rifle-dominated battlefields while mobile German infantry wiped out the two documented French cavalry charges with accurate rapid fire from cover:

[78]Kegan, John. *The Face of Battle—A Study of Agincourt, Waterloo, and the Somme*, (London: Jonathan Cape Ltd., 1976) London: Penguin, 1978; p. 149.

[79]Angelo, Col. Edward Anthony.; p. 13.

[80]O'Rourke, Matthew J. p. 10.

[81]Berriman, Capt. M. W. *The Militiaman's Manual and Sword-Play without a Master. Rapier and Broad-Sword Exercises copiously explained and illustrated*; (...), New York: D. Van Nostrand, 1861 (2nd ed.); p. V.

"Probably no saber cut any infantryman and no infantryman had occasion to defend himself with his bayonet. The era of traditional shock action seemed to have ended, and cavalry, a large target in any case and usually unable to take cover, had lost its tactical role."[82]

Which, of course, didn't keep the same thing from happening again in 1941, as becomes evident from the war reminiscences of the late Otto Günther Klusmann:

"Unforgettable and worth mentioning—because completely anachronistic and incomprehensible for someone who did not witness the event—is the defense of a mêlée of the 4th Mongolian Cavalry Division (stirrup to stirrup with sabers drawn) in our divisional section on November 17, 1941 near Mussino (southwest of Klin) by means of our artillery's ricochet shooting, whose devastating splinter effects reduced the 2,000 riders and their horses into only a few dozen, which then were cut down by machine gun fire. We did not have a single wounded on our side."[83]

Fighting by committee

In this situation, it may strike you as odd that army departments all over the Western world were arguing about what type of sword should be used in mounted conflict:

"Those in favour of the cut claimed that a cut with skill and weight behind it would do more than the thrust to put a man out of action, and that it was easy after the cut to recover quickly to come on guard. In later years, (…) the general opinion seems to have been that the thrust should be used for the charge, and the cut in the mêlée, for at close quarters it is difficult to use the thrust."[84]

In 1909, the British opted for the new thrusting sword, which was modified and adapted for the U.S. cavalry in 1913. This happened at a time when one machine gun crew could defend itself successfully against an entire cavalry squadron.

Knowing too well that their sabers, rifles and revolvers had become useless against even a single sniper with a repeating rifle, cavalry officials made one last valiant attempt to regain some luster by reviving their most anachronistic weapon—notwithstanding the fact that at the dawn of World War I, edged weapons had been playing a negligible role on European battlefields for at least 150 years.

Contemporary military manuals illustrate how little attention had been given to the actual use of the edged sidearm in combat situations. The *Regulations for the Prussian Cavalry*, translated from the German in 1757, for example, give detailed information about the most important cavalry tactics, in particular the "caracole." A brief description of this cavalry offensive makes clear what an inferior role the sword played even in what we today consider the heyday of cavalry battles:

During the caracole, the first and second ranks of a hussar squadron would unleash six waves of small-arms fire on the enemy. The first rank of the first

[82]Jones; p. 401.

[83]Klusmann, Otto Günther. —"Begegnungen im Kriege 1939/45," in *Mitteilungen Hannovera Göttingen*, Göttingen: Corps Hannovera; #83 (August 20, 1990); p. 33.

[84]Ffoulkes, Charles. *Arms and Armament—An Historical Survey of the Weapons of the British Army*, London: George G. Harrap & Co., 1945; p.30.

division would advance and fire their carbines. Then the second rank would advance before the first and fire; the first rank would then advance again and fire one pistol, again followed by the second rank; then the second pistols of the first and second ranks would be discharged, consecutively.

Afterwards, the first division would gallop back to reload and align with the left wing of the second division. This game would be repeated by the second and third divisions. Then, and only then, do we find one laconic sentence about the use of the sidearm:

> *"When the third Divisions have fired their carbines and pistols, and begin their retreat, the second Divisions are to advance about thirty paces upon a gallop sword in hand, at which distance they are to raise themselves off their saddles, and make a stroke."*[85]

It appears that the techniques of "making a stroke" did not change considerably between the late 18th and early 20th century. In fact, only the terminology is different if you compare Henry Angelo's *Hungarian and Highland Broadswords*, published in London in 1799, and the *Provisional Regulations for Saber Exercise of the United States Army* of 1907. The latter still teaches all classic saber guards and parries, and only advises to

> *"aim at the most exposed part of the body, his [the opponent's] sword arm, and if that cannot be reached by a direct attack, endeavor to mislead him by making a distinct feint at some part of the body the parry for which exposes the arm, and then cut at the arm with the true or false edge of the blade."*[86]

Military fencing

Seitz argues that military fencers did not concern themselves with a methodical study of the use of the saber until the 1790s.[87] Even then, the primary aim was to achieve a tactical result with the combined impact of a troop's edged weapons. Speed and force of a squadron's communal shock action determined the result, not the fencing skills of the individual. The cut was the simplest, most natural and most forceful attack with the saber.

By 1845, organized military fencing in central Europe could be separated into three systems. The first was the contemporary school of the smallsword (*Stoßrapier* or *Stoßdegen*), which was mainly practiced by officers. The light smallsword was useless in battle but was carried as a status symbol, identifying its bearer as an officer and a gentleman. The practice weapon was the foil, and training was mainly preparation for duels.

The second system was that of the curved-blade saber. This was the general issue edged sidearm for enlisted men and nearly exclusively a cutting weapon. Practice was first conducted on the "fencing bench", and then on horseback. Its system featured a limited repertoire of guards and parries, allowed for hardly any direct thrusts, and for effect relied heavily on the shock and impact trauma of its heavy blade.

The third system, commonly called cut-and-thrust, was practiced with a variety of heavy, straight-bladed weapons: the spadroon or shearing sword, the

[85] Faucitt, William (ed.). *Regulations for the Prussian Cavalry* (London, 1757), reprint: New York: Greenwood, 1968; p.124.

[86] *Provisional Regulations for Saber Exercise*, p. 37

[87] Seitz, Heribert. *Blankwaffen II*, Braunschweig: Klinkhardt & Biermann, 1968; p. 387f.

broadsword, or the army rapier (*Armee-* or *Haurapier*). Cuts were aimed mainly at the sword arm and the face of the opponent, although fencing practice could include the chest as target. [88]

These weapons could be used for thrusts, but their main function was to cut, usually from a hanging guard. (This system is the precursor of the German Schläger fencing, which was developed after the French Revolution, when the aristocratic smallsword had fallen into widespread disuse.)

Transfer of authority

By the 1890s, however, army fencing masters and amateur lovers of the sword—even the legendary Sir Richard Burton—had begun to advocate the thrusting sword for the cavalry. It appears that many of them were academic fencers with limited combat experience outside the salles or maybe the duelling grounds.

Even though most were experts in the use of the lightly curved cavalry saber of that period, many had started teaching the newly developed Italian *sciabola di terreno* or duelling saber, the straight-bladed predecessor of the modern sports saber. These masters were trained in the pedestrian art of fencing (as opposed to the equestrian military skill), which to this day maintains that the thrust is more quickly executed than the cut. And they began to apply their experience on the *planche* to mounted combat in the field.

One of the most famous proponents of the thrust weapon was Louis Rondelle, a former French zouave in the war of 1870/71, who was trained as Maître d'Armes at the Fencing Academy at Joinville-le-Port. In 1889, he was appointed fencing master of the Boston Athletic Association.

He held that the sabers in use in the 1890s were not suitable for either offensive or defensive because their blades were too heavy and the handles too short. The ideal cavalry saber would be straight, with a steel guard well protecting the hand, and be used mainly for the point thrust. He favored discarding all cuts except for those directed at the bridle hand and the rein, but instead would teach the point thrust in all positions and for all conditions:

The Patton Skewer (1913)

"A heavy saber deals a heavy blow but may not cut at all. (. . .) The saber cut sometimes wounds seriously, often lightly or not at all, and rarely kills; whereas it uncovers the body of the assailant and exposes it to the Point Thrust of the enemy, which latter thrust has the advantage of being easily executed in every direction without exposing the body. It is the most rapid of execution, the most dangerous, and the most difficult to parry of all saber strokes. In all the great wars of the Empire the French cavalry won its invincible reputation by this Point Thrust, which at all times and places is superior to the cutting stroke." [89]

[88]Heck; p. 546f.

[89]Rondelle; p. 214.

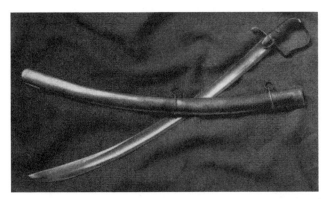

The Classic Cleaver (1796)

Rondelle doesn't know that this same "invincible" French cavalry complained to Wellington about the use of the heavy curved saber that the British used exclusively as a cutting weapon:

"In 1773 the 15th, and later the 8th, Light Dragoons rehilted their swords with stirrup hilts. The sword was in use in the campaigns against Napoleon, and it has been stated that it caused such terrible wounds that the French protested to Wellington against the use of this 'barbarous' weapon."[90]

This saber type remained in use in the German army until 1914. The effectiveness of this weapon even in the hands of troops with no formal training is illustrated in a footnote to the English translation of Col. Marey-Monge *Memoire sur les armes blanches.*[91]

"The author (Col. Marey) all through his work speaks of the old British Light Cavalry Sword as an admirable weapon for cutting, and in his judgment is remarkably confirmed by the following interesting extract from Captain Nolan's book on Cavalry:[92]

'When I was in India an engagement took place between a party of the Nizam's irregular horse (...) My attention was drawn particularly to the Doctor's report of the killed and wounded, most of whom suffered by the sword, and in the column of remarks such entries as the following were numeruous: 'Arm cut from shoulder.' - 'Head severed.' - 'Both hands cut off (apparently at one blow) above the wrists, in holding up the arms to protect the head.' - 'Leg cut off above the knee, &c.' ... And now fancy my astonishment! The sword-blades they had were chiefly old dragoon blades cast from our service. The men had remounted them after their own fashion. The hilt and handle, both of metal, small in the grip, rather flat, not round like ours when the edge seldom falls true; they all had an edge like a razor from heel to point, were worn in wooden scabbards, (...)

An old trooper of the Nizam's told me the old English broad blades were in great favour with them, when remounted (...) I said, 'How do you strike with your swords to cut off men's limbs?' - 'Strike hard, sir!' said the old trooper. 'Yes, of course; but how do you teach them to use their swords in that particular way?' - 'We never teach them any way, sir; a sharp sword will cut in any one's hands.'"[93]

[90]Graham, Col. H.. *History of the 16th Light Dragoons (Lancers)*, n.p.: 1912; i. p. 245; as quoted in Ffoulkes, p. 40.

[91]Marey-Monge, Guillaume. *Memoire sur les armes blanches*, Strasbourg., 1841. English translation by Maxwell, Henry Hamilton. *Memoir on Swords*, London: John Weale, 1860.

[92]Nolan, Capt. L.E. *Cavalry: Its History and Tactics*, London, 1854 (2nd ed.); p. 110-112.

[93]Maxwell; p. 9f.

It was in the hands of these native soldiers that the sword regained some of its historic glamour:

> *"In the various wars between Turkey and Russia, the Turkish and Circassian cavalry, armed with scimitars and yataghans, committed such havoc among the Russians that the ponderous cuirassiers were wont to seek shelter from the terrible blades of their foes, behind infantry and masses of artillery. During the war on the Punjaub, the Sikh horsemen not only met the English cavalry hand-to-hand, but individual soldiers challenged English dragoons to meet them in single combat."*

In one of these encounters, at Chillianwalla, a Sikh cut down and unhorsed three English dragoons in succession, and would doubtless have committed more damage had he not been shot down.

The history of the same battle furnishes another striking illustration of the relative value of the point and edge of the sword.

> *"A dragoon of the Third Regiment, charging with his squadron, made a thrust at the Sikh next to him; the sword stuck in the lower part of the body, but did not penetrate sufficiently to disable him, when the Sikh cut back, hit the dragoon across the mouth, and took his head clean off."*[94]

Point vs. edge

For sure, the argument of point vs. thrust could only be proven at the price of blood. And sometimes, the results were all but clear, as the following account bears out:

> At the Battle of Talavera, in 1809, *"I saw [Harry Wilson] engaged hand-to-hand with a French dragoon; I saw him (...) give and receive more than one pass, with equal skill and courage.*
> *Just then a French officer delivered a thrust at poor Harry Wilson's body and delivered it effectually.*
> *I firmly believe that Wilson died on the instant; yet, though he felt the sword in its progress, he, with characteristic self-command, kept his eye still on the enemy in his front, and raising himself in his stirrups let fall on the Frenchman's helmet such a blow, that the brass and skull parted before it, and I saw the man's head was cloven asunder to the chin.*
> *It was the most tremendous blow I ever saw struck; and both he who gave, and his opponent who received it, dropped dead together. The brass helmet was afterwards examined by an order of an officer, who, as well as myself, was astonished at the exploit; and the cut was found to be as clean as if the sword had gone through a turnip, not so much as a dent being left on either side of it."*[95]

The point attack from horseback relied heavily on the element on surprise. But if the point was anticipated, as in the example below, it—like other techniques

[94]O'Rourke; p. 96f.

[95]from Stoqueler, J.H. *The British Soldier* (1857), in Regan, Geoffrey. *The Guinness Book of Military Anecdotes,* New York: Canopy Books, 1992, p. 17.

that can be anticipated with reaonable certainty—quickly became a liability. The Sepoy Mutiny provided the follwing example:

> *"It is the creed of these men [of John Nicholson's elite Pathan's Guards encamped outside Delhi in 1857] that to be individually in action without accounting for someone is a matter of shame.*
>
> *In pursuance of this doctrine, we saw two of the bodyguard, out on our right, apparently challenge two of the Bengal Cavalry to single combat; anyway, the challenge was accepted, and the four rode at each other, the Pathans on their ponies, their tulwars waving in circles round their heads, their loose garments flowing.*
>
> *The Bengalees sat erect on their big horses, their swords held ready to deliver the 'point', a stroke no regular cavalryman comprehends, and he does not in his sword exercise learn to parry the thrust.*
>
> *For a moment all eyes were on the four combatants: the thrust was delivered, but instead of piercing the bodies of the Pathans, it passed over them, for they threw themselves back on their ponies, their heads on the crupper, their feet by the ponies' ears, and in that position swept off the heads of the Bengal cavalrymen. Instantly the ponies wheeled round, the men straightened themselves in their saddles, and they passed from our vision."*[96]

Patton's folly

Most cavalry soldiers, of course, could not be expected to possess the equestrian artistry of Pathans. This realization is what a young, ambitious American lieutenant was to use as the foundation for one of the most hyped and only recently most controversial systems of edged-weapons combat ever designed.

The U.S. Army's *Saber Exercise* of 1914 was prepared by Second Lieutenant George S. Patton, Jr., 15th Cavalry, Master of the Sword at the Mounted Service School for the two-edged model 1913 saber.

Like its British predecessor of 1909, this weapon was designed predominantly for the thrust. Patton redefined the role of the saber from a weapon of both offense and defense to one of purely offensive character:

> *"The saber is solely a weapon of offence and is used in conjunction with the other offensive weapon, the horse. In all the training, the idea of speed must be conserved. No direct parries are taught, because at the completion of a parry the enemy is already beyond reach of an attack. The surest parry is a disabled opponent."*[97]

Emphasis was put on guards rather than parries. And "faulty" attacks, such as cuts, high points, low points, or inaccurate points as well as the seeking of the opponent's blade were prohibited. Patton explains:

[96]Wilberforce, R.G., *An Unrecorded Chapter of the Indian Mutiny*, 1894, in Regan; p. 188.

[97]*Saber Exercise*, 1914; p.5.

"On foot, at the walk, it is quite possible to make this sort of a parry and still have time to touch; but, mounted, at a gallop, a man who seeks the blade of his foe and parries it may escape uninjured, but so will the other man. The speed of the horses is such that the enemy will be out of reach before a trooper can make an effective lunge at him, whereas if he disregards the other's saber and lunges at his body, he will, in so doing, force his adversary's saber aside and transfix him. Moreover, the very idea of seeking the saber so as to parry it is taking a defensive frame of mind and is contrary to the offensive cavalry spirit."[98]

The charge, according to Patton, is *"an extended position deriving all its great effect from the momentum of the horse. (...) In combat, (...) the difference in time between a touch with the point and a cut with the adverse edge will usually be sufficient for the spasmodic contraction caused by the entrance of the point to render the cut ineffective."*[99]

The Hokey Pokey according to Patton (1914)

Compare this limited use of the saber to the role defined only a few years earlier by the Austrian Bartunek—who defines the saber as a weapon of war designed to deal blows whose effects could be felt through thick uniform cloth or helmets, and that were heavy enough to parry blows even with gunstocks, and finally allowed a few forceful cuts![100]

Patton's system may have been close to the reality of mounted combat of his day, considering this period's overall lack of classic cavalry battles. But it excluded any *corps-à-corps* action at close distance as the one described by witnesses of the Crimean War.

The main weakness, however, is its lack of flexibility. Patton's system is the modern equivalent of medieval and Renaissance jousting, which only works under highly artificial conditions. It presupposes equally armed and attired opponents with similar if not identical levels of skill. A saber-wielding horseman who was not trained to seek and parry the weapon of his opponent was dangerously outclassed by the longer reach of polearms as used by uhlans or lancers:

"The lance—in fact all long weapons—should be considered as a weapon of attack, an opponent, with a sword for instance being alway within yours, whilst you are out of his reach."[101]

Against the breast-plate of a cuirassier, his point attack would have been useless.[102]

Some historians still take exception with this view, considering Patton's system the best possible system, considering that land warfare is won primarily by maneuver. Undoubtedly, there is some truth to the fact that the point of a hefty 40-inch blade, barreling along by virtue of a ton of of moving horseflesh, certainly is not an easy problem to solve.

[98] *ibid.*, p.19-20.

[99] *ibid.*, p.20.

[100] Bartunek, Josef. ***Ratgeber für den Offizier zur Sicherung des Erfolges im Zweikampfe mit dem Säbel***, Esztergom, Hungary, 1904; p.26: *"Der Vorschriftssäbel ist jedoch eine Kriegswaffe, eine Waffe, welche die Bestimmung hat, durch die Wucht ihres Auffallens selbst auf Tuchbekleidung, Helm, etc. zu wirken, Gewehrstösse und Schläge abzuwehren, endlich im Handgemenge einige wenige, aber dafür tüchtige Hiebe zuzulassen."*

[101] Angelo, E. A.; p. 18.

[102] Patton argues the opposite: *"Against a lance, the charge with the point is superior to the charge with the edge. In the first place, the lance point can be deflected at a greater distance from the body; thus giving the swordsman the longest possible path in which to get the necessary deflection, while the sword at the same time slips along the shaft of the lance with the point in line for the lancer's body who thus not only has his attack parried, but also his life menaced. Should the trooper on the contrary, sit up to use the edge, he must make his parry when the lance is not over two feet away from him, so that the path the point has to go, while being deflected, is reduced between six and seven feet, while the size of the deflection is the same as before and at the same time the attention of the lancer is not disturbed by the threat of the blow."* from Patton, Lieutenant G.S., Jr. —"Mounted Swordsmanship," in ***The Rasp***, 1914. (Copyright 1996-97, The Patton Society).

But then, it is also true that in any charge, be it of infantry or cavalry, it is rare for blades to actually cross. One side or another will break first—and run. That's why it is essential that any charge be executed with the most aggressive methods.

Any attack is to be preferred to a parry-riposte from a psychological standpoint. Attacks with the edge involve a much finer timing than attacks with the point, which simply require that the point be kept in line. Consequently, a point attack is the logical best method for training common cavalry trooper with limited training time available.

Patton did intend to use his saber technique in combat. Probably the most telling notes are from the Mexican Punitive Expedition of 1916, when Patton engaged in repeated debates with General Pershing about the feasibility of charging with pistols. Patton held that a proper charge had to be made blade-in-hand, while Pershing, relying on Civil War experience, argued that the pistol was perfectly adequate.

Patton actually attempted to stage a charge with sabers. Patton's superiors gotwind of it and forbade it, but the attempt was made to actually use the M-1913 saber in combat.[103]

Linear motion

Disregarding the element of psychological bluff that undoubtedly would have influnced the outcome of a charge with the point (and in which Patton put a lot of trust), the mechanics of the system still argue for a very different outcome. Even if executed properly, Patton's system stops working at the very moment of successful penetration. Patton provides guidelines about how to withdraw the saber from the stationary practice dummy.

But he overlooks that the attack was directed against a target that was moving toward the attacker at the same speed. The impact of two speeding bodies would drive the blade deep into the body of the opponent.

Sabers frequently were tied to the wrist of the trooper by a thong to prevent loss in battle. If his blade had transfixed the opponent, his best bet would be to bail out and let go of the weapon—thus disarming himself! If he decided to hang on, he faced two deadly threats: At best, he would break his wrist or dislocate his sword arm as he raced past his falling enemy. At worst, his dead opponent would drag him off his own horse—making him an unarmed foot soldier in an ocean of falling saber blades and trampling hooves. Considering this, the point-in-line charge would be suicide if the enemy charged in ranks more than one deep.[104]

Furthermore, the thrust requires a linear forward motion with a straight arm that carries the point into the target. In sports fencing with the foil, épée and saber, this forward motion is provided by a lunge or flèche; during Patton's charge, it is provided by the movement of the galloping horse.

While standing or wheeling, however, the fighter must needs "punch" or stab with his blade to make up for his lack of forward impact. He loses essential point control and accuracy, without being able to adequately compensate for the lack of linear impact. The fighter also exposes his arm and elbow to the opponent during the pumping motion of the arm.[105]

[103]Most of the above arguments were made in a letter to the editor by Michael McDaniel, published in *Hammerterz Forum*, vol. 3 # 4/vol. 4 #1 (Spring/Summer 1997), p. 17.

[104]Compare also Conwell, Charles. —"Was Patton Right?," in *American Fencing*, vol. 42, #2; p. 16; and Ffoulkes, p. 30.

[105]Craig—and thus the English experts whose work Craig so shamelessly copies—explicitly warns against the dangers of this action: *"For in bending the elbow, the sword arm is exposed; a circumstance of which the opponent will ever be ready to take his advantage, as a cut in that quarter may be made with the greatest security; and if it be well directed, with the most fatal effect, as it at once decides the issue of the contest."* (p. 8) and *"These are faults which beginners are extremely apt to commit, and which expose the swordarm to be completely disabled."* (p. 22)

Matter of intent

A blow with the heavy saber may not always have resulted in lethal wounds, but the impact of the heavy weapons must have been devastating. Even the slender blunt blade of the German practice Schläger can break bones, as many a German Corps student with torn or loose-fitting fencing cuffs has found out.

It must also be noted that continental European police officers in the 1800s rarely carried sharpened sidearms but used their blunt hangers and sabers as steel truncheons. (There is also evidence that the 18th-century smallsword outside the salle and the duelling ground was frequently used as a non-lethal steel rod.) The heavy curved saber therefore combines the characteristics of both the butcher's cleaver and the medieval war club. [106]

At close quarters, the best targets for the cut are bridle arm and reins, the sword arm, and face and neck of the opponent. Cuts in the high line—prime, high tierce and high quarte—were impractical as they would be caught by the enemy's headgear. The neck would typically be protected by the stiff collar of the uniform against direct cuts. However, a heavy hit against the neck was able to incapacitate. Hits to the face would blind the enemy by their heavy blood flow, and, more importantly, have devastating psychological impact.

(To Patton's credit, it must be mentioned that he made provisions for the cut:

"The Cavalry Sword Model 1913, is an ideal thrusting weapon and at the same time, one which can give a cutting blow at least one third harder than our former saber, while the sharpened back edge makes it much easier to withdraw from a body than would be the case if it were single edged."[107])

Patton's decision to make do without parries is particularly remarkable, considering that even Rondelle could not conceive of successful saber fencing without a solid knowledge of parries:

"It is uncontestably true that in the case of the saber a good parrier always wins. Strong in parries, he never fears the adverse attack. He waits for it and even provokes it, that he may have the advantage of a Time Thrust or a good riposte, which, made within distance, will invariably count."[108]

Retrospectively, it appears that the decision to adopt the straight-bladed thrusting weapon for the cavalry, and to train the trooper exclusively in the thrust, was influenced more by academic considerations than actual experience of the battlefield. The abstract experience of salle fencers was applied to the tasks of fighters whose needs to survive in battle conditions were far more complex.

Due to the fact that a mounted trooper had to be able to defend and attack to all sides in whatever limited chance he had to find himself in close combat, the two-dimensional linear system of Patton seems particularly inadequate. It combined the disadvantage of the lance (lack of flexibility and limited use for close-range defense) with those of the sword (short reach).

(It might be arguable how prudent it was to publicize Patton's exclusive focus on the point in print. Given that the point requires an unsuspecting and untrained opponent to be successful, hostile intelligence services would probably have passed on the information to the respective authority.)

[106]It has been pointed out that many military sabers don't actually have an edge, thus were useless for cutting. This is certainly true for blades worn as dress sidearm after World War I. But in many armies, edged weapons designed for action (except for the bayonet) were only sharpened at the time of mobilization. (See Angolia, John R.. *Swords of Germany 1900/1945*, San Jose, CA: R. James Bender Publishing, 1988; p. 56.)

[107]See Patton; "Mounted Combat".

[108]Rondelle; p. 213.

In World War I, however, it was difficult to disprove the perceived advantage of Patton's saber versus the classic curved pattern:

> "*The amount of use to which the new sword was put was, of course, negligible, it having arrived at a time when tactics were being so changed by the advance of new and improved weapons that the massed use of cavalry and, indeed, the use of cavalry charges, was becoming more of a folly than a useful manoeuvre.*"[109]

Latham records a single episode in which this straight-bladed sword was used in World War I:

> "*Lieutenant Gordon Flowerdew of Lord Strathcona's Horse gained his Victoria Cross in France on 30 March 1918. He led three troops of cavalry to the charge, passing over both lines of the enemy, killing many with the sword. Then, wheeling about, charged them again. The enemy broke and retired. This very gallant officer died of his wounds the next day.*"[110]

This incident, of course, illustrates nothing more than cavalry's superiority in riding down footsoldiers, with riders stabbing or hacking at infantry from an elevated position. And that is where the effectiveness of Patton's system would have to be sought:

> "*In practicing the use of the point as prescribed it must always be remembered that it is for the use of the many in combats of opposing masses. It is in no way fencing, but the use of the sword is to quickly accomplish a tactical object; the quick and complete defeat of the enemy. (. . .) It's object is to teach, as quickly as possible, a large number of men the most efficient way of handling their weapon in a combat that will last for minutes and be famous for centuries.*"[111]

It may have been Patton's good fortune, and that of his men, that the Patton Skewer, that "ultimate cavalry sword," never had the chance to put lives at risk in battle—not more, at any rate, than an enemy hand grenade...

[109]Latham, John Wilkinson. *British Military Swords from 1800 to the Present Day,* New York: Crown, 1966; p. 51. Latham, of course, discusses the British 1909 model cavalry sword, which was similar in design to Patton's.

[110]Latham; p. 35, note 4.

[111]See Patton; "Mounted Combat".

INTERLUDE:

COMMENT COMBAT:
Mensur

Mensur with bell-guard Schlägers (Berlin, 1911)

Ultimate Male Bonding:
A Schläger Mensur at Göttingen, AD 1987[112]

> *"To face an adversary in armed combat is one of the most exciting experiences in life."*
>
> **Aldo Nadi**

A last command, a brief clash of steel—then glasses clink and cigarette smoke and fragments of conversation swirl like fog through the dimly lit room. A half-hundred men push toward the counter in the corridor to have their beer mugs refilled by the stocky bartender. A pledge wearing a blue cap starts vigorously cleaning splatters of bright red from the hardwood floor.

I listen to the muted buzz of the crowd through the high glass doors that separate a small winter garden from the *Fechtsaal* or fencing hall of the Corps Brunsviga in Göttingen, Germany. Then the doors burst open, and a dozen or so of my Corps brothers lead in one of the combatants. Blood drips from underneath his blond hair into a thin rivulet down his neck, his face is sweaty and puffy, but he is grinning from ear to ear. Waving to me, he disappears behind a gaggle of agitated dark blue suits.

[112]Amberger, J. Christoph. —"Ultimate Male Bonding," in ***Hammerterz Forum***, vol. 3, #3 (Winter 1996/97); p. 8f.

It is my turn now. I am already wearing the long-sleeved black Kevlar shirt. Knof, my second, enters the room, carelessly dropping his heavy helmet on the ground, picking at the buckles that keep his long padded gauntlets fixed to the tattered leather plastron. An oblong apron protects his loins. Three horizontal strips of colored felt are sewn to it: red-blue-red, the ancient colors of the Corps Hannovera. Nonchalantly, Knof pulls a pack of Marlboros and a Zippo lighter from a hole in the felt. For a fleeting moment, I wonder what else he has hidden in there.

Attention, along with the mail shirt, shifts from the wounded fencer to me. The awkward fingers of my Corps brother Frisch start wrapping my neck with stiff silk bandages. I choke and cough, but the expert wrapper, a medicine student from Emden in Eastern Frisia, remains unimpressed: bandages have to sit tight to prevent blades from getting caught in between cloth and skin.

The mail shirt is pulled over the Kevlar and velcroed shut. What an improvement over the old silk-padded leather plastrons that I fought my first couple of bouts in! But that fleeting feeling of comfort and mobility doesn't last. A broad, stiff bandage is strapped to my neck. My chin juts out, my eyes nearly pop from their sockets under the pressure. Am I turning blue? Slowly, the choking pressure subsides. A leather apron with inch-high ridges is hooked into the chain mail and tied around my thighs. Helping hands thrust my right arm through a padded cuff and connect it to a steel-reinforced glove. A black leather square is buttoned to my left shoulder. I am ready to go!

My opponent is already sitting on a chair in the center of the hall. The backs of his Corps brothers shield him from inquisitive glances from our side.

Leisurely, the spectators are taking their places. All of them wear gaudy caps, and most have woven silk bands in the color combinations of their respective Corps across their chests. The bright red patch of Hannoverians' heads is visible at the far end of the hall. One by one, most of my companions leave me, tapping my shoulder and wishing me *"Waffenschwein!"*[113], luck at arms.

I am seated on a chair opposite my opponent. In the center of the battlefield, Knof and the other second are selecting an umpire from among the more experienced and respected fencers in the crowd. Weapons in hand, helmets tucked underneath their arms, they announce the combatants and type of encounter in ritual phrases. The umpire, a Saxon who goes by the nickname of "Silver Curl," requests Silentium. The room falls mute.

At the center of a hall crammed full with people—some standing on tiptoes, on chairs and tables just to catch a glance over the closed ranks and shoulders of the men in the first rows—with a hundred interested eyes directed at me and with close and trusted friends to my left and right, I suddenly experience a feeling of solitude such as a man left alone in the woods must feel at nightfall. It is oppressing and dense, a primal emotion of apprehension and instinctive alertness that drains all learning and art from the mind and only leaves a tiny voice of reason piping in the void. The feeling is intense and existential: Within a few moments, a razor sharp blade will flick at my head, six times in two seconds, for round after round after round.[114] And it is only myself, being the examiner and the examined at once, that will get me through, not by spooling off some body of theoretic knowledge, but by taking ultimate control of myself, of my body, of my mind, of my reflexes, of my blade. At that moment I know I cannot fully rely on the skills and

[113]This literally means "weapon swine," related to the German expression *"Schwein haben"*—to be lucky.

[114]The Göttingen *Comment* for a "Persönliche Contrahage" (PC) calls for 40 rounds at 6 cuts each. As cut and parry occur simultaneously, a round takes only between 2 and 3 seconds of highly focused bursts of energy. While there is indeed a gentlemen's agreement not to aim hits below the line of the cheek bones in a normal *Bestimmungsmensur* (40 rounds at 4 cuts each), the more rigorous rules for the PC allow "low cuts" aimed at the cheek. Rules differ greatly from city to city, ranging from 4-8 cuts per round, and 30-80 rounds per Mensur, depending on the character of the encounter.

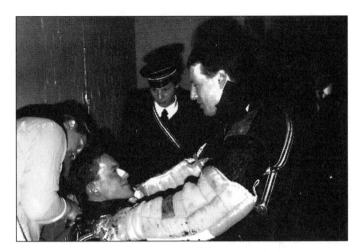

Fitting the neck brace

techniques I have mastered with the Schläger during the past two years. All that is left is the mechanical imprint of the drill—and a latent desire deep in my throat to sell my hide as dearly as possible.

For a moment I am wondering what the hell I am doing here. I'm hot and uncomfortable. My mouth is dry and a whole colony of butterflies seems to populate my stomach. Then it dawns upon me. Two fundamental truths about human nature—my nature—rapidly gain cohesion: Deep inside, underneath all that Kevlar and mail, I know I'm a coward. If I could, I'd be bounding out of here like a jackrabbit on a pogo stick.

But here's where the second realization sets in: I'm also a moron. There's no reason for me to be here. There's no prize to be won, no credits to be accumulated. In fact, I stand a good chance of having my face and head cut up in every direction—leaving indelible scars that will mark me as an anachronistic elitist or a nutcase in the eyes of most my uninitiated contemporaries. Still, I'm free to leave even now. I could wrestle off the bandages and make for the exit, and that ocean of curious eyes and bright caps would part before me like the Red Sea did for Moses. But I don't. I stand firm, dig in my heels, set my teeth, and in a gesture of near bovine defiance, lower my forehead.

Once again, I feel clumsy hands take charge. The *Paukbrille*, or fencing goggles, are pressed over my eyes. They look like a small iron skiing mask, with a beak-like projection for the nose. Inch-high steel ridges are soldered around the eye openings, jutting out from the notched surface. Instead of clear glass or plastic, steel mesh protects the eyes[115].

"Talk about tunnel vision...," I start thinking, but then the leather straps are tightened so hard I feel my skull sutures creak and thought grinds to a standstill. A small circular leather pad is strapped to the crown of my head, where a previous opponent's blade had left a nasty scar. The lower part of my face, my forehead and scalp remain unprotected. Someone thrusts my Schläger into my right hand. My index finger gropes for the leather sling inside the red-blue-red basket hilt, pulls it tight. Ring finger and pinky nestle into the curve of the D-shaped knuckle-guard, the pommel pressing into the root of my thumb to establish something resembling a pistol grip. The shark-skin handle and glove seem to merge. I am ready. There is no way in hell I could be less comfortable.

[115]Depending on local rules, the ears can be protected by additional leather straps. In some cities, such as Braunschweig, a leather flap protects the cheek against low cuts.

In my immobile state, I am placed, pushed, moved, like a piano, opposite the enemy. The seconds measure a blade's length distance between sternum and sternum. A captive of my own body and its outlandish gear, the only thing I can see through the wire mesh is my opponent's face. The protruding beak of his goggles gives him the nightmarish appearance of a sweating giant raptor. His double-edged Schläger is razor sharp. And for all I know he will go for the gusto, that is, my face. Brown eyes flicker at me uncertainly. Good, he seems nervous. Time for some psychological warfare. I stare into his eyes and affect an arrogant smile. If only my mouth wouldn't twitch like that . . . and could I have a sip of water to peel my tongue off the roof of my mouth?

Meanwhile, the seconds have gone into position. My right arm and Schläger point straight up, the point at a slight angle toward the head of my opponent, as is my habit.[116] The padded cuff over my right biceps is pressed to my ear. I thrust up my head. It is less a gesture of defiance—although it sure must look like it. It's a necessity: I have to be able to watch the forte of his blade.

Knof's blunt blade locks mine right above the basket. Then there is a second that lasts for minutes, in which I can only feel my stomach and my adam's apple, both pulsating and slightly unstable. Through the current inside my ears, I hear the commands:

> *"Hoch, bitte!"*
> *"Hoch!"*
> *"Legen sie aus?"*
> *"Sie liegen aus!"*
> *"Los!"*

The seconds dodge. Time stops. Then the moment races on: Blades clash, my weapon taking on a life on its own: One, two, three, six slashes in rapid succession, heavy as lead at first, then lightly cutting the stale air with vicious hisses. Baskets clank and leather thuds. I feel something cold flick at my left cheek; try to cut under my opponent's parry. Then, a blink of an eye after the last command:

> *"Halt!!"*

The seconds jump in. My blade is knocked off-balance as Knof's Schläger and swordarm shoot up to provide a protective umbrella against cuts after "Halt." Extending arm and blade upward from the hanging guard I finished in, I slowly lower my weapon to the right in a wide arc. Roether, my roommate, catches the descending sword just below the hilt. He starts rotating my hand at the wrist to relax the sword arm: A well-intentioned superstition. Another attendant, wearing a butcher's chain mail glove, disinfects my blade with a sponge and Lysol. Tiny scraps of yellow, sheared off by the razor edge, have to be picked from the steel with caution after he is done. Upon brief examination, my cheek seems to be intact, only slightly nicked by my opponent's flat hit.

> *"Hoch bitte!"*
> *"Los!"*

[116]This initial guard position is called the *Steile* (steep) Auslage. Other cities such as Würzburg have the *Verhängte* (hanging) *Auslage* as the starting position.

This time I try to break his time with a *Schleife*, a combination of sweeping moulinets.[117] In the seconds-long burst of rattling steel, I manage to get under his guard, pull through and ... my blade leaves a red welt across his cheek. This could have been the decision. I could be out of my steaming armor and at the counter, drinking in streams of cold, life-affirming beer in a moment. But unfortunately, I, too, occasionally hit flat. Still, my opponent appears shaken. His associates request a brief intermission for him to sit down. I watch him examine the bruised cheeck with his bare left hand, checking for blood. I fully intend to take advantage of this blow to his fighting morale.

Next round, the same again. But I have become too cocky, to the detriment of my cover. My sword arm veers to the right during the first moulinet, leaving the left side of my head open and setting the stage for an even less-covered low quarte. My mistake is punished immediately: Within a second, two horizontal quartes hammer into my left temple, a bit more than an inch apart. Oddly detached, I feel the double tap of the blade; then Knof jumps in.

Something cold runs down my face. I can taste blood. My own blood. A doctor moves up in front of the two meshed tubes that constitute my range of vision, gently dabbing a piece of gauze at the wounds. I briefly wonder how hot my face must be that fresh blood actually feels cool on my skin. But only for a moment. The doctor is done, slaps my shoulder and grins. Not bad enough to be taken out. The Mensur goes on. And on.

An infinity of rounds later I am exhausted. I feel like I have entered a dream, a dream in which my actions are as futile as trying to fend off rain drops by waving a stick over my head. But this is real: The chain mail drags my shoulders down and I nearly have to push from my legs to raise my sword arm. Knof keeps whispering combinations into my ear that I should try.

But I've stopped listening: What does he know. Every action of mine hits leather or steel, is parried intentionally or unintentionally by the blur of my opponent's arm and weapon. I feel I am scraping the bottom of my barrel. I am bleeding liberally from three cuts in my head, and I can't tell if it is blood or sweat that runs down my face to splatter into a puddle on the floor. Viscous red stalactites of coagulating blood seem to be forming on my chin and I think my opponent even nicked the fringe of my ear! And he himself hasn't received a scratch. Only a purple smudge on his cheek marks the place where my blade hit flat a millennium ago.

> *"Hoch bitte!"*
> *"Los!"*

This time I try a "dessin" I learned from the swashbucklers of the Corps Normannia in Berlin. It is called a *"Stirnzieher,"* a relatively basic pattern of cuts, high quarte, a high tierce with incomplete recovery, and a pulled-through horizontal quarte into the angled tierce. Timing is crucial. If timed right, this combination breaks his tempo after the high tierce and would lay open his entire forehead to my blade for the fraction of a second.

I try. I succeed. I miss. A tuft of hair gently whirls, then floats through the air like dandelion parachutes. My energy level suddenly is sky high again: Explain that to your hairdresser! My opponent seems confused, doesn't know where it came from. A good sign. For me, at least. I know I have to forcefully maintain this state

[117]This particular combination, the *Bonner Schleife* (lit.: "Bonn bowtie"), begins with a high quart from cover that draws into a reverse moulinet through low tierce that is immediately converted into a drawn-through low quarte (*"Zieher"*).

of alertness. Its a matter of time now. My face is burning. I can't wait to hear the seconds' command. Inside my head, I repeat the syncopated rhythm of the combination, over and over again:

"Pom-pom-ka-WOOM-boom."

But I can't repeat it immediately. I've got to wait, take the pounding blade as low on my forte as possible, while riposting with rapid quartes—throwing in a crisply-cast Hakenquart across his elbow toward the end of each set. But two rounds later I try it again. His aggressive power appears to be decreasing, leaving his face pale, with large red blotches on his cheeks. Apparently he stops breathing for the duration of the round, for two, three seconds at a time, that is. This can eat into your oxygen reserves.

This all enters my mind at once. I am experiencing the adrenaline-induced hyper-awareness of a fighter at the end of the match: I notice he stopped using more sophisticated combinations and dessins, and is brutally pumping quartes against my surprisingly stable and high guard. His sword arm is punching toward me, the basket hilt rotates only a foot away from my head. That's bad for his cover. And bad for me because the force of his cuts makes the full length of his blade whip flat over my arm, hitting the back of my head and my shoulders, no matter how high I set up my guard. The force of the whipover twists steel: His second already had to straighten his blade twice. It is painless, given the insensitivity that comes with fight, but disconcerting. One of us will snap. Soon. I focus on my dessin again: "Pom-pom-ka-WOOM-boom. Pom-pom-ka-WOOM-boom." Then the seconds pick up where they left off:

"Hoch bitte!"
"Los!"

Again. Pom: High quarte, Pom: high tierce, ka: a quick turn of the wrist, a whipping moulinet into the horizontal quarte pulled through while pushing my arm to the utmost left ... WOOM ... and I've got him. That's it. The "boom," an afterthought in the dessin, already hits padded leather: The seconds have simultaneously burst into action, all but knocking me over backwards. But I still can see my opponent's sweat-drenched face. A hair-fine line appears across his forehead, five, six inches long. Then a red curtain falls, turning his face into a mask of oily scarlet, from which the inch-high rims of the goggles stick out black and ghoulishly.

Commotion. My opponent disappears behind the tattered leather back of his second. The doctor approaches, looks and shakes his head. A moment later the second will turn around, request silence while unhooking his gauntlets, and courteously thank for a fair fight.

Suddenly all the tension that has drained me for an hour has evaporated, my lungs expand, and a breeze seems to cool my face. And not even the prospects of having needles shoved through the gaping fringes of my cuts can dim the elation. I know I won't feel a thing: the combination of wound shock and adrenaline will take care of anaesthesia.

At that moment, an invisible bridge links me to generations and generations of men of all ages and races and creeds who realized the pathetic core of their own humanity in armed confrontation—undistorted by the layers of fads and culture that civilisation has deposited on the surface. I know that for the rest of my days, my outlook on life and its challenges will reflect that one primal experience, of facing a hostile opponent with steel in my hand.

PART TWO

GRID OF STEEL:
THE SPHERES OF COMBAT

The text in its unadulterated original spelling, reads *"Wie schmeckt dir Fechter dießer Stoß! Mich dünckt du gebst dich gar zu bloß, Und könnest nicht wo[hl] auch parirn, Nach recht, nach kunst, den Degen führ'n, bleib weit davon, so hast du's gut. Weil niemand dort dich treffen thut."* Which loosely translates into: "How, fencer, does this thrust taste to you, I think you leave yourself open too much, And if you can't parry well, either, wield the sword according to law and to art, stay far away from it, then you'll do fine, as nobody will hit you then."

The fencer on the right, presumably starting from the German Guard has deflected the Fool's thrust with his left hand (a technique that was to survive in German thrust systems well into the 1890s.) His padded point hits the Fool's nose, giving him the professional appearance of John Wayne Gacy minus the rainbow wig for a short but undoubtedly painful moment.

And as his Fool's cap is knocked off his head, he is to realize that you either learn how to parry or are better off staying away from the fencing strip altogether.

Der Fecht-Narr (The Fencing Fool), from Abraham a Santa Clara (a.k.a. Megerle, Ulrich.) ***Centi Folium Stultorum in Quarto, oder Hundert Ausbündige Narren***, Wien: Megerle and Nürnberg: Lercher für Weigel, 1709.

PART TWO

Wager of Battle
French miniature from
the 15th century

Grid of Steel:
The Spheres of Combat

In his autobiography *The Living Sword*, the Italian master Aldo Nadi devotes an entire chapter to a "Critique of American Screen Swordsmanship". Suffice to say, the Maestro has little esteem for such silver screen icons as Errol Flynn, Tyrone Power, or Douglas Fairbanks, Jr. who *"know little or nothing of the science of fencing. While they do their stuff on the screen as well as they can, and their best is often pitiful, it should be made exceedingly clear that none of them could hope to make the eight-man finals of any novice fencing contest in most states of the Union..."*[1]

His scathing review culminates in the advice that *"any and all of the director's ideas concerning the duel should be sifted and studied by the fencing master; and if the latter finds them sound and in keeping with the dignity of the sword, the chances are that in their final execution, they will emerge quite improved."*[2]

At the core of Nadi's resentment is a sentiment alien to no red-blooded swordsman. It is probably as old as fighting itself—traceable in the vitriolic remarks of George Silver regarding True and False Fight (the latter, of course, practiced by Saviolo and Bonnetti) and in the disdain thrust fencers of all periods have mustered for cut fencers.

[1]Nadi, Aldo. *The Living Sword,* Bangor, ME: Laureate Press, 1995; p. 367.

[2]ibid., p. 374.

Even today, it survives in modern sports fencers' opinions about Schläger fencing; that of re-enactment fencers about sports fencers and recreational fencers; and in the opinions of all fencers combined about the art of the stage fencers: The others' systems are not REAL fencing!

To outsiders uncoached in the appreciative and critical skills of observing a fencing bout, this integrated system of mutual disdain is hard to understand. After all, most people couldn't distinguish the systems involved in, say, a fight with broadswords, a smallsword duel, a 1930s Hollywood flick, or a local sports fencing event if their lives depended on it.

The uninitiated may plead ignorance of swordplay in his defense. The respective sword aficionado, however, is not too far removed from this lack of exposure: Most of his criticism is based on close familiarity with a particular subset of edged weapons combat—and ignorance of all others.

And then, of course, popular usage of certain terms certainly offers very little help in clarifying matters

The meaning of life

Duel, n. *A formal ceremony preliminary to the reconciliation of two enemies. Great skill is necessary to its satisfactory observance; if awkwardly performed the most unexpected and deplorable consequences sometimes ensue. A long time ago, a man lost his life in a duel.*

Ambrose Bierce,
The Dictionary of the Devil

Take the word "duel", for example—probably the most abused term describing any kind of confrontation from a soccer penalty kick shoot-out, to batteries of artillery slugging it across the trenches of Verdun.

For the last 300 years, the only correct use of the term was to denote a ritualized armed encounter to settle matters of honor. A duel could be fought to the death, until a pre-determined number of cuts or shots were exchanged, or until first blood was drawn (i.e., a bleeding wound of pre-determined depth or width decided the outcome.)

The duel is inseparably tied to the notion of honor, a concept that is difficult to fully comprehend from a modern point of view.

Thomas Hobbes defined that *"honorable is whatsoever possession, action, or quality is an argument and sign of power (. . .) Nor does it alter the case of honor whether an action, so it be great and difficult and consequently a sign of much power, be just or unjust, for honor consists only in the opinion of power."*[3]

Without getting any more detailed or specific, one of the last codices of honor published still echoes Hobbes' 17th-century summary:

> *"Honor is a) the inner value of a man that is based on the proper ethical mindset and carriage, b) the acknowledgment and noticeable respect of this value through others."*[4]

[3]Hobbes, Thomas. **Leviathan** (1651), Indianapolis: Bobbs-Merril Educational Publishing, 1958; chapter 10; p. 83.

[4] *"Ehre ist a) der sich auf anständige sittliche Gesinnung und Haltung gründende innere Wert des Mannes, b) die Achtung und erkennbare Anerkennung dieses Wertes durch andere."* Verein Alter Corpsstudenten (VAC) **Ehren- and Waffenordnung,** 1937; p. 7.

Honor at its most visceral is an intangible commodity representing public and individual expectation of the degree of power the honorable individual is expected to wield. It is a measure of the determination not to be forced to do another man's bidding as long as one is alive and able to wield a weapon. The word of honor can be pledged or pawned as security for a promise, a loan etc. If the promise is broken, the party pledging his honor loses it much like a foreclosing borrower on a mortgage loses his collateral.

(The VAC's *Ehrenordnung* of 1937 (!) explains this in so many words:

"Who is guilty of breaking his word of honor has lost its honor and no longer can be a Corps student.")

Men of honor

"It is too bad that death often results from dueling, for duels otherwise help keep up politeness in society."

Napoleon Bonaparte
(to Gaspard Gourgaud at St. Helena, 1815-18)

Ignoring the mystic determination of right and wrong by divine intervention during the ordeal, and the balance of raw justice demanded and established by blood revenge, the duel is an entirely worldly affair:

"Honor and revenge have no alliance."[5]

Honor is the recognition and consciousness of a man's social and personal dignity and value that transcends the individual and applies to his family and household. (Beating another man's servant, or even dog, was reason enough for a challenge.)

The sidearm not only represented a visible back-up of one's personal claim to freedom.[6] But in the scabbard, in the holster of the other man, it also provided a clear demarcation of where exactly that liberty ended. Expanding your space into that of an opponent could only be achieved at the risk of facing his sidearm in deadly conflict.

Consequently, being without honor meant being without power and an honorless individual would be hard pressed to find the trust and esteem necessary to continue undisturbed in his previous social or power position. Loss of honor was equal to moral bankruptcy. The honorless individual will be treated much the same way as someone who declared financial bankruptcy applying for an unsecured personal loan.

Life without honor is deemed to be impossible. Only public functionaries and officials can refuse all challenges since their duty to their office takes precedence over their personal interest. Private trustees, on the other hand, and *"professional gentlemen, on whose energies or talents, the lives, fortunes, or reputations of their clients may depend, can never justify their fighting duels, without making a full and timely surrender of their trusts."*[7]

[5]Hamilton, John. *The Only Approved Guide Through All the Stages of a Quarrel Containing the Royal Code of Honor; Reflections on Duelling; and the Outline for a Court for the Adjustment of Disputes*, London: Hatchard & Sons; Liverpool: Bentham & Co., and Dublin: Millikin, 1829; p. 2.

[6]Interestingly, this symbolism survived World War II until German Re-unification in 1990. When I bought my first bell-guard Schläger back in 1985 in my home town of West Berlin, Allied law still prohibited anyone in West Berlin from owning a gun or sword... theoretically even a long kitchen knife was illegal. This was a remnant of 1945 when the specter of the Wehrwolf was lurking in the shadows of the shattered city. The symbolism of occupation law transcended the practical military and paramilitary implications. Of course, chances of a Berlin Brunhild with a broadsword attacking a U.S. or British tank were slim. But it sent a message: The defeated, the un-free, have no right to bear arms, no matter how outdated and useless these might be. On post-war Berliners, this message was lost. After all, apart from the wild post-World War I years, individual liberty in Germany had always been subordinated to the state.

[7]Hamilton; p. 4.

Can't get no satisfaction

"One sword keeps another in its sheath."
George Herbert, *Outlandish Proverbs, 1640*

Truthfulness is the key characteristic of the gentleman. Giving the lie, i.e., calling someone a liar, not only questions the veracity of a statement but also attacks a tangible and all-important social asset. The attacker is attempting not only to damage the reputation of the accused, but in doing so endangers his entire moral credit rating, the very essence of life and position in society. He must be dealt with in a matter that repudiates the accusation—by throwing one's life and bodily integrity into the balance.

"Satisfaction" therefore does not refer to the intellectual satisfaction of "winning" a duel or asserting right or wrong by victory or defeat. The very fact that the combatants show up, engage in the fight, clears them of all insinuations against their honor, independent of the outcome of the duel.

But this also poses a problem. To avoid inflationary use of the duel for petty disputes solved by inflicting petty injuries, the rules had to be strict, yet vague enough to deter the casual duellist.

Trivial pursuit: Épée duel Lifar vs. de Cuevas. Whatever passes for honor is restored by a scratch to the elbow. (From Baldick; ***The Duel***, image 31 c).

Delegation of responsibility

It is important to note that in the last stages of the duel as a social self-cleaning mechanism, the directly involved parties relinquished nearly all decisions to their representatives... the seconds and the doctors.

The duel with saber or duelling sword provides the last scenario for hostile antagonistic combat with swords in 20th-century Western Europe. The rules, particularly those written by Central European masters of ceremony like Barbasetti, muster all the self-righteous bluster against frivolous duels (i.e., those where the parties settle for First Blood) that raised Central European index fingers are capable of: A duel has to be fought until one of the parties received one or several "incapacitating" injuries.

Oddly enough, all authors I examined avoided specifying what exactly is meant by that favorite term "incapacitating." There are no physiological details, check lists, or definitions. In tome after tome, it becomes evident that "incapacitating" is not a matter of medical or physiological condition, but predominantly one of individual opinion or judgment on the side of the seconds.

What the doctor ordered

In Germany and the Austro-Hungarian Empire (the latter borrowing heavily from Italian trend setters like Barbasetti), final judgment about the severity is rendered by the attending physician(s) and approved or disapproved by consensual decision of the seconds.

The physicians in turn are bound by their honor not to terminate severe duels because of a "slight" injury. (In fact, during these duels, they are not allowed to intercede until one of the fighters has dropped to the ground or is so badly injured that he cannot continue. Still, even here the fight could be interrupted by the second.)

Duel triage

Here are a few examples straight from the sources:

Hergsell, Gustav[8] (1891):

- Page 74: *"If the motives for the duel are of a less serious nature, or both opponents only took refuge in arms due to a wrong interpretation of the points of honor, the seconds have to agree that the fight will be continued no further after the first injury, even if it is light. This condition will have to be communicated to the duellists just before the fight."*

- Page 75: *"Who is responsible for judging the seriousness of an injury? It seems like it is the doctor, yet we found the following rule in the duelling rules: 'The ability or inability to fight will be determined by the seconds, with the doctor having an advisory role.' We believe we have to agree with those who think: 'The fight can only be terminated as a result of the unanimous decision of seconds and doctors.' (...) It is not up to the doctor to decide if the fight is to be ended, he only has to judge the severity of the wound."*

Barbasetti, Luigi[9] (1898):

- Paragraph 114: *"The duel is only an unavoidable solution of a matter of honor, and if insults of a serious and severe nature between two individuals have been passed, the measurement of satisfaction for it*

[8]Hergsell, Gustav. **Duell-Codex**, Wien, Pest, Leipzig: Hartleben, 1891.

[9]Barbasetti, Luigi. (Ristow, Gustav transl.) **Ehren-Codex**, Wien: Verlag der Allgemeinen Sportzeitung, 1898.

cannot be diminished, nor can conditions be negotiated that are apt to make the combat look ridiculous; thus the exemption of certain cuts or the thrust, as well as the application of [defensive] bandages are fundamentally inadmissible. (...)"

- Paragraph 122: *"In duels for complete incapacitation ("bis zur vollständigen Kampfunfähigkeit") it is permissible to continue the fight with the left hand, or vice versa, if the other arm is injured. In such duels the use of a padded leather glove can be demanded to avoid that the duel be terminated because of a slight injury to the hand."*

- Paragraph 128: *"Each of the parties will provide a doctor and everything necessary for potential medical assistance. The presence of two doctors is often imperative, be it to judge the nature of a wound, or be it to help to render immediate medical attention to both fighters."*

- Paragraph 131: *"In duels for complete incapacitation you will need to have— apart from the selected weapons—another pair of more dangerous weapons at hand, for use in case the combat cannot be continued with the former and it would become necessary to terminate the affair otherwise. (It is not rare that in a saber duel one of the opponents gets injured on his hand and— notwithstanding the wound being slight—it becomes impossible to use the hand for combat. Then the duel is to be continued with pistols.)"*

- Paragraph 150: *"If the offending party in the duel for complete incapacitation is injured on the right arm, he is obliged to continue the fight with the left hand."*

- Paragraph 157: *"In duels for complete incapacitation, the continuation of the fight after an injury depends on the judgment of the doctors."*

- Paragraph 162: *"If the doctor has an imperative vote and declares the injury as one that would prohibit the continuation of the fight, the seconds are not allowed to permit that the duel be continued."*

- Paragraph 176: *"If a duel is to be fought for complete incapacitation, the doctors cannot provide assistance or render a judgment—aside from immediately necessary staunching of the blood flow—until one of the fighters has dropped to the ground or is unable because of a heavy injury—thus not from exhaustion!—to continue the fight. (...) The doctors are not allowed to terminate the duel because of false compassion or another reason when one of the fighters has only been injured lightly."*

Ristow, Gustav[10].(1909):

- Paragraph 167: *"If the injured party can only continue the fight under unfavorable conditions because of heavy loss of blood or severity of injury, the seconds are obliged to stop the fight."*

- Paragraph 204: *"If one duellist becomes incapable to use weapons because of high-grade excitement, or becomes unconscious at the first sight of blood, the seconds have to terminate the duel with the respective protocol."*

The delegation of responsibility is evident even in the specialized scenario of the Mensur—a scenario that by virtue of compulsory defensive weaponry excluded life-threatening injuries.

Just for kicks, here are a few 19th- and early 20th-century regulatory samples from Schläger and saber Mensur-*Comments*… similarly vague, with even more emphasis on the role of the physician.

Würzburg[11]:

- Paragraph 18: *"A Mensur (or saber duel according to student custom) can be declared finished if a fencer is* abgeführt *(declared unable to continue the fight), i.e., if the second declares to the umpire that his fencer is unable to continue the fight because of a bloody hit* (Blutiger) *received according to the rules* (commentmäßig). *A bloody hit is any bleeding cut wound received above the nipples and underneath the fencing cravat in a place not covered by defensive weaponry. The umpire has to decide, after hearing the doctor's opinion who has to pledge his word of honor, if a debilitating hit has been received."*

Dresden[12]

- Paragraph 69: *"A wound counts as a bloody one* (Blutiger) *only if blood runs over the wound fringes."*

Pan-German *Comments*:

- Paragraph 20[13]: *"The* Abfuhr *(termination) occurs when a fencer has received cuts causing a loss of blood that make further standing impossible or that could imperil the life if another hit lands in or next to a cut."*

- Paragraph 67[14]: *"If an artery is severed by a* commentmäßig *cut, second, witness and doctor have to pledge their word of honor that the bleeding will not be stopped by tourniquet or other blood flow-interrupting means."*

[10]Ristow, Gustav. *Ehrenkodex*, Wien: Seidel & Sohn, 1909; (1st edition).

[11] *Würzburger S.C.-Paukcomment*, Würzburg: Universitätsdruckerei von H. Stürtz, 1891; (III. Vom Ende und der Suspension der Schlägermensuren.) p.7.

[12] *Dresdner Paukkomment: Bestimmungen zur Regelung schwerer Ehrenhändel*, Dresden: A. Dressel, 1912; p. 18.

[13]Schmied-Kowarzik, Josef and Kufahl, Hans. *Duellbuch*, Leipzig: J.J. Weber, 1896; p. 330.

[14] *Offizieller Paukkomment einschließlich des Säbel- und Pistolenkomments für die deutschen Universitäten und Hochschulen*, Leipzig-Reudnitz: August Hoffmann, 1907; p.26; "Von den Verwundungen"); in Setter, Jürgen (ed.) *Paukkomments: Eine Materialsammlung*. Erlangen (?): Schriftenreihe der studentengeschichtlichen Vereinigung des CC (# 25), 1986.

A bleeding wound, heavy or light, on either side was an indication that the intent and determination on both sides was serious. The German students said *"Hat ein Schmiß gesessen, ist der Tusch vergessen"*—if blood has been drawn, the insult is forgotten. Only vendettas that entangled personal hostility with questions of honor undertook a duel to the death.

This, of course, was the theory. But the duel was a proof of gentlemanly behavior, of how a man carried himself through the challenge and subsequent procedure. Thus, it contained a strong element of peer pressure. Which did not make much of a difference to duels being touchstones of honor:

> *Private duels are and always will be honorable, though unlawful, till such time as there shall be honor ordained for them that refuse and ignominy for them that make the challenge. For duels also are many times effects of courage, and the ground of courage is always strength or skill, which are power; though for the most part they be effects of rash speaking and of the fear of dishonor in one or both of the combatants, who, engaged in rashness, are driven into the lists to avoid disgrace.*[15]

By the book

> *"When you meet your antagonist, do everything in a mild and agreeable manner. Let your courage be as keen, but at the same time as polished, as your sword."*
>
> **R.B. Sheridan**; *The Rivals* iii, 1779

Being a para-legal way of regulating social interaction, the characteristic sign of the duel is the presence of a written or unwritten set of detailed regulations—the Code Duello.

A proper duel had to involve seconds and doctors, later on even umpires and witnesses, to set it apart from armed assault. Offensive and defensive weaponry had to be predetermined and equal, the allocation of weapons being conducted by chance. In later forms of the duel, like in the German duel with basket-hilt sabers, even the number of cuts was prescribed.

This heavy regulation was required to establish a level playing field: Not every gentleman could be expected to be an expert swordsman. The duel with cold steel is not so much a play of skill but of aggressive energy. And even here the disparity between opponents could be so severe that a fight with swords could turn out to be quite an unappetizing affair. Pistols suddenly started to look attractive...

The example of the duel serves to illustrate how many factors could influence the setting of a combative confrontation long before the seconds actually measured the distance between the fighters. Yet up until now, most of the determining peripheral factors have never been taken into consideration when analyzing a particular combative scenario.

[15]Hobbes; p. 84.

The origins of rules

Even though the roots of the art of fencing (and thus, those of the modern sport) are deeply entangled with the preparatory effort for antagonistic combat, substantial differences in the fighting style of competitive bouts and actual duels remain. What is permissible during the bout today may have been imprudent (not to say downright foolish) on the duelling ground.

Modern épée fencers, for example, no longer have to worry about actual injuries, so attacks below the waist-line can be executed more freely and frequently than they would have been possible or desirable in an actual duel with smallswords or épées de combat.

Aldo Nadi commented on the alienation between real combat and the abstract art of fencing:

> "True, the same weapons are used in both [sports fencing and duelling]. Yet, but for the technical foundations, they constitute two different worlds hardly compatible with each other. (...)"[16]

The rules of modern fencing were derived from late forms of ritualized armed encounters that were strictly regulated by codices of honor, and enforced by seconds, umpires, and the nemesis of spectators. These dictates of prudence and caution translated into the fixed regulations and target definitions as fencing developed from a fighting art into a competitive sport. Barbasetti probably put it best in his *The Art of the Foil*:

> "The art [became] a sport rather than a pure and direct preparation for combat. This sport has become quite complicated and it has become necessary to regulate it by rules and former conventions, to make it artistic. This explains the origins of the rules."[17]

The modern sport of fencing currently is the most prevalent form of edged-weapons combat. During the last century, it has shed every element of antagonistic combat — since it lacks the intention to put an opponent out of combat by way of physical injury.

Sports fencing is heavily imprinted by the availability of body protection that makes actions possible hat no actual fighter would have dared to undertake at any point in history. Accordingly, apart from the épée (which may find practical application in the equally strictly regulated *Comment* environment of the 19th century duel), no modern fencing weapon is practical as a weapon for antagonistic combat scenarios.[18]

[16]Nadi. *On Fencing*, p.24.

[17]Barbasetti, Cav. Luigi. *The Art of the Foil*, New York: Dutton, 1932; p. 170.

[18]It is noticeable how quickly agonistic practice systems—such as singlestick or Dussack—completely disappeared once the weapon it was to exercise were no longer used in actual antagonistic confrontation. Modern sports fencing is the only exception, having thus far survived more than six decades after the duelling sword and *sciabola di terreno* became collectibles.

INTERLUDE

ANTAGONISTIC COMBAT

Navaja fighter using
his hat to parry (1849).

An Unregulated Duel to the Death with Navajas[19]

Both opponents grasped their cloaks and stepped into a small courtyard behind the tavern, which by now had filled up with numerous spectators of both sexes, attracted by the animated altercation. Nearly all by itself, a large circle had formed around the fighters—and from the moment that the knives were drawn and the cloaks wrapped around the left arm, they stood without a sound in focused attention.

Some women at first wanted to assuage the opponents with their wailing, some uninvited advisers tried the same with their counsel. But calls of *"quieto"* (quiet!) and "let them go, they know why", "don't get involved with stuff that ain't your business" resounded from all sides, and thus the thrust-upon mediation had been refused.

Both opponents stood facing each other. The older one stood erect, the left arm with his *manta* held in front of his chest like a shield, the knife pointing down in his lowered muscular fist. The rolled-up sleeve provided a view of the muscular brown arm. His steadfast, courageous glance measured up the enemy, against whom he appeared to want to act mainly defensively.

Resting on his left knee, right foot set back, his left arm—hung with his *capa*—thrust away from him, the younger one was preying with glowing, vengeance-seeking looks for an opening to attack the powerful enemy.

[19]from Kufahl, Hans and Schmied-Kowarzik, Josef. **Duellbuch**, Leipzig: J.J. Weber, 1896; p. 199f.

When the other remained unmoveable, he began to stalk him like a tiger cat, hiding his movements behind his cape, which covered him like a curtain. Finally he dared to pounce at his opponent like a tiger. But this one evaded the thrust with a small volte, caught the knife on his *manta*, and returned a thrust with his navaja against the attacker, which hit the right arm pit, but did not penetrate deeply.

The injured man, disregarding his wound, jumped back, and the older fighter called that this was enough, that he didn't want to have mass read for the souls of two brothers—because this combat had originated for the sake of avenging the killed brother.

Even more incensed by the sarcasm and his injury, the other hissed his *"carajo"* in reply, and despite the bright blood running from his armpit across his chest and hip, he appeared not at all to be ready for reconciliation, but rather for a second, more decisive attack.

The witnesses of the duel had barely noted this when the injured man jumped with a powerful lunge at his opponent, ran under him, and with his wide knife delivered a thrust into his lower body that the other one had no time to parry. With a muted scream he reached for the wound, swayed, and fell to the ground. With one cut, the knife had opened up the body in a foot-long incision, so the entrails came out.

The perpetrator, after having picked up his coat and hat, had disappeared through the circle of spectators, without anyone attempting to stop him.

MEN OF IRON

Urs Graf,
"Landsknechte" (1514)

T he International Hoplology Society defines a combative system as *"a body of organized, codified, repeatable movement patterns, techniques, behavior, and attitudes, the primary intended function and planful design of which is to be used in combative situations."*

In addition to the objective and descriptive approach, however, I believe that the internal context of any combat scenario ought to be approached from the most basic and yet, most neglected element: the individuals involved.

The protagonists in any fighting scenario are living, breathing human beings whose actions more often than not depend less on proprioceptive conditioning, their mastery of motoric and strategic skills, than on the subjective psychological effect of the situation. While the outsider may focus mainly on the weapons and biomechanical responses exhibited, combat activity itself is first and foremost a combat of minds and wills.

The role of angst in single combat

Combat situations are high stress scenarios. The level of stress is determined by the subjective evaluation of the opponent and the subjective perception of risk to one's own welfare and bodily integrity.

According to the working definition brought forward by John Keegan in his remarkable book *The Face of Battle*, single combat is characterized as hand-to-hand fighting of individuals:

> *"Single combat demands, by definition, equality of risk and fore-knowledge of the consequences. It also appears to presuppose consent by both parties (it was in that chivalry saw its glory.)"*[20]

A crucial element of single combat is mutual consent. This need not mean voluntary consent. Entering a combative situation as an active participant implies that other options—such as running away, deserting, or passively submitting to violence—have been rejected in favor of active defense or counter-attack. Involuntary consent can be coerced by discipline, threat of court martial, even anticipated ostracism.

But before consent can be given to join in edged-weapons combat, it is necessary to examine the element of individual fear. After all, this most formidable hurdle to actually entering into serious single combat first needs to be overcome to make consensual engagement in battle possible at all.

Garden of fear

The French 19th-century military theorist Ardant du Picq[21] stated that most soldiers fight out of fear of the consequences of not fighting—either punishment, even death, meted out by a firing squad—and then of fear of not fighting well (i.e., not surviving the fight).

A subtle but even more powerful coercion often emanates from the fear of being disregarded by one's fellow fighters, endangering one's *"reputation as a man among other men."*[22] In civilian life, peer pressure could be exerted by the nemesis social opinion—as would be the case for a declined challenge or breach of etiquette during an affair of honor.

This phenomenon is already documented in Homer's *Iliad* where *"the driving force is called honor,"* i.e., a preoccupation with the hero's status in the eyes of other people:

> *"Possessions and property are an outward sign of 'honor'; (…) A hero will not court death—indeed it in no way increases his honor to be killed. He will not fight for his country, nor for his leader; but he will die rather than lose face. So he will fight bravely in the front rank because the eyes of the others are upon him."*[23]

[20]Kegan; p. 145.

[21]du Picq, Ardant. **Battle Studies**, New York: Macmillan, 1921, based on the French original from 1870.

[22]Marshall, S.L.A. **Men Against Fire**, New York: William Morrow, 1927, as quoted in Keegan; p. 71.

[23]Willcock, M.M. **The Iliad of Homer**, London: Macmillan, 1978; p. xiii.

(The Greeks used the term *timé* to describe this complex interaction between self-esteem and peer acceptance.)

Considering that strong elements of fear are present in most serious armed conflicts, consent implies at least an intuitive if not rational weighing of alternatives, a conscious decision to set aside fear and choose fight over all other options— including that of letting yourself be killed without making an attempt at defense.

Paralysis of fright

Any fight scenario that involves the actual possibility (if not probability) of injury or death subjects the fighters to a veritable cocktail of competing, barely containable emotions. These include panic, extreme anticipation, passive and active aggression. [24] For the sake of argument, I will refer to this complex nightmare as "personal fear."

The degree of fear encountered by an individual fighter may vary according to the level of intuitive expectation and possible severity of injury. The exaggerated focus on the opponent and the opponent's weapon tends to trigger an equally distorted perception of subjective risk. Ritualized encounters, such as ordeal, duel, or Mensur, maintain and sublimize high fear and stress levels over prolonged periods, whereas the emotion triggered by ambush and unexpected ("self-defense") encounters is more immediate.

In combat with edged weapons, fear's paralyzing force can be documented from historic sources [25]. It quickly becomes obvious that no matter how high the level of skill and mastery in play with blunt weapons, most of the fighter's conditioned responses get overlaid by natural, barely controllable reflexes as soon as the mind of the combatant focuses on the potential destructiveness represented by the opponent's sharp weapon. Friedrich von Schiller described this mental state in his *Jungfrau von Orleans*:

> "And never erring in the shaking hand, the sword rules itself as if it were a living spirit." [26]

Mind over matter

An example that vividly illustrates this can be found in Aldo Nadi's account of his duel as published in *American Fencing*. [27]

A photograph taken during the duel shows Nadi attacking the sword arm of his opponent Adolfo Contronei. What is most interesting, however, is the fact that Nadi's left foot is off the ground—not only inches but well over a foot high! One would expect to see this movement in raw beginners who are practicing their first lunges with the foil. But in a champion of the stature and level of mastership achieved by Nadi, this basic blunder would be difficult to explain unless the element of fear is taken into consideration.

[24] Given my own experiences with sharp edged weapons combat — which are, of course, limited, entirely subjective and not representative — I believe the role of aggression in antagonistic combat scenarios may be negligible, as the dominant element tends to be the instinct of self preservation.

[25] It is interesting to note that most first-hand accounts of high-stress antagonistic combat scenarios are very vague about the actual techniques, sequences, and details of the fight. This might indicate that the actual motorics of the fight are steered from a different level of consciousness than during practice bouts. It could also explain why drills for antagonistic combat focus on imprinting short clusters of simplified action that occurs independent of (or at least non-reactive to) the opponent's action.

[26] Schiller, Friedrich von. *Die Jungfrau von Orleans*, Act II: *"Und nimmer irrend in der zitternden Hand regiert, Das Schwert sich selbst, als wär' es ein lebend'ger Geist."*

[27] see *American Fencing*, Boulder, CO: USFA, vol. 42, #4 (April, May, June 1992); p. 19.

[28]See **American Fencing**, Boulder, CO: USFA, vol. 43 (July, August, September 1992); p. 6.

[29]Martincic, Albert. **Kevey und seine Fechtschule**, Graz (Austria); Self-published, 1983; p. 19: *"Unnatürliche Anspannung und starke Konzentration verursachen leicht eine Verkrampfung der Muskulatur."*

[30]Martincic; p. 30: *"Die Angst macht langsam und erzeugt Defensivität."*.

[31]Nadi's shortcomings of form during the duel have been explained plausibly by some of his students: *"Stop-thrusts, according to Maestro Nadi, must be performed going forward, to meet the attacker, thereby gaining time on his attack. To gain time on the attack, it is not sufficient to make the thrust from immobility, by merely extending the arm. If the front foot is not moved, then the body must be leaned forward with the thrust.*

It would be a mistake, of course, to execute a retreat simultaneously with the stop-thrust— any advantage gained by the leaning forward of the body would have been lost. With the épée, however, because of the extended target and the vulnerability of being hit even after hitting first, a step back (or a jump back) may be necessary, and is made immediately after the stop-thrust, by lifting the rear foot and starting the movement of the rear leg backwards, while leaning the body forward for the thrust.

I might add that Maestro Nadi advocated following up virtually every épée stroke with an immediate second thrust — sometimes referring to such combination as a "double shot". Used in conjunction with stop-thrusts, this second thrust may follow so quickly that the rear foot, raised for a (half) step back, remains airborne (though not motionless) during the process.

(note continued on p. 85)

Nadi's student Weldon Vlasak wrote in a letter to the editor:

"As a former student of Nadi, it is very difficult for me to believe what I saw in these photographs. Nadi was always the picture of perfection. He never raised his left foot as shown in the first picture. A flat left foot is one of the first things that he taught. Further, his right foot is askew in both photos— another blunder. Further, his right arm and hand are not characteristic. This hand was held high, fingers together, straight, and pointed towards his head."[28]

Nadi's near perfect conditioning could have been all but destroyed by the pervasive element of visceral fear and a sky-high level of adrenaline. The photographs taken during his duel illustrate that *"unnatural alertness and strong concentration easily cause a cramping of the muscles."*[29] Martincic, in his wonderful analysis of Kevey's system, repeatedly points out that *"fear makes slow and generates defensiveness."*[30]

(These observations, by the way, are at the core of the theory of proprioreflexive conditioning as embraced by most modern sports fencing training programs.)[31]

Nadi is fully aware of what went on during the encounter with Contronei. Without envy or embarrassment, he concedes that fencing and using swords in a duel with the actual danger of injury or death being present are fundamentally different. He comments on the alienation between real combat and the abstract art of fencing:

"In a duel, the fencer is compelled to execute an ultra-careful form of fencing, which, indeed, is an almost unworthy expression of the science he knows. No matter how courageous and great, the all-out movements with which he nearly always scores in a bout would be unthinkable in a duel, because it's far too risky."[32]

More than he is willing to admit in his memoirs, the swashbuckling Italian champion has been reduced to the same situation as the average junior member of a German duelling fraternity. An off-hand comment later on sums up the dominating sentiment of the duellist in combat:

"Young man, you must never be touched. Otherwise, the blood now coming out of your arm may instead be spurting from your chest."[33]

Where Angelo feared to tread

Nadi, you might argue, at the time of his duel is a young, Italian hothead—but a product of the 20th century: The Olympic sports fencer *par excellence*. But the duel with sharp duelling swords is already an anachronism.

How would an 18th-century master have regarded the usefulness of Olympic or Olympian expertise in antagonistic combat?

None less than Henry Angelo found himself running as fast as his legs could carry him to keep two of his students from killing each other in a duel with smallswords:

"Here was a commencement, far different to those methods they had previously practised before me in the Haymarket, as caution and skills are necessary when opposed to the point of a sword. It was not now a button covered with leather—a lesson to the many I have seen violently rushing on, who, after repeated efforts, have succeeded in giving a hit. This is not fencing. It is not scientific in the school, and is dangerous in the field.

As I mean soon to write my opinions of what I have experienced during the space of fifty years, and of the French school, where the science is practiced more for self-defence than as an accomplishment; whereas here [i.e., in England] it is more for exercise, for the improvement of the carriage, and the promotion of health, so well recommended by Sir John Sinclair."[34]

Angelo has watched enough students of his—soldiers, officers, gentlemen—go to their deaths wielding a sword for self-defence in the dark streets of Paris and London, or on muddy, misty duelling grounds to know why he doesn't want the two men go at it in earnest. He also is businessman enough to realize that the death of either duellist might pose a major problem to his livelihood.

Preparing to die

Would-be duellists, had at least an inkling of what psychological pressures they would be facing. After all, in Central Europe, the First Blood principle was held in low esteem—which meant a debilitating injury was required to terminate the duel. And for every fencing master preparing a prospective duellist for the most frightening experience of his life, there was at least one approach on how to beef up the psyche of the fighter.

(continued from p. 84)

I think it would be fair to say that the picture in Figure 5 was snapped at some point between the start and finish of a stop-thrust movement. Yes, the maestro was caught with his left foot off the ground. But he appears to be in control and not off balance. Whether that foot actually completed the first half of a step back, or was subsequently brought forward to a position close behind the right heel, is immaterial."
(from a Letter by Alexander Rivera, published in *Hammerterz Forum*, vol. 3, #2 (Fall 1996), p. 19).

[32]Nadi; *On Fencing*, p. 29.

[33]ibid.

[34] Angelo, Henry. *Reminiscences of Henry Angelo*, London: Kegan Paul, Trench, Trübner & Co., 1904; vol. 2; p.230.

Still, the actual danger triggering the fear was hard to re-create. De Beaumont observed:

"An épée bout cannot, however, be made exactly to resemble a duel, because the wearing of protective clothing and a mask destroys most of the psychological effect of naked steel. When the writer was a member of the Salle Mangiarotti in the 1920s, training someone for a duel was a common occurrence. The method used was to fence stripped to the waist, without masks and with especially long points d'arrêt. No one who has had this experience will retain the illusion that normal épée fencing with masks and jackets can be made to resemble a duel." [35]

The duel proper died with a whimper after World War I. A few paunchy Frenchmen took a shot at reviving it in the fifties, without being able to capture as much as a sparkle of its dashing history. [36] In the West, the German Mensur remains as one of the last living traditions of antagonistic swordplay—and as such the only source to gage the psychological effects of pre-combat and combat fear.

The following passage describes the phases of self-assertion, doubt, fear, and surprise that are integral parts of the Mensur experience, as valid today as they were a century ago:

"The Fuchs [37] *means to show himself a plucky fellow in the presence of his patron Mossy Head. He can scarcely await the time of his first encounter. Secretly glowing with heroic purpose, he hastens to the field of honor; sees there his antagonist surrounded by a crowd of sympathizers; among the philistines who have crowded in, he recognizes his own over-curious landlord.*

The surgeon unpacks his apparatus, with dignified and earnest air, although, in fact, this surgeon is a practical joker and takes out ten times as many instruments as necessary. The Fuchs is taken aback, begins to feel uncomfortable, in spite of himself loses some of his previous confidence. A tremor runs trough his limbs. The Mossy Head, a connoisseur in Foxes, marks this in his protégé and reproves him with a quieting look. The Fuchs recognizes this, makes a hypocritical show of pulling himself together, but for all that cannot prevent a slight weakness in the knees. At last the stiff leg-bandage, perhaps sticky with blood, is put on; his arm is carefully wrapped like a child in swathing clothes; a heavy thick pauking cravat is tied around his neck, and the surgeon affects great solicitude.

Of course, when the command 'Los!' is given, he has forgotten all the points and advice of his patron, and just hacks away blindly. What his opponent is doing—whether he guards or attacks—he does not know. What he himself is doing, he knows just as little, until there is a cry of 'Halt!' and the seconds interpose. Whether he or his antagonist is hurt, he has no idea. In fact, while this thing was going on, he did not know if it was day or night, for the blood which streamed over his eyes. While the surgeon is examining his head, he asks, with astonishment: 'Am I wounded?' The surgeon replies: 'And how!'

Now, for the first time, he begins to recover from his excitement." [38]

[35] de Beaumont, C.L. *Fencing: Ancient Art and Modern Sport* (London: Nicholas Kaye, 1960) South Brunswick and New York: A.S. Barnes & Co., 1971; p. 108.

[36] One pre-war example, the 1938 encounter of Edouard Bourdet and Henri Bernstein, was recorded in *Life* magazine. Bourdet, sporting an impressive Homburg-style hat, is fly-fishing for an opening with his épée, blade whipping backwards. No wonder he ended up with a scratch on his arm, which led to a photogenous hospital-bed reconciliation...

[37] *Fuchs* (lit.: fox) is the term for a pledge or freshman member of a duelling fraternity who has not yet fought a sharp Mensur.

[38] see Wilcox, M. "Dueling at a German University," unattributable, post 1882; p. 599 ff., in the author's collection. (Could be identical with "Dueling at Jena University," in *The Hawk*, Feb.2, 1892, as listed in Thimm.) This passage is an adaptation from Roux, Friedrich August Wilhelm. *Deutsches Paukbuch*, Jena: Mauke, 1867; p. 79f — in which Roux, in his characteristic sarcasm, draws a quick vignette of the reality of the Mensur, as opposed to the ideal of technical and mental perfection he and his dynasty of fencing masters attempted to instill in their students.

(The duelling students used this state of mind to play practical jokes on their pledges. On occasion, two Foxes would be squared off against each other in a sham match. The typical high level of stress, fear, and excitement made the poor guys oblivious to the fact that they had been armed with blunt blades. Between rounds, an attendant would squeeze out a sponge with water over their heads—while seconds and doctors made serious faces as they gingerly examined their heads. Finally, a bucket with cold water would be emptied over the confused fighters in a subtle display of wit and amicable humanitarian concern...)

Great expectations

A certain level of individual fear—be it only the heightened adrenaline level experienced before a sports fencing tournament— is present in all encounters with edged weapons that are fought with intended results (as opposed to scenarios intended to produce an intended effect, such as in theatric fencing).

Practice bouting and proprioreceptive conditioning serves to control some, in certain cases most of the subjective fear that is being experienced.

Duel
Asselin vs.
de Saint-Victor

Primal emotion

If you have never faced a hostile opponent's sharp blade, you will tend to underrate the effects and influence of personal fear on individual skill level and coordination. The difference between facing a foil, saber, or blunt practice Schläger and seeing yourself face to face with a live blade is about as dramatic as encountering a black bear safely behind the moat and steel bars of a zoo—and running into the same animal in the rain and fog of a Shenandoah Valley night:

Much like the grunting and growling of the bear is enhanced by the lack of visibility—and the heart-pounding apprehension of a brush with primal chaos—, the eye of the fighter encountering a hostile opponent's steel for the first time magnifies the unyielding, heinously sharp point, or the jagged, wavelike reflections of the edge, translating the impression into instant anticipation of the stinging slice that will change your physiology for ever...

It was this kind of fear that had to be mastered in the face of battle, either by natural inclination or by conditioning, much to the chagrin of some anti-duelling pamphleteers who lambasted the duellist's decision to overturn dictates of sanity and conscience to face his opponent:

"That a certain kind of coolness, and deliberation may exist in connexion with all this untractable obstinacy, we are not disposed to question. But their existence here, form the most terrible feature in the man's whole character. They give tranquillity to his frightful purpose, permanency to his rash resolve, undeviating conduct to the paroxysms of a persecuting hatred, and a fatal certainty to the final action. But under these manifestations, they reflect no honour, or semblance of courage that the assassin may not claim, who can direct his knife with steadiness to the palpitating bosom of his victim."[39]

In many people, civilization has built up a strong barrier against consciously inflicting injuries on others. (Despite my seven Mensuren, I feel compelled to apologize for every cut with the sports saber that I feel hit my opponent a tad too hard.) Take the pioneer of sword and sorcery fiction and father of Conan and Solomon Kane. While his gore-splattered super-human heroes wreak red ruin on entire armies with their blood-dripping blades, he himself is somewhat less sanguine:

"Howard was fascinated by Price's discussion of the martial arts, such as fencing. He later wrote [H.P.] Lovecraft regretting the fact that fencing masters were rare in Texas and that, when he and a friend tried to teach themselves using army swords as foils, he ran his sword through his friend's hand. After that, he never tried to fence again."[40]

It was exactly these un-civilized qualities Patton had in mind when he defined the mental attitude that his ideal cavalryman would have the natural inclination to assume before the charge:

"And we expect that a man (...) shall, in an instant, the twinkling of an eye, divest himself of all restraint, of all caution and hurl himself on the enemy, a frenzied beast, lusting to probe his foeman's guts with three feet of steel or shatter his brains with a bullet. Gentlemen, it cannot be done, not without mental practice.

That is why it is easier to attack on foot than to charge mounted. It seems more refined. There, in front, are those dear futile bushes of maneuvers, the bullets sing and whisper but there is more time to get used to them. It takes courage, higher moral courage to walk to death than to gallop at it. But, it is the form of courage which our civilization has given us. It is the courage of the burning house; not of the bloody nose.

Therefore, you must school yourself to savagery. You must imagine how it will feel when your sword hilt crashes into the breast bone of your enemy. You must picture the wild exaltation of the mounted charge when the lips draw back in a snarl and the voice cracks with passion."[41]

But even the most macho fighter would be subject to the sobering influence of cold steel, as Bartunek observes:

"During the duel, when the bare chest suddenly is exposed to the threat of the opponent's sharply honed weapon, nature—which wild fencers or brawlers try to deny—demands its rights, so that most are induced to the instinctive parry, rather than cutting simultaneously."[42]

[39]Colton, Walter. **Remarks on Duelling**, New York: Jonathan Leavitt and Boston: Crocker & Brewster, 1828; p. 26.

[40]deCamp, Sprague et al.. **Dark Valley Destiny: The Life of Robert E. Howard, The Creator of Conan**, New York: Bluejay Books, (1961) 1983; p. 305.

[41]Patton, Major George S., Jr. "The Cavalryman", 1921 (Copyright 1996-97, The Patton Society).

[42]*"Im Duell, wo der entblösste Oberkörper plötzlich der Bedrohung durch die gegnerische scharfgeschliffene Waffe ausgesetzt ist, tritt die Natur, die [wilde Fechter oder Raufer] verleugnen wollen, wieder in ihre Rechte, so dass die meisten, statt mitzuhauen, zur instinktiven Parade verleitet werden."* See Bartunek; p.33.

The Austrian echoes comments of Joseph Swetnam's, made 300 years before:

"But I say there is great odds betwixt fighting in the field and playing in a fence-schoole, for in the field being both sober, I meane if it be in a morning upon cold blood, then every man will feare to kill as to be killed, againe a man shall see to defend either blow or thrust in the field then in a fence-schoole, for a man will be more bold with a foile or a cudgell, because there is small danger in either of them."[43]

Mastering fear could provide a short-cut to terminating the duel: Henry Angelo, after breaking up the above-mentioned duel of Monsieur Chevalier vs. Mr "M'D—t" (McDermott?), sums up the observations he made during the first bout:

"The Frenchman, endeavouring to intimidate his adversary, kept making a noise; though he made the first lunge, he took good care to be out of distance at the time, whilst the other, whom I had often seen not so cool and collected with a foil, now, with all that sang froid, laughed and cried 'poh!' on his first receiving the attack, and at Chevalier's not coming nearer. This faire semblant of the one to appear courageous to frighten, or the other's fierté, could not have continued long; the result may have been dangerous, or fatal."[44]

Grain of salt

I stated above that fencers who never faced a hostile opponent's sharp blade are prone to underrate the pervasive effects of self preservation, stress, and anticipation on a fighter's state of mind. I also would like to remind you that the cathartic element of antagonistic combat centers on overcoming that fear.

Indeed, most Comment scenarios—like the duel proper or the Mensur—focus heavily on building up pre-combat stress by having the combatants live in ever-increasing anticipation for hours, days, or even weeks. During the day of the encounter, the routine of the normal day is replaced by the somber rituals of seconds, witness, and umpires, even the doctors, each more disconcerting than the other.

The German poet Hanns Heinz Ewers, himself a veteran of several heavy saber duels, countless Schläger Mensuren, and a pistol duel in which both participants ended up drilling holes into the cold morning air of the Kottenforst near Bonn, works his experience during these encounters into his novel *Alraune* and his short story *"Der tote Jude"*. In both instances, one of the duellists is unable to control his bowels as he steps up to his position.

Yet both men remain in their places to fire—and in one case, kill—despite their bodies' violent rejection of the situation. And thus many, if not most fighters manage to have their conscious will overcome their self-preservation instincts in the moment the combat begins in earnest. At that point, the Olympian skill level in using a particular weapon may have decreased by fifty, seventy, even ninety percent.

But it is this moment of the will emerging to rule the body that represents the true victory—and sole purpose—of most *Comment* combat set-ups. This state

[43]Swetnam, Joseph. *The Schoole of the Noble and Worthy Science of Defence*, London: Nicholas Okes, 1617; p. 5.

[44]Angelo, Henry. *Reminiscences*; p. 231.

of mind will not only determine the fighter's own retrospective attitude toward the fight, when even severe wounds are discounted as coincidental in contrast to the personal victory, it frequently determines the actual outcome of the bout.

Of course, it may work both ways... and unless a man is actually put to the test, it is impossible to predict when or if this emergence of the will as the dominating engine of combat will take place: If it fails to occur, every subsequent detail of the fight will further erode the moral foundations of the unlucky fighter until his self is washed away in a flood of uncontrollable chaos.

A very vivid picture of this degenerative process is included in Otto Julius Bierbaum's[45] *"Gamasche, der Pommernfuchs"*.[46] And since the awareness of just such an erosion taking place within yourself is one of the most prevalent fears of any Mensur fencer I know, I believe this account encapsulates the true nature of any *Comment* combat:

Henry, nick-named Gamasche ("Galoshes"), is a young millionaire who for some reason unfathomable even to him joined a duelling fraternity, the Corps Pomerania. Supported by Böhle, a veteran "two-ribbon-man" (i.e., a member of two different fraternities) and his second Kuttler, Henry is getting ready to fight his first Mensur as a pledge, against another first-timer, a pledge of the Corps Frisia:

> *"The great hall in which the Mensuren were to take place was filling up slowly, while Henry, who was up for the first bout, was being bandaged up. Nonetheless, he felt utterly alone. Suddenly, he realized that he had absolutely nothing in common with all those people, that all this was essentially alien to him.*
>
> *Only when Böhle approached, he felt that there was someone who was part of him. And only Böhle's words made it it into his consciousness; what the others around him said, particularly what Kuttler did not tire to preach to him in endless repetitions, was only empty noise, hollow sound, muted gushing.*
>
> *'So how do you feel,' asked Böhle, who didn't like Henry's apathetic looks at all.*
> *'How am I supposed to feel? Not at all!' Henry replied.*
> *'Does the neck brace sit alright?'*
> *'Probably. At least I can't breathe.'*
> *'The goggles are cutting in a bit. But no matter, Galoshes, you'll get used to it.'*
> *'No, it's alright. Nothing matters at all. Even this disgusting stench of old blood that gets into my nose from the neck brace...'*
> *'It'll pass.'*
> *'Might as well stay...'*
> *'Man. Don't be so horribly apathetic. Would you like me to get you a drink?'*
> *'Yes, please. Cognac.'*
> *'Feel better now?'*
> *'Don't really feel bad at all. I just don't get the point of this thing.'*
> *'Quiet.'*
> *'I'm so angry I want to shout.'*
> *'Good! Get angry! Anything but this damn apathy.—Let me tell you something, Galoshes. This is something important now. Pull yourself together, to the utmost! Stand like a piece of wood, and do not leave out a single cut! Deliver an impeccable Mensur. And tomorrow you resign. Then you may do it. I'll fight everyone who says anything against it. But now, for God's sake, do not give any reason for offence.'*

[45]Otto Julius Bierbaum (1865-1910) was a popular writer specializing in student life. In 1887, he was accepted into the Corps Thuringia at Leipzig, and thus was experienced in the use of the bell-guard Schläger. This story takes place in Jena, Germany, thus also involving bell-guard Schlägers rather than the basket-hilt variety—even though the mention of a sling points at the basket.

[46]Bierbaum, Otto Julius.— "Gamasche, der Pommernfuchs," in Conrad, Heinrich (ed.) ***Das Duellbuch***, München: Georg Müller, 1918; p. 330f.

Henry felt that a friend's concern motivated these words, and he found
support in them. He now even could—what he had fearfully avoided up
until this moment—turn his glance to the opposite side, where his opponent
stood with a free smile and executed a whistling cut through the air.

Of course, he shouldn't have done that. To him, this was an absolutely
gruesome picture. The vague fear, which had manifested itself in dull apathy,
turned into downright fright of something definite, personal: Of this agile,
tall, strong human over there, with this horrifyingly long Schläger that whistled through the air like a whip. His apathy dissipated; now something
welled up inside him, something pressing, something captive that looked for
a way out. Henry's eyes began to dart back and forth, as if he himself was
looking for an exit.

But even a vice couldn't have gripped him tighter than his battle gear
and the presence of all these murmuring, whispering, laughing strangers,
who themselves were like tied down, and, with stern or laughing demeanor,
represented the Priciple that united and dominated them: The Principle of
Overcoming Bodily Fear.

There was no escape. To admit one's fear would indeed have required a
moral sovereignty that would have counter-balanced any cowardice of the
body—because it would have proved more than an over-abundance of bodily
fear, namely real individual courage as opposed to the courage of peer pressure.

One has only found courage like this in men who after their first laughter
or terror, depending on what excited their courage, were venerated and
admired as saints. Even behind the holy courage of St. Francis of Assisi may
have been a cowardice of the body, when he declared in the face of all the
beautiful young ladies of his home town: My bride is poverty, and left the
locale with ha-ha-has and hee-hee-hees.

Such and similar thoughts went through the head of the deviant member-
of-two-Corps Böhle when he noticed what was now going on in Henry's face.

Henry himself only felt one thing: 'Now, I'll be lead to the slaughter.'
He stood on the chalk cross of the Mensur [47] without knowing how he got
there. His left hand mechanically closed tightly around the pulled-through strap
of the fencing apron, his right arm rested in the arms of the Assisting Pledge [48],
his eyes were staring as into a maelström of fog.

Now someone put his Schläger into his hand and whispered: 'Why don't
you put your finger through the sling, goddamn it.'

He did that. Someone put his cap on his head for the round of honor. [49]
From far, far away, he heard a voice: 'Silence for a Menusur with Schlägers
with wraps and bandages between Frisia and Pomerania.' Then the command:
'Silence for the round of honor! Bind the blades! They're bound! Go!—Halt!'
The caps were removed.

Now it was serious.

'Silence for the first round! Bind the blades! Go!'

Henry closed his eyes and waved his Schläger around in the air. But his
opponent cut in earnest.

'Halt.'

It was the opponent's second who had called—and now added: 'I request

[47] In pre-WWII practice, the positions of the Mensur participants were staked out by chalk marks on the floor. Stepping back over the mark (as in a retreat) meant disgraceful termination of the bout.

[48] To avoid tiring of the right arm—weighed down by a massive cuff and steel-reinforced gloves—and to control the descending arm with the sharp blade after each round, an Assisting Plege (Schleppfuchs) or close friend of the fighter supports the sword arm before and between rounds. From my own experience, I believe that a well-trained fencer does not require assistance to get his arm up... but I would have to admit that one and a half foot of honed edge always can do with an additional safety catch.

[49] The Ehrengang, or round of honor, marks the opening or close of a Mensur, depending on local rules. It consists of a test run, with the seconds going through their phrases. The fighters either remain motionless in the Steile Auslage, or briefly clash the blades together.

that a bloody hit on the quarte side be announced by the opposing party.'[50]

Henry felt something warm running down the left side of his head and that someone was figering around in his hair. Then a whisper reached his ear: 'You're asleep! Follow through with your cuts and don't go back into cover after only half a blow!'

"Why 'Halt'?"
Inquisitive second, from an early 20th century postcard.

'How weird,' thought Henry, 'now I've been hit and didn't even feel it; this thing isn't that bad after all.'

And he ventured to open his eyes. There went his boldness again!

His opponent seemed even more gigantic to him than just a moment ago, and all the whispering that was done over there did not bode well at all. Why was this horrible brute grinning and nodding? What was he up to? No, it was much more sensible to close the eyes again. But he intended to follow through with the cuts.

'Bind the blades.'

Henry shut his eyes so tight that it turned deep, dark night around him.

'Go!'

Splat! Splat! — Good lord, what was that? That brute was thrashing him with cudgels!

Henry had to bite down hard not to scream in pain.

His opponent had hit him with two flat blows, twice, right on the spot where he had received the small bloody one in the first round.[51]

'Halt!'

Again it was the opponent's second who had interjected.

'Probably two bone splinters,' Henry thought, as much as he was able to think because of the pain.

'Why halt?'

'I would like to inquire if the opposite side is still fencing.'

Henry had indeed preferred to remain covered and had not returned the first or second blow.[52]

Now it no longer was a whisper near his ear, but a hiss: 'Man, you don't do anything but lurk! Hit, goddamn it, or...'

'We request a break, the neck brace is too tight.'

Kuttler saw the smirk triggered by his Mensur-lie, and this enraged him even more. He tore wildly at the brace and thus loosened the buckle a bit. Then he continued hissing: 'It's a bloody disgrace the way you're acting. You deserve that he slaps you with the flat blade left and right. Hit, I say!' He was just grinding his teeth now. Then: 'We request continuation of the Mensur.'

'O God, o God! Don't hit the same spot again,' Henry thought. And: 'Hit! Hit! Cover doesn't help at all.'

'Bind the blades! Go!'

This time Henry hit blow upon blow simultaneously with his opponent,

[50]During the bout, the seconds not only act as enforcers of the rules and protectors of their fighter, they frequently engage in verbal needling of the opposing party in the fashion of trial lawyers.

[51]This may seem like deliberate cruelty, and without a doubt is interpreted as such by Henry, but the flat hits not only are indicative of Henry's faulty cover, but also of his opponent's lack of experience and skill.

[52]Most German *Comments* today stipulate that the tip of the blade has to be constantly in motion after Go! Remaining passively in cover (called *lauern*—to lurk, to prey) would mean immediate exclusion from the bout.

*and he continued to hit, even though it splatted again twice, not in the least
less painful than before, o God, no, not less painful at all.*

'Halt!'

This time Kuttler had called Halt.

*To the question 'Why: Halt?', he responded growling: 'The neck brace
has loosened.'*

*A sunny smile radiated over everything that pledged allegiance to Frisia's
banner, while Pomerania stood in grim gloom.*

'What the hell is the matter now,' thought Henry. 'I didn't leave out a cut.'

*He was enlightened quickly. Kuttler pulled his neck brace together that his
breath halted and grunted like a wounded boar. 'Wait . . . do not retreat back
into the brace! You'll rather suffocate! And if the least bit happens now,
we'll kick you out right here and now. Never seen such a goddamn mess!'*

*He was so enraged that Herr von Spöckhoff had to seriously admonish
him not to lose his bearing.*

*Meanwhile, Böhle helped the now completely demoralized Henry to some
cognac and whispered into his ear: 'For God's sake, head up! Chin firmly onto
the neck brace! Put your self out forward as much as possible*[53] *and stand firm,
firm, firm. The thing'll be over in a flash.'*

*'Be over! Be over! Be over!' Henry idiotically repeated to himself. His
constricted neck hurt just about as much as his head, whose left half had
visibly swollen up. The original small bloody one from the first round was
gaping apart as a consequence of the subsequent flat hits, and was bleeding
strongly. Henry was convinced that his skull was laying bare. And even while
he now kept his eyes open, he fearfully avoided to look at the Terrible One,
who was torturing him so viciously.*

*He was full of fright and horror and distictly felt that there was not
a soul in the hall who had compassion with him. In his painful emotional
overextension, the smiles of the Frisians seemed like the grins of demons,
who were feeding on his disgrace—their triumph—and would accompany
his complete annihilation with resounding laughter.*

*This was the low point of his life. He felt like a whipped dog waiting for
that last kick, and he only had the one wish to be liberated from this horribly
constrictive neck brace as soon as possible, and thus to be free from this entire
horrible nightmare in full daylight. His fear now was limitless. It completely
filled him, he did not have the faintest hope for any somehow bearable outcome,
and yet he did not in the least think that one thought, that he could simply say:
I don't want any more; let me go, I am a coward. Despise me as much as you
want, but I do not want to be a caricature of your courage.*

'We request continuation of the Mensur.'

*Kuttler shouted it overly loud, but made such a twisted face that you
could see how little confidence he had. His mind was made up: At the first
bloody hit, at the most minute scratch, he would declare the* Abfuhr.[54]

'Bind the blades! They're bound! Go!'

Splat! 'Halt!'

*Kuttler threw away his weapon. The Assisting Pledge neglected to prop
up Henry's arm which now sank down heavily and remained hanging
obliquely so that the point of his Schläger touched the floor.*

[53]Leaning forward while standing on the fixed, short distance of the Mensur means reducing the distance between fighters. Thus, the chances of a sharp hit are somewhat reduced. Or so you think...

[54]Termination of the Mensur as the result of an "incapacitating" wound.

The second of the Frisians put is left up to the broad rim of his cap as if shading his eyes, and said with dry sarcasm, yet seemingly very seriously and correct:
'I request someone check out if the opposing fencer is still present in the hall.'
O sweet revenge! That beautiful million-dollar pledge of the Pomerania now was done in for good. To take an entire step behind the crux[55]: that was a bit much!
After this insult, Kuttler felt better: He declared termination and, as soon as the umpire had announced the outcome, stepped up to the impertinent Frisian with a cold but highly correct greeting, growling:
'You will hear from us.'
The Frisian returned the greeting not any less correctly and replied:
'Very well; it will be no small pleasure to us.'
They measured each other with a coldly courteous glance and turned around. And behold, the Spirit of the Pro Patria Suite hovered festively through the hall.[56]
None of the Pomeranians exchanged a word with Henry. Only Böhle stepped up close to him as if by chance, as Henry was groaning while being mended and said: 'I'll go over to your place and wait for you. There's nothing left but getting out of here unnoticed. Ex est volupta.[57] "

Given the slippery slope of this degenerate mental process into complete demoralization, it is not surprising to me that the ordeal regarded the outcome of a fight as divine judgment: Any fighter who had to overcome the additional drag of a guilty conscience—and the never-ending period of anticipating divine wrath—must have been at a disadvantage to beging with—his defeat a logical consequence of his misdeed.

The other man

The element of fear and anticipation decreases dramatically with any minute that does not elapse between the awareness that an encounter will inevitably take place, and the actual face-off. Most antagonistic scenarios that do not involve a *Comment* of sorts, that occur spontaneously or with minimal premeditation, revolve around factors other than personal fear.

The most important, in my opinion, is the success or failure to immediately grasp and interpretation of the situation in all its consequences.

Training conditions the fencer to expect a certain behavior from his opponent. This expectation is a preeminent factor in the personal evaluation and classification of the imminent combat scenario and in the external development of the fight itself. Expecting an opponent to behave in one way or the other is not without danger. Often, being right or wrong determines who's going to live or die at the end of an encounter—before the actual fight has begun.

Take the German patriot and poet Theodor Körner, for example. A member of Lützow's Freicorps, he was one of the most popular and romantic figures of the German war effort against Napoleon.

Before he joined the volunteer partisans lining up in the great patriotic struggle against the French, Körner had studied at the Bergakademie (mining academy)

[55] i.e., the chalk cross on the floor that marked the position.

[56] A Pro Patria Suite pitches all or a pre-determined number of fighters from one Corps against an equal number of fighters from the other Corps in a series of bouts fought under rules providing for more cuts per round, more rounds per bout, and less restrictions on target area.

[57] "Fun's over."

of Freiberg, where he belonged to a student fraternity (probably the Landsmannschaft Montania) from 1809-10.

As his contemporaries attested, he had fought a number of duels and Mensuren with straight-bladed broadswords. His estate even included a sheet in which he had summarized a very basic "*System der Hiebe*," a system of cuts.[58]

The way students fought at Freiberg in Körner's day was roughly equivalent to the military spadroon and broadsword styles of the period. The sketch of the weapon used in his "System" indicates a classic cut-and-thrust sword closely resembling a spadroon, which in combat is aimed mainly at upper body, arms, and thigh of the opponent, without the Schläger's later preoccupation with the opposing head and face.

But Freiberg's duelling was regulated by a strict code of honor. It allowed and excluded certain cuts, prescribed a certain number of rounds that had to be fought, as well as stated that for a round to be valid, a bleeding wound had to be scored.

It is no longer possible to find out what kind of a fencer Körner had become at Freiberg. In fact, it is utterly unimportant. Because his acquaintance with the heavily regulated fencing scene at university had conditioned Körner to expect a certain behavior from his opponent—a behavior that was as strictly bound and enforced as the actual exchange of cut and thrust on the duelling grounds. More importantly, it provided for a standardized, no-surprises set-up that eliminated the actual need to assess the situation.

Reality bites

For Körner, his sense of honor and conditioned expectation proved fatal. Willingly or unwillingly ignorant of the fact that he had left the dictates of the *Comment* and entered the wilderness of war, he allowed a captured French officer to hang on to his sidearm in deference to his rank. As could be expected, he received three feet of Klingenthal steel through his body for his trouble at the first opportune moment—leaving him to die like a dog because he had been unable to correctly gauge his opponent's behavior.

It is interesting that the French officer was allowed to hang on to his sword—the symbol of his rank and social standing, which to the naive German poet-turned-soldier must have implied a mutual acceptance of where and on which occasions this symbol could be used as a weapon. His lack of circumspection and cynicism did not apply to the Frenchman's firearms. Even though pistols were as common as sabers to settle disputes of honor among German students, they had been confiscated because they had been identified as weapons of war in their proper context.

All's fair in love and war

"With a worse man speak not / three words in dispute,
Ill fares the better oft / when the worse man wields the sword."
The Poetic Edda: *Hávamál*, verse 125

[58]See Textor, Horst-Ulrich. — "Die Bergakademie Freiberg und das Brauchtum ihrer Studenten (1765-1845)", in *Einst und Jetzt,* vol. 41, München: Verein für corpsstudentische Geschichtssforschung, 1996; p. 234f.

Swetnam records a similar incident:

> *"I remember a tale as I heard out of Germany, thus it was, the Master and usher of a school had upon occasion appointed the field, and their weapon was each of them a two-handed sword, and meeting at the place appointed, said the Master 'Thou art not so good as thy word.'*
>
> *The usher asked him why. 'Marry,' said he, 'thou promisest to bring nobody with thee, and yet looke yonder what a number of people are comming towards thee.'*
>
> *The usher no sooner looked about, but the Master smote off his head, and afterwards meeting with some of his friends said 'I have taught my man a new tricke in the field,' said he, 'which he never learned before.'"*[59]

Again, the usher is oblivious to the fact that the plane of combat has shifted from the competitive measuring of skill he was used to from the daily sparring and the Fechtschulen, to that of antagonistic combat to the death—unwitnessed, without a rule or regulation to protect the participants.

Seduction of art

"Hitting is not important. Hitting and hurting is."

Dunraj Seth,

foundry shop foreman and
martial artist at Benares, India

Closed combative systems that condition the use of clearly defined (or even standardized) weaponry in defined, replicable environments also condition the fighter to expect certain maneuvers, and to respond to them within the parameters of the system. This enables system-immanent growth of complexity and sophistication.

Hergsell warns his readers against *"underestimating a naturalist gifted with great physical strength, otherwise it could be the case that the fencer who is accustomed to conventional* [regelrechte] *attacks with be conquered by the uninhibited attacks, the ruleless application of violence."*[60]

In mismatched combat, there's also the temptation to equate accomplishment in any one system with superior ability in general. Nadi, an international champion in the competitive systems of foil, épée, and saber, receives the first wound (of several) in his duel against Contronei—a middle-aged newspaper editor twice his age. Had this been a first-blood duel, Contronei could have been considered the "winner"—if the notion of winning were indeed compatible with the duel proper.

Contronei, who faced the twenty-four year old Nadi in 1923, appears to have had a gift for provoking duels with internationally acclaimed fencers. In the aftermath of the 1924 Olympics, he fought another duel, this time against Italo Santelli's 27-year old son Giorgio—who had invoked the Code Duello to fight for his 60-years-old father.

The duel was fought in the town of Abazzia near the Hungarian border with heavy sabers. Santelli must have landed a tierce of quarte in the side of Contronei's

[59]Swetnam; p. 37.

[60]Hergsell. **Duell-Codex**, p. 83.

forehead, upon which the duel was terminated after only two minutes of combat time. (Nadi's duel had taken 6 minutes of total fighting time.) [61]

Santelli must have perceived the 45-year old amateur Contronei (who was the fencing critic for an Italian newspaper, *"with considerable knowledge of the sport"*[62]) as a real threat to his father, a veteran fencing master and coach of the Hungarian Olympic team.

To become dangerous to a master of the art, a fighter's inexperience— and therefore, his unpredictability—would sometimes serve as well as an equal or superior level of skill. That's why the fencing books and duelling tracts throughout the centuries tend to warn against the naturalists and the *"unferme"* fencers— amateurs whose unorthodox way of handling their weapons made them as dangerous as champions to the duellist.

When ignorance is bliss

"The danger is death if ignorant people procure a combate."
Thomas Churchyard,
"Epistle Dedicatorie"
to di Grassi's ***True Arte of Defence***[63]

Sir William Hope devotes considerable space to the problems posed to the artistic fencer by "Ignorants". To Hope, the danger of Ignorants lies both in their unpredictable behavior, and in the elimination of natural responses in fencers with an incomplete grasp of the art.

An elementary understanding of the Art, according to Hope, makes the incomplete fencer abandon the offensive in favor of the defensive—of which he typically has limited understanding. With the offensive thus all but eliminated, a rash and furious Ignorant may easily gain the upper hand:

"There are but few good Sword Men to be found, and many get the name of Artists when they are really but ignorants; for if a Man hath but a moneth or six weeks at a Fencing School, presently he is said to understand this Art, and when such a person as this is engaged against an Ignorant, in stead of having any Advantage by what he hath been taught, I can assure you he hath rather the disadvantage, because what he hath learned hath put away his Natural and forward Play, and maketh him understand the hazard there is in being too forward. (...) he hath the disadvantage of the altogether Ignorant, in so far as he is not so forward, because he knoweth the hazard of it; wheras the other's ignorance maketh him more forward, and so is the occasion of his mastering the other, who getteth the name of an Artist. (...) And therefore he is rather he worse of that little Art that he hath (...) I say if an Ignorant meet with such a person, he will find that he hath but too great Advantage of him, if he come to meake use of Sharps: Yet Ignorants will sometimes overcome those who understand this Art very well."[64].

Again, the centuries do little to detract from the value of experienced advice. Bartunek, writing in 1904, still echoes this experience:

[61] Wallechinsky, David. *The Complete Book of the Olympics*, New York: Penguin, 1984; p. 247. Wallechinsky portrays Contronei as the captain of the Italian foil team. Given Contronei's age and the fact that his name does not appear in the team line-up, this must be an error.

[62] Nadi. *On Fencing*, p. 24.

[63] Grassi, Giacomo di *His True Arte of Defence* (London, 1594) in Jackson; *Three Elizabethan Fencing Manuals*; p. 4

[64] Hope; "Epistle to the Reader."

"Even the best fencer should never forget that in dangerous situation weaker characters can be driven into a condition of raging courage by the thought of impeding annihilation. (. . .) History has shown that even experienced tournament fencers, who even had passed several duels victoriously, succumbed to inferior opponents only because they felt secure and superior.

As such a feeling immediately results in a dropping of attentiveness and a simultaneous reduction in combat and mental energy, this may have sinister consequences. Thus one should never underestimate an opponent, because only few mortals are preordained to reach the heights of ideal perfection."[65]

Clearly, swordplay for artistic purposes and swordplay intended to dispatch an opponent as soon and swiftly as possibly not only have different objectives, but also demand a different mental approach from the fighter. In life-and-death fights, results were all that counted. This accounts for the importance of the *botto secreta* through all ages in which combat to the death was a more likely scenario than extended engagement in ritualized Olympic or Olympian environments.

[65]Bartunek; p. 146.

INTERLUDE

ANTAGONISTIC COMMENT COMBAT

Duel between officers
at Saumur.

The Épée Duel
Romano vs. Liscotti Rome, A.D. 1898[66]

On the thirty-first of January, 1898, I was called upon to act as director of another duel which resulted from a Signor Romano challenging a Signor Liscotti after the latter had refused to withdraw certain "offensive public expressions." This combat was called with the *spada* (rapier or épée) and under the following rules:

- The duellists would wear a gauntlet to protect the wrist.
- They would be allowed to strap the sword to the wrist if they desired.
- Because of the low winter temperature the duellists would be permitted to wear a light undershirt to protect the body from the waist up.
- The duel would continue until one or both of the adversaries should be incapacitated because of serious wounds.
- The seconds and witnesses, besides the director, would be authorized to halt the combat, taking full responsibilities as to the consequences.
- The duel would be fought near the Tomb of Cecilia Metella.

The contestants and watchers met shortly after 8. a.m. It was a cold, foggy morning, with an icy breeze blowing from the northwest, yet the duellists, with centuries of tradition behind them, stood majestically erect and immobile as they were reminded of their duties as gentlemen in combat. Both were members of the

[66]in Huber, *Fundamental Swordsmanship*, p. 27f.

87

Bersaglieri, the flower of the Italian Army, and both were swordsmen of strength and cunning.

After calling them to take their distance I placed my sword between the points of their weapons and ordered them to be on guard. Then, thinking that I was sending on of these fine men to his death, I withdrew my blade and said, "Start!"

The two eyed each other intently for a moment. Then they began to feint, to advance slightly, to withdraw a little. It was easy to see they realized that a false step, a rash movement of the blade, would mean death. Neither tried these bold, furious attacks one sees too often in the salle d'armes of America.

The first three bouts had to be stopped because in each one the combatants sidestepped out of the established limits. By the fourth bout, despite the cold, both were perspiring; their arms seemed to be tired, their bodies tense. Suddenly, Romano's lunging rapier passed Signor Liscotti's neck by a fraction of an inch— the thrust failed only because Signor Liscotti instinctively dodged in the nick of time. Signor Liscotti had grazed Signor Romano's forearm and the latter, stung, had risked the near-fatal lunge. As Signor Romano lightning-like withdrew his blade, his adversary again struck at the forearm. This time the rapier entered at the wrist and penetrated the entire length of the forearm, the point protruding several inches past the elbow.

Signor tried to disengage his adversary's sword but could not. The surgeon ran up and withdrew the blade, while a nurse applied disinfectant to the incision.

The vanquished man then thanked Signor Liscotti for having given him satisfaction and the affair was declared closed. Honor had been satisfied without serious crippling or death.

2. THE TOOLS

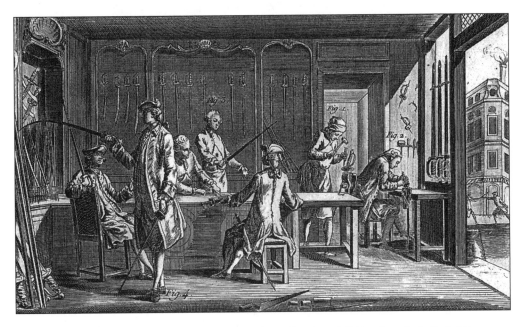

A blade for every job: "Fourbisseur," from Diderot, Denis and d'Alambert, J. de R. (edd.). — "Fourbisseur" in *Encyclopédie méthodique ou dictionnaire raisonné des sciences, des arts, et des métiers*, Paris and Amsterdam, 1751-75.

I n 1885, the historians Faudel and Bleicher published the description of a bronze sword reportedly found, along with other bronze artifacts, near Krautergersheim in Alsace (then Germany). Of the original hoard, only the sword had been preserved: The thrifty finder had been using it for a long time... to trim his hedges.[67]

Nadi would have bristled at this. After all, he couldn't help but vent his rightful indignation against the misappropriation of the sword in the movie *Scaramouche*:

> *"Obviously forgetting that his men were armed with swords, and that it was with these weapons that they were supposed to try to kill, the director had the truly brilliant idea of having a French marquis start cutting backstage, with his sword, a not inconsiderable number of ropes holding up as many colossal scenery counterweights, so that these would fall from above upon the adversary. In his own sweet time, the latter would return in coin, or I should say in weight, doing exactly the same thing in monotonous and quite incredible repetition. Having thus defiled the dignity of the sword by degrading it to the lowliness of the ax, each man, (...) waited for the fall of this engine of destruction. (...) Most unfortunately I am terribly sorry I cannot continue to relate the proceedings, because at that point I was compelled to leave the theater in a hurry."[68]*

[67] Cowen, J.D. —"Das Schwert von Krautergersheim (Elsaß)," in **Germania**, vol. 30, #3/4 (1952), p.381.

[68] Nadi, Aldo. **The Living Sword**, Bangor, ME: Laureate Press, 1995; p. 372.

Nadi's bluster roots in the long tradition of the sword's elevated symbolism, first as the hallmark of the wealthy warrior, then as the cruciform emblem of the knight and defender of the faith, and later, as the status symbol of the gentleman of leisure. You just don't clip your hedges or saw at ropes with the queen of weapons...

Confessions of a sword abuser

I admit it. I have opened bottles using a saber guard or blade... beheaded a wine bottle with a stuck cork using a basket-hilt saber... and my battered bell-guard Schläger was my one all-round household tool back in my Göttingen days... its blade cutting everything from wallpaper to salami, its knuckle guard serving as a makeshift hammer.

But all the symbolism and dignity of the weapon aside: A sword is a poor substitute for even a Swiss Army knife when it comes to its versatility and effectiveness as an all-round tool.

Butler's Hudibras, armed to the teeth with a basket-hilt broadsword and dagger, in Hogarth's classic engraving.

And yet, throughout history, the sword appears to have been used for purposes it most definitely was not designed for. Dark-Age Teutonic warriors and their rioting drunken 17th-century scions reportedly beat their blades into rocks and walls—to provide illumination by flying sparks. Butler describes the rapscallion Hudibras as abusing his trusty Toledo equally for domestic and manly chores, much in the same way American GIs turned their steel helmets into multi-purpose tools:

"With basket-hilt, that wou'd hold broth,
and serve for fight and dinner both.
In it he melted lead or bullets..."[69]

And the Pilgrims were known to use their swords to "hew and carve the ground a foot deep."[70]

Swords into plowshares

It goes without saying that the knuckle-guard of a bell-guard Schläger makes a poor hammer—for the simple reason that it was not designed for pounding nails into drywall, but for keeping the opponent's blade from turning your fingers into tater tots.

There are indeed edged weapons that are specifically designed to double as a weapon and a tool. There's the fachine knife of the 19th-century artillerist, whose serrated back doubled as a powerful saw... the gunner's stiletto, etched with intri-

[69]Butler, Samuel. *Hudibras, in Three Parts, Written in the Time of the Late Wars. Corrected and Amended with Additions*, London: T.W., 1726; p. 32. (Canto 1, Part 1, lnn. 351-390.)

[70]Peterson, Harold L. *Arms and Armor of the Pilgrims*, Plymouth, MA: Plimoth Plantation, Inc. and the Pilgrim Society, 1957; p. 11.

cate conversion tables... the machete, as handy for chopping bananas or sugar cane as in taking a swipe at an enemy's neck.

But most swords are designed with only one specific purpose in mind.

Take the common foil as an example. Today, few people perceive a difference between the two main varieties of this weapon, the good old mechanic foil, and its electric cousin.

But as recently as 1961, old-school fencers would consider the electric foil the Fourth Weapon.[71] Indeed, the electric scoring apparatus has changed foil play, not only by restricting the influence of chauvinist, corrupt, or plain incompetent judges on the outcome of a bout, but also by modifying the techniques used:

"With the ordinary foil there was a certain amount of prejudice regarding stop-hits and redoublements in particular. Unless the fencer executing them gained an appreciable and evident period of time on an adversary's attack, or riposte, he was seldom given priority or the benefit of a doubt. Convention, as often as not, had the advantage over common sense. It was a prejudice comparable to that still current in the early part of the century, when foilists deemed that it was not quite 'cricket' to retreat. The step back was commonly referred to, in those days, as the ninth parry. Knowing that a president of jury would only award a stop-hit, a remise, or a redoublement when not to do so would have caused him to be treated with ridicule, it was not surprising that foilists fought shy of these movements."[72]

At its best, the steam foil is a perfect training tool for artful agonistic competition: No weapon is as unforgiving when it comes to point control. Just try this: Put an eye-hook into a golf ball and suspend it from a wire or string to the level of your sternum. Then pick up a vintage foil with the characteristic narrowly tapering #5 blade. Take distance and attempt to hit the golf ball squarely with the point.

You will notice that any punching or stabbing movement (as opposed to the proper straight thrust executed by straightening the arm with an advance or lunge forward) will set the foible and point of the blade into wild oscillations that make it all but impossible to land a solid center hit. Any sloppiness is punished immediately. Try the same with a more recent blade—one with the stiffness of an electric foil— or an épée, and you will notice that the weapon has become much more forgiving...

The point of the exercise: The classic foil is designed for scoring a touch using proper technique. The electric foil and épée are designed to score a touch, plain and simple... Like all weapons, they are tools designed specifically with one particular purpose in mind.

Apples and oranges

Sci-Fi and fantasy author Fritz Leiber, himself a fencer trained in the sports weapons, wrote about his hands-on experiences with some military weapons:

"I do fence with the three weapons and I have owned workaday sabers, both the fairly comfortable ones of the Civil War and the ponderous straight blades issued by the U.S. Cavalry just before World War I, which I can liken only

[71] see Crosnier, Roger. *Fencing with the Electric Foil*, London: Faber & Faber, 1961; p. 13.

[72] Crosnier; *Electric Foil*, p. 18. Crosnier goes as far as to bring the decline of the dominant French and Italian schools into context with the spread of the scoring apparatus, which put more value on simple attacks, athletic ability, and eroded the influence of chauvinist judges.

to skewers suitable only for broiling roast-size shish-kebab. I have occasionally toyed with one of the latter in the manner of Fafhrd, handling it as a foil rather than a broadsword, but I find it really is better for thrusting; if you swing it, making a great swashing stroke, you're very apt to fall down."[73]

Patton's saber, like any other heavier straight-bladed broadsword[74], obviously does not handle with the whipping grace of a foil. It is heavier, its balance point is further down the blade (not an inch away from the guard, as in the modern foil), making it a rather slow weapon if commandeered to do a foil's job.

(To use it effectively, the technique has to be modified: Altenstein recommends that straight-bladed broadswords of the pallash style—Patton's model is nothing else— be used with a *"combination of cut and thrust fencing"*[75], requiring only steps back and forward, and without the foil's lunges, balestras, and those nice, narrow circular parries.)

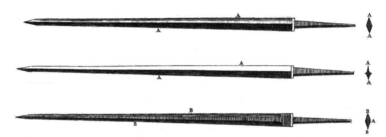

18th century blade forms

Tool time

Standardized sports weapons are perfect tools within their regulatory framework. But as soon as you use them in a way they weren't designed for, they fail to perform— much the same way a Phillips head screwdriver will not work in a regular slot screw.

If you look at a sword as a tool—an implement specifically designed to perform specific mechanical tasks, you have to allow for Colonel Marey-Monge's observations between the differences between weapons and tools proper:

"Tools used for cutting differ from arms used for the like purpose, as the latter require to be light to admit of rapid motion in attack and defence,—to be shaped for defence,—to reach to a distance—and finally, to be conveniently portable in a scabbard."[76]

The tasks assigned to a sword thus can be segmented into offensive and defensive functions, with different parts of the weapon serving one or several purposes simultaneously.

[73]Leiber, Fritz. —"Fafhrd and Me," in deCamp, Sprague (ed.). **The Spell of Conan**, New York: Ace, 1980; p. 130.

[74]In German, the terms Kürassierdegen, Pallasch, or Felddegen are applicable, denoting straight-bladed cavalry weapons pre-dating even Patton's British prototypes.

[75]Altenstein, Axel von. **Der Fechtsport**, Leipzig: Grethlein, c. 1911; p. 105.

[76]Marey-Monge; p. 44.

The hilt, for example, serves both passive and active defensive functions: It passively protects the hands, and—in some systems— allows for active defence (e.g., by turning the guard to catch a blow). Elements of the hilt also serve offensive functions, such as providing leverage in a cut, or, like the spur-like outgrowth on Central European saber hilts, to catch and control an opposing blade.

(Swords also could have other specific purposes. Rapiers, smallswords, and combination weapons frequently were designed and ornamented to impress or reflect status, as well as scare off potential opponents—or just nicely set off a new velvet coat in drawing room society…)

The most prominent offensive feature of an edged weapon is its blade, whose tasks have traditionally been segmented into Thrust and Cut.

Of course, nothing is ever quite that simple. For one, there are two kinds of thrust, each facilitated by a different blade design: There's the classic foil thrust in which the point moves in a straight line. But there's also the thrust in which the point describes a curve.

If the intent is to score a touch—without injuring the opponent—a straight blade with a button will do. But if the intent is to deal the opponent a nasty wound, a curved blade may actually be more useful for thrusting than a straight one:

> "In the position of 'Guard' the point is higher than the wrist; to give point, the latter is lowered smartly, and the wrist is advanced at the same instant. This double motion causes the point to describe very nearly a cycloid, the curvature of which is analogous to, but in the inverse direction to that of our blades, approaching to the curve of the yataghan (the sword of the foot soldier of the East. It is short, slightly curved: It's cutting edge is concave.)
>
> This shape is so well adapted to the object in view that in France, in duels with the sword, those who wish to make use of the point particularly hold the curved sword upside down, so that in the position of 'Guard' the edge is upwards; thus, to gain the advantage of a curvature of blades, analogous to that described by the point, the combatant sacrifices the use of the edge and the defensive effect of the hilt. It is further to be observed that in holding the sword in any other way, the impulse resulting from the two motions is so directed, that the point penetrates as though its angle were nearly double."[77]

(Indeed we find this position depicted already in the Messer segments of Dürer.)

Accordingly, we may assume a simplified grid of specific tasks underlying blade design:

A. Thrust:
1. Linear Thrust:
a) penetration by incision and separation
(i.e. making use of a cutting edge)
b) penetration by separation only
(pointed blade, such as in a duelling épée)
c) percussion (blunt "touch" in fencing)

[77] Marey-Monge; p. 58.

2. Circular Thrust:

a) penetration by incision and separation
   (i.e. making use of a cutting edge)
b) penetration by separation only
c) percussion (blunt "touch" in fencing)

B. Cut:

a) penetration by incision and percussion
b) penetration by incision and laceration ("slicing")
c) percussion ("touch")

Give and take

The design of a blade aims to facilitate one or several functions:

"[In striking with cutting weapons,] the velocity causes the edge to penetrate; the blade enters the wound by thrusting aside the parts divided, while these again close in. (...) The blow of a man acts by contusion and laceration; the edge of a sword, by incision only. The point acts by incision and separation. The vertex of the angle having penetrated, the edges, if they be sharp, divide the substance by incision, while the thickness of the side faces acts by separation. If the point be blunt at both edges, it penetrates by separation."[78]

Even among weapons designed for the specialized task of cutting, there are clear differences as to their effectiveness:

"The curved British sword has likewise great capacity for cutting; the grip and the hilt are well constructed (...). The blade is of good steel and well tempered; it has great percussive force, is light, and takes a fine edge. This weapon is inferior to the Mameluke saber in cutting moderately soft substances: much more so for delicate strokes, such as cutting a handkerchief in the air, or a sheet of paper placed flat on the table; but it is perhaps superior to it in its effect on hard substances, such as cutting the ashen shaft of a lance—that is to say when the stroke should fall like an axe to avoid friction. (...) The British sword, as a European arm, has the fault of being in no way calculated for thrusting."[79]

[78]Marey-Monge, Guillaum*e. Memoire sur les armes blanches*, Strasbourg., 1841, English translation by Maxwell, Henry Hamilton. Marey-Monge, Guillaum*e, Memoir on Swords* etc., London: John Weale, 1860; p. 84.

[79]Marey-Monge; p. 42.

Obviously not thrusting weapons: Bronze and iron hacking swords from the iron-age Balkans (from Randall-MacIver, David. ***The Iron Age in Italy: A Study of these Aspects of the Early Civilization which are neither Villanovian nor Etruscan***, (Oxford: Clarendon Press, 1927) Westport, CT: Greenwood Press, 1974; p. 112 and 146.)

Chicken and egg

As Altenstein's above-mentioned recommendations regarding "fencing" with straight-bladed broadswords indicate, you have to adapt your technique to the shape of your weapon—or vice versa. Executing immediately incapacitating blows, for example, requires a weapon designed for such purpose, but also a technique that serves the underlying intent:

> "*Direct (short) cuts might be able to cause gaping wounds during the duel, when the opponent's upper body is bare, but it is not practical to assume that in hand-to-hand combat or in any hostile encounter, this kind of cut would put an opponent hors-de-combat, or even kill him.*
>
> *In hand-to-hand combat, you will always have to use fully swung cuts [i.e., moulinets] to have any effect; for example, to cut down a hostile foot soldier, you will only achieve this if you succeed to not only cut through his head gear, but also cleave a gaping cleft into his skull.*"[80]

Trade-off: The opening caused by the molinello was worth the added force.

This explains why Barbasetti is still pictured executing wide moulinets or *Schwingungen* from the elbow.[81] He—who was also the author of a popular Code Duello[82]—may have exposed his sword arm to time cuts during this motion. But most of the students at his pricey establishment at the St. Annahof belonged to the upper crust of the Austrian officer corps, and only this movement could have provided enough impact to do serious harm to an opponent.

As this intent to harm the opponent faded into obsolescence, both technique and hardware adapted to the new situation: The modern sports saber no longer intends to represent a threat to the physical integrity of the fellow-fencer—and in fact, cannot present a danger apart from freak accidents.

Martincic's brief synopsis of the gradual shift of the rotational point for the execution of cuts[83] with the sports saber illuminates the shift of intent from this weapon's original purpose as a weapon of antagonistic confrontation to one of agonistic, competitive sports:

[80] "*direkte (kurze) Hiebe] können zwar im Duell, wo der Oberkörper des Gegners entblösst ist, klaffende Wunden erzeugen, doch es ist nicht anzunehmen, dass man im Handgemenge oder überhaupt bei feindlichen Zusammenstössen einen Gegner mit solchen Hiebe sofort kampfunfähig machen oder gar töten wird.*
Man wird daher im Nahkampfe stets nur mit Aufbietung aller Kraft angeschwungene Hiebe führen müssen, um überhaupt eine Wirkung zu erziehlen, da man, um z.B. einen feindlichen Infanteristen niederzuhauen, dies nur erreichen wird, wenn es einem gelingt, nicht nur dessen Kopfbedeckung mit dem Säbel zu durchschneiden, sondern auch einen klaffenden Spalt in die Schädeldecke zu hauen." See Bartunek; p. 28.

[81] Barbasetti, Luigi. **Das Säbelfechten**, Vienna: Verlag der Allgemeinen Sportzeitung, 1899; figg. 9, 11, 13, 15.

[82] Barbasetti, Luigi. **Ehren-Codex**, Vienna: Verlag der Allgemeinen Sportzeitung, 1898.

[83] Martincic, Albert. **Kevey und seine Schule**, Graz: H. Kunz, 1983; p. 39.

Cuts from the shoulder were intended to cut through defensive armor and inflict as much damage as possible by the sheer force of the impact.[84] Radaelli shifted the axis to the elbow for use with the *sciabola di terreno*, a pure comment weapon frequently used for first blood duels—not the destruction of the opponent. Igalffy of the Viennese Neustadt then moved the axis further down to the wrist, only to be overtaken by the modern school of the saber whose main force is generated from the fingers (before being shifted to the middle of the blade or even the point.)

The plopping sound of a flat blade grazing an opponent's lamé that today precedes the triumphant bleep of the scoring apparatus would have had no effect at all on the outcome of an actual duel or mêlée. Martincic highlights his remarks about the finger-generated cuts of the modern competitive sports saber technique:

"This way, the opponent cannot be injured."

Which, of course, is what friendly competition is all about.

[84]See also the remarks on the utility of the heavy cavalry saber in combat, in Bartunek; p. 26.

INTERLUDE

OLYMPIAN COMPETITIVE COMBAT

The Lady in the Park:
An Épée Bout, c. 1920[85]

I had a cup of tea, then stepped out onto the narrow balcony, gazed into the eventide summer park. Somewhere I heard bright female voices, then a ringing and rattling of metal—but couldn't see a thing. I noticed that the balcony, which started at this room, ran around the rounded corner of the house, and I followed it to see what was going on.

And now I observed a very curious spectacle.

Linden trees in full blossom, whose scent carried up to me. Underneath, two human beings, fencing with *épées de combat*[86], on the ground a couple of blades, chest plastrons, fencing masks, coats, kerchiefs. Just in the corner of my eye, positioned so I could see her entire face, was Elsa Krüger. Dressed weirdly enough. High, gray leather riding boots with little silver spurs, then a silver grey and green brocade gown as medieval princesses may have worn it riding out for a boar hunt—on stage or in reality, what do I know.

Long sleeves, buckskin gloves with high cuffs, the gown fitting tightly and fully exhibiting the shape of her body down to the hips. But then, getting wide and broad, cinched in front at the knees, so you might see the boots, to the back flowing in to a two, three yard long train. Matching a flat, large hat, turned up in front, with long, bobbing ostrich plumes at the side. The épée matched the outfit. It looked like a riding whip. No fencing mask, no breast plastron.

A gown for horseback riding, not for the fencing loft.

Facing her, a boy. The costume of a squire: black and purple. High tricots, short and poofy knee pants, laced with silver. Velvet jacket, but with a strapped – on chest protector. No hat; the narrow fencing mask over his face, from which a plentitude of blond curls sprang forth over the shoulders. Leather gloves. A costume fit for fencing much as that of the Krüger woman was inappropriate.

One round had just been finished; they were getting ready for another one. *"A loro!"* the bright voice of the Krüger woman rang out—they went on guard. The blades touched, and immediately the blond boy began his game. The gowned lady exhibited a deep inside opening, he thrust into it, but received a parrying time thrust, which was followed immediately by a reply in quint.

"Toccato!" the Krüger woman called.

"Niente affatto!" was the reply—but obviously the curly-haired boy had been hit.

Even though he was constantly attacking, lunging again and again, the woman was gaining more and more ground. Her train didn't seem to impede her in the least; it was amazing how she kicked it back with a quick movement of the foot. Inch by inch she forced her opponent back. She intentionally neglected her cover, inside and outside, above and underneath the hand. The boy noticed that

[85]from "Armer Freddy" by Hanns Heinz Ewers, in **Ameisen**, München: Georg Müller Verlag, 1925; p. 403f.

[86]Ewers uses the term *"Stossdegen."*

quickly enough, but his rapid thrusts were much too soft, the blade of the experienced lady caught them with ease in the half forte. The entire foible of her blade, however, was constantly threatening the squire; he parried, caught her thrusts, but only by yielding ground. Now she chased him around in a circle, ligating, traversing—it was a wonderful sight for an old fencer such as myself.

All of a sudden she jumped backward, right into her train—I will never understand how she managed not to get entangled in the heavy brocade with her spurs. In the blink of an eye she pushed forward again, catching a well-intentioned, yet much too feeble low tierce, binding and reprising, which again cost the boy a couple of inches of ground. Close to the linden tree she had driven him, he couldn't go back, was forced to advance.

And now that she had all the advantages of the defensive over the attacker, her great mastery of the art was truly exhibited. The blond boy fought laudably, obviously fired by the one single wish to hit his mistress at least once. In that he was not in the least bit perturbed that she wore neither mask nor plastron, it was obvious that he was used to this kind of fight with her. Without inhibition he aimed his thrusts at chest and face; despite the leather button of the blade a hit would have been able to injure badly.

But the lady with the plumed hat appeared if not invulnerable, then at least unhittable. The heavy disadvantage of her opponent, namely that his arm was weak and that all his thrusts were not strong enough, she masterfully used to her own advantage, tempting him again and again with feints and treacherous openings, only to parry always in time.

Then a glorious flanconnade. *"Toccato!"* she cried.

"Gia!" the boy replied.

He threw away the épée, tore off the wire mask. The Krüger woman opened the straps of the chest plastron on his back and it dropped to the ground: There I saw that this slender boy was a girl. And I understood why his thrusts had been so feeble.

The trained lady took a silk kerchief from her bosom, wiped the blond squire girl's beading sweat drops off her face. Quavering she stood there, shaking from head to foot; big tears rose in her eyes. The Krüger woman put her arm around her shoulders, kissed her tears off her eyes.

"You fought gallantly!" she said. "Very gallantly, Julia!"

The girl did not reply, she nestled her little head to the bosom of her friend, who tenderly caressed her blond curls. But then she looked up again, called laughing through her tears: "You wait! Next time!"

Holding each other tightly, they walked toward the castle.

3. THE THREAT

The dreader end.
duel Dichard vs. de Massas.

. . . a dashing man with a pencil mustache on a staircase, his rapier point weaving an invisible web of death between himself and a savage squad of goateed warriors wearing breastplate and morion. There's a feint in the high line, a clanging of blades in the low, faster, more accurate than in real life . . . high again, low again, a corps-a-corps with blades locked. Then a lunge, a triumphant yet relaxed smile . . . a banderole—and a warrior goes down with a maximum of arm flailing and grimacing . . .

You've seen it on late-night movies and ten-dollar video tapes. Chances are the image was so powerful it got you started on the arduous road to mastering the sword in any or all its modern incarnations.

It doesn't matter if the bad boys running with pikes in the background move their legs just a tad too fast. (Heck, the scene was shot at slightly higher speed.) It doesn't matter if the morioned moron goes out of his way to open him self up to parry a cut too weak to cause more than a *ping!* on his helmet. It doesn't even matter if the banderole glances off the cuirass as it "kills".

After all, it's the movies.

Swordplay on stage and on screen have imprinted the modern perception of fighting with edged weapons more than any competitive event ever could. So pervasive was its influence that it swayed the opinions even of those in charge of training men to kill with the sword. . . from horseback and on foot.

On the fatality of sword-inflicted wounds

But fighting with swords is a messy affair. Its reality involves gaping flesh wounds, cut muscles, broken bones, spouting blood and severed limbs—stuff you couldn't or wouldn't want to show before an audience until the guts-'n'-gore genre of action movies took off in the 1970s.

The dramatic requirements of a staged death were simple: An acoustically and visually pleasing display of choreographed swordplay... a cut or, even better, a thrust that appeared to disappear in the opponent's costume... and then a quick or prolonged farewell to leave the audience drenched in cathartic tears or awash in rightful triumph, depending on the moral qualities of the victim.

Deaths to please the eye

The thrust remained the most popular shortcut to Hades on stage. It credibly could claim mortal injury with a tastefully minimal display of gore. And in its linear line of travel, it also served as an allegory for divine justice if the bad guy was at the receiving end. Jove's thunderbolt, after all, travels along straight lines and not along the trajectory of the edge and point during the cut.

This is the way Hal kills Hotspur in Shakespeare's *Henry IV*; thus Iden kills Cade, and York kills Clifford in the same play. Thus Richmond kills Richard in *Richard III*; thus Tybalt takes out Mercutio and Romeo takes out Tybalt and then Paris in *Romeo and Juliet*. Thus Hamlet kills Laertes.

Stage deaths were clean deaths designed to gratify the audience esthetically and emotionally. Death and injury in antagonistic combat, however, even in the somewhat refined environment of the duel, follow sobering and often sickening reality.

For one, the human body often proved frightfully resilient even to divine justice.

Take the duel between Sir Edward Sackville and Lord Bruce, fought in 1610.[87] Sackville recounts the damage mutually inflicted on each other by the fighters:

> *"I made a thrust at my enemy, but was short, and in drawing back my arm I received a great wound thereon, which I interpreted as a reward for my short shooting; but in revenge I pressed in to him, though I then missed him also, and then receiving a wound in my right pap[88], which past level through my body, and almost to my back.*
>
> *And there we wrestled for the two greatest and dearest prices we could ever expect trial for, honour and life; in which struggling my hand, having but an ordinary glove on it, lost one of her servants, though the meanest; which hung by a skin, and to fight yet remaineth as before, and I am put in hope one day to recover the use of it again.(...)*
>
> *Myself being wounded, and feeling loss of blood—having three conduits running on me—which began to make me faint, and he courageously persisting not to accord to either of my propositions, remembrance of his former bloody desire, and feeling of my present estate, I struck at his heart, but with his avoiding missed my aim, yet passed through the body, and drawing out my sword repassed it through again, through another place; when he cried, 'Oh! I am slain!' seconding his speech with all the force he had, to cast me."*

[87] from Anonymus. ***Reflections on Duelling and on the Most Effectual Means for Preventing It***, Edinburgh: W. Creech, 1790; p. 52f., and page xi of this book.

[88] Pap = nipple.

A large cut (or puncture wound?) on his sword arm, a thrust through his chest, a finger cut off... aware of his fading strength due to bloodloss, which will render him temporarily blind, then unconscious after Lord Bruce cries uncle… yet Sackville fights on to defeat the uninjured opponent.

The failure of even multiple thrusts to put either opponent instantly out of action is reminiscent of Silver's scolding remarks on the Italians' focus on the point:

"I have knowne a Gentleman hurt in Rapier fight, in nine or ten places through the bodie, armes, and legges, and yet hath continued in his fight, and afterward hath slaine the other, and come home and hath bene cured of all his wounds without maime and is yet living."[89]

Oddly enough, Silver's arch-rival Saviolo fully agrees with him for once. But he also indicates that he knows the importance of strategic fight psychology in addition to the mechanics of incapacitation:

"Every little blowe in the face stayeth the furie of a man more than anie other place of his bodie, for being through the bodie, it happeneth often times that the same man killeth his man notwithstanding in the furie of his resolution: but the blood that runneth about the face, dismayeth a man either by stopping his breath, or hindering his sight."[90]

Saviolo, who prefers the thrust as being "more lethal", is realistic and experienced enough to know that it can be irrelevant to the outcome of a fight. A superficial slash across the forehead, however, could pack enough psychological punch to wrap up business.

This insight was to hold true until the modern era: The saber duel Terrone vs. Flauto in 1896[91] was terminated by a gaping cut in Flauto's forehead that probably had him see red. Adolfo Contronei's injury in his fight against Giorgio Santelli also was sufficient to terminate the duel — a high tierce or high quarte against the forehead that probably blinded him by the volume of blood.

Martial speculation

When the sword lost its main purpose as a weapon of antagonistic combat in the 19th and 20th century, armchair warriors began to engage in a free-for-all philosophical struggle that pitted thrust vs. cut.

Comfortable that debates about the "lethality" of sword fighting systems never could be proven by scientific experiment, a declaration of superiority of a particular method was arrived at by compiling theoretic analysis and anecdotal evidence: The thrust by definition had to be "more lethal" than the cut.

This now commonly accepted thesis, however, has a terminal flaw: Fighters in antagonistic combat scenarios do not use definitions to dispatch each other. They use tools specifically designed for narrowly-defined purposes to achieve specific objectives against a human opponent's psyche and physiology – an opponent whose actions and motivations are often unpredictable, erratic, uncontrollable because of competing instincts, emotions, and psychological pressures.

[89]Silver, George, *Paradoxes of Defence*, London: Edward Blount, 1599; p. 21. In Jackson, James L. *Three Elizabethan Fencing Manuals*, Delmar, NY: Scholar's Facsimiles and Reprints, 1972; p. 519.

[90]Saviolo, Vincentio. *His Practice*, London: John Wolff, 1595; in Jackson; p. 261f.

[91]see Huber, Ted. *Fundamental Swordplay*, Ann Arbor, MI: Edwards Bros., 1939; p. 24 f; Terrone, Leonardo F. *Right and Left Hand Fencing*, New York: Dodd Mead, 1959; p. 8 f., and on p. 159. of this book

Duel du Lau vs. des Perrières.

Murderous intent

It should be noted that the intent to actually kill the opponent is not necessarily implied in antagonistic scenarios. In fact, it appears that the decision to kill the opponent rather than rendering incapable of fight requires an additional element of conscious deliberation that transcends the mere struggle for absolute dominion and survival. Some *Comment* scenarios attempted to rule out the death of an opponent both explicitly (Mensur) and implicitly (for example by prohibiting seconds from imposing conditions that made the death of one or both combatants probable).[92]

Entering an antagonistic scenario, however, requires at least the implicit acceptance of a coincidental or accidental kill due to the unpredictable nature of fight.[93] This attitude is fundamentally different from agonistic scenarios, where death and injury (for example through broken blades, as in the fatal accident of the Soviet fencer Smirnoff in 1983, whose mask was pierced by a broken foil that penetrated his brain through the eye) are indeed unacceptable accidents whose occurrence and recurrence is sought to be ruled out by expanding the protective quality of offensive and defensive weaponry.

The 1881 duel of Saint-Victor vs. Asselin[94] serves to illuminate the unpredictability of antagonistic combat. Fought with sabers, the seconds had agreed to exclude the thrust during the duel. A contemporary illustration shows the duellists to be wearing padded masks, but no bandages or even gloves to protect neck, torso, arms, and hands. (See also page 75.)

Despite the exclusion of the point, Asselin was killed by a thrust into the belly. St. Victor claims to have executed the thrust without premeditation in the heat of confused action.[95]

Killing by the thrust

The ability to kill required not only the proper mindset, but the proper hardware.

There are indeed numerous instances that document instant death as the result of a thrust with the duelling sword—even though the number of duels

[92]See Frevert, Ute. *Ehrenmänner: Das Duell in der bürgerlichen Gesellschaft*, München: C.H. Beck, 1991; p. 206.

[93]The only exception are ritualistic combat scenarios like the Mensur, where the configuration of the offensive and defensive weaponry is intended to exclude life-threatening injuries.

[94]Veaux, Baron de. *Les duels célebres*, Paris: Éd, Ronveyre, 1884; p. 97f.

[95]I have repeatedly pointed out Barbasetti's observation that saber duels in which the thrust is allowed (i.e., where both combatants are aware that there's no regulatory agreement to protect them from the possibility) are usually terminated by an injury to the lower sword arm.

involving the death of one party was small compared to those in which both duellists survived, Schmied-Kowarzik and Kufahl's list of deadly encounters in France late in the late 1800s points out how dangerous the duelling sword was:

1864: Épée duel de Froideford vs. Gaëtani. Gaëtani killed in second round.
1876: Épée duel Ollivier vs. Feuilhuade. Ollivier killed.
1877: Épée duel Hugues vs. Daime. Daime wounded in first round, dies instantly.
1880: Épée duel Olivares vs. Lardi. Lardi killed.
1882: Épée duel Dichard vs. Massas. Massas killed by thrust into throat.
Also: Épée duel: Mareillet vs. Piat. Mareillet killed.
Also: Épée duel Daudier vs. Marseul. Daudier killed.
1885: Épée duel Chapuis vs. Dekeisel. Chapuis killed.
1886: Épée duel Caze vs. Viguier. Caze dies on the strip.
1889: Épée duel Pierrotti vs. Belz de Villas. Pierrotti killed.

This is not surprising. After all, the weapon itself is designed for antagonistic combat. Its point can indeed be described only with the over-used cliché of "needle-sharp". It will snag veins, arteries, and muscles on its path through the body, tearing them as the blade progresses.[96] (A blunted tip, such as that of the modern sports saber, will push them aside rather than tearing them.[97]) The resulting damage is a function of organs hit and depth of penetration.

It always is hard to gauge, however, if the fatalities were indeed the result of a premeditated intent to kill, or if they occurred coincidentally. Schmied-Kowarzik and Kufahl recount one instant of a deliberate intent to kill:

This is the story of a man from Marseille, who avenged the death of his bride, parents, and family at the hands of the Jacobites and Bonapartists first as a corsair and slaver, and then as a notorious duellist. He picked his victims by their choice of reading... readers of the *Figaro* and the *National.* And he made sure he killed his opponent:

"If I thrust en quarte, I pull out with a barely perceptible shift of hand position into tierce, or vice versa. That kills. He'll forever stay down.(...) because the lung then is damaged, and sepsis will follow."[98]

It should be noted that this kill could be considered a secondary fatality. The opponent was put *hors-de-combat* not by an immediately fatal injury but by a combination of physiological incapacitation and conditional/regulatory incapacitation (probably the doctor's decision). Death occurs long after the encounter is over and thus has no direct effect on the outcome of the duel.

(Other documented secondary kills were probably coincidental rather than intentional:

1879: Épée duel Koechling vs. Liebenberg. Liebenberg dies a few days later of his injuries;
1884: Épée duel Puyflitz vs. Civry. Puyflitz dies two days after receiving wounds that did not appear life threatening.)

[96] The French "service duel" of non-commissioned officers at the beginning of the 19th century frequently used duelling swords whose blades were equipped with a cut-in thread at a certain distance below the point. A bolt would be screwed onto these blades to prevent dangerous depth of penetrations. Duels stipulated in detail if they were to be fought with our without these bolts *(émoucheté),* allowing officers to settle petty matters of honor in style without depleting the ranks of valuable fighting men.(See Schmied-Kowarzik and Kufahl; p. 183.)

[97] I recall a sports saber blade penetrating my sword hand between ring and small finger, sliding across the back of my hand underneath the skin for a good two inches without leaving anything but a puncture wound.

[98] Schmied-Kowarzik, Josef and Kufahl, Hans. **Das Duellbuch**, Leipzig: J. J. Weber, 1896; p. 158.

Robust physiology

But even the most murderous intent was not a reliable guarantee for killing the opponent. After all, a successful kill depended as much on skill as on sheer luck. Bartunek, a contemporary of Barbasetti at a time when the Italian competitive systems had began their triumphal march into Central Europe, is himself drawn to the modern systems, without discounting the viability of the traditional schools. He comments:

> *"The thrust is only then a certain thing if it penetrates the internal organs, not when it gets stuck somewhere on a bone."*[99]

You could say that given the physiological variants of the opponent's body, a deliberate attempt at an instant kill with a thrust into a "vital point" could be compared to trying to impale an airborne fly hovering behind a curtain—with a fifty-fifty chance of killing after hitting the fly. And frequently, a fighter scoring that "sure kill" found himself incapacitated or killed by his victim.

Physiology of fight

The very stress of a serious combat scenario causes changes in the body's physiology that actively counteract some immediate effects of injury. The body *"starts getting physically ready for danger, with increased blood flow to the arms and legs (for fighting or running), release of the chemical cortisol (which helps blood coagulate more quickly in case of injury), lactic acid heating up in the muscles (to prepare them for effort), focused vision, and increased breathing and heartbeat to support all these systems."*[100]

In his thesis *Duelling: Swordplay and the Wounded Adversary*, Frank Lurz rounds up the most insidious candidates responsible for death in edged-weapons combat:

> *"Death from stabbing and incising (. . .) wounds is mainly brought about through five mechanisms: massive hemorrhage (exsanguination), air in the bloodstream (air embolism), suffocation (asphyxia), [collapsed lung] (pneumothorax), and infection."*[101]

Even if major arteries are cut and severe loss of blood is taking place, an injured fighter can remain fully conscious for 2 to 30 seconds, with death occurring within 3 seconds and two minutes.[102]

Lurz sums up the situation with precision:

> *"The immediate consequences of wounds to a duelist inflicted by sword thrusts or cuts were unpredictable. While historical anecdotes of affairs of honor and twentieth-century medical reports show that many stabbing*

[99] *"(...) da der Stoss nur sicher ist, wenn er in die Organe eindringt, nicht aber irgendwo an einem Knochen stecken bleibt."* See Bartunek; p. 30.

[100] de Becker, Gavin. *The Gift of Fear*, NY: Little, Brown & Co., 1997; p. 112.

[101] Lurz, Frank. *Duelling: Swordplay and the Wounded Adversary, A Thesis Presented to the Faculty of the Military Fencing Masters Program*, San José State University, 1996; p. 20.

[102] Applegate, Col. Rex. *Combat Use of the Double-Edged Fighting Knife*, Boulder, CO; Paladin Press, 1993; p. 18.

Any which way you can:
At the Battle of Nürnberg, 1502.

victims collapsed immediately upon being wounded, others did not. While a swordsman certainly gained no advantage for having been wounded, it cannot be said that an unscathed adversary, after having delivered the fatal thrust or cut, had no further concern for his safety. Duellists receiving gravely serious and even mortal wounds were sometimes able to continue effectively in the combat long enough to take the lives of those who had taken theirs."[103]

As the following example from 14th-century Scotland illustrates, this could even occur when inherently superior weaponry (polearm vs. sword) was involved:

"Lindsay had run one of them, a strong and brawny man, through the body with a spear, and brought him to the earth; but although in the agonies of death, he writhed himself up, and with the spear sticking in his body, struck Lindsay a desperate blow with his sword, which cut him through the stirrup and into the bone, upon which he instantly fell and expired."[104]

Reviewing historic accounts, it appears that the most successful strategy to end an encounter was to aim not at the instant kill but at the immediate physical incapacitation of the enemy, achieved by destroying his capacity to wield a sidearm by loss of limb or destruction of the control center. (If executed with sufficient severity, death would follow within a tolerably quick time frame by exsanguination.)

In battlefield scenarios, the cut with ax and broadsword would often have drastic results. In 1689, for example, General Mackay's defeat at Killiecrankie at the hand of the Highlanders again painted a savage picture of the ferocity of their cutting swords.

[103]Lurz; p. 55.
[104]In *History of the Highland Regiments, Highland Clans, etc. from Official and other Authentic Sources*, vol. 1, Edinburgh: Thomas C. Jack, 1887; p. 68.

The battlefield was scattered with mutilated bodies *"hewn down by the Highlanders. Here might be seen a skull which had been struck off above the ears by a stroke from a broadsword—there a head lying near the trunk from which it had been severed—here an arm or a limb—there a corpse laid open from the head to the brisket; while interspersed among these lifeless trunks, dejectaque membra, were to be seen broken pikes, smallswords and muskets, which had been snapt asunder by the athletic blows of the Lochaber axe and broadsword."* [105]

Down and soon to be out: Ordeals could be just as bad for your health as the battlefield.

The antagonistic use of the cut was intended to have immediate incapacitating effects on the opponent. Silver elaborates:

> *"But the blow being strongly made, taketh sometimes cleane away the hand from the arme, hath manie times been seene. Againe, a full blow upon the head or face with a short sharpe Sword, is most commonly death. A full blow upon the necke, shoulder, arme, or legge, indangereth life, cutteth off the veines, muscles, and sinewes, perishes the bones: These wounds made by the blow, in respect of perfect healing, are the losse of limmes, or maimes incurable forever.*
>
> *And yet more for the blows: a full blow upon the head, face, arm, or legs, is death, or the partie so wounded in the mercie of him that shall so wound him.*
>
> *A blow upon the hand, arme, or legge is a maime incurable; but a thrust in the hand, arme, or legge is to be recovered. The blow hath manie parts to wound, and in everie of them commaundeth the life; but the thrust has but a few, as the bodie or face, and not in every part of them, neither."* [106]

This, of course, echoes some plates from Talhoffer's use of the Messer (roughly comparable to the falchion), where the over-eager attack against the opponent's head is punished by a time cut that takes off the sword hand (plate 228) and is followed by a lethal cut into the skull (plate 229). [107] Sutor still includes the severed hand as a technique for rapierplay, with the variant of piercing the sword hand as an advanced technique. [108]

[105]ibid. p. 376n: *"Many of Mackay' officers and soldiers were cut down through the skull and neck to the very breast; others had skulls cut off above their ears like nightcaps; some soldiers had both their bodies and cross-belts cut through at one blow; pikes and smallswords were cut like willows."*

[106]Silver; p. 21.

[107]Hergsell, Gustav. **Talhoffers Fechtbuch as dem Jahre 1467**, Prague: self-published, 1887.

[108]Sutor, Jakob. **Neu Künstliches Fechtbuch** (1610), (Stuttgart: J. Scheible, 1849) Limburg an der Lahn: San Casciano Verlag, 1994; p. 75, p. 87.

Talhoffer, plate 228   plate 229

The brutal efficiency of the cut is also illustrated by a grainy black-and-white photo from the turn of the century reprinted in Baldick's *The Duel* [109] which shows a duellist with a cavalry saber standing over the body of his opponent—whose severed head stares from the grass a few feet away.

Losing your head.
(After Baldick.)

Lethal impact

I have already illustrated some of the horrible effects of sword cuts above. But let me get back to the Death of King Arthur for a moment: Even as he feels his father's spear pass through his body, Mordred lunges forward into the shaft and *"right so he smote his father, King Arthur, with his sword held in both hands, upon the side of the head, that the sword pierced the helmet and the tay of the brain. And therewith Mordred dashed down stark dead to the earth. And noble King Arthur fell in a swoon to the earth."* [110]

With his skull split (probably through the protective layer of a helmet!), Arthur survives the fight, at least for a few feverish days—the time it takes for the boat to arrive to take him to Avalon.

[109] See Baldick, Robert. *The Duel,* (London: Chapmann & Hall, 1965) London & NY: Spring Books, 1970; fig. 26(b). The most recent reprint of this excellent book is now also available from Barnes & Noble.

[110] Malory, Sir Thomas. *Morte Darthur,* (London: Caxton, 1485) in Kermode, Frank et al. (edd.). *The Oxford Anthology of English Literature,* New York, London, Toronto: Oxford UP, 1973; vol. 1; p. 453.

Is this the stuff of legends ... swords cutting not only through rock, like Roland's Durendal, but through steel and bone? Or are such horrid sword injuries the common fare of the medieval, even Renaissance or Baroque warrior? Thus, did Mallory, a seasoned rogue and warrior himself, model the Death of Arthur on what he personally witnessed on the battlefields of his day?

The most extensive study into the forensic evidence of medieval battle injuries was conducted by Bengt Thordemann, who analyzed the dead of the mass graves of Wisby. [111]

Thordemann marvels at the powerful cuts that sheared through skulls, arms, legs:

> *"Fig. 170 demonstrates the berserker rage which overcame the warriors in the heat of battle. It shows in situ the lower extremities of a man who had both lower legs cut off, probably by a single blow. (...) It is almost incomprehensible that such blows could be struck. (...) several crania have been found in which the coif had been cut to pieces and the blow had partly penetrated to the bones of the cranium."* [112]

But what Thordemann attributes to berserk battle fury apparently was not uncommon in other parts of Europe as well. A recent exhibition at the Wilhelm-Fabry-Museum in Hilden, Germany—tellingly titled "Silent Witnesses of their Suffering"—included a number of pathological exhibits with tell-tale signs of cut injuries to the heads of people in the Middle Ages. [113]

Moon of skulls

Skull injuries caused by blows can be separated into a) blows with sharp instruments and b) blows with blunt instruments.

Sharp and half-sharp cuts—such as those dealt by a sword or battle ax—typically leave two marks in the skull: A smooth, incision-like surface, and a jagged fracture whose rim is pushed outside. [114] The defect is larger on the outside than on the inside. Other indicators are microscopic, crescent-shaped splinters along the injury, as well as channels and elevations caused by notches in the edge.

The effects of a sharp cut on the human cranium. (After Czarnetzki)

If the blade was twisted after entering the skull, a whole piece of bone can be levered out—enlarging the area of the injury.

Depending on the brain damage suffered as a consequence of the cut, skull injuries can kill immediately. If the dura mater (Mallory calls it the "tay") is severed, survivors of the primary injury faced infection and inflammation, which usually led to death within a short time. Infections and—temporary—survival can be recognized by impressions by the imprints of new blood vessels, especially

[111] See Thordemann, Bengt. *Armour from the Battle of Wisby, 1361*, Stockholm and Uppsala: Kungl. Vitterhets Historie och Antikvitets Akademien, 1939; vol. 1, chapter iv "The Skeletons", pp. 159f.

[112] Thordemann; p. 164f.

[113] Injuries to bones suffered by living persons ("intravital" injuries) cannot be distinguished from those that occurred shortly after death.

[114] Czarnetzki, Alfred (ed.). *Stumme Zeugen ihrer Leiden: Paläopatholgische Befunde*, Tübingen: Attempto Verlag, 1996; p. 184-194.

on the inside on the skull.[115] The blunt and sharp trauma of a blow to the head can rupture blood vessels inside the skull. The resulting bleeding into the cavity can pressure on brain tissue, which could result in brain damage even if it was survived originally.

Skull and bones

In his book, Czarnetzki includes four skulls that show the marks of sharp sword cuts:

• **Case 1.** A 40- to 50-year old male from Lichtenstein in the Odenwald (Germany), 14th-16th century. His skull exhibits the traces of a sharp cut, dealt frontally from the upper right. (This would correspond to a head cut in quarte, dealt by a right-handed opponent.)

A direct consequence of the impact was a fracture in the skull which virtually extended the cut across the side of the head. Incredibly enough, this cut was survived briefly, as newly formed bone within the fracture proves. The perforated surface structure, however, indicates that death probably occurred shortly afterwards, probably as the result of inflammation.

• **Case 2.** A 50- to 60-year old male from Vaihingen, c. 12th-14th century, with two separate defects on the left side of the frontal bone. The upper one exhibits a clean, horizontal cut which resulted in a large, nearly square piece of bone being broken out of the skull. The lower cut only took off a surface shard of bone, while damaging the interior bone structure. Here the upper half was cut out, the lower half broken.

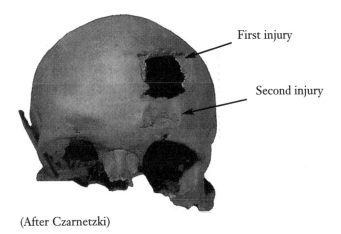

First injury

Second injury

(After Czarnetzki)

It seems that this man received the upper injury first. The blade must have been twisted in the wound, probably in an effort to dislodge it from the bone. The second injury occurred flat across the skull.

The angle of the first cut is inconclusive to decide if the blow was executed in a flat, near-horizontal (maybe back-handed) arc, or if it maybe was dealt from an elevated position (on horseback). The second injury is even more puzzling, since it must have been dealt when the victim was still in nearly the same position—which is difficult to imagine since the first cut was probably sufficient to immediately kill this man, or at the very least knock him off his feet.

[115]Czarnetzki; p. 187.

• **Case 3.** A 30- to 40-year old male from Vaihigen, c. 12th-14th century, with a near-vertical defect in the left upper rear of the skull, caused by a sharp frontal cut. The weapon penetrated (and cut through) the skull at an oblique angle, breaking out a large piece of bone. The broken-out piece, however, has re-ossified with the skull, indicating that this injury was survived.

• **Case 4.** A 30- to 40-year old male from Vaihingen, c. 12th-14th century., with a deep, near vertical cut in the frontal bone. The weapon entered the skull from the left side, breaking out the right-hand rim. The injury shows traces of an inflammatory process, but nearly all fragments have healed and refused with the bone, indicating that the man survived for a long time.

An earlier exhibit at the Württembergisches Landesmuseum at Stuttgart back in 1983[116] featured

• **Case 5.** A 40- to 50-year old male from Kirchheim (no date, grave #410) with an overlapping shard of the frontal bone. The gaping cut, which completely severed the bone, was caused by a sword cut from the left side. It thoroughly healed.

• **Case 6.** A 20- to 30-year old male from Kirchheim (grave 234), with a vertical cleft in his frontal bone which partially cut through the bone into the interior. The wound healed completely without infection.

• **Case 7.** A 40- to 50-year old man from Kircheim/Teck (Martinskirche, Grave 1) with a large, gaping cut in the right side of the skull caused by a sharp cut from the front, which cut through bone and dura mater and resulted in an open brain injury. The wound shows signs of bone healing, death probably occurred after a few weeks as a result of infection and inflammation.

• **Case 8.** A 30- to 40-year old man from Hermaringen, with one cut across the frontal bone and into the left part of the back of the head. The nicks of the blades are still visible. This man must have died immediately.

• **Case 9.** A 30- to 40-year old man from Donzdorf (Grave 49). His left lower jaw was laid open to the roots of his molars. At the angle of his left jaw his a smooth defect with thin, diagonally occurring shards. The first frontal cut removed part of the jawbone, but was not lethal. The defect at the angle of his jaw indicates a sharp cut that grazed the bone but cut deep into his neck, probably killing him immediately.

[116]Czarnetzki, Alfred (et al.). *Menschen des frühen Mittlealters im Spiegel der Anthropologie und Medizin*, Münster, Bonn, Liestal: Württembergisches Landesmusem, 1983; p. 45f.

• **Case 10.** A 40- to 50-year old male from Oberschmeien with a sharply defined arched defect above the left temple and in the left back of the head. Results of two sharps cuts that removed large parts of the skull and cut deep into the skull.

Anglo-Saxon parallel

These observations concur with those of S.J. Wenham's study of Anglo-Saxon skeletons at Eccles, Kent:

"The skulls had damage in the form of linear injuries to the brow, temple and crown (mostly to the left). Many seem to have been the result of a downward (vertical and angled) chop. One man (Victim II) had suffered as many as eleven blows to the head and a further five to the neck, ten to the back and three to the arms, which were such as to make him unable to hold any weapon or shield." [117]

Pollington is quick to draw conclusions to the fighting style from the skeletal evidence:

"Right-handed men holding their shields at chest height in their left hands can most easily attack the left sides of their opponents' heads, shoulders and arm. Cutting strokes would be the most effective, though well-aimed thrusts could be deadly if they were to land properly. Three of the six skulls examined had cuts to the mid-left brow or pate, consistent with fatal dueling wounds, although they could just as easily have been sustained in battle." [118]

But the evidence is inconclusive. If the intent inherent in a combat scenario or confrontation is inflicting death or serious injury, we are dealing with antagonistic combat for survival or dominion.

This rules out any intended matching of weaponry and fighting style—thus reducing the applicability of the findings to individual combat scenarios: Despite the evidence on the skulls, we cannot determine if the man suffering the injury was armed—or if the party inflicting the wound did not take full advantage of all possible means. It is impossible to tell if a man met his death in single combat or if he was ambushed, if he was armed or not, or if he might have been a pedestrian attacked by a horseman.

The only thing we can safely deduct from the grisly remains of the victims of medieval swords is that not only were there wielded with enough strength to destroy steel and bone alike (thus belying the commonly-held belief that thrust fencing was "developed" because cuts were ineffective against armor)—but that the human body frequently managed to recover from the most dangerous of all wounds, open skull-brain injuries.

Still alive

While decapitation probably is the only way of stopping an opponent dead in his tracks, even cuts with the broadsword were no guarantee for instant success. General Mackay's nephew was still able to ride away from the battle (and presumably fight) with eight broadsword wounds in his body.

[117] Quoted from Pollington, Stephen. ***The English Warrior from earliest times to 1066***, Hockwold-cum-Wilton: Anglo-Saxon Books, 1996; p. 187.

[118] Pollington; p. 188.

And the German *Waltharilied* sings of Walther, who after the loss of his sword hand shifts his shield to the right, draws his second sword and continues the fight with his left hand, to knock out Hagen's eye and six teeth before the opponents amicably put their differences aside.[119]

On the other hand, putting an opponent *hors-de-combat* did not always require that one opponent was killed or dismembered. Applegate echoes Silver's remarks about the interaction of knees, pommels, elbows, "coddes" and the opponent's morale when he writes:

> *"The psychological and shock effect of a thrust or slash to the stomach-groin area is very effective and usually will cause the recipient to lose his mental balance and control, even if it is not immediately fatal."*[120]

Sutor takes this on step further in his advice on the *langes Schwert*. He recommends that the fighter caught in a corps-a-corps drop his blade, grasp the opponent's knees, headbutting him in the gonads while tripping him by pulling him toward him.[121]

Conclusion

The concept of a combat system's a-priori "lethality" appears to have limited value to determine how efficiently and how fast an opponent can be neutralized.

Neither thrust nor cut—while certainly dangerous and potentially life-threatening to the fighters—can claim a monopoly on being the most effective means to neutralize the opponent. In fact, it appears as if the belief in the superiority of one particular technique contained the danger of overconfidence, which might prove more lethal to a fighter than enemy steel.

[119]A nice summary is provided in Nickel, Helmut. —"About the Sword of the Huns and the 'Urepos' of the Steppes," in *Metropolitan Museum Journal*, vol. 7, 1973; p. 131.

[120]Applegate; ibid.

[121]Sutor; p. 18. See also p. 234

INTERLUDE

COMPETITIVE COMBAT
Playing the Prize

Dussack fencers (1594)

A Fechtschule in Late 16th-Century Germany[122]

I t is evident from old fencing manuscripts that a precise distinction was made in those days between the exercise of arms on the fencing floor and the contests which were held publicly, the so-called Fechtschulen.[123]

Fencers from the era of guilds did not like to be observed during training, and did not appear in public until they had attained full mastery.

We could adduce many further proofs that public competitive fencing bouts were called "Fechtschulen" and that this is not a case of misunderstanding by us as inheritors of the tradition, but we will content ourselves with an additional passage from Rösener in which fencing students are taught among other things to behave modestly on the "teaching ground," not to "recklessly" destroy "any weapon,"

> *"And should not mock anyone else at all,*
> *In exercise, it is forbidden.*
> *And you should not beat anyone bloody*
> *who is just beginning to fence."*

From this it can be seen that fencers were to show restraint in the training school and use their weapons with caution, so that serious wounds would not occur. In the Fechtschulen, however, such wounds were often required to obtain a prize.

[122]Schmied-Kowarzik, Josef and Kufahl, Hans. ***Fechtbüchlein***, Leipzig: Reclam, 1894; pp. 137f. (Translation by Dr. Ann Martin.)

[123]*Fechtschule* literally means "fencing school". The term is used both for training establishment and for a very characteristic public fair that combined display of skill and fighting for prize money, as well as providing opportunity for guild fencers to accumulate experience necessary to compete for the prescribed number of bouts necessary for reaching the coveted degree of Provost or Master.

For the sake of simplicity, a rule had been introduced for the larger public fencing displays that a prize would be granted to the one who had inflicted a bleeding wound on the head of his opponent.[124] On the one hand extensive rules of combat could be avoided, on the other hand, agreements between the fencers would be circumvented. The wound was decisive and could not be hidden; this avoided troublesome amounts of writing, of which people were not very fond at that time.

How simple this requirement was in comparison with the regulations for prize fencing today! How frequently hits are denied today, how attentive the judges must be not to miss any movement, and how complex prize and exhibition fencing is at the present, with its many paragraphs and points and evaluative marks.

As mentioned above, it is possible that competitions on foot took place very early; the first descriptions are found in the 16th century.

While the two fencing societies of the *Marxbrüder* and the *Federfechter* were teaching accomplished fencers in every German city using trained masters, virtuosi of the art of fencing were traveling from city to city holding exhibition fights in which the best fencers could show their skills. All presentations in the area of fighting ability were followed with the greatest attention, and the whole populace took a lively interest in the flowering of the art of defence.

It can be seen from a manuscript of the Germanic National Museum in Nuremberg, "Fechtschul Rhymes," that in 1579, for example, a Fechtschule was held every Sunday from 26 April to 4 October; so there must have been not only a sufficient number of fencers, but also quite a large circle of onlookers to cover the cost with the entrance fees.[125]

Even if special fencing houses[126] were being built in other cities, these public exhibition fights are most often read of in the case of Nuremberg, the city in which the masters of the sword were first given certain documented rights by Friedrich III, including permission to "hold schools."

Generally these Fechtschulen were held in inn-yards, in the Egidierhof, in the Heilsbrunnerhof, and in the Golden Star, until the Fencing House was built in 1628.

We will now use what we ourselves have found written about such Fechtschulen in other places to describe such an exhibition combat and cite some of it from the original texts, to give the reader a faithful picture of the events at a Fechtschule

A fencing-master who wanted to give a "fencing school" first had to demonstrate his qualification as master of the sword with the municipal council of the city in question and apply to be granted the use of an open space for the purpose.

If permission was granted and the day and hour set, then he could proclaim his intentions at the city's Rathaus by posting a notice.

On this notice the letter of privilege of the *Marxbrüder* was generally printed—if the fencing-master belonged to that society—and the Free Fencers of the *Feder*[127] were invited to appear in force to measure themselves against the *Marxbrüder*.

Although the Federfechter obtained their first letter of privilege from Rudolph II in 1607, this society had been acknowledged as of equal standing long ago, and their masters of the sword could also obtain permission from the city authorities, even though the *Marxbrüderschaft* did everything in its power to make their fencing schools impossible, because they encroached upon their privileges.

Under the notice of the master of the sword whose school we are going to describe was written:

[124] This, of course, corresponds to the "broken head" of Victorian singlestick, and to the *"Anschiss"* rule of the German Mensur prior to the Imperial era, when an inch-long or inch-deep bleeding wound sufficed to terminate even serious encounters.

[125] Given the system of financial transactions surrounding the more aristocratic tournament, it would surprise me if entry fees indeed were the only source of revenues for those putting on the Fechtschule.

[126] Authors' Note: *"One of the largest of these houses was the Fechtschule in Breslau, which was torn down about 20 years ago,"* i.e., in the 1870s.

[127] *Feder* in German means "feather" or "quill". Grimm et al. postulated that *"Feder"* also was a slang term for rapier, an assumption that cannot be supported with a shred of evidence. Karl Wassmannsdorff derived the term "Federfechter" from Veiterfechter, or fencers of St. Vitus. This could be adduced by two or three examples. Schmied-Kowarzik and Kufahl, however, point out that the coat of arms of the Federfechter featured a quill, thus rendering etymological calisthenics redundant.

"Whoever wants to see this art
should come up to the Golden Star,
About two hours before noon,
and he will find as much room as he wants."

A fair Sunday morning has dawned. Everyone is getting ready to go to church, to which the bells are solemnly summoning them. The streets are animated, young and old in festive garments make haste to do their duty and then to have something to eat. The best is saved for last, the real, genuine Sunday treat: the Fechtschule. The whole city has been looking forward to it for a week, since everybody knows someone in it, some a brother or a son, some a husband or a friend. And so after mass, all the streets and squares are full; the young lads can hardly wait for the moment when the procession goes by.

It is spring, the sap has risen in the trees, blossoming branches hang down into the streets. And as the gnarled branches feel that it is time to stretch, to expand and to grow, so too the young people are driven outdoors by a feeling of strength; they want to measure themselves against one another in combat. The birds sing their spring greeting from the branches into the blue air, the girls walk up and down in threes in front of the houses, giggling and waiting for their friends and neighbors. Everyone, everyone is lingering in the streets, for soon the players are to come by as the head of the procession of fencers which the onlookers will join. But anyone who wants to have a good place has to go on ahead.

Finally, the familiar melody of the city cornet players rings out from the Rathaus tower, and immediately drumbeats and piping are heard. There they are already! The boys greet them with yells of delight. First, the constable of the council, and the groundsmen with leather *Dussacken*, then the players and a troop of fencers, then a young boy with the parade sword, then a grey-bearded servant with a red velvet bag, heavy and well-filled, which a patron of the one holding the fencing school, a count living nearby, has sent so that prizes of two gulden can be given to the victors for inflicting a wound.

Behind him, the fencing-master paces proudly, the image of strength and agility. Then, another procession of fencers and finally the servants who are carrying the fencing weapons. All find themselves in the midst of a swarm of boys who run ahead of the procession and then allow it to pass by them again—now imitating the powerful steps of the greybeard, now mocking their acquaintances who are passing by so solemnly, teasing one, pulling another by the doublet, singing mocking verses about those who hesitate, overflowing with youthful high spirits.

The groundsmen had already had to intervene a few times because the procession was being held up by the boys, i.e. they had taken their leather *Dussacken* in their hands and made as if to strike out with them—but where were the boys now? Far ahead!

A festive mood everywhere, lifted by the colorful garments of the holiday and the clear blue sky, and in no way clouded by the fact that three surgeons with the tools of their trade have joined the procession and hope to earn good money today.

Meanwhile the procession has reached the appointed place. A large courtyard strewn with sand, surrounded on three sides by spacious buildings and closed off on the fourth by a board fence, behind which the boys' heads can be seen; they have already taken possession of their ancestral free seats. They peer over curiously;

115

sometimes one of the tow-headed lads vanishes—he had to give way to a stronger who now occupies the empty space.

The city council, a few exalted personages and "all womanhood" sit on chairs and benches which have been set up in the broad curves of the pathways, while the populace, who paid little or nothing, takes up a position behind stretched-out ropes.

The city constables stand alongside. A drum roll resounds, the servants carry the weapons into the space and spread them out on the ground according to the master's directions, and he takes up an ornately decorated staff, the sign of his standing.

He swings the staff around his head and walks all around the space, passing by the council members; he bows deeply, then when he reaches the middle he stretches out his sinewy form, leaps back and forth, threatens with the staff and shows the agility of his body.

The players play a piece while he catches his breath. When it is over, he strikes the staff against the ground three times, the drummer plays—then silence falls. And now the master opens the Fechtschule with a loud, penetrating voice:

"Through the power and might of the Imperial Majesty of our all-gracious lord, whose privileges and freedom have been graciously grant-ed and ceded to me, Peter Hauer, Master of the Long Sword, with the permission of the high council of this city, to set up a free public Fechtschule, with all knightly weapons present here in this place: So then, let all good fellows who are here present and have learned the knightly art of fence and are experienced in it, and who intend to bring joy and entertainment with due submission to the high-born gentlemen, the honorable company of knights and all the ladies with their skill, come forward unhindered to fight for the established prize, to keep the fitting passages of arms according to the honorable ancient custom of fencing. And I am minded and determined to keep myself unprejudiced towards all such good fellows, as befits an honor-loving master of the longsword, and to guard and protect them against and in opposition to arrogance and impropriety.

"Yet all men should know what is to be forbidden in this fencing school, such as Ort, button, point, *Einlauff* [128], breaking of an arm, violent push, reaching for the eyes, stone-throwing and all dishonorable devices which many no doubt know how to use, but I cannot mention them all, and have never learned them; and let no one strike either above or below the staves. [129] Guard and protection is to be extended to each, as well as to all the rest, and likewise I wish to request that if two of you bear hatred and envy towards one another you will not fight it out in this school, but where it has power and might.

"And if one or more good fellows are present (excluding the noble order of knights, which I have no intention of dishonoring) who might desire that the combat be for money or something worth money (regard-less of the fact that I have not much money), or for a good blow, dry or wet [130], that they should come forward in good heart and spirits following the custom of the justice of the sword, and set to freely, do not spare their swords, but their own fingers, and strike between the ears where the hair is thickest, and strike me too, seeing that I am also a good man."

[128] Authors' Note: "*Ort* =sword point; *Einlauff, i.e. the oppo-nent's penetrating one's defenses while pushing the weapon aside, after which there was wrestling, which often turned to "dishonor-able tricks," such as reaching for the eyes or breaking an arm.*"

[129] Authors' Note: "*The fencing master stretched out his staff between the fencers if they attacked one another violently, which interrupted the combat immediately.*" The staff as the symbol of the umpire is trace-able in ancient Greece, and survived in the umpire's épée well into the 20th century.

[130] i.e., bloody.

This long opening was supported by drumbeats during the important sections. Thereafter, at the repeated urging of the fencing master, young apprentices and also men of more advanced years come onto the field, put aside their cloaks, hats and weapons, and some also the outer doublet, and pick up some fencing weapon[131] from the ground as they await an opponent.

But none of them wants to start; it is not hesitation or lack of courage—only that no one wants to be first.

Around the holder of the *Fechtschule*, who is a master of the longsword of the brotherhood of St. Mark, twenty *Marxbrüder* have gathered from the town and its surroundings, who wish to "offer their points" to the free fencers of the Feder; but since twenty-six *Federfechter* are present, so that they would have an advantage over the twenty *Marxbrüder*, after a short conference three *Federfechter* go over to the *Marxbrüder* to make the numbers equal.

Since no one has yet come forward, they "freshen" themselves for the combat with taunting rhymes, either sung or spoken. These taunting rhymes, as far as their content is concerned, understandably move within narrow confines; with almost identical expressions one's own brotherhood is exalted to the skies and the opposing company is damned, or general remarks on swordsmanship, courage and other topics are repeated in bad verses.

After this, a beginning had to be made; the honor of the two fencing societies required it, and two stepped forward with longswords, just in front of the place where the council members were sitting: the *Federfechter* a young man with curly blond hair, tall and slender, and the *Marxbruder*, an older, powerful fellow with dark hair and a stocky figure, the former nimble and swift, the latter reflective, but not slow.

Sutor (1612)

Scarcely had the *Marxbruder* taken up his stance in the rechter *Ochs* when the *Federfechter* struck a blow from the rechter *Zorn*, which the former countered with a Zwirch. But the *Federfechter* follows up swiftly from the *Tag*, while the sturdy *Marxbruder* drives up at the fists of his opponent with the heart of his blade, thereby weakening the stroke, pushing the man back and adding a long stroke which the blond fencer eludes by a powerful leap backwards.

There is clamorous applause after this bout, which is fought with great rapidity. Encouraged by this, the *Federfechter* presses his counterpart with the "defensive stroke." The other takes up the stroke on the long blade and simultaneously strikes with the short blade with a *Zutritt*, so that the point hits the head and the first bloody cut can be "confirmed" by the fencing master, who immediately stretches out his staff between the two. The blond man, for whom the first *rote plume* has

[131]This means they could pick and choose from among the long sword, *Dussack*, sword, dagger, halberd, long staff—all weapons used in the Fechtschulen.

117

blossomed, leaves the *Fechtschule* area through a small side door, accompanied by a boy, and enters a spacious room where the surgeons have already made all necessary preparations to meet the challenges which will confront their skill.

(There were no antiseptics in those days. People were satisfied with cleaning the wound, bringing the edges together as well as possible and bandaging up the victim, and the healing proceeded *per primam.*)

While the *Federfechter* meditated on his misfortune in the surgeons' room and regretted his over-hasty ardor, the *Marxbruder* outside had received shouts of acclamation, the ladies had thrown a small wreath down to him, and the greybeard with the red silk bag had approached him solemnly and handed him the first four silver gulden, which he tucked away in his belt after a brief expression of thanks as money well-earned.

After the first pair, who fought alone, several pairs stepped forward simultaneously, this time with different weapons.

Two with long staves excited general attention by the skill with which they handled these long weapons, sometimes laying them on the left shoulder, sometimes letting them sink to the ground, striking swift blows, skillfully directing those which bore powerfully down on them to the forte and deflecting them.

Finally, one of them was careless and suffered a bump and a small bleeding cut just over the right eye, which earned his opponent two gulden; he followed the path which the first loser had taken.

The fights with *Dussacken* were lively, long-lasting and the most numerous, largely because there was no immediate danger of death. For the opposite reason, sword fights were rarer.

The fencing master and some *Vorfechter* [132], also equipped with staves, had their hands full separating heated fencers, who immediately stopped fighting when the staff was stretched between them.

Even if it sometimes may have happened that the fencing master held out his staff to favor someone when it was not strictly necessary to protect him, but only to prevent the other from seizing the advantage, yet the proceedings seem always to have been conducted with great exactness and justice.

The surgeons' room was full by now. Fencers wounded by the sword had their heads bandaged and were sitting on a bench against the long wall, while the *Dussack* fencers "had great rising stripes on their faces and heads, so that at times they looked unrecognizable," covered their lumps with damp cloths and thronged together in a cor-

Sutor (1612)

ner. Two of the latter were already prepared to reenter the lists, and were just discussing how they planned to be victorious this time. "Was sehrt, das lehrt," [133] as the proverb so rightly says.

A continual change in fencers kept the onlookers in a state of perpetual tension. There was particular applause for two *Dussack* fencers who made twelve passes without either of them being beaten, which of course did not cause the red bag to open in sympathy. But it had to pay out the promised prize without any battle to a giant, as tall as a tree, who stood there with his halberd and found no opponents. [134]

Suddenly there was a commotion. A furrier's apprentice had offended against a prohibition by recklessly thrusting the pommel of his sword into his opponent's face.

The fencing master took the sword from his hand and by throwing it down at his feet forbade him from taking up any weapon at all. The one who was publicly branded in this way crept away and was "soundly thrashed" in the gateway by some *Federfechter* and their relatives who had followed him [note: word for word according to the fencing-school rhymes of 1579], which of course was used by the furrier's friends as an excuse to join in. The fist fight might have drawn even more people in if the groundsmen had not completely cleared the space with their leather *Dussacken* in a few seconds.

They struck out without mercy wherever they could find a mark, and people naturally withdrew from these blows, which were painful but not dangerous, inflicting only disgrace and mockery, with suitable rapidity. Finally, after the graybeard's bag has been emptied, the fencing master steps forward, in order to execute some bouts with one or two who might wish to do so, as he had already mentioned at the opening of the school.

He takes up a sword and gives his staff to one of the champions. A counterpart steps forward and faces the master, who initially tempts him forward by weak counterstrokes and hesitant attack and would certainly have done him some harm if the champion had not "brought down" the staff and ended the fight. A second and third opponent fare no better in *Dussack* fighting, and only the fourth gained the advantage over him in the rapier, because he was already overly tired.

The fencing arena has been cleared, the guests are departing, and the wounded, who have waited for the end, also creep towards their homes by side streets. But the victors and those who are not too badly wounded gather around a table set up in the courtyard to recover from the exertions of the day and to refresh their thirsty throats.

"The one who is lucky will sing in the evening," so says one of the Fechtschul rhymes, and indeed cheerful song rings out, given a higher blessing by the innkeeper's message that the exalted patron has donated a keg of beer.

[134]Authors' Note: "*The prize was appointed for a weapon; if one of the fighters took up a weapon from the ground and no opponent presented himself, he received the set amount.*"

4. THE ENCOUNTER

The Tree of Battles
(French, 15th century)

According to the preceding considerations, I have enhanced existing classifications of combat scenarios involving edged weapons by adding a few new categories: First and foremost is the concept of objective and subjective risk, as well as the concept of projected intent. (Projected intent is the subjective individual interpretation or assumption of what the antagonist's intentions are, which correlate closely with the perceived risk he poses.)

The two main distinctions in combative edged-weapons systems are antagonistic and agonistic scenarios. In antagonistic scenarios, the opponent is considered hostile, posing a real or imagined threat to life, bodily integrity, or status. In agonistic scenario, the level of hostility is low. The opponent is either a competitor (sports fencing) or even a collaborator (theatric fencing).

I.   Antagonistic combat

All antagonistic fight scenarios are carried by highly divergent intents or motivations:
    1.) to achieve absolute dominion over the opponent
    2.) self-preservation

Both intents can coexist simultaneously, a) with or b) without implicit adherence to a set of rules that is characteristic of Comment combat scenarios. Intent can be conscious and unconscious.

All antagonistic combat scenarios share one single objective: To end the combative situation as quickly as possible by neutralizing the opponent.

Neutralization of the opponent can be achieved by

1.) killing him
2.) precluding further continuation of combat due to
   a) physiological incapacitation
   b) conditional/regulatory incapacitation (first blood, doctor's decision)
3.) disarmament
4.) forcing the opponent' capitulation or flight by
   a) exerting psychological pressure (resulting, for example, in dodging or *"Kniesen"* during a Mensur)
   b) cumulative non-incapacitating injuries
   c) a combination of mutually perpetuating psychological stress and physical injury (duel Nadi vs. Contronei)

Antagonistic scenarios can be segmented into the following groups:

A: Combat for absolute dominion and/or survival

"In the midst of extreme violence, there is only action. Remember, we aren't talking about a sport here, where you can have the luxury of a referee, strategy from the corner, and rules to protect you."

Greg Jones,
Predator Training

"If your bayonet breaks, strike with the stock; if the stock gives way, hit with your fists; if your fists are hurt, bite with your teeth."

M.I. Dragomiroff,
Notes for Soldiers, c. 1890

The fight for dominion or survival is entered either as an aggressor or defender, implying voluntary, or direct or indirect (coerced) consent. Combative activity can take place between one (or several) attackers and one or several defenders, or among attackers and counter-attackers (mêlée). It can occur either spontaneously (rencontre and ambush) or with premeditation (ordeal).

A perfect—if fictitious—example of antagonistic combat is given by Tobias Smollet in his picaresque novel *Roderick Random*. Apart from a remnant of habitual *Comment* courtesy, this fight has it all: The seeking and taking of unfair advantages, the use of different, unmatched weapons, as well as the utter lack of regulation or target restrictions:

"As soon as I set foot on terra firma, my indignation, which had boiled so long within me, broke out against Crampley, whom I immediately challenged to single combat, presenting my pistols, that he might take his choice:

He took one without hesitation, and before I could cock the other fired in my face throwing the pistol after the shot. I felt myself stunned, and imagining the bullet had entered my brain, discharged mine as quick as possible, that I might not die unrevenged; then flying upon my antagonist, knocked out several of his foreteeth with the butt-end of the piece; and would certainly have made an end of him with that instrument, had he not disengaged himself, and seized his cutlass, which he had given to his servant when he received the pistol.

Seeing him armed in this manner, I drew my hanger, and having flung my pistol at his head, closed with him in a transport of fury, and thrust my weapon into his mouth, which it enlarged at one side to his ear.

Whether the smart of this wound disconcerted him, or the unevenness of the ground made him reel, I know not, but he staggered some paces back: I followed close, and with one stroke cut the tendons of the back of his hand, upon which his cutlass dropt, and he remained defenceless. I know not with what cruelty my rage might have inspired me, if I had not at that instant, been felled to the ground by a blow on the back part of my head, which deprived me of all sensation. "[135]

Scenarios:

Battlefield combat (mêlée), combat of champions, rencontre.

Motivation/Intent:

a) achieving domination by neutralizing the opponent or as many opponents as possible as fast as possible;

b) self-preservation by neutralizing the opponent or as many opponents as possible as fast as possible.

Projected Intent:

Opponent is perceived as lethal threat to one's own life; the assumed intent usually coincide with a full or even exaggerated personal identification with the highest possible risk level.

Conscious awareness
of risk and level of consequence:

Full or latent awareness of death or serious injury.

Fear Level:

High.

Stress Level:

High.

Objective risk:

Death or serious injury.

Combative systems:

Coincidental, mainly dominated by spontaneous, primary response, dictated by coincidental offensive or defensive weaponry, environment, state of mind; can be preconditioned to a degree by drill and experience. [136]

[135]Smollett, Tobias. *The Adventures of Roderick Random*, (1748), Oxford & New York: Oxford University Press, (1979) 1981; p. 210.

[136]In specific cases, coincidentially similar weapons may imply the use of a similar combative system, thus presenting the possibility of *comment*-like combat. For example, a spontaneous life-and-death rencontre between gentlemen armed with and trained in the use of smallswords would probably resemble a smallsword duel or even training match in all but the fighter's perception of risk and fear level.

Taboos:

None, encounters are uncontrolled and unsupervised, often unwitnessed; each fighter attempts to achieve any advantage over the opponent, including control of time and space (ambush), physical characteristics (size), or weapon-immanent advantages (cavalry riding down infantry.)

Weapons: [137]

a) & b) mismatched or coincidentally matched

Level of skill:

Coincidental, large variants.

B: *Comment* combat

Comment combat (from the Germanized French word *"Comment"*, meaning "set of rules") implies voluntary or indirectly coerced consent. Combative activity usually takes place between two individuals or detailed groups of individual. It occurs with premeditation, with equality of risk and foreknowledge of the consequences. [138] *Comment* scenarios contain the possibility that the physical outcome of the fight could be assumed to have been achieved by the intentional absence of one of the combatants.

German thrust Mensur with Degen ("Pariser"), c. 1850.

Scenarios:

a) Legal institution: Ordeal
b) Social institution: Duel
c) Prize fight with sharp weapons
d) Ritualistic combat: Mensur

Motivation/Intent:

To kill, control, or disable the opponent while adhering to a clearly defined, enforced or implied code of behavior.

[137] We define a weapon here as a) offensive, actively defensive: edged tool specifically designed to effect death, injury, damage, or control in combative situations; b) passive defense: garments or device worn or carried to limit potential damage or injury inflicted by opponent's offensive weaponry.

[138] Kegan; p. 145.

Projected Intent:
Opponent is perceived as threat to one's life or bodily integrity.
Conscious awareness of risk and level of consequence:
Full or latent awareness of death or serious injury.
Fear Level:
High.
Stress Level:
High.
Objective risk:
Death or injury.
Combative systems:
Equally matched, dictated by offensive and defensive weaponry, environment, state of mind; preconditioned by drill and experience. Strong ritualistic element. Specific combative systems are specializations of practice systems.
Taboos:
Enforced or implied notion of "fair play", i.e., adherence to set of rules; selected target areas are protected by defensive weaponry.
Weapons:
a) & b) intentionally matched.
Level of skill:
Intentionally similar.

II. Agonistic combat

Competitive combat implies voluntary consent. Combative activity usually takes place between two individuals or detailed groups of individuals. It occurs with premeditation.

The critical difference between agonistic and antagonistic is the attitude toward the opponent, who is perceived as partner (in Olympian scenarios) or non-hostile or even friendly competitor.

A: Competitive combat

Scenarios:
a) "Olympic": sport/recreational combat: sports fencing, competitive kendo, SCA pageants & "wars". Olympic scenarios focus almost exclusively on competitive "winning" or assertion of superior skill level.

SPORTFECHTEN
E.von Ciriacy-Wantrup
GRETHLEIN & Cº·LEIPZIG-ZÜRICH

b) "Olympian": conditioning combat: practice for *Comment*, dominion, or competitive combat (kendo, "Pauken", singlestick, medieval & Renaissance tournament), period or retro-sport.[139] Olympian scenarios, named after the immortal denizens of snowcapped Olympus, are the sand-box games of the active fencers. They take place on a low level of competitiveness, and with near complete absence of consequence. There's usually nothing at stake, and nothing to be gained except for the individual's reaffirmation of being good at something.

c) Playing the prize.

Motivation/Intent:

To competitively assert superiority of skill ("winning") and achieve control by scoring a predetermined number of clearly defined objectives while adhering to a clearly defined, enforced, or implied code of behavior. Potential of "winning" by default or by external manipulation. [140]

Projected Intent:

Opponent is perceived as competitor for control

Conscious awareness of risk and level of consequence:

Remote possibility of injury, complete absence of hostile intent; no disadvantageous physical consequences are tied to the termination of the encounter. (Exception: the "broken head" in public singlestick competitions or the German Fechtschulen.)

Fear Level:

Low.

Stress Level:

Low to medium.

Objective risk:

Remote, controlled possibility of injury.

Combative systems:

Equally matched, dictated by convention and environment (which is standardized and replicable by clearly defined spatial dimensions); preconditioned by drill and experience.

Taboos:

Enforced notion of "fair play", i.e., adherence to set of rules; selected target areas are protected by defensive weaponry.

Weapons:

a) and b) intentionally matched and standardized, specifically designed to eliminate risk of injury; consensual disarmament, e.g. by restriction of defensive & offensive repertoire ("covering target" in fencing).

Level of skill:

Intentionally similar.

[139]Period or retro-sports inlude recent efforts to revive and reconstruct historic fighting systems.

[140]Former World Foil Champion Allan Jay wrote: *"As a 'steam foil' international, I well remember that a French or Italian foilist had only to shout 'hé la' and a hit was scored against his opponent. Not only this, but with four judges, it was virtually inevitable that at least one judge was of the same nationality as one of the competitors in the pool. In this event, it often occurred that the decision of one or more judges was dictated by the interests of his fencing compatriot."* In his Preface to Crosnier, **Fencing with the Electric Foil**, p. 11.

B. Theatric combat

Scenarios:

    a) stage combat (unbroken sequence)

    b) film combat (broken sequences)

    c) re-enactment fencing

Motivation/Intent:

    To create a premeditated, replicable, choreographed effect for the spectator.

Projected Intent:

    Opponent is perceived as non-competitive collaborator, not as opponent.

Conscious awareness of risk and level of consequence:

    Remote possibility of injury, complete absence of hostile intent;
    no disadvantageous physical consequences are tied to the termination
    of the encounter.

Fear Level:

    Zero.

Stress Level:

    Low.

Objective risk:

    Remote, controlled possibility of injury.

Combative systems:

    Selective elements applied in sequence or out of sequence to create effect
    in a controlled and specifically designed environment that has been
    arranged and choreographed to achieve the desired effect.

Taboos:

    In absence of hostile or competitive intent, risk is minimized. Safety of
    the opponent is a paramount concern.

Weapons:

    Intentionally matched or mismatched, specifically designed to eliminate
    risk of injury while creating desired effect.

Level of skill:

    Intentionally similar.

While these categories still require further expansion and fine-tuning, they already allow a much closer comparative evaluation between edged weapons combative systems. This may be less entertaining than musings about who'd come out on top in a match of Nadi vs. Musashi, or cutlass vs. foil. But I believe they allow for a more accurate classification of systems.

INTERLUDE:

ANTAGONISTIC COMBAT:
Comment combat

Mensur with dish-hilt rapiers.

A Dish-Hilt Rapier Mensur at Jena, c. 1840

From his long-cut velvet coat
He produced the rapier[141] blades
Which in solid leather sheaths
Had been kept with prudent care.
5   Yet the other took in secret
from his brightly colored waistcoat
Forth the circular, flat guard
And they screwed into the dish-hilts
Carefully the pointed blades
10   Which like horsewhips made of steel
Whistled through the air with glee.
The freshmen[142] now had done their duties,
Others came to help to bandage:
Carefully placed on the armpit
15   And upper arm the axillaris,
Strapped around the loins the apron,
And gingerly wound 'round the neck
A light and soft and silken kerchief.
Then the seconds stepped forth,
20   Turned to face each other squarely,
Thrust the rapiers out toward each
Other, level with the point in line,
Measured thus the length of blade,
From the tip down to the hilt,
25   Then they stepp'd out with the left foot

[141] The original German calls it "Degen"—the generic term for thrust and cut-and-thrust weapons.

[142] First-semester members of fraternities.

as far backward as they could.
Took good notice of the place,
Marked the spot with sharpened blade
Then they measured out the circle,
30   That narrow space for duellists,
Which these even during vaulting
Could not traverse by one hair's width.
For combat now the scene was ready,
And futile seemed the seconds' labor
35   To put the quarrel by in peace.
Into the circle the assistants
Now were leading the two fighters,
Placing rapiers in their hands,
And quickly then both seconds jumped
40   Aside to mark the duel's start.
Then each of them stepp'd to the left
of the hostile party's fighter,
Holding up the walking stick
To lunge with speed and certainty
45   Warding off thrusts after "Halt!"
"Bind blades!" sounds the other's order.
And the fighters, stretching forward,
Cross the blades in readiness.
Commands then ring out: "Ready! Go!"
50   Resounding widely 'cross the field.
Quick as lightning there the quarte thrust
Whips forth above the en'my's arm,
Heinz, who's very well aware of
His opponent's dark intent
55   To flaunt deceptive lack of cover,
To then finish off his man
With the counter tempo thrust,
Who then would defend in vain.
Yet the other parries nimbly
60   With an outward-disengage,
Quickly then in half-quarte into
Heinz's well-considered offense,
Thrusting also with a quarte
Across the arm; — Yet counter-timing
65   Heinz opposes with a tierce, and
Then, in hanging second guard,
And with the timing of his foot,
The foe's attack slides off the blade,
'Cause with half a thrust he found him
70   Still in middle-distance range.
But the seconds both did jump in
With the canes to ward off swiftly
The worst of all thrusts — time thrust.
"Halt!" each second shouts out loudly,

75   And their sticks knock up the blades.
      Now both fighters took a break,
      But not for long they stayed at rest.
      "Bind blades!" the command resounded
      And again the blades were crossed.
80   "Go!" and Ruge, whose turn it now was to thrust first,
      Threw a half high quarte at Heinz.
      Skillfully and proud Heinz parried
      With a circular cavation;
      And to himself he was saying:
85   "The Devil take your quartes, my friend,
      Now I'll try you with the feint."
      Accordingly, he feints in quarte
      Over the opponent's right arm,
      And then, with all his force, he thrusts
90   Full-fleeting inside quarte against him.
      But with a solid quarte parade,
      The foe grasps for the outside feint
      From a hanging seconde guard,
      Tying now opponent's fleeting
      quart thrust to his own.
95   From his hand, straight like a candle,
      Flies into the air — up ten feet! —
      Heinz's rapier, staying airborne;
      Like an arrow whistling down then,
      and remaining — dish hilt bobbing —
100   Firmly lodged in the ground.
      During rapier's flight the crowd had
      Jumped safely out of harm's way.
      And Heinz now stood disarmed.

The dish-hilt rapier

At the eve of the French Revolution, the dish-hilt rapier (German: *Tellerrapier*) had been obsolete in almost all of Europe for about a hundred years. Only in Germany was this weapon able to survive until at least 1845.

Its main users were fraternity students, who wielded the weapon in comment combat, particularly at the universities of Leipzig and Jena. These schools had a particularly high rate of divinity students who couldn't risk facial scars in view of their careers, but rather preferred a perforated lung.

The target was mainly the sword arm of the opponent, even though dangerous, sometimes fatal chest wounds (called *Lungenfuchser*) were commonplace. Anecdotal reports point out that a single thrust would frequently cause four bleeding wounds, in cases when the blade penetrated and perforated both the lower and upper arm of the fencer. The swaggering Jena Burschenschaft students in particular were famous for wearing their sleeves rolled up over their elbows in public to show off the multitude of tiny puncture scars they had received in battle.

Dish-hilt rapier duels were usually conducted according to the first blood rule, for one round. Only a round in which someone received a bleeding wound counted. Other than the forerunners of the *Schläger* and saber, the dish-hilt rapier was never carried in public, but assembled on the duelling grounds. It was later on superseded by the French-style epée de combat and, for less serious quarrels, by the bell-guard *Schläger*.[143]

Song of the sword

The above passage is a rare and anonymous description of a rapier duel in Jena, Germany, that appears to have taken place in the first half of the 19th century.[144]

The author uses the terms *Degen* and *Schläger* (literally "beater" from German: *schlagen*, to beat) for the weapon, which echoes etymological speculations of Egerton Castle that the word *"rapier"* may actually derive from a supposedly dialectal German word *rappen* which according to Castle also means "to beat."[145]

The weapon, however, is unrelated to the modern basket-hilt Schläger and ought to be properly called a dish-hilt rapier.

The duel takes place between two Jena students, Heinz and Ruge. The anonymous author must have been a personal friend of Heinz', since he is using his Christian name, which would have been unusual among strangers. The opponent, Ruge, is only mentioned once by his family name. The duel seems to have come about as the result of an insult. Ruge appears to have been the insulted party and, thus, the challenger, since Heinz as the challenged is allowed the first thrust. The seconds are obliged by the code of honor to try to patch up things between the opponents. Usually, however, a peaceful solution did not come about at this stage, and we have to take the amount of "trouble" the seconds went to straighten things out with a grain of salt.

Each second is armed with a *"Ziegenhainer,"* stout canes or walking sticks. The distance between the fighters is one blade's length, measured from point to hilt. The seconds also determine the size of the battleground by stepping backward with their left foot, marking the point with their blades on the ground and using the demarcation to determine a circle that would restrict the fencers' range of action (*Kreismensur*).

The fencers, by punishment of disgraceful termination of the duel, are prohibited to step over the line. Other than during the Schläger or saber Mensur, the seconds take position next to the opponent, not to the left of their own fencers.

The duel proper in this case consists of two rounds. The first thrust of each round is regulated. Every action taken leaves the impression of great forethought and careful plotting of the Gang or round.

The duel is terminated after Heinz is disarmed. This reflects duelling regulations according to which the duel is terminated after a bleeding wound has been received ("first blood") or one opponent is disarmed as a consequence of a deliberate action of the opponent.

Disarmaments were a mainstay of the Kreußler school fencing, which dominated German thrust fencing from the early 1700s to the early 1900s.

[143]For a detailed description of bouts with the dish-hilt rapier, refer to Schmied-Kowarzik, Josef & Kufahl, Hans *Duellbuch*, p. 234 ff.

[144]Ibid, p. 247 f.

[145]In my opinion a very sophomoric derivation....

PART THREE

ADVENTURES IN LOST COMBAT ARTS:

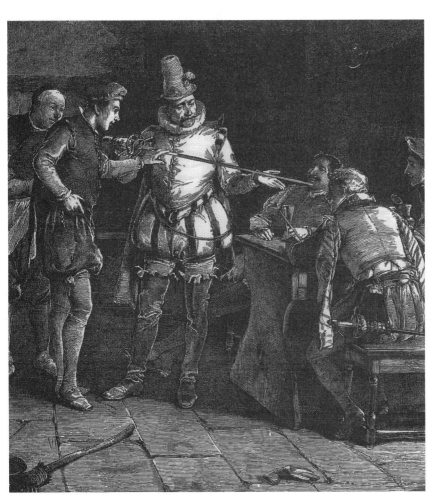

Bobadil's Toledo

On the multi-culti reading lists of modern academia, students are more likely to encounter the plight of bisexual rural Nicaraguan coffee roasters than the dramatic and literary heritage of the Shakespearean era. Too bad, because they are cheated out of this pensive dead-white-male bonding scene from Ben Johnson's ***Every Man in his Humour***:

"Bobadil: ... It is the most fortunate weapon that ever rid on poor gentleman's thigh...

Stephen: I marle [wonder] whether it be a Toledo or no.

Bobadil: A most perfect Toledo, I assure you, sir."

Johnson, who lived at Blackfriars in 1598, 11 years after Rocco Bonnetti had died in "Thospital", is said to have modelled Bobadil on the shifty, unfortunate Italian who set heaven and earth into motion not to square off against the Masters of Defence. This is a Victorian engraving of the scene.

ADVENTURES IN
LOST COMBAT ARTS 1

RECONSTRUCTING ANCIENT MARTIAL ARTS

Two-handed sword practice
after Egenolph (1558).

Fencing historians like to date the beginning of an organized Art of Fencing in the Renaissance.

There is a good reason for it:

"Since all contemporary schools of fencing in the western world are derived from Italian and French sources, focus in [Maestro Gaugler's The History of Fencing] is on treatises published in those countries. Rapier play in the other two early schools, the German and the Spanish, in fact, closely resembles the Italian model."[1]

Also, early sources are at best scattered manuscripts, or bits and pieces and fragments of arcane references only grad students in their 15th semester of preparing their dissertations might ever have heard of—rather than proper books printed in any decently sized print runs.

There are other obstacles. Masters like Liechtenauer actually made a point of keeping their instructions as cryptic and unintelligible to outsiders as possible. Accordingly, fencers imprinted by the modern versions of the art and without the urge to research the early schools of the sword, gladly embrace the assumption that before the Spanish and Italian fencing masters popularized the rapier and thrust fencing, there must have been a void of skill and technique, the obvious lack being made up by brute strength.

[1] Gaugler, William. *The History of Fencing: Foundations of Modern European Swordplay,* Bangor, ME: Laureate Press, 1998; p. xv.

But much like the martial artists of the Orient, Europe's warriors and knights, even its burghers and peasants practiced systems of self-defence that combined small and long arms with very effective elements of wrestling, throwing, boxing and kicking.

Circumstantial evidence

Tracing or reconstructing extinct martial arts requires more than a fair share of speculation. It seems that at least some early fighting systems traceable in recorded history preserved elements of religious or at least shamanic exclusivity that prohibited outsiders from learning and passing on jealously guarded secrets. In non-literate societies, this means that an art would cease to exist (and be lost to the antiquarian) when the native masters were unable or unwilling to pass on their knowledge.

There are several indications that the fighting arts and metalworking professions in medieval Europe were at least as advanced as those in, say, Japan or China. Not only are there interesting parallels in two-handed sword techniques with the Bidenhander and the Japanese katana. [2] But the sword smiths of both regions had developed alloys and metalworking techniques to produce blades that according to legend could cut steel.

Wieland's sword Mimung was an example of a compound nitrate, phosphate and iron sword. [3] It reportedly cut iron like butter. Japanese swords were known for being able to cut even through musket barrels:

"A Japanese sword blade is about the sharpest thing there is. It is designed to cut through tempered steel, and it can. Tolerably thick nails don't even make an interesting challenge. In the 1560s one of the Jesuit fathers visited a particularly militant Buddhist temple—the Monastery of the Original Vow, at Ishiyama. He had expected to find the monks all wearing swords, but he had not expected to find the swords quite so formidable. They could cut through armor, he reported, 'as easily as a sharp knife cuts a tender rump'. Another early observer, the Dutchman Arnold Montanus, wrote that 'Their Faulchions or Scimeters [sic] are so well wrought, and excellently temper'd, that they will cut our European blades asunder, like Flags or Rushes...' (...) Montanus's story can be checked and has been. The distinguished twentieth-century arms collector George Cameron Stone once took part in a test in which a twentieth-century Japanese sword was used to cut a modern European sword in two. And there exists in Japan right now a film showing a machine-gun barrel being sliced in half by a sword from the forge of the great 15th-century maker, Kanemoto II. If this seems improbable, one must remember that smiths like Kanemoto hammered and folded and rehammered, day after day, until a sword blade contained something like 4 million layers of finely forged steel. Or rather, until the edge of the blade did. The rest was of much softer steel. (...) This technique of varying the hardness was one that European smiths never perfected, which is why European swords were never as sharp." [4]

[2] Galas, S. Matthew. — "Kindred Spirits: The Art of the Sword in Germany and Japan," in *Journal of Asian Martial Arts*, vol. 6, # 3, (1997); p. 20f..

[3] See Daeves, Dr. ?. "Die Untersuchung altdeutscher Eisenteile," in *Rundschau deutscher Technik*, vol. 20, no. 26, June 27, 1940, as quoted in Ritter-Schaumburg, Heinz. *Dietrich von Bern—König zu Bonn*, München and Berlin: F.A. Herbig, 1982; p. 20. To create the sword Mimung, Wieland forged a sword, filed it down into metal shavings, mixed them with flour, and fed them to geese he had starved for three days. He then collected the birds' excrement, welded the undigested metal together, and made another sword.

He repeated the process three times, finally forging a sword that "cut iron like clothes." Tests conducted by German metallurgists before and during WWII proved not only that the welding of carbon-enriched steel filings improved the cutting ability and compound stability of the weapon, but that the nitrates contained in the bird dung also caused a considerable increase in hardness—which made Mimung a weapon that reportedly was superior even to modern spring steel products.

[4] Perrin, Noel. *Giving Up the Gun: Japan's Reversion to the Sword, 1543-1879*, Boulder, CO: Shambala, 1980; p. 11f.

Perrin's account is, to steal a phrase from Fr. Klaeber, so enthusiastic *"that one might wish it could be forthwith assented to."* But that poses some problems: For one, he takes George Cameron Stone by his word—whose book is so riddled with mistakes it is only good as a quarry for pictures. And he is part of a neo-Western academic tradition that is frequently over-zealous to dismiss European history and culture(s)[5], so that even a second-hand report of a piece of celluloid can credibly double as evidence!

Now, only a fool would argue that Japanese swords are not horrific weapons—in some cases breathtaking pieces of the sword maker's art that combine metallurgical perfection with pure artistry. (Even though my references only wanted to commit themselves to a "few thousand" layers of hammered steel per rod... not four million.)

But they're not made for splitting armor—at least not Western-style plate armor. The curvature of their edges makes them ideal for draw cuts through soft materials. Yet sharpness is not an indicator of armor-splitting capability—otherwise you could buy six-packs of can opener replacement blades at your supermarket check-out counter.

There is also ample evidence—literary and iconographic—that Western steel was quite capable of cracking steel helmets, even cut through other blades or gun barrels (see page 106)—even though this would certainly not be the target of choice for a swordsman.

Hank Reinhardt, who has probably broken, bent, notched, and warped more sword blades than any single man in the 20th century, has convincingly argued that this myth—perpetuated in World War II with machine-gun barrels—is pious nonsense:

"I have been assured, frequently in fact, that Japanese blades are so strong and tough that they never break, nick or bend. Well, they break, they nick, and they bend. They frequently nick quite badly. Damascus steel is a superior steel, or it can be when done by a superb smith. But even a superior steel is still steel and will respond like steel. One sad fact is that the harder the steel, the more likely it is to chip and nick. A softer metal will bend, flatten or otherwise distort. When this happens, it is relatively easy to pound or file a new cutting edge. When a chip leaves a gap, not much can be done. A piece can be reforged into the blade, but this also requires that the blade be retempered."[6]

And to fully sink Perrin, European sword smiths were crafting Damascus sword blades from steel rods of varying hardness since the Dark Ages. Only recently did metallurgists of the German steel giant Thyssen attempt to create an authentic replica of an Ottonian sword using the damascening techniques of Frankish sword smiths.[7] And Italian metallurgists analyzed the blade structure of a 12th-century battle sword, discovering that it, too, was intricately constructed from layers of steel of varying hardness expertly crafted to reach the objectives of hardness, flexibility, and sharpness.[8]

[5]Indeed, some modern academics are even unaware that there's more than one European culture....

[6] Special reprint of Reinhardt, Hank. —"Hype—As Ancient an Art as Swordmaking," in *Knives '87*, n.p.: DBI Books, 1987.

[7]see Pothmann, Alfred (ed.). *Das Zeremonialschwert in der Essener Domschatzkammer,* Münster (Germany): Aschendorff, 1995.

[8]Panseri, C. *Ricerche metallografiche sopra una spada da guerra del ii secolo,* Milano: Assoziazione Italiana di Metallurgia, 1954.

The layering of steel in
a 12th-century sword.

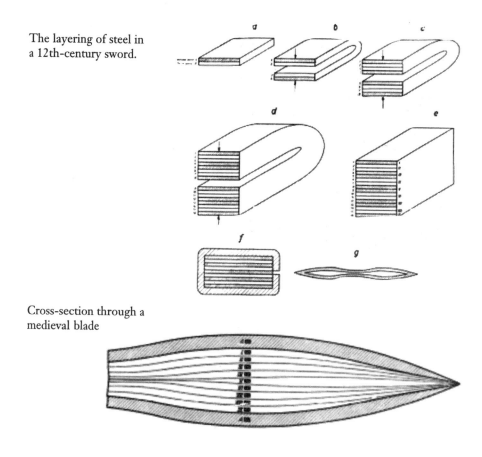

Cross-section through a
medieval blade

Martial cultures

The fencing manuals of the Germans Talhoffer (1443), Dürer (yes, Albrecht Dürer compiled a fighting manual, around 1512), Paschen (1658), and the Dutchman Nicolaes Petter (1674), illustrate joint locks, throws, kicks, and other techniques that we have come to expect from the Asian arts.

Modern remnants of organized martial arts can be found in France, in the systems of *bâton* and *canne* (in Britain thriving as quarterstaff and singlestick into the present century), or in the predecessors of savate, which only died out in the middle of this century, having been superseded in popularity first by French boxing, and today, by the Asian martial arts.

Even relatives of the notorious *nunchaks*, developed from flails, can be traced in Europe, where their use as a weapon was taught at least up to 1610, when Sutor represents them as *Pflegel*.[9]

In William Hogarth's *Chairing the Member* (1754) we still find the flail used as a weapon in a truly negative election campaign. It is impossible to say if the young partisan wielding it is breaking the head of his opponent according to art, however, or just uses the implement as a layman's shortcut to blunt impact trauma.

(An anecdotal reference from the late 19th century even suggests the practice was alive and kicking in southern Europe as little as a hundred years ago:

[9]Dr. Karl Wassmannsdorff ridicules the idea that the flail was taught systematically. (See Wassmannsdorff, Karl. *Aufschlüsse über Fechthandschriften und gedruckte Fechtbücher des 16. und 17. Jahrhunderts,* Berlin: R. Gaertners Verlagsbuchhandlung, 1888.) However, European armories still hold many documented war flails. There are also many iconographic sources depicting pairs of flail fighters in the context of the widely practiced arms—for example on a frieze under the eaves of the city council building at Breslau (now Poland), or in a recently discovered mural at Schloss Ambras near Innsbruck (Austria).

"In Italy, there used to be the tradition—in cases when the stiletto insufficient for revenge — to brawl with a curious percussive tool. A thick, 60-90cm long staff carried three, 30cm long sticks, which were weighed down with lead and iron rings, fixed like on a flail, which served for attack and defence as it was kept in swinging motion. These flagelli appear to have been specially effective against several attackers, or when one tried to elude the guards."[10]

Hogarth (1754)

Runic riddle

One of the earliest enigmatic clues to shamanic martial arts originated in Iceland. The *Edda*, one of the few literary monuments of Germanic paganism, features two verses that have been interpreted as being indicative of a close link between warrior arts and native cults:[11]

"A third [rune] I know, if great is my need / Of fetters to hold my foe. / Blunt do I make mine enemy's blade, / Nor bites his sword or staff. (...) A fifth I know, if I see from afar / An arrow fly 'gainst the folk, / It flies not so swift that I stop it not / If ever my eyes behold it."[12]

The catching of a flying arrow from mid-air is a feat that is well-documented in Oriental martial arts. And the upper tiers of the Icelandic heroes frequently catch spears from mid-air and redirect them against the enemy who threw it. The techniques of evading a blade or staff rather than parrying with the blade are reminiscent of Aikido. Some of these evasive maneuvers (such as vaulting and even throwing) were still integral parts of 18th-century smallsword techniques.

This knowledge is transmitted by a "rune" a magic symbol obtained by Wotan/Odin himself at the cost of his one eye (by the way, a typical fencing master injury). Only an initiate into magic lore would be able to pass on this knowledge... a master... a shaman... a priest. In Scandinavia and other parts of Northern Europe, weapons are frequently marked with runes. Spear points are named "Charger", "Target rider", "Asir Arrow"[13]... the symbold carved by rune masters, keepers of Odin's magic lore.

(It might not be coincidence that the Parker and Laud Chronicles mention that in 605 (viz. 607) when *Æthelfrith led his levies to Chester and there slew a countless number of the Welsh; (...) two-hundred priests were also slain there who had come thither to pray for the Welsh host."[14]* A slew of 200 shamans praying (or directing the fight?)—and then slaughtered wholesale—maybe to prevent further uprisings?)

[10]Schmied-Kowarzik and Kufahl; *Duellbuch*, p. 201.

[11]See also Pennick, Nigel. *Practical Magic in the Northern Tradition*, Guildford, England: The Aquarian Press, 1989; pp. 123f. Most practical conclusions presented in this New-Age paganism book are speculative and should be taken with a grain of salt.

[12]*The Poetic Edda: Hávamál*, verses 149 and 151.

[13]Pieper, Peter (Pit). — "Runen," in *Symbole und Zeichen*, Bremerhaven (Germany): Landkreis Cuxhaven, 1991; p.88.

[14]see Garmonsway, G.N. (ed.) *The Anglo-Saxon Chronicle*, London: J.M. Dent & Sons (Everyman's Library), (1953) 1990; p. 22/23.

For all occasions

Like many Oriental arts, early European manuals still include a wide array of weapons and empty-hand techniques in their fighting repertoire.

In Germany, Talhoffer's codices are all about raw antagonistic combat. Apart from knowing how to handle a variety of staff and bladed weapons, a fighter had to know throws, chokes, lock joints, and holds. Hitting is not the primary concern of Talhoffer's lovingly drawn fighters... blocking, securing the threatening weapon by locking the arm, and then immediately dealing an incapacitating cut or thrust (the latter often guided by both hands) is what it is all about.

In Italy, Fiore di Liberi's *Fior Battaglia* [15], one of the first printed volumes on the art of defence, is a compendium that combines wrestling, unarmed fight against the dagger, sword fighting of armored and unarmored men, pike against pike, pike against war club, armed men fighting with war hammers, lance and sword fighting of mounted men, wrestling on horseback, lance from horseback against foot soldier, pedestrian fight dagger vs. sword. [16]

The Austrian historian Karl Lochner comments snidely that Fiore *"verliert sich endlich in Phantasiekämpfen"*—gets lost in fantasy fights. What Lochner carelessly writes off to the imagination of an overzealous writer, however, represents reality-based possibilities of armed and unarmed encounters a man had to be prepared for. By presenting defense techniques performed with tools and implements of daily life, the Master indirectly commented on the quality and integrity of his system:

If an opponent wielding superior weapons could be neutralized by a fighter trained to use whatever makeshift weapons were at hand, the martial arts system by definition had to be superior to other techniques applied in matched encounters. The "tricks" depicted in these early sources (and criticized today by modern historians as indicative of lacking scientific sophistication) are really indicators for the existence of a systematic approach to teaching and practicing martial arts!

Homer's papyrus trail

Systematic European fighting arts seem to be as old as fighting itself. References to martial arts abound in Greek and Roman literature: Contemporary sources on the Greek *pancration*, for example, document elements of wrestling, boxing and kicking that are surprisingly similar to the modern "Ultimate Fighting" and bareknuckle contests currently fueling the ire of politicians and do-gooders in search of a cause.

Suetonius mentions that Tiberius was able to pierce an apple with his index finger, a technique referred to as spear-finger in some modern Asian systems. The gladiatorial games and schools, where fighters were systematically trained in highly specialized fighting systems, have never been analyzed in regard to technical detail—although one of our Adventures will introduce us to one of their techniques.

Of course, lack of clear-cut evidence invites speculation about the extent and character of these arts. But a closer examination of the techniques alluded to in the sources provides clues not only to the fighting prowess of the heroes, but also to some of the techniques they employed.

[15]Fiore di Liberi. *Il Fior Battaglia, Duellatorum in armis, sine armis, equester, pedester*, Milano, 1410; facsimile by Francesco Norvati, 1902.

[16]See also Galas, S. Matthew. —"The Flower of Battle, An Introduction to Fiore dei Liberi's Sword Techniques," in *Hammerterz Forum*, vol. 2, #3 (Winter 1995/96); p. 18f.

The following is an example taken from the most widely read piece of literature in antiquity, Homer's *Odyssey*, whose descriptions of fights could date the existence of systematic martial arts as far back as the Greek bronze age.

Here's the story: Odysseus, disguised as a beggar, has finally arrived at his court in Ithaka. The suitors force him to square off against Iros, a bronze-age welfare king:

"So now Odysseus made his shirt a belt / and roped his rags around his loins, baring / his hurdler's thighs and boxer's breadth of shoulder, / the dense rib-sheath and upper arms. Athena / stood nearby to give him bulk and power. (...) / Poor Iros felt a new fit of shaking take his knees. / But the yard-boys pushed him out. Now both contenders / put their hands up. Royal Odysseus / pondered if he should hit him with all he had / and drop the man dead on the spot, or only / spar, with force enough to knock him down. / Better that way, he thought—a gentle blow, / else he might give himself away. / The two were at close quarters now, and Iros lunged / hitting the shoulder. Then Odysseus hooked him / under the ear and shattered his jaw bone / so bright red blood came bubbling from his mouth, / as down he pitched into the dust, bleating, / kicking against the dust, his teeth stove in." [17]

What reads like an archetypical brawl between hero and buffoon actually opens up a world of speculation about ancient martial arts: Both men take on a similar stance, hands raised. It is odd that Homer, a keen observer, should say "hands" rather than "fists."

A modern parallel can be found in the native French martial art of *savate*, which today is synonymous but not identical with modern French boxing, and originally combined open-hand and kicking techniques. [18] Odysseus, his rib cage tight and dense—is he exhaling like a martial artist before the assault, or simply crouching to make his ribs overlap for maximum protection, like a 19th-century saber fighter?—ponders whether to kill the opponent with a single punch or merely knock him out. He decides in favor of the latter, fearing to reveal his hidden identity.

But what exactly would have given him away?

Would a killer punch have identified the beggar as more than just another experienced beerhall brawler? Maybe as the initiate of an exclusive aristocratic fighting art? As a man with the Zen and *ch'i* (and implied breathing technique!) to later on not only draw a bow no other man could handle but then shoot an arrow not through one axe but through a dozen?

Iros attacks. Odysseus doesn't even bother to evade or block—but immediately hooks the opponent under the ear, shattering the lower jaw. Just how did he do that?

A straight, open-handed hit combining rotation and whiplash energy from shoulder, elbow and wrist can pack a painful knock-out punch—a well-known practice not only in Asian but also European fighting arts.

But Odysseus has not only mastered breathing, concentration and punching techniques. He also appears to have a solid knowledge of pressure points His deliberately chosen target coincides with Tegner's nerve center #25:

[17] Homer. **The Odyssey**, Book xviii, ll. 80-120, [translated by Robert Fitzgerald,] New York: Random House Vintage Classics, (1960) 1990; p. 337f.

[18] See also —"Last of the Great Savate Men," in Gilbey, John F.. **Secret Fighting Arts of the World**, Rutland, VT & Tokyo: Charles E. Tuttle Co., (1963) 1989; p. 116f.

"In this area there is a concentration of nerves. The target is behind and up under the jawbone. (...) A jabbing or punching blow results in considerable pain. The extended knuckle or fingertips can be used."[19]

The *Iliad* and *Odyssey* are chock full with vivid fighting descriptions. In fact, *"Homer has a very clear idea of what he is describing. He and his audience understood fighting, and liked to hear about it."*[20]

Dance, monkey boy, dance!

Other Classical sources allude to the "Pyrrhic Dance," which was practiced by some of Xenophon's men prior to battle.

There were regional differences in the choreography of these dances, as becomes obvious in the following passage:

"After they had made libations and sung the paean, two Thracians rose up and began a dance in full armour to the music of a flute, leaping high and lightly and using their machairas; finally, one struck the other, as everybody thought, and the second man fell, in a rather skillful way. (...) After this a Mysian came in carrying a light shield in each hand, and at one moment in his dance he would go through a pantomime as though two men were arrayed against him, again he would use his shields as though against one antagonist, and again he would whirl and throw somersaults while holding the shields in his hands, so that the spectacle was a fine one. (...)

And the Paphlagonians, as they looked on, thought it most strange that all the dances were under arms. Thereupon the Mysian, seeing how astounded they were, persuaded one of the Arcadians who had a dancing girl to let him bring her in, after dressing her up in the finest way he could and giving her a light shield. And she danced the Pyrrhic Dance with grace.

Then there was great applause, and the Paphlagonians asked whether women also fought by their side. And the Greeks replied that these women were precisely the ones who put the King to flight from his camp."[21]

Exhibitions of martial skills in war dances undoubtedly were not a reflection of a generally high level of martial arts training. In Xenophon, they were part of a carefully orchestrated pep rally aimed at boosting the morale of the home team, impressing those who needed to be impressed, as well as providing distraction, entertainment and ritualistic reaffirmation to the fighting men. (In this regard, they did no more or less than a Van Damme or Steven Segal movie.)

In the above example, the Greeks even use them as a means of gunboat diplomacy—by implying that even their dancing girls were so skilled in the martial arts that they were able to mop the battleground with the enemy king and his generals.

The Pyrrhic's ritualistic element remains evident in the civilian practice of the dance later in the Roman Empire. Claudian's poem of the sixth consulate of Honorius gives a picture that is about as enigmatic as it is tantalizing:

[19]Tegner; p. 44.

[20]Willcock, M.M. *The Iliad of Homer*, London: Macmillan Education Ltd., 1978; p.xiii.

[21]Xenophon. *Anabasis* (transl. by Brownson, Carleton L.), Cambridge, MA and London: Harvard UP [Loeb Classical Library], (1922) 1992; vi.1.11-15, p. 440f.

"Here, too, the warlike dancers bless our sight,
their artful wand'ring, and their laws of flight,
and unconfus'd return, and inoffensive fight.
Soon as the Master's Clack proclaims the prize,
their moving breasts in tuneful changes rise;
their shields salute their sides, or straight are shown
in air high waving; deep the targets groan
struck with alternate swords, which thence rebound,
and end the concert and the sacred sound."

It is impossible to trace a potential continuity of the Pyrrhic Dance into modern times, since it is nearly impossible to reconstruct the actual system itself. Also, the term could have been applied to a variety of systems.

We know that the sword was held in great veneration among the Germanic tribes, and that there were ritualized dances involving both sword and spears:

"However, accounts of similar exercises by Irish warriors with spears
and swords were a form of training for agility." [22]

But it is worthwhile mentioning that the 1737 edition of the *Antiquities of Rome* contains the following observation:

"Julius Scaliger tells us of himself, that while a youth, he had often danc'd the
Pyrrhic before the Emperor Maximilian [23], *to the amazement of all Germany:*
And that the Emperor was once so surpriz'd at his warlike activity, as to cry
out, "This boy either was born in a coat of mail, instead of a skin, or else
has been rock'd in one instead of a cradle.[Poet. lib. 1, chap. 18.]" [24]

Rome's pugilistic pastimes

Among the Romans, another martial arts system survived far into the days of the Empire. Virgil's *Aeneid*, for example, illustrates a fight with the caestus that is as brutal and skillful as any modern bloodsport:

"Then having spoken thus he cast in the midst two
gauntlets of vast weight with which brave Eryx had
been accustomed to bear his hand in battle and to
stretch his arm in the hard skin.
Their minds were amazed; seven great skins of huge
oxen were stiffened with inserted lead and iron. Dares
himself stands dazed before it all, and utterly refuses
to fight, and the high-minded son of Anchises turns
over and over the weight and the immense folds of the
gauntlets. There the aged man uttered these words
from his breast:

[22]Scott, B.G. *Early Irish Ironworking*, Belfast, 1990; p. 193; as quoted in Pleiner, Radomir. *The Celtic Sword*, Oxford and New York: Oxford UP [Clarendon Press], 1993; p. 35 (note 35).

[23]Maximilian died in 1519.

[24]In Kennet, Basil. *Romae Antiquae Notitia: or, the Antiquities of Rome. In two parts,* London: 1737 (10th ed); p. 264f.

'What if anyone had seen the gauntlets and armor of Hercules himself and the sad contest on this very shore? Your brother Eryx formerly bore these arms. You see them even now stained with blood and scattered brains. With these he stood against the great Hercules; I have been accustomed to these, when my better blood gave me strength, nor yet had envious age had sprinkled the grey on both my temples. But if Trojan Dares refuses these our arms, and it is determined by the pious Aeneas, if Acestes our adviser, then let us equal the fight. I yield to you the skins of Eryx; banish fear; and you put on the Trojan gauntlets.'

Speaking those words he threw back from his shoulders the double coat and stripped the great joints of his limbs, his great bones and arms, and great he strode forth in the midst of the sand. Then the father descended from Anchisa raised the equal gauntlets and bound the hands of both with equal arms.

Forthwith each stood erect on his toes, and undismayed raised his arm high into the air. Backward they drew their towering heads, far from the blow, and they mingled hands with hands, and tried to provoke the contest: the one better in the motion of his feet, and relying on his youth; the other powerful in limbs and size, but his weak knees fail him trembling, a sickly shaking shakes his vast joints. The men hurl many wounds among themselves, in vain: they redouble many hits on their hollow sides, and cause great sounds to emanate from their breasts, and the frequent hand wanders around their ears and temples: their jaws crash under the severe blows.

Entellus stands heavy, and unmoved in the same posture; only with his body and watchful eyes he avoids the weapons. Dares as one who besieges a lofty city with engines, or sits under arms around a mountain fort, now with art wanders over these, now those approaches, and all the place; and baffled presses on with various assaults. Entellus, rising, shows his right hand, and on high he raises it. Dares quickly foresees the blow approaching from above and, with his active body escaping, withdraws.

Entellus spends his strength on the wind; and himself heavy and forthwith falls heavily to the ground with vast weight; as sometimes a hollow pine torn up by the roots falls either on great Erymanthus or great Ida. The young men from Troy and Sicily arise with anxiety; a shout goes forth to heaven; and Alcestes runs up first, and pitying his friend of equal age, lifts him from the ground.

But the hero, not slowed down and not frightened by the fall, returns more active to the contest, and rage arouses his power; then shame inflames his strength and conscious courage (conscia virtus), and burning he drives Dares headlong through the whole plain. Now redoubling his blows on the right, now on the left.

There is no delay or rest. As grains of hail rattle on the rooftops, the hero, with dense-falling blows, strikes often and turns Dares with each hand. Then father Aeneas did not suffer his anger to proceed further, and Entellus to rage with bitter anger; but he put an end to the battle, and snatched wearied Dares, soothing him with words, and speaking these things:

'Unhappy man, what great madness hath possessed your mind? Do you not perceive other powers, and that the gods are changed? Yield to the god. And he spoke and ended the battle with his voice.

But his faithful companions lead Dares to the ships, dragging his feeble knees and throwing his head on each side, vomiting clotted blood from his mouth, and teeth were mingled in blood. And called in they receive the helmet and sword, they leave the palm and the bull to Entellus. Here the conqueror, elated in mind, and proud of the bull he said:

'O man born of a Goddess (Aeneas) and you Trojans, know these things, and what strength has been to me in my youthful body and from what death you have saved Dares recalled.'

Saying this, he stood opposite the front of the bullock, which stood as prize of the contest. And high with his right hand drawn back, he poised the hard gauntlets between the horns and dashed them into the bones, the brains being broken."[25]

Fighters weaving, feinting, evading—but strong enough to knock in the skull of an ox: What does Mike Tyson have that Entellus didn't—apart from shoulder-length gauntlets weighed down with lead and studded with spikes?!

The fight with the caestus appears to have remained confined to comment scenarios—and practiced by professional athletes whose personality cult was about as developed as that of modern athletic entertainers. But Poliakoff adduces Plutarch, who *"insisted 'that all these activities [boxing, wrestling, footrace] are imitations and exercises of war' and explained that the custom of breaking a section of the city wall for the triumphal entry of an Olympic victor is a sign that walls are of no great importance to a city that has men capable of fighting and winning.' He drew the same connections between combat sport and hand-to-hand fighting that Lucian and Philostratos did, adding that the Spartans lost the battle of Leuktra to the Thebans because the Thebans were better practiced at the palaestra."*[26]

Statements like this one by Plutarch may be overly nostalgic: Greek decadence was blamed on the palaestra as often as athletic achievements were credited with excellence of the battle field:

"Regardless of the value of combat sport in the training of soldiers, popular opinion saw in it the demonstration of courage, tenacity, and resourcefulness in a potentially hazardous situation, and many citizens viewed it as beneficial to the security of the city. (...) Sport provided a useful and enjoyable kind of indirect training for warfare. But the most serious military societies, Sparta and Rome, trained for war more directly and reduced the role of sport or condemned it. They recognized that it was an inefficient, haphazard training, and the seemingly undisciplined combat events were particularly suspect."[27]

The absence of ancient European martial arts from the collective memory of the 20th century can be attributed to several factors. First and foremost, their mostly oral mode of transmission (and the secrecy in which some systems were practiced and taught) made sure all traces were lost once the last masters had died. And that even those masters or systems that left literary sources were at the mercy of academic philistines unable to interpret references outside of the context of their disciplines.

[25] P. Virgilius Maro. *Aeneid*, Book v, in Hart, Levi and Osborn, V.R. *The Works of P. Virgilius Maro*, Philadelphia, David MacKay Co. [Classic Interlinear Translations], 1882; pp. 136f.

[26] Poliakoff, Michael B. **Combat Sports in the Ancient World: Competition, Violence, and Culture,** New Haven, CT: Yale UP, 1987; p. 97.

[27] ibid.

INTERLUDE

COMMENT COMBAT
Ordeal/Wager of Battle

Before the Ordeal
After Paulus Kal (c.1400)

Much Ado About Nothing:
The Legal Pageantry of the Ordeal[28]

Comment scenarios rely heavily on a codified framework that regulates the behavior of the men involved. In some cases, the framework can take over to a degree that the individuals initially involved in an altercation completely fade into the background.

The wager of battle was a rare legal avenue to solve property disputes even in Tudor England. Yet its roots go far into the dawn of time. In fact, it might have been part of an ancient Indo-European legal tradition that survived—and still may be surviving—in remote parts of the world. There is at least anecdotal evidence that this time-honored was alive and kicking only a few decades ago, in Manipur, India, in Cachar District:

> *"Land disputes were usually not taken to court because of the long delay in settlement and the immense cost of litigation. The traditional method of settling such land disputes was to hire a champion who would sit on the disputed land from dawn to dusk. If the opposing party sent their own champion, there would be a duel and the part whose champion won the duel would own the disputed land."*[29]

[28]After Stow, John. *The Summarye of the Chronicles of Englande (...) abridged* (London, 1573) in Berry, Herbert. *The Noble Science: A Study and Transcription of Sloane Ms. 2530, Papers of the Masters of Defence of London, Temp. Henry VIII to 1590*, Newark, DE: U of Delaware Press, 1991; p. 9f. The fact that an account of this incident also appears in Lord Chief Justice Dyer's *Cy ensount ascuns nouel cases* (London, 1585) might point at the rarity of wagers of battle even in the late 1500s.

[29]Kenoyer, Jonathan Mark. "Thangkairol; Manipuri Sword Fighting of Eastern India," in Kiyota, Minoru and Lee, Jordan (edd.). *Personal Growth through Martial Arts: Studies in Kendo, Fencing, and Indian Swordsmanship*, Madison, WI: Center for South Asia Publications, 1997; p. 61.

The following account from 1571 London puts to rest two commonly held assumptions: Conventional wisdom today holds that the Masters of Defence were barred from acting as champions in wagers of battle. But Naylor, who also appears in Sloane 2530 as "Nayler", and who is the flamboyant protagonist of the wager, is an accredited Master—and as such mentioned several times in the membership rolls between 1568-87. And judging from the degree of showmanship he exhibits, he apparently is no novice at this game.

The other assumption is that a wager of battle only could end when one fighter—even if he was a stand-in or hired champion—was killed or, if he was only disabled, would be punished by having his sword hand chopped off before being executed. Both champions here leave the lists in one piece, even though the case is decided by the absence of one of the litigating parties.

"The 18th day of June and the fourth of Trinity term of 1571, there was a combat appointed to have been fought for a certain manor and domain lands belonging thereunto, in the Isle of Harte adjoining to the Isle of Sheppey in Kent. Simon Lowe and John Kyme were plaintiffs and had brought a lawsuit against Thomas Paramore, who offered to defend his right by combat, whereupon the aforesaid plaintiffs accepted to answer his challenge, offering likewise to defend their right to the same manor and lands, and to prove by combat that Paramore had no right nor good title to the same manor and lands.

Hereupon the said Thomas Paramore brought before the judges of the Common Pleas Court at Westminster one George Thorne, a big, broad, strong-set fellow. The plaintiffs brought Henry Naylor, Master of Defence, and servant to the right honourable Earl of Leicester, a proper, slender man, and not as tall as the other. Thorne cast down a gauntlet, which Naylor took up.

Upon the Sunday before the morning the ordeal was to take place, the matter was stayed and the parties agreed that Paramore, being in possession, should have the property, and was bound 500 pounds to consider the plaintiffs, which sum, upon hearing the matter, the judges were to award. The Queen's Majesty was the taker-up of the matter, in the following manner. It was thought good that for Paramore's assurance, the order should be kept touching the combat, and that the plaintiffs, Lowe and Kyme, should make default of appearance, but that yet such as were the surties for Naylor, their champion's appearance should bring him in and likewise those that were surties for Thorne, should bring in the same Thorne in discharge of their bond, and that the court should sit in Tuttell Fields.

There, a plot of ground was prepared, 21 yards square in size, double-railed for the combat, outside of which, on the West side, a stage was to be set up for the judges, representing the Court of Common Pleas. Scaffolds, one above the other, were constructed all around the lists for the people to stand and watch. Behind the side where the judges sat, there were two tents, one for Naylor, the other one for Thorne.

Thorne was there early in the morning. Naylor arrived at about seven o'clock via London, wearing a doublet and a pair of galligaskin breeches, all of crimson satin, cut and rased. His stockings were of knit crimson silk, and he wore a hat of black velvet with a red band and a red feather. Before him went four drummers, playing all the way. The gauntlet cast by George Thorne was carried before Naylor upon a sword's point. His baton, a staff an ell in length, tapering toward horn tips, and his shield of hard leather were carried behind him, by Askam, a yeoman of the Queen's guard.

He went into the palace at Westminster, and staying not long in front of the hall door, came back into King's Street, and so along through the sanctuary and Totehill Street into the field, where he stayed past nine o'clock. Then Sir Jerome Bowes brought him to his tent. Thorne had retired to his tent with Sir Henry Chenye long before.

About ten o'clock, the Court of Common Pleas removed and came to the place prepared. The Lord Chief Justice with two of his associates was seated. Then Lowe was called solemnly to come in or else to lose his suit. After a certain time, the surties of Henry Naylor were called to bring in the said Naylor, champion for Simon Lowe, and shortly after, Sir Jerome Bowes, leading Naylor by the hand, entered the lists with him, bringing him down that side by which he entered, being on the left side of the judges until he came to the side right next to the judges. There he made his curtesy, first with one leg, then with the other. Whereupon he passed on until he came into the middle of the place. Here he made the like obeisance, and then passing on until he came to the bar, he made another curtesy and his shield was held up aloft over his head.

Naylor took off his stockings and, bare-footed and bare-legged to the ankles,[30] except for his silk trousers, the sleeves of his doublet tied up above the elbow, and bare headed came in as afore said.

Then the surties[31] of George Thorne were called in to bring in the same, and immediately Sir Henry Chenye, entering at the upper end on the right-hand side of the judges and used the like procedure in coming down his side as Naylor had before on the other side. So coming to the bar with like obeisance, he held up his shield. Proclamation was made that no one else should touch the bars nor presume to come within the same, except those appointed.

This solemn procedure being finished, the Lord Chief Justice recounted the manner Simon Lowe had filed his suit and the reply Paramore made, and how Paramore had challenged to defend his right to the land by combat by his champion George Thorne, and of the acceptance of the trial at arms by Lowe with his champion Henry Naylor.

Then, because of Lowe's default to appear, he ruled the property to Paramore and dismissed the champions, acquitting the surties of the bonds. He also willed Henry Naylor to render the gauntlet again to George Thorne. Naylor answered that his Lordship might command him anything, but willingly he would not render the said gauntlet to Thorne except he could win it. Further, he challenged the said Thorne to play with him half a score of blows, to show some pastime to the Lord Chief Justice and the other there assembled. But Thorne answered he came to fight and would not play. Then the Lord Chief Justice, commending Naylor for his valiant courage, commanded them both quietly to depart the field."

[30]In 13th- to 15th-century Central European manuals depicting wagers of combat, the fighters enter the lists apparently sewn into tight-fitting *cuir-bouilli* armor. They, too, however, go into battle barefooted and bare-handed (i.e., without gauntlets or gloves.)

[31]warrantors

ADVENTURES IN
LOST COMBAT ARTS 2

THE DIALECTICS OF DEATH

Roman vs. barbarian.
Italian cameo (1685)

I f you are a fencer, you will agree that few things in life are as intellectually gratifying as a successful point-in-line: A feint attack with second intention, a pause, a retreat that prompts the opponent to counter too enthusiastically, overlooking the subtle straightening that lines up shoulder, elbow, wrist, and point. A tempting opening protected by a sneaky point whose neutralization requires the cleansing battut: then the upward twang that twists straight steel into a graceful arc as the opponent lumbers into the trap.

In modern athletic competition, the point in-line is rewarded by a red or green light and a vulgar buzzing that in a remotely Pavlovian way indicates a point in your favor. In mortal combat, it means a puncture wound that can kill immediately or by lingering sepsis—a week, a month later.

Socrates was a master of the point-in-line and the second- and third-intention attack. Not, of course, with the foil or saber, kopis or phasganon, but with arguments, questions. He needled his opponents, had them rush into his well-placed traps again and again—until the festering wounds caused by his pin-pricks had them writhing in tortured anger.

And then they turned to swat the gadfly. Refused to engage in play with him. Made him drain the hemlock like a good little boy. Proved once and for all that art can kill, once the artist actually starts to believe that the outside world can be manipulated by the abstract principles and machinations he believes to have mastered.

Or so it may seem.

Divine windbag

Yet his very death was Socrates' final point-in-line. Playing the same kamikaze game as a migrant Aramaic rabbi was to engage in four hundred years later, he lured his enemies into a trap that he had baited with his own worthless life. And, bumbling like a junior sabreur fully convinced that athletic prowess will carry off the laurel, they ran into, impaled themselves in his point. Flaunting his life as the terminal opening, the fatal chink in his armor, Socrates achieved the ultimate revenge, condemned his enemies to eternal disgrace and humiliation while catapulting his own parasitic existence onto snowcapped Olympus.

You could look at fencing as combat not only of iron, but of wills, of intellects. It is a game of short-term tactics and long-term strategies, of controlling and directing the opponent's actions, of snaring and entrapping—much like chess or the art of debate.

The connection between ferrous and verbal combat reaches far into the past and back again into the present. Norwegian sagas describe drinking banquets of chieftains and their retainers whose martial exploits would be followed by battles of wit and cleverly barbed insult—a tradition called *"knattern"* (rattling) kept up today by some duelling fraternities in Germany, particularly at Göttingen and Heidelberg. And Icelandic padrones such as Njal used their retainers' fighting prowess on par with their knowledge of the law and Byzantine diplomacy to keep the thirn Norn from prematurely clipping their household's thread of light...

In the 17th and 18th centuries, courtiers practising the art of fencing engaged in "conversations with blades," where a bold argument was enveloped, disengaged and redirected against the opponent in a resounding riposte in a game defined by conventions determining the boundaries of the acceptable.

The same boundaries that create the space in which art and fundamentally friendly competition thrive can also put their practicians into mortal danger. This is exactly why back in 1599, the English martial artist George Silver advocates that candidates for the Master of Defence, at the end of their 14 year-long training,

"play with such weapons as they professe to teach withall, three bouts apeece with three of the best English Maisters of Defence, & three bouts apeece with three unskilful valiant men, and three bouts apeece with three resolute men half drunke. Then if they can defend themselves against these maisters of Defence, and hurt, and go free from the rest, then they are to be honored, cherished, and allowed for perfect good teachers, what countrey men soever they be: but if anie of these they take foile, then are they imperfect in their profession, their fight is false, & they are false teachers, deceivers, and murtherers, and to be punished accordingly, yet no worse punishment unto them I wish, than such as in their triall they shall find."[32]

It is not only the awareness of the limitations of art that differenciate the artist from the impostor. It is the capability to adapt the style of fighting to the opponent—and survive. This is the weakness of the Italian rapier entrepreneurs who used political influence and appeal to the high-end market to push aside the rights, privileges, and traditions of the Masters of Defence:

Their system's viability and practicability was limited to the close confines of the artificial, regulated combat environment of the duel.

[32] Silver, George. *Paradoxes of Defence*, London: Edward Blount, 1599; p. B2; in Jackson. *Three Elizabethan Fencing Manuals;* p. 501.

If pitched into an unregulated, unarranged fight with opponents moving, defending, attacking according to unorthodox, incalculable principles, rapier fighters exposed only to the rarified principles of the fencing academy were doomed. Silver's mocking words could have been spoken on the occasions of the Bonnetti vs. Bagger or Ieronimo vs. Cheese encounters, which left the Italian incapacitated or dead after squaring off against native English provosts:

> *"Now, o you Italian teachers of Defence, where are your stoccatas, imbroccatas, mandritas, puntas & punta reversas, stramisons, passatas, carricados, amazzas, and incartatas, and playing with your bodies, your feet a little aside, circle wise winding of your bodies, making of three times with your feet together, marking with one eye the motion of the adversary, and with the other eye the advantage of thrusting? What is become of all these juggling gambalds, apish devices, with all the rest of your squint-eyed tricks, when as through your deepe studies, long practises, and apt bodies, both strong and agilious, you have attained to the height of all these things? What then availeth it you, when you shal come to fight for your lives with a man of skill? You shall have neither time, nor place, in due time to performe any of them."*[33]

The same holds true for Socrates. He takes on enemies whose intellectual capacity and limited willingness to follow the old cobbler's lead make them unpredictable and thus hard to manipulate along the lines of the Socratic truthfinding process.

The fighting philosopher

In the *Apology*, his refutation of Meletus' accusations are masterpieces of semantic and contextual entrapment that indicate a level of fighting spirit a modern shyster would be proud to call his own.

Socrates plays on ambiguities—and skillfully manipulates Meletus into admitting to the major and minor premises of his syllogisms. John Burnet characterized his way of verbal combat as *"dialectical fence."*[34]

This is a rather well-chosen term, particularly if you take into consideration Aldo Nadi's observations that

> *"the steel is the medium through which the fencer is able not only to read at prodigious speed his adversary's brain, but to look into his heart as well. (...) Within the first minute of combat, the great fencer can read an opponent's thoughts as in an open book, and evaluate his daring, even though he has never seen the man before. The fencing strip is the mirror of the soul. Unerringly, it portrays the character of the individual. From the psychological viewpoint, you may learn more about a man fencing with him a couple of times than through hours of conversation."*[35]

But at court, Socrates is matching the foil of his dialog against the sawed-off shotguns of his accusers. His artful argumentative manipulations are received with

[33]Silver. *Paradoxes;* p. 55; in Jackson; p. 553.

[34]Plato. *Euthyphro, Apology of Socrates and Crito* (transl. Burnet, John), Oxford: Oxford University Press, (1924) 1974; p. 117.

[35]Nadi. *On Fencing;* p. 11.

predictable results: Like a champion synchronized swimmer caught in a flash flood, his chances of survival are minimal.

In this situation, Socrates transcends the mere struggle to survive. He can afford to gamble his life—doomed to brevity by nature at any rate—and devote his final efforts to revenge: precise, vicious, premeditated, malicious, almost mephistophelian in its strategic conception and execution.

Socrates cannot force his terms on his opponents in court. He refuses to turn tail, escape Athens using the influence and money of his students. Because Socrates is a fighter. The only way left to him is to raise the stakes, turn the tables on his enemies, carry the fight onto a playing field more familiar to him.

Instead of fighting for his life as his opponents expect him to by allowing them to dictate the method of his style, Socrates cuts bait. He carries war and bloodfeud into hyper-reality. He targets the souls of his enemies, their family altars, their *lares praestites*, *familiares*, *privati*, and *patrii*, whose reputation and memory he aims to destroy for millennia to come.

Suddenly, the myth of the proto-Christian, the meek Socrates—heaping coals on the heads of his enemies by willingly submitting to the law—appears in a different light. Socrates' death and triumph becomes the quintessence of Western warrior barbarism: Like his compatriots at Marathon and Thermopylae, like the Nibelungs who died sword in hand in the flaming inferno of Etzel's court, like the Germans holed up on Monte Cassino, or Mordred who, dying, pulled Arthur's spear through his own guts to get close enough to brain his father with his sword, Socrates fulfills his heroic destiny.

This is the stuff epics are made of, a grim and savage will to destroy one's enemies, avenge one's own death even as you die—with a determination as fiercely heroic and murderously suicidal as the grey gods of Asgaard's last stand against the hellish legions of the Ragnarök.

Twilight of the cobbler

Heroics seem to come easily to Socrates. And why not: In the *Apology* (ln. 28 e) there are a number of references to Socrates fighting background. Apparently he participated as an active combatant in at least one battle. He may have been involved in the fighting which accompanied the founding of Amphipolis in 437 B.C., when he was about 32 years old.

Burnet sums up:

"If he took part in the siege of Samos in 440 B.C. [mentioned in Crito] it is pretty safe to assume that he saw service elsewhere between that and Potidaea. Whichever view we take, the three battles are out of their chronological order, but it is perhaps easier to assume that Potidaea and the earlier battle of Amphipolis have been transposed than that this has been happened with Delium (424 B.C.) and Amphipolis (422 B.C.)."[36]

[36]Plato. **Euthyphro, Apology of Socrates and Crito** (transl. Burnet, John); p. 120.

At Delium, Socrates was 42 years old. On this occasion, the Athenian forces under Hippocrates had 7,000 regular hoplites, Socrates among them.

Modern opinion about the quality and competence of the hoplites' fighting prowess varies considerably. Armed with shield, helmet, cuirass, greaves, the main offensive weapons were a seven-foot spear and a short sword:

"The completeness and quality of their equipment made up the only professional attributes of the Greek hoplites. Militiamen, they had full-time occupations as farmers, artisans, and tradesmen, furnished their own armor, had engaged in some training, and tried to keep in good physical condition. (...) The tactical formation adopted by the Greeks supported their morale in the frightening experience of combat, the spearmen standing shoulder to shoulder at least four and usually eight or even more ranks deep."[37]

Ancient armor and fighting styles

Jones and other military historians have no high opinion of the fighting prowess of city-state hoplites.

Apart from re-interpreting literary monuments, details of lost fighting styles can be deduced by critically examining samples of armor. The guru of U.S. arms and armor, Bashford Dean, for example, broke important ground in this field in his *Handbook of Arms and Armor* (1915). In regard to the Greek hoplite, his findings let one assume that the Hellenic warrior indeed practiced a highly sophisticated and athletic martial art:

"Altogether, the panoply [of Greek armor] was designed to hamper as little as possible the movements of the wearer. And if a modern, or, still better, a mediaeval soldier could have observed the individual attacks at Marathon or Platae, he would probably have been dumbfounded at the suddenness of the charges, the rapidity of the thrusts, and the quickness with which the heavily armored Greek dropped to his knee, rose, or feinted. I have seen no comment of the supreme activity of the Greek soldier in battle, but his armor gives the clearest proof that he specialized his equipment in this functional direction.

There was no reason why he should not have worn more complete armor, and if he did not protect his abdomen and thighs it was because he wished to keep unhampered his movements in running, leaping, twisting, bending, and stooping. Note, for example, the details of his greave: its ends show that it was formed so as to restrict as little as possible the varied movements of knee and ankle.

That his sword arm was bare showed that he would not embarrass it even with the weight of a leathern sleeve; for to retard the movement of his arm the fraction of a second might cost him a fatal wound. The use of the shield does not mean, indeed, that it was unnecessary for the soldier to protect otherwise the abdomen and thighs: certainly his sword arm was exposed, yet was unprotected, and his corselet fitted too closely the lower ribs and marked out too accurately the limits of the muscles which function in stooping, to have been developed as a mere accident. In fact, even when armor of the thighs is present it is of a special form so as to hinder little their activity."[38]

[37] Jones; p. 2.

[38] Dean, Bashford. *Handbook of Arms and Armor, European and Oriental, including the William H. Riggs Collection,* New York: The Metropolitan Museum of Art, 1915; p. 28f.

155

Dean may have overstated the degree of actual flexibility pitched battle in the pushing, shoving hoplite phalanx would afford the fighter. (In fact, both Plato and Aristophanes repeatedly comment on the clumsiness and discomfort of the armor—which was usually not custom-tailored to the wearer but would be handed down from father to son, or taken off a fallen enemy.)

Still, modern historians have slowly come around to acknowledge that the single combat between hoplites was not the rustic banging and bashing of bronze against bronze earlier generations of historians have alleged.

Hoplite power

Hanson sums up the hoplite experience:

> *"Few types of infantry battle in the West have required quite the same degree of courage, of nerve in the face of mental and physical anguish, as this, its originl form, in which armed and armored hoplites advanced in massed formation with no chance of escape. (...) A man could focus all his courage upon one pure burst of frenzied activity; for an hour or two he overcame the limits of physical and psychological endurance."*[39]

Athenian intellectuals of the time had a firm rooting in the world of the fighting man:

> *"Most Greek writers knew battle firsthand (...) in Aristophanes or Plato we hear often of the bothersome clumsiness of hoplite armor or the need to stay in rank during the fighting. (...) Hoplite battle was second nature to nearly all these writers."*[40]

Aeschylus the dramatist, for example, considered his experience as hoplite on the battlefields of the Persian wars so crucial to his being that his epitome does not even mention his fame as a playwright. It is a simple reminiscence on his bravery in battle.[41]

Socrates, however, was no ordinary fighter. In the *Symposium*, Alcibiades himself describes the actions at Potidaea, which he attended as Socrates' commanding officer:

> *"I had the opportunity of observing his extraordinary power of sustaining fatigue. His endurance was simply marvelous when, being cut off from our supplies, we were compelled to go without food.*
>
> *On such occasions, which often happen in time of war, he was superior not only to me but to everybody; there was no one to be compared to him. Yet at a festival he was the only person who had any real powers of enjoyment; though not willing to drink, he could if compelled beat us all at that; wonderful to relate, no human being had ever seen Socrates drunk; (...)*
>
> *His fortitude in enduring cold was also surprising. There was a severe frost, for the winter in that region is really tremendous, and everybody else either remained indoorss, or if they went out had on an amazing quanity*

[39]Hanson, Victor David. *The Western Way of War: Infantry Battle in Classical Greece,* NY: Alfred Knopf, 1989; p. 25.

[40]Hanson; p. 45f.

[41]It reads "Under this monument lies Aeschylus the Athenian / Euphorion's son, who died in the wheatlands of Gela. / The Grove of Marathon, with its glories, can speak of his valor in battle. / The long-haired Persian remembers and can speak of it, too." (Aeschylus, *Vita* [Lattimore translation])

of clothes, and were well shod, and had their feet swathed in felt and fleeces; in the midst of this, Socrates with his bare feet on the ice and in his ordinary dress marched better than the other soldiers who had shoes, and they looked daggers at hime because he seemed to despise them."[42]

Later, as the Athenian army is routed, Alcibiades again encounters Socrates not as the proto-Christian sage, but rather as the battle-hardened fighter who shows that he knows more about fighting and battle psychology:

"I was wounded and he would not leave me, but rescued me and my weapons. (…) There was another occasion on which his behavior was very remarkable—in the flight of the army after the battle of Delium, where he served among the hoplites–I had a better opportunity of seeing him than at Potidaea, for I was myself on horseback, and therefore comparatively out of danger.

He and Laches were retreating, for the troops were in flight, and I met them and told them not to be discouraged, and promised to remain with them; and there you might see him (…) just as he is in the streets of Athens, stalking like a pelican, and rolling his eyes, calmly contemplating enemies as well as friends, and making very intelligible to anybody, even from a distance, that whoever attacked him would be likely to meet with a stout resistance; and in this way he and his companion escaped–for this is the sort of man who is never touched in war."[43]

Alcibiades and Socrates had been old acquaintances. In the formative phase of their relationship, there is yet another circumstance that illustrates the fighting qualities of the supposedly meek philosopher: He is also an expert wrestler! Alcibiades explains:

"Afterwards, I challenged him to the palaestra[44]*, and he wrestled and closed with me several times when there was no-one present. I fancied I might succeed in his manner. Not a bit; I made no way with him."*[45]

[42] Plato. ***Apology, Crito, Phaedo, Symposium, Republic*** (transl. Jowett, B.), New York: Walter J. Black, 1942; p. 212.

[43] Plato. ***Apology, Crito, Phaedo, Symposium, Republic*** (transl. Jowett); p. 213.

[44] Athletes in *palaestra* practised the *exercitum*, or *pentathlum*, which included running, wrestling, and jump/hurdle. Greek wrestlers tried to grab each other's feet as their bodies had been made slippery by wrestler's ointment (oil and wax).

[45] Plato. ***Apology, Crito, Phaedo, Symposium, Republic*** (transl. Jowett); p. 209.

[46] Plato. ***Lysis, Symposium, Gorgias*** (transl. W.R.M. Lamb), Cambridge, MA and London: Harvard UP [Loeb Classical Library], (1925) 1991; Symposium 217 C.

Even if recent translators have interpreted the last two sentences[46] as relating to Alcibiades' supposed homosexual overtures, it becomes evident that Socrates' intellectual prowess and strategic approach to annihilating his enemies are those of a fighting master. Combine this insight with a passage from Xenophon's speech before the assembled Greek fighting force, and a different picture of Socrates emerges:

[47] Xenophon, **Anabasis**, iii. 1. 43; p. 195.

[48] Gajkowski, Matthew. **German Squad Tactics in WWII**, n.p.[West Chester, OH?]: privately published, 1995; p. 42. Swetnam also records an incident in which the fleeing opponent managed to get himself killed by committing the cardinal mistake of the sword fighter, turning your back to your opponent: *"In Plymouth, one Captaine Treherne and Captain Egles fell out about nothing in a manner, the cause was for that one of them was denied lodging, where the other did lie by the good wife of the house, for it may bee she affected the one better than the other, and two dogs and one bone commonly can never agree well together.*

But they fell out about such a trifling matter, and at the door in the street they fought, and in the first bout, Treherne was downe in the gutter. And Egles there in presence of many might have killed him, but stayed his hand, and suffered him to rise again.

But then Treherne assaulted Captain Egles most furiously, and it so chanced that with a blow Egles rapier broke, and then running into a house to save himselfe, Treherne ran him into the backe and killed him."

[49] Plato. **Euthyphro, Apology, Crito, Phaedo, Phaedrus** (transl. Fowler, Harold North), Cambridge, MA and London: Harvard UP [Loeb Classical Library], (1917) 1995; p. 137. (Apology 39 B.)

[50] Tyrtaios, ii. 21ff.

"I have observed that those who are anxious in war to save their lives in any way they can, are usually the very men who meet with a base and shameful death. While those who have recognized that death is the common and inevitable portion of all mankind and therefore strive to meet death nobly, are precisely those who are somehow more likely to reach old age and who enjoy a happier existence while they do live."[47]

This coincides with observations found in the U.S. tranlation of an anonymous German Wehrmacht training manual from the early 1940s

"It is essential that the infantryman does not lose his nerve. Running away is the worst thing he can do, for in all probability he will be shot."[48]

This experience underlies Socrates' own words in the *Apology*:

"For neither in the court nor in war ought I or any other man plan to escape death by any possible means. In battles, it is often plain that a man might avoid death by throwing down his arms and begging mercy of his pursuers; and there are many other means of escaping death in dangers of various kinds if one is willing to do and say anything. But, gentlemen, it is not hard to escape death; it is much harder to escape wickedness, for that runs faster than death. And now I, since I am slow and old, am caught by the slower runner, and my accusers, who are clever and quick, by the faster, wickedness."[49]

Even in his advanced age, facing the crushing superiority of his accusers' clout, Socrates acts like an infantry fighter. He choses to die the way he fought as a hoplite, facing his enemies and dealing death even as he submitted to the Law:

"Let him take a wide stance and stand up strongly against them, digging both heels in the ground, biting his lip with his teeth, covering thighs and legs beneath, his chest and his shoulders under the hollowed-out protection of his broad shield, while in his right hand he brandishes the powerful war-spear and shakes terribly the crest high above his helm."[50]

He may have been the most articulate and most radical hoplite of his generation. But given the startling similarities in the Way of the Warrior and Socratic dialectics, it seems to me that the traditional judgments on the qualities of Mediterranean fighting systems will have to be rethought and put into a new perspective.

INTERLUDE

COMMENT COMBAT
Duel

The Saber Duel
Terrone vs. Flauto, Rome, A.D. 1896[51]

Still in my twenties and an officer in the Italian Navy, I[52] had been attached to the Navy Department in Rome, as at the time the most competent adviser in reading the reports of the various captains commanding all the ships of the Italian Navy, where new men had to take their practice course at handling and shooting with newly invented complicated pieces of artillery, from machine guns to guns weighing 106 tons each; and had been studying at the Scuola Militare Magistrate di Scherma, which is the national fencing school conducted by the Army.

Partly because of my writings as a disciple of the great republican philosopher, Joseph Mazzini, I had been accepted as a member of exclusive intellectual and social circles in the capital. This, coupled with my reputation as a fencer, appeared to have aroused resentment among a certain class of men, particularly fencers, because I had never participated in their social life and escapades.

One day at a social gathering, the son of a renowned duellist, and himself a fine, brave fencer, took occasion to address a rude remark to me so that everyone in the room could hear. Conversation immediately ceased and the ladies and gentlemen present stood tensely awaiting my reply. As calmly as possible, I said: "Only an ill-bred person could talk to me like that."

The young man, Guido Flauto by name, immediately shouted: "Withdraw and apologize!" to which I replied that I had weighed every word that I had uttered and felt they had been deserved. He departed and a few hours later two of his friends presented to me his challenge so that I could uphold my words at the risk of my life.

[51]Huber; p. 24f. This account is also reprinted in Terrone, Leonardo F. *Right and Left Hand Fencing,* New York: Dodd, Mead, & Co., 1959; p. 8.

[52]Meet Leonardo F. Terrone.

Commendatore Parise [53], founder of the national fencing school, scenting that this was not merely a personal quarrel but rather a manifestation of a social feud, since Signor Flauto was a Neapolitan and I a Piedmontese, and also because of my popularity as a writer and public speaker, asked for my permission to be present at the meeting of the seconds. Having obtained it, he sent my seconds to ask if I would not modify my expressed judgment of the challenger. This I was not able to do.

It was therefore decided that we should fight the next day with sabres, the weapon selected by the challenger; that our forearms should be protected so that a wound below the forearm would not cause the stopping of the duel and that, as a social privilege, some notable representatives of the national school should be present. In fact, Signor Gaudini, one of its distinguished teachers, was chosen to direct the battle.

We met in the Eucalyptus Grove of the Trappist Friars, near the Catacombs, at 1:30 o'clock on the ninth of April, 1896. What transpired is best told in the succinct account drawn up by the seconds and witnesses:

> *"The combat lasted fifteen minutes and had six distinct bouts.*
> *In the first one, Signor Flauto was slightly wounded just above the elbow of the right arm.*
> *In the second, Signor Terrone was slightly wounded near the elbow.*
> *The third bout had to be stopped because the two adversaries had sidestepped toward the trees.*
> *In the fourth bout, Signor Terrone was wounded for the second time, this one being a rather long incision just above the elbow of his right arm.*
> *The fifth bout had to be stopped because, following a most deliberated attack from Signor Terrone, Signor Flauto withdrew rapidly and in disorder beyond the limit agreed upon.*
> *In the sixth bout Signor Terrone renewed his attack and inflicted a wound upon the face of the withdrawing Signor Flauto. The surgeon declared the wound so severe as to prevent the possibility of a continuation of the duel.* [54]
> *The proceeding of the duel was strictly within the best chivalrous rules. As soon as he returned to his senses, Signor Flauto expressed his unlimited esteem for Signor Terrone and wished to thank Signor Terrone for having given stern satisfaction; and, though his eyes were temporarily closed, extended his hand. Signor Terrone took it in a friendly grip and the incident was closed."*

After some time, Signor Flauto, meeting Signor Terrone publicly among sportsmen from all parts of the world gathered in Ancona for the International Fencing Tournament of 1900, climbing on a chair, called the attention of the ones present and said:

"Gentlemen, there has just arrived among us Signor Terrone—the man who, at the risk of his own life, correctly as well as intrepidly and nobly, caused the long indelible scar on my forehead."

And there was nothing but admiration in his voice."

[53] And this is Masaniello Parise, one of the fathers of the modern sports saber.

[54] Cuts to the forehead, particularly if executed with the *sciabola di terreno*, are rarely dangerous enough to terminate a duel for purely medical reasons—unless, of course, the temporal artery is damaged. The inevitably heavy bloodflow would have impeded Flauto's ability to see—an assumption supported by his "temporarily closed" eyes. In Schläger Mensuren where this kind of injury is frequent, some fighters today apply Vaseline around their goggles to keep blood from running into their eyes.

Saber duellists fighting *"sine"*, i.e., without goggles, typically were advised to keep their foreheads lowered during the fight—not only to keep blood from interfering with their vision, but also to avoid eye injuries by letting the opponent's blade be deflected by eyebrow ridges and frontal bone.

ADVENTURES IN
LOST COMBAT ARTS 3

Roman gladiator at the Post.

The Way of the Gladius

In Roman military training, some recent studies suggest that there was also a systematic approach to teaching the practice of the gladius in the Roman army.

The gladius is usually described as a thrusting weapon. However, its design points at a general use for cut and thrust, used in combination with the long shield, or scutum. The shield was also used in the offensive: Legionnaires rushed into hand-to-hand combat *"striking opponents with their shields to unbalance them and then stabbing them with their swords. (...) Normally, the scutum was held out horizontally in front of a man. The soldier stood behind it in a slight crouch, his left leg towards the enemy, and his right side turned away."*[55]

Hunter B. Armstrong, the editor of *Hoplos*, summed up the techniques that might have been used in hand-to-hand combat with gladius and scutum.

> *"The length of the gladius' blade is such that thrust and effective penetration (through any type of armor) would be primarily a function of body displacement rather than by extension of the arm. The most efficient use of the point would be with the blade and hand held low, elbow at an angle closer to 90 degrees, rather than extended straight, with the upper arm held close to the side to allow the body weight to effectively augment the power of the thrust."*[56]

[55]Goldsworthy, Adrian Keith. *The Roman Army at War, 100 BC—AD 200*, Oxford: Clarendon Press, 1996; p. 218f.

[56]Armstrong, Hunter B. — "The Way of the Gladius," in *Hammerterz Forum*, vol. 3, #2, (Fall 1996); p. 9. A previous version was published in *Hoplos,* vol. iv, #4 (August 1985).

The one surviving reference for a combative system of the gladius appears in *De re militarii* by the Roman author Flavius Vegetius Renatus. Vegetius, writing around A.D. 490, mentions a system of combative training which he calls armatura. However, it remains unclear if it was a general training system or a true combative system.

Vegetius describes the basic sword training that preceded the more advanced armatura: [57]

> *"We are informed by the writings of the ancients that, among their other exercises was that of the Post. They gave their recruits bucklers woven with willows, twice as heavy as those used on real service, and wooden swords double the weight of the common ones. They exercised them with them at the Post both morning and afternoon.*[58]
>
> *This is an invention of the greatest use, not only to soldiers, but also to gladiators. No man of either profession ever distinguished himself in the circus or field of battle who was not perfect in this exercise. Every soldier, therefore, fixed a post firmly in the ground, about the height of six feet. Against this, as against a real enemy, the recruit was exercised with the above mentioned arms, as with the common shield and sword, sometimes aiming at the head or face, sometimes at the sides, at others endeavoring to strike at the thighs or legs. He was instructed in what manner to advance and retire and in short how to take every advantage of his adversary, but was thus above all particularly cautioned not to lay himself open to his antagonist while aiming his stroke at him.*
>
> *They were likewise taught not to cut, but to thrust with their swords. For the Romans not only made a jest of those who fought with the edge of that weapon, but always found them an easy conquest. A stroke with the edges, though made with ever so much force, seldom kills, as the vital parts of the body are defended both by the bones and armor. On the contrary, a stab, although it penetrates but two inches, is generally fatal. Besides in the attitude of striking, it is impossible to avoid exposing the right arm and side; but on the other hand, the body is covered while a thrust is given and the adversary receives the point before he sees the sword.*[59]

A codified exchange of strikes and counters frequently characterizes combative training systems. Given the purpose of the gladius as a predominantly military close-combat weapon, it may be safe to assumed that a comparable sparring system was practiced in the armatura.

Unfortunately, no written description of this process appears to have survived:

> *"But the very fact that the training had a name, and that this name was applied to a very specific level of training, is indicative that armatura were a very specific combative system, not just a general term used to describe recruit training."*[60]

[57]Vegetius Renatus, Flavius. *On the Military Institutions of the Romans* (transl. Clark, John), Harrisburg, PA: The Military Service Publishing Co., 1944; p. 19f.

[58]Post training continues today for Schläger practice.

[59]This, of course, points out that the "thrust" has nothing in common with that of the rapier, smallsword, and the modern fencing weapons, but rather is a ripping stab from behind the protection of the shield. The leading leg of the shield-armed fighter is usually the left leg. The modern thrust, of course leads with the right leg, with the sword and point in plain sight of the opponent.

[60]Armstrong; p. 20.

The art of war

Tacitus reports that the Germans who took on Germanicus used their spears to *"strike thick and fast, and to direct the point to the face."*[61] When Agricola in Britain faces off against superior British forces, battle reports indicate high levels of mobility on the side of the British, as well as effective tactical adaptability on the side of the Roman footsoldiers:

> *"The battle began with fighting at long range; the Britons, with their long swords and short shields, showed determination and skill in evading or brushing aside the Roman missiles, while on their own side they launched dense volleys of spears; until Agricola ordered four battalions of Batavi and Tungri to bring things to the sword's point and to hand-to-hand fighting; a maneuver familiar to them from long service and embarrassing to the enemy, whose shields were small and swords too long; for the British swords, without points, did not admit of locked lines and fighting at close quarters. Accordingly when the Batavi began to exchange blows hand to hand, to strike with the bosses of the shields, to stab in the face, and, after cutting down the enemy on the level, to push their line uphill, the other battalions, exerting themselves to emulate their charge, proceeded to slaughter the nearest enemies."*[62]

Combining their strategic advantage of advancing in a closed shield wall, using their superior defensive armor both for offence and defence, and fully taking advantage of their opponents' short-comings, Agricola's Germanic auxiliaries are able to trounce the highly trained British warriors.

It probably should be pointed out that the British forces may not have been all individually armed with swords:

> *"Swords were much less common weapons than spears. Their production was a skilled and expensive affair and swords were therefore rare beyond the Roman Empire, though they seem to have been relatively common within it. (...) A small increase in the use of swords would not make any significant difference to barbarian warfare; although swords would make individual barbarian warriors more effective against armored troops, increasing the small number of men with swords would not allow the barbarians to do anything they could not already do. The spear remained the weapon of the majority throughout this period."*[63]

As Goldsworthy emphasizes, the actual duration of these hand-to-hand encounters may not have exceeded 15 to 20 minutes, with the first line doing the lion's share of the fighting[64] —after the barbarians' supply of primary weapons (spears) would have been reduced by the preceding medium-range volleys.

The number of enemies who would have to be encountered sword against sword might accordingly have been much less than the original forces. Agricola's choice of the Batavi and Tungri to close and break the British front lines might indicate that some troops were better at this kind of job than others... masters of the armatura excelling in a tactical scenario equally masterfully exploited by the general...

[61] *Tacitus, in Five Volumes (vol. III)*, Cambridge, MA: Harvard UP and London: William Heinemnn Ltd., (1931) 1979: Goold, G. P. (ed.). *Annals*, II, 14; p. 404/405.

[62] *Tacitus, in Five Volumes (vol. I)*, Cambridge, MA: Harvard UP and London: William Heinemnn Ltd., (1914) 1980: Hutton, M. (ed.). *Agricola*; 36; p. 93.

[63] Elton, Hugh. *Warfare in Roman Europe A.D. 350-425*, Oxford: Clarendon Press, 1996; p. 67.

[64] Goldsworthy; p. 224.

INTERLUDE

Halliburton sporting
Khevsoor armor (1935).

Sword and Buckler Fighting among the Lost Crusaders

When the 20th century kicked off in Europe, pockets of backward populations remained virtually untouched by industrialization and the advances in communication. Some of these isolated sub-cultures still retained traces of fighting systems that even the great cultural levelers of the century, Communism and Fascism/Nazism, required decades to eradicate.

A the fringes of civilized Europe, in the ranges of the Caucasus mountains, the American traveler Richard Halliburton (1900-1939) heard a curious tale in 1935, when he visited the city of Tblisi in the then Soviet republic of Georgia.

Georgia on my mind

In 1915, a year after the outbreak of World War I, the citizens of Tblisi woke up to watch a troop of mounted warriors ride down the cobble-stoned streets. They were armed with rusty chain armor, sword and buckler, and carried rifles of amazing antiquity. They called themselves the Khevsoor. Their mission: Upon learning that their Czar was at war, they wanted to put their swords at his disposal.

These men hailed from a remote region of the Caucasus—and area cut off from the outside world by ice and snow for a full nine months out of each year.

The Khevsoor considered themselves the direct descendants of a party of crusaders who got separated from a larger army and got stranded in this remote area. Indeed, Halliburton believes to have recognized French and German fragments in the otherwise unintelligible dialect of the people.

Legend of the Lost Crusaders

It remains unclear what crusade brought on the unfortunate exile... if a contingent of fighters indeed made up the entire original land-wrecked party, or if only a handful of men was accepted into an indigenous population. There's no record on the social status of these men, if they were knights, common soldiers, or maybe just entourage. Indeed, since the very existence of these people currently cannot be corroborated, it is tempting to write the whole story off as a hoax, at best to colorful local mythology.

But Richard Halliburton's works exhibit little creative imagination. And since his is the only published account of a Westerner having visited the region and observed some of the more picturesque traditions, I am tempted to believe at least the description of what he witnessed[65]:

> "On first reaching the land of the lost Crusaders, I had hoped to find every man wearing his famous coat of mail. I didn't find a single one. Instead they all wore a homespun cross-embroidered shirt over baggy trousers. But on the wall in every house, the armor hung beside the shield and gun. The sword itself, varying from twelve to thirty inches in length, each man carries constantly.[66] It is as much part of his dress as his sheepskin hat, or the ornamental row of cartridges across his chest.
>
> Seeing how interested we were in the chain armor, the village elders took half a dozen suits and let me examine them and try one on. The entire outfit, including shield and sword, weighs about thirty pounds.
>
> Each mesh coat is made of some twenty thousand tiny iron rings and goes on like a night shirt. The sleeves are short, but mesh gauntlets cover the forearms. With each suit goes a bag-like chain helmet with a hole cut out for the face. A flap folds over, so that the entire head can be protected. For the shins there are likewise mesh greaves. Consequently when completely arrayed, the only parts of the body vulnerable are the knees and thighs.

[65]Halliburton, Richard. *Seven League Boots*, Indianapolis: Bobbs-Merrill Co., 1935; p. 214f.

[66]The photo of Halliburton shows him posing in mail shirt with buckler, and a 19th-century Mameluke-style saber. Other fighters carry regionally made weapons of the qama and Kindjal patterns. This hodge-podge of styles is to be expected from a tribe without more than basic metalworking capabilities.

Khevsoor combat
Note the low crouch!

The original mesh is terribly rusty, as the owners no longer understand how to preserve it. The newer coats are made from copper wire stolen from the telegraph line along the highroad. It is both cleaner and lighter than the iron but offers by no means as good protection.

The Khevsoors have not worn their coats of mail into battle since their famous march into Tiflis in 1915. The chief reason is that those who finally did join the Czar's army found that modern bullets have no respect for copper wire mesh.

But for duelling, which remains an accepted way for settling all disputes, the contestants still clothe themselves in their armor. Also they enjoy fighting for fun. Like their forefathers, the Crusader knights, they have a passion for putting on their iron shirts and going at each other with broadswords. Fighting, both in good and bad humor, in this land where books are unknown and where other forms of sport or diversion simply do not exist,   is the only means they have of expressing themselves.

Sunday is reserved for getting drunk and duelling.

For our benefit two of the Khevsoor braves decided to put on a show. We all went to a little plateau outside the village where the duellists faced each other. There is no referee, as everybody has known and followed the rules for centuries. Unlike the jousting in the Middle Ages, when ladies were such important features in the tournament, the Khevsoorian duellists permit only men to watch. However, there is an age-old custom that permits a woman to stop a duel at her pleasure by appearing on the scene and tossing her handkerchief between the two combatants.

The fighters crouch with one knee bent almost to the ground. Their small round shields, embossed with a big cross, are used to parry rather than receive the blows of the opponent's sword. The duellists jump about with astonishing agility, circling and jockeying for position like fighting cocks.

Recklessly, the swords thud on leather shields, crunch on chain armor, or clash as they strike together. But unlike similar duels in German universities, wounds are rare, since the head and face, where most of the blows fall, are not exposed. There is no slit even for the eyes. The fighter must see as best as he can right through the mesh screen of the helmet flap.

The duel I witnessed was, of course, friendly. Though both fighters were well oiled on home-made barley brandy and didn't hesitate to attack with full vigor, a couple of bruises were the worst that happened.

When, however, anyone actually inflicts a wound, either in friendly or in angry battle, the victim must be compensated in cows. The village elder measures the wound in barley seed, and for every seed it will contain the guilty swordsman must pay one cow."

Fact or fantasy?

My attempts to verify the existence of the Khevsoor remained futile. There are some indications that mesh armor can be documented in the Caucasus in the 20th century.

The total absence of plate armor could point at Persian rather than European influences.

Even the clues to the fighting techniques are few and far between. The knees are kept bend, nearly touching the ground, the fighters are crouching lower than in comparable European sword and buckler systems. The leather bucklers are used to deflect rather than block, and the cuts are light enough not to break bones—and judging from Halliburton's account must have been dealt at a speed that made their acoustic impact more easy to track than visual observation.

The question remains what the point of the bout was. If injuries were punished and all body parts were covered by mail, there must have been an implicit way of measuring competitive ability that may not have been communicated to Halliburton.

ADVENTURES IN
LOST COMBAT ARTS 4

Gladiators

"Renaissance" Sword Techniques in A.D. 150!

I n regard to sword fighting, a recent discovery appears to support the assumption that the fighting arts of classical antiquity were indeed as well developed
as those of the Renaissance—belying Garrett's laconic comment that *"during
the Greco-Roman era the styles of fighting were primitive; the strongest arm and the
heaviest weapon prevailed. Feints of attack were unknown and combatants often struck
at the same time, rendering both helpless."*[67]

The term Renaissance—rebirth—implies a second installment of previous
phenomena, in this case, of the culture and art of Greco-Roman antiquity. And
when it comes to swordplay, the Renaissance was indeed a rebirth rather than a
new beginning—as can be illustrated by one particular technique that represents
the assumed superiority of Renaissance fencing systems over the ancient systems
—the famed *Coup de Jarnac.*

(This is, of course, the tradition. Bataillard's summary of the official documentation only mentions that the fighters used thrusts more than cuts and that
Jarnac managed to repeatedly strike his opponent behind the ham.)

Sir Alfred Hutton ascribes the *Coup de Jarnac* to the influence of an Italian
fencing master, Capitano Caizo, who *"judging from the nature of the instruction
which he imparts to his pupil, must be an adept in the precepts of the renowned Achille
Marozzo."*[68]

This much-touted maneuver supposedly originated during the famous duel[69]
in which Guy de Chabot, Lord of Jarnac, fought his opponent, François de
Vivonne, Lord of Chastaigneraïe, with sword and buckler in the presence of Henri II
on July 20 1547.[70] To vanquish the superior opponent, Jarnac feinted a head cut,

[67]Garrett, Maxwell R. and
Heinecke, Mary F. **Fencing,**
Boston: Allyn and Bacon,
1971; p. 98. The last sentence
of the passage is particularly
mystifying—as simultaneous
"a tempo" attacks do occur not
only in modern fencing, but
in systems such as Schläger
fencing as well, without being
considered indicative of the
respective system's lack of
sophistication.

[68]Hutton, Alfred. **The Sword
and the Centuries,** (London:
Grant Richards, 1901)
Rutland, Vermont: Charles E.
Tuttle Co., (1973) 1980; p. 48.

[69]The use of the term duel
may be inappropriate in this
particular context, since the
fight actually took place in the
presence of the sovereign—
an arrangement incompatible
with the paralegal character
of the duel proper. The entire
staging of the event indicates
that this fight must have been
closer to an ordeal or wager
of battle.

[70]See also Bataillard, Ch.
**Du duel, consideré sous le
rapport de la morale, de
l'histoire, de la législation
et de l'opportunité d'une loi
répressive. Suivi de combat
et duel de la Chasteneraye
et de Iarnac,** Paris, 1829.

169

drawing up his adversary's shield, then dropped the blade under the left leg of Chastaigneraïe, hamstringing him. Chastaigneraïe, too stubborn to admit defeat, refused help and bled to death on the field.

But what Hutton regards as a manifestation of sophisticated Renaissance sword techniques appears to have been known to gladiators in the outskirts of the Roman Empire as early as the second century A.D.

Classic technique

Lucian (c. A.D. 120-190), the satirist from Samosata on the Euphrates, is one of the wittiest and sharpest observers of his period. He started out as an apprentice sculptor, then turned to rhetoric and traveled through Gaul and Italy as a lecturer and instructor. Lucian settled in Athens. He later fell on hard times that forced him to accept an administrative post in Egypt.

Nowhere in my fencing and swordplay library—not even the rambling displays of erudition of Sir Richard Burton—have I encountered a mention of the following passage,[71] which in a few sentences introduces us to some basic tactics and techniques of Mediterranean swordplay in antiquity. In my opinion, Lucian's description once and for all blows all those fencing historians out of the water who claim that early fencing systems were inferior or less developed than, say, Renaissance rapier schools.

Raw deal

In Lucian's dialogue "Toxaris," two Scythian friends—Toxaris and Sisinnes—from what today is the Crimean Peninsula, are in the process of traveling from their home country to Athens, because of Toxaris' "desire for Greek culture." Their ship puts in at Amastris, a Black Sea port in Pontus, Asia Minor, in what would be modern Turkey. Here, they are burglarized and left destitute, unable to continue their travel or to return to their home country.

For a few days, the young men eke out a miserable living by hiring themselves out to carry lumber at the port. One day, however, Sinsinnes encounters a procession of "high-spirited, handsome young men" in the market place. These had been enrolled to fight single combats for hire and were to carry out their combats on the next day.

Sisinnes wants to fight for the prize so his friend and blood brother can continue his journey. From their last money, they buy tickets. And after

[71]Lucian. — "Toxaris, or Friendship," in *Works in 8 Volumes* (transl. Harmon, A.M.) Cambridge, MA: Harvard UP and London: William Heinemann Ltd., [Loeb Classical Library], (1936), 1972; vol. v; p. 199f.

"watching wild beasts being brought down with javelins, hunted with dogs, and loosed upon men in chains, the monomachoi (gladiators) entered, and the herald, bringing in a tall youth, said that whoever wanted to fight with that man should come forward, and would receive 10,000 drachmas in payment for the encounter. Thereupon Sisinnes arose, and, leaping down, undertook to fight and requested arms. On receiving his pay, the 10,000 drachmas, he promptly put it in my hands, saying: "If I win, Toxaris, we shall go away together, with all that we need; but if I fall, bury me and return to Scythia."

While I was lamenting over this, he was given his armor and fastened it on, except that he did not put on the helmet but took position bareheaded and fought that way. He himself received the first wound, an under-cut in the back of the thigh, dealt with a curved sword, so that blood flowed copiously. For my part, I was already as good as dead in my fright.

But he waited until his opponent rushed upon him too confidently: Then he stabbed him in the breast and ran him through, so that on the instant he fell at his feet.

Himself laboring under his wound, he sat down upon the body and his life almost left him, but I, running up, revived and inspirited him. When at length he was dismissed as victor, I picked him up and carried him to our lodgings. After long treatment he survived and still lives in Scythia, with my sister as his wife; he is lame, however, by his wound."

Curved-bladed swords in the Greek context

Lucian describes the sword used by Sisinnes' antagonist as curved-bladed (kampulos)—thus predominantly a cutting weapon. The fact that he highlights the curved weapon in the hands of the prize fighter could indicate that Sisinnes himself may have wielded a straight-bladed weapon, maybe the classical phasganon/xiphos—the straight-bladed and double-edged cut-and-thrust sword of Classical Greece.

Curved swords were rare weapons in Greece. Most prominent among them is the kopis, a cutting sword often associated with the machaira, but with a convex cutting edge of the blade, much like the Iberian falcata or the modern Ghurka kukri. The machaira, on the other hand, is a single-edged, pointed war knife slung from a baldric or belt along with the xiphos. Its heavy, curved blade was large enough to make it the ideal weapon for both infantry and cavalry. It was also used for sacrificial and domestic purposes. Another Greek curved sword is the harpé. Its prominent characteristic is a large spur on the concave cutting edge of the blade. The Romans called it ensis hamatus or ensis falcatus. It also appears as a sacrificial weapon.

Of course, the Mediterranean cultures in the second century A.D. are neither truly Greek nor truly Roman in the sense of classic scholarship. Particularly Asia Minor, where this particular fight took place, was a true melting pot of Hellenic, Italic, Oriental, Celtic, and Semitic cultures.

Gladiatorial shows originally were a Roman phenomenon, more or less alien even to the Greeks. Amastris, located in the region of Pontus, had a strong Greek tradition and population, but had been part of the Imperium Romanum for a long time, adopting and adapting to Roman administration and culture.

Roman-style circenses even in provincial transit ports such as Amastris probably featured the same types of gladiator as the main arenas in Rome. Accordingly, the weapons used by *monomachoi* in Amastris could have conformed to Roman rather than Greek traditions. The only hint Lucian provides in regard to the weaponry and consequently the type of gladiator encountered by Sisinnes is the curved-bladed sword—which corresponds to a passage in Juvenal's vitriolic satires:

"nec murmillonis in armis nec clipeo Gracchum pugnantem aut falce supina."[72]

The Murmillo's equipment contained both the round targe as well as the falx supina (lit.: "recurving sickle"), a Roman fighting knife with a concave cutting edge.

Scythian traditions

Sisinnes and Toxaris are Scythians, a warlike people from what today would be Southern Russia. The sword played an important role in Scythian religion. Earlier in the text, Toxaris swears by "the Wind (Anemos) and the Sword (Akinakis)", wind being the source of life, the sword being the cause of death.[73]

The characteristic Scythian sidearm is the akinakes or acinacis, which had been the predominant Central and West Asian sword from at least the seventh century until the second century B.C. Frequently illustrated in Achaemid Persian and Scythian art, the characteristic P-shaped mount of the akinakes (which allowed the wearer to suspend the weapon from a wide belt on the right side) continued to be used on Sarmatian and Sassanian long swords and is eventually found on Sui and Tang [Chinese] dao.

The short akinakes had a straight, double-edged blade 34-45 cm (14-18") in length and was used until the second century B.C., when it was gradually replaced by the long, single-edged iron sword of the Sarmatians.[74]

Herodotus (c. 485-425 B.C.) reports on the ancient Scythian Ares cult that closely involved the sword:

> *"In every district, at the seat of government, Ares has his temple; it is of a peculiar kind and consists of an immense heap of brushwood, three furlongs each way and somewhat less in height. On top the heap is leveled off square, like a platform, accessible on one side but rising sheer on the other three. Every year a hundred and fifty wagon-loads of sticks are added to the pile, to make up for the constant settling caused by rains, and on the top of it is planted an ancient iron sword, which serves for the image of Ares. Annual sacrifices of horses and other cattle are made to this sword, which, indeed, claims a greater number of victims than any other of their gods. Prisoners of war are also sacrificed to Ares."*[75]

Toxaris and Sisinnes, of course, are "modern" Scythians who may be no longer aware of the symbolic backgrounds of their ancestral religion. (Toxaris' failure to recognize the symbolic unity of the Scythian war god and the sword he swears by may be indicative of this cultural alienation.) But still, from the fight described by Lucian it appears that Scythians remained formidably proficient with their sidearms.

Anatomy of a wound

As little as we know about Hellenist fighting techniques, one could assume that the basic stance of fighters in a life-and-death situation would be facing each

[72]Juvenal. *Juvenal and Persius* (transl. Ramsay, G.G.), Cambridge, MA & London: Harvard University Press [Loeb Classical Library], (1918) 1990, p. 175. (Iuvenalis Satura VIII, ln. 200-201): *"Gracchus fighting, not as a murmillo, nor with round shield and scimitar"*—scimitar, of course, being the well-intentioned anachronism to be expected by a non-hoplologist.

[73]Lucian; pp. 164-65.

[74]See also Richardson, Thom. "China and Central Asia," in Coe, Michael D. (ed.) *Swords and Hilt Weapons*, New York: Weidenfeld & Nicholson, 1989; p. 176-77.

[75]Herodotus. *The Histories* (transl. de Sélincourt, Aubrey), Harmondsworth, Middlesex and New York: Penguin Books, (1954) 1984; p. 290. (Book IV.)

other. Sisinnes' refusal to wear a helmet preordained his head as the most worthwhile target area for his opponent—who probably feinted a head attack, drawing up Sisinnes' shield, then dropping his blade in pronation into the low line and cutting upward behind the left leg.[76]

The first crippling injury dealt in the fight is an under-cut to the back of the thigh. Depending on the configuration of the blade, the wound would have been caused by slicing (a modern saber-style blade) or by chopping or tearing (facilitated by the kopis or harpé configuration). An undercut to the back of the thigh, however — even if it could have been helped by the angle of the kopis' cutting edge—is a sophisticated and complex maneuver that requires absolute blade control, speed, balance, and timing, as well as an excellent knowledge of vital points.

The muscles on the back of the thigh (in Lucian: ignuan) are an important target in both empty-hand and edged weapons systems. Also referred to as hamstrings, this package is made up of the biceps femoris, the semitendinosus and the semimembranosus, which attach to the pelvis and lower leg, not to the femur. They are responsible for straightening the hip and bending the knee. A blunt blow to the belly of these muscles will partially paralyze them, temporarily weakening the leg. (A strong enough blow can even affect the underlying nervus ischiaticus.) These muscles provide a difficult target in edged weapons combat:

"Under rare conditions, the hamstrings may be presented as a knife or bayonet target. Severing them produces immediate collapse of the leg and permanent crippling."[77]

According to the text, Sisinnes' leg does not collapse. This may indicate that the hamstrings were not severed but only cut, causing a painful and heavily bleeding wound and impaired mobility. Given the nature of the injury, the footwork of Sisinnes must have been extremely compromised.

Consequently, it is unrealistic that he may have evaded the next attack by side-stepping. He may have pivoted on his sound leg (assuming that he was right-handed his left leg would have been damaged) or evaded the blow by a body movement. This indicates that his opponent may have attempted a downward cut at the head, rather than a diagonal or horizontal cut.

This evasive maneuver was sufficient to throw the gladiator off balance for a brief moment—another indication for a full-forge vertical cut aimed at the head that carried the gladiator's point into a low line. Sisinnes immediately takes advantage of the resulting opening for what could have been a point-in-line. Lucian clearly differentiates two times of this action: The passive point attack (maybe executed by straightening the arm with the point in line) that results in a hit, and the "running through"—facilitated maybe by a lunge-like forward shift of body weight. The opponent dies on the spot.

The latter circumstance is particularly interesting in regard to the target area: Despite the widespread belief that any thrust is by definition lethal, only very limited vital points produce the immediate gratification of instant death. Sisinnes must have hit a vital organ, such as the heart, or a major artery and fully destroyed it by running the blade through.

"Toxaris" indicates that early edged-weapons combat systems were at least as effective and sophisticated within their respective hoplological contexts as 16th-century Italian rapier schools or the French foil techniques of the 18th century.

[76]This technique, minus the shield action, continued to be used well into the late 19th century. It is illustrated best in Henry Angelo's sequentially illustrated manual for cutlass and broadsword, as well as in late 19th-century sports saber techniques dealing with the thigh cut. The proper evasive maneuver for this attack is "shifting the leg" as described in a previous chapter.

[77]Mashiro, N. *Black Medicine—The Dark Art of Death: The Vital Points of the Human Body in Close Combat*, Boulder, CO: Paladin Press, 1978; p. 78.

INTERLUDE

ANTAGONISTIC COMMENT COMBAT
Duel

Duel de Béville vs. Chimay

Life Imitating Operetta:
An Old-World Melodrama in
Jackson Park, Chicago 1891 [78]

Baron Rudolf Kalnoky de Korös-Patak, nephew of Count Kalnoky, Prime Minister of Austria, fought a duel at daybreak yesterday, in Jackson Park at Chicago, with an unknown Southerner, who is believed to be the son of a prominent son of Atlanta, Georgia. The weapons used were rapiers. [79]

Baron Kalnoky arrived at Chicago a month ago. The object of his visit was a mystery to all except to Mr. Carlson, the manager of the Richelieu Hotel, to whom he partly told his story. He said he was at one time a staunch defender and passionate admirer of Queen Natalie of Serbia during his visits to the Austrian capital. He had also been the chosen companion of the gay [80] young Prince Imperial of Austria; and on the suicide of the Prince he was driven into wilder dissipations, and finally sought change in America.

By accident he met with Miss Mattie Atherton, a member of the Duff Opera Company during their last Chicago engagement, and fell madly in love with her. She kept before him the fact that she could never become his wife, because her heart already belonged to another, for whom she would soon quit the stage. Baron Kalnoky followed her from Chicago to Louisville, where he met another candidate for her affections. The rivals returned to Chicago together on Friday night, and dined at the Richelieu Hotel. Kalnoky's companion drank too much wine, and a quarrel ensued, the Baron knocking down his rival for speaking disrespectfully of

[78] from *Pall Mall Gazette*, May 25, 1891.

[79] i.e. *épées de combat*, similar to the modern sports épée.

[80] "gay," of course, in the sense of "merry," "carefree".

175

the woman he loved. An hour afterwards a friend of the Southerner appeared with a note demanding a meeting. Kalnoky at once accepted, and details were arranged on Saturday night. Kalnoky's second selected rapiers as the weapons to be used, the Baron being unfamiliar with the use of the pistol.

Before the duel the Austrian expressed a desire to Mr. Carlson to die in the duel. If he did, he said, it would obviate the necessity of his taking his own life. His wild life had been the occasion of his being disowned by his own family, and suicide was the only recourse left to one who was without a home and without love. He then settled his bill, and left word that if he did not survive the duel all his belongings should be sent to the woman for whose honor he fought. At 4 o'clock yesterday morning he went to the rendezvous, taking with him a prominent young physician who resides in Prairie Avenue, and whom he formerly knew when the latter was a student in Vienna.

At 6:20 the combatants were facing each other, stripped to their shirts. After some sharp fighting the Southerner succeeded in inflicting a slight wound in the Baron's leg. Later, the Baron, by a clever lunge, pricked the skin of his antagonist's shoulder. Up to this time both men had fenced with care. Suddenly, however, to the horror of the seconds, Kalnoky appeared to slip, and literally fell upon his adversary's sword, which entered his neck.

A stream of blood gushed from the wound. The seconds at once stopped the combat and the Baron's wound was dressed by his friend the physician. The Southerner fled. All attempts to identify him have failed. It is known, however, that he boarded the train for Cincinnati two hours later. The Baron's whereabouts is a secret. His friends say that his life is not in immediate danger, but Mr. Carlson fears that the Baron will make an attempt on his own life.

ADVENTURES IN
LOST COMBAT ARTS 5

Didrik vs. Wideke
(12th-century relief from Zürich)

Barbarians at the Gates

Knowledge of the human anatomy paired with technical fighting skills can be taken as a telltale sign of a high level of martial arts in any culture. That this level existed not only among the Hellenic tribes that sacked Troy but also among the peoples today labeled "barbarians" can be gleaned from classical sources.

The period we now refer to as the Middle Ages presents many problems for the reconstruction of early martial arts. Until the publication of fighting compendia, the sources are obscure. Often, a passage in a chronicle, an illustration in a codex are the only clues a researcher has to supplement the evidence of offensive and defensive weaponry. In this field of "paleo-hoplology" (the study of ancient fighting systems) the line between speculation and factual documentation is as blurry as Boris Yeltsin's view of Lenin's Tomb after Happy Hour...

Ancient myths contain many tempting hints at martial initiation rites. The Ossic myths from the Central Caucasus include references that some researchers have brought into context with ancient Indo-European myths that appear in old Scandinavian tales. [81]

Syrdon, a Caucasian from the clan of the Nartes, has been closely linked to the Old Norse god Loki. In the Nartic myth cycle, Syrdon once offered up his son to the other Nartes to use him as a target for archery practice, demanding an ox from them if they were not able to hit him. Indeed, the boy could not be hit, eluding the missiles successfully until Syrdon's enemy Soslan appears—who kills him with the very first arrow.

A similar story line can be found in Snorri Sturluson's *Edda* story of Baldr's death—the prelude to the Ragnarök or Twilight of the Gods—which the philologist Jan de Vries explicitly links to warrior initiation scenarios:

[81] See Dumézil, Georges. *Loki*, Darmstadt: Wissenschaftliche Buchgesellschaft, 1959.

...meanwhile, back at Asgaard

Baldr, the son of Odin, was the most popular and brightest of the divine host at Asgaard. He was also invulnerable, as his mother had taken the oaths of all things on earth that they would not hurt him—all things except for a lowly mistle twig. Being the rustic rubes they were, the Teuton gods amused themselves shooting arrows at young Baldr, lobbing rocks and missiles at him, even using him for sword practice. But they could not harm him. Until Loki had the blind Hoedr shoot just that mistletoe at him...

Testing the skills of a young warrior by subjecting him to the most fierce assault at arms would remain part of European weapon masters initiation rites for centuries. The rigorous exams of the Marxbrüder and Masters of Defence, for example, the challenges at singlestick at English country fairs, are but late incarnations of this custom—notwithstanding that the ability to dodge flying arrows must have been an extremely rare and highly regarded skill even in the realms of the ancients' mythic past.

The Nartic cycle of myths shows warriors practicing running, rock throwing, archery, even unseating an opposing horseman with a single push of one's hand.[82] Apart from the latter feat, which could be regarded as an under-equipped fore-runner of Renaissance jousting, these "sports" remained fixed parts of popular festivals such as the Highland Games or the central European *Schützenfest* until today. Competitive sports like this served to tie up the energies of the stronger, more aggressive young men in inter-clan gatherings... much like they still were among Montenegrin tribesmen in the 1970s, who served as the subject of study for Christopher Boehm's *Blood Revenge*.[83]

The show must go on

These martial arts on foot and horseback were already ancient when Karolus crowned himself emperor. We find a most illuminating sample of the martial expertise of "barbarian" warriors performed by Totila, the charismatic 6th-century Ostrogothic king who put his spatha's blade uncomfortably close to Rome's jugular, in front of two opposing armies.

(The narrator of the following passage, by the way, had little reason to take Totila's side: Procopius was part of the Byzantine forces under Narses that lined up to do battle with the Goths that very day.)

> *"But Totila now went alone into the space between the armies, not to engage in single combat but to prevent his opponents from using the present opportunity. For he had learned that the two thousand Goths who had been missing were now drawing near, and so he sought to put off the engagement until their arrival by doing as follows.*
>
> *First of all, he was not at all reluctant to make an exhibition to the enemy of what manner of man he was. For the armor in which he was clad was abundantly plated with gold and the ample adornments which hung from his cheek-plates as well as from his helmet and spear were not only of purple but in other respects befitting a king, marvelous in their abundance.*

[82]ibid, p. 178.

[83]Boehm, Christopher. *Blood Revenge: The Enactment and Management of Conflict in Montenegro and other Tribal Societies*, Philadelphia, PA: University of Pennsylvania Press, (1984, 1987) 1991; p. 99f.

And he himself, sitting upon a very large horse, began to perform the dance under arms skillfully between the armies. For he wheeled his horse round in a circle and then turned him again to the other side and so made him run round and round. And as he rode he hurled his javelin into the air and caught it again as it quivered above him, then passed it rapidly from hand to hand, shifting it with consummate skill, and he gloried in his practice in such matters, falling back on his shoulders, spreading his legs and leaning from side to side, like one who has been instructed with precision in the art of dancing from childhood. By these tactics he wore away the whole early part of the day."[84]

(To put this into proper perspective, consider that an early 17th-century correspondent of the Fuggers found it worth mentioning that a circus rider performing at court was able to draw and sheath a sword in full gallop!)

These warriors were so skilled and so well conditioned in the martial arts that they were able to fight for extended periods of time against overwhelming odds. Another Ostrogoth, Teias, is a good example of the stamina of these fighters, even if he did not survive the fight. His main weapons, spear and shield, are standard weapons for the average Teutonic fighter of his age, requiring a high level of practice and expertise in pole-arm techniques.

"Now the battle began early in the morning, and Teias, easily recognized by all, stood with only a few followers at the head of the phalanx, holding his shield before him and thrusting forward his spear. And the Romans saw him, thinking that, if he himself should fall, the battle would be instantly decided in their favor, all those who laid claim to valor concentrated on him—and there was a great number of them—and they all directed their spears at him, some thrusting and others hurling them.

He himself meanwhile, covered by his shield, received all their spears in it, and by sudden charges he slew a large number. And whenever he saw that his shield was filled with spears fixed in it, he would hand this over to one of his guards and take another for himself. And he continued fighting in this manner for the third part of the day, and at the end of that time his shield had twelve spears stuck in it and he was no longer able to move it where he wished and repel his assailants.

So he eagerly called one of his bodyguards without leaving his post so much as a finger's breadth nor giving ground nor allowing the enemy to advance, nor even turning round and covering his back with his shield, nor, in fact, did he even turn sidewise, but as if fastened to the ground he stood there, shield in hand, killing with his right hand and parrying with his left and calling out the name of the bodyguard.

And the guard was now at his side with the shield, and Teias immediately sought to take this in exchange for the one weighed down with spears. But while he was doing so his chest became exposed for a brief instant of time, and it chanced that at that moment he was hit by a javelin and died instantly from the wound."[85]

[84]Procopius. ***History of the Gothic Wars*** (transl. Dewing, H.B.), viii.xxxi.17 f., Cambridge, MA and London: Harvard UP [Loeb Classical Library], (1928) 1992; p. 373f.

[85]ibid; p. 413f.

Wooden weapons

Since before the Roman Iron Age, the armory of the European warrior consisted mainly of pole arms and staff weapons: javelin, spear, lance, and staff—as well as highly specialized wooden swords.

During excavations at the Großes Moor between Damme and Hunteburg in Lower Saxony—about 10 km distance from Kalkriese, where the battle of the Teutoburg Forest is now thought to have taken place—several long wooden artifacts were found in August 1992 in the debris of a *Bohlenweg*, a trail made from wooden boards that was being excavated at the time. Archaeologists thought they were part of the wooden construction.

Chances are that this assumption would have remained unchallenged, if it hadn't been for Dr. Pit Pieper, a forensic archaeologist at the Heinrich-Heine-University of Düsseldorf.

During a discussion at the 1995 German Archaeologists Congress in Oldenburg, a replica of one of the artifacts was held up by one of the investigating scientists. Pieper saw no connection between the preceding lecture about wooden pathways and this obviously recent implement. He volunteered the opinion that this obviously represented a wooden blade with grip and pommel—thus, a kind of wooden sword, roughly analogous with the late medieval Dussack. (Only that the latter had a better grip construction.)

Master of his craft

A quick demonstration with this weapon illuminated *Haue* (cuts), *Huten* (parries), *Läger* (guards) as practiced with the Dussack, the hand-and-a-half sword, and the two-handed sword for the benefit of the archaeologists present—and sent Pieper off on a research venture that could revolutionize fencing history.

Pieper discovered that the replica he encountered at Oldenburg was not the only one of its kind. There were three or four similar pieces, all found in a charred section of the *Bohlenweg* near Damme. All had been sent to Schleswig for restoration and conservation. Exact replicas of each piece had been made prior to conservation. (A wise decision, considering the artifacts lost up to 30% of the mass during the process.)

Furthermore, there were three comparable wooden artifacts from the same area that had been discovered in 1892, all identified as carved pegs (*Pflöcke*).

The inventory

Further research revealed that some of the unidentified wooden implements could be categorized as weapons, most of them blunt, club-like impact weapons. Four of them, however, could only interpreted as swords.

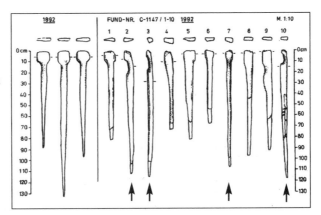

Weapon #2 described as "Sword", tip only lightly fragmented, handle cavation for 4 fingers; length: 112 cm; width of spine c. 4 cm; weight 1410 g. Cutting edge slightly flanged.

Weapon #3 described as "Rapier (Panzerstecher)", point slightly fragmented, handle narrow, cylindrical; length: 117 cm, rectangular; Handle length: 7 cm, blade width: 3 cm; weight: 1779 g; scorching in upper and lower areas.

Weapon #7 described as "Rapier (Panzerstecher)", barely fragmented, cylindrical handle; length: 107 cm, Length of pummel: c. 12 cm, width of pummel 7.5 cm, pommel thickness c. 5 cm; weight: 1242 g; square blade

Weapon #10 described as "Sword", blade fragmented by impact of cuts, handle "rarefied" (?); length: 118 cm, length of handle: 10 cm, blade width: 6.5 cm, spine: 34.5 cm; weight: 1484 g.

All weights and measurements before conservation!

Using 14 C carbon-dating, the finds from the Bohlenweg were pinpointed to a mean average of 2035 +/- 35 years, corresponding to the dendrochronological period between 50 B.C. and A.D. 15.

Morphology

Because of the presence of edges and points, all four sword-like weapons from the 1992 and three samples from the 1892 excavation can be considered cut and thrust weapons in the widest sense.

The blade morphology of four of these weapons (including all 1892 samples) could point at a predominant use as thrust weapons, whose broad bulbous widening at the grip end would allow to put the full body weight behind a thrust.

(Weapon #7 and the 1892er weapons could also have been used as mace if gripped by the blade. This blow with the pommel was later called *"aus dem Tag"*, executed from above against the head of the opponent. Another term for it was *Donnerschlag*—thunderclap.)

Weapons # 2, 3, and 10, however, described both as swords (*Schwerter*) and *Rapier/Panzerstecher*, have clearly defined edges whose morphology corresponds with modern weapons especially designed for the cut.

(A quick note on semantics. The word "cut" in English is used both synonymously with "blow" (German: *Hau* or *Hieb*), i.e., the blunt or sharp splitting impact of the edge, and in the sense of "slicing" (German: *Schnitt*), i.e., inflicting an injury by the incisive action of the blade that is caused and enhanced by the drawing motion of the arm and the curvature of the blade. [86])

Especially Weapon #3, characterized by a concave curve of the edge (what was later to be called a *Sensenschwert*, lit.: scythe sword) appears to reflect an extraordinary knowledge of percussive machanics. It roughly compares with an 108 cm long iron Danish sword from the Merovingian era. [87] But even more strikingly, it resembles the shape of the Turkish yataghan—which in itself reflects a high development of edged weapons sophistication.

According to Marey-Monge, the yataghan's blade *"acts by the weight of the part A [i.e., the foible], and the velocity due to the lightness of the weapon. Its curvature does not assist the cut."* [88] However, it *"is an excellent weapon for infantry; it cuts and thrusts well"*. [89] And due to its raised point, it was particularly suited for the curved thrust.

This shape makes full use of Marey's observation that *"in a cut made with full velocity, the blade at the moment it comes in contact with the body struck should lie in the direction of the fore-arm; it strikes in a direction nearly perpendicular to the prolongation of the origin of the blade. The greater the inclination of the part of the edge which strikes to that line, the greater will be the length of the mark left on the blade by the wound."* [90]

(Burton later commented that the yataghan's *"beautifully curved line of blade coincides accurately with the motion of the wrist in cutting."* [91])

The differentiation between cutting, thrusting, cut-and-thrust and percussive cutting weapons represented in this small sample belies modern-day assumption that Northern Europeans were oafish churls ignorant of the thrust and the mechanics of the sword in general.

The context

In A.D.15, six years after Germanic tribes under the Cheruskian Arminius (aka Hermann der Cherusker) smashed the invading Roman legions under Varus into red ruin in what is now known as the Battle of the Teutoburg Forest, Germanicus reportedly led a punitive expedition against the Germans. His mission: punish the offenders and recover and bury the remains of the dead Romans.

He succeeded in the latter, erecting a huge tumulus of the mortal remains. In his account of the campaign—which culminated in a sound thrashing of the Germans—Tacitus mentions the *pontes longi* (long bridges) in the vicinity of the encounter—a term that could refer to the long stretches of *Bohlenweg* across the North German moors.

The dating of the wooden implements, the location of the site, the excavation's proximity to Kalkriese, now though to have provided the setting for Varus annihilation, as well as the traces of battle use (cuts with metal weapons) on the weapons indeed could be interpreted that these weapons indeed could have been used by warriors fighting against Germanicus.

[86] See also, Marey-Monge, Col. (transl. Maxwell, Henry). *Memoir on Swords*, London: John Weale, 1860; p. 34: *"The blow of a man acts by contusion or laceration; the edge of a sword, by incision only. The point acts by incision and separation. The vertex of the angle having penetrated, the edges, if they be sharp, divide the substance by incision, while the thickness of the sides acts by separation. If the point be blunt at both edges, it penetrates by separation."*

[87] Demmin, August. *Die Kriegswaffen in ihrer geschichtlichen Entwicklung von den ältesten Zeiten bis auf die Gegenwart*, Gera-Untermhaus: Eugen Köhler, 1891; p. 341; fig. 59.2

[88] Marey here is discussing the use of the yataghan as an executioner's weapon. "Cut" here comprises the element of slicing, not exclusively the percussiove effect of the blow.

[89] Marey-Monge; p. 80.

[90] Marey-Monge; p. 13.

[91] Burton, Sir Richard. *The Book of the Sword*, London: Chatto & Windus, 1884; p. 134.

The use of the wooden swords itself allows for further speculation about the exact dating of the combative action whose traces are visible on some of the weapons. A newspaper article[92] quotes Pieper as saying that the Germans may have lost so many weapons against Varus that they had to use wooden swords as quick fixes—thus indicating that the weapons had seen action after Varus' illfated expedition.

This makes sense. But it must be considered that the Germans encountered during Germanicus' punitive expedition may have had nothing in common with those who annihilated Varus' legions.

Not only was Arminius' alliance a hodgepodge of tribal chieftains whose united effort could be focused on one communal effort before unraveling in petty Teutonic squabbles. The Germanic way of war at that point in time also centered around seasonal bursts of warlike activity, mainly aimed at plunder and booty.

In fact, the use of wooden weapons (six years after the battle) can be interpreted entirely differently—and yet support the date of A.D. 15.

After crushing Varus, the surviving warriors most certainly would have plundered the dead Romans, and carried off any artifact of value or practical application. Swords, due to their rarity among the Germanic tribes, would have been especially prized. (Metal implements may have been so scarce in Germania at the time that probably no scrap of enemy metal remained unrecycled.)

The forces encountered by Germanicus may not have been made up predominantly of Teutoburg veterans. Rather, they could have been recruited from fresh young warriors from the neighboring tribes who had not yet had the opportunity to acquire the coveted iron weapons from their slain enemies. This may also have accounted for their apparent inexperience in allowing themselves to be outmaneuvered and slaughtered by the Romans.

The right stuff?

In his report, Pieper speculates that the wooden swords—while definitely not misappropriated agricultural tools—must have been makeshift weapons, *"naturally inferior to the opponents' iron weapons."*

Pieper points out correctly that Roman legionaries were trained in the armatura, which included sword fighting training with the gladius. He believes that the direction of cut marks left on one of the clubs (2 parallel incisions) and on Weapon #10 (3 cuts from the same direction, plus one that took off part of the tip point at the legionaries' use of short, forceful beat attacks (battuts) against the

opposing blade, aimed at removing the dangerous points of the Germanic weapons or beating the weapon out of the way before closing in for the ripping upward attack with the gladius.

Both arguments appear not quite bullet-proof, however. For one, the Germanic wooden weapons cannot by definition be considered inferior to those of the Romans.

[92] *Welt am Sonntag*, March, 16, 1997.

Anyone who has ever blunted a hatchet while shaping a piece of dried oak will be aware that in certain cases, weapons made from oak are a definite match against iron or even steel weapons, even armor. (In fact, the incisions at near the handle of Weapon #10 could have been made *after* the tip of the sword was shorn off. They are much shallower and thus could indicate that the opposing edge was considerably blunted by the first cut.)

Furthermore, these cuts may not necessarily have been dealt in hand-to-hand combat of wooden sword vs. gladius. Leaving marks of this depth on a piece of dried oak requires a considerable amount of force, which may not have been caused by the short gladius, but rather by a horseman's spatha, swung with full force from horseback against the weapon raised in defense and maybe even suppured by both hands.

Superiority by definition

Lacking the slicing edge, the wooden swords could have made best use of a cleaver-like percussive effect, designed to break bones and crush tissue upon impact (particularly against the legs, arms, and neck of the legionnaire) rather than leaving clean, saber-like cuts.

If anything, they have a wider reach—negating the material advantage of the short cut-and-thrust gladius—and greater weight behind them, combining the functions of mace and broadsword.

The points are fire-hardened, and clearly designed to inflict maximum damage during penetration, again with the advantage of distance. Even after losing their points, the weapons would remain fully functional as war clubs, whereas a short sword with a broken point has little to offer to its wielder than two nicked hair-fine lines of edge. The tight, strong fibers of oak also pose an acute danger of entrapping and wedging an enemy blade in a chopping action into the grain— which then could be wrested from the hand or broken.

But swords would have been a secondary weapon at any rate, used only after the fighters would have closed in "fencing" distance. Another weapon found in the vicinity, would have had a far more devastating effect in the medium range.

Referred to as *"hasta ingens"* and *"hasta enorma"* (enormous lance) by Tacitus, a specimen was found and identified in the respective dig. (See below.)

While this weapon has thus far not been analyzed in detail, its very measurements indicate that it was a horrific implement of war: 2.5 m (nearly 8'!) long, 10 cm wide, with a "clipped" point 50 cm long. (Given the position of the handle, the illustration might actually show the lance upside down.)

It is not hard to put this murderous weapon in context with Tacitus' remark about *"hasta ingentes ad vulnera facienda quamvis procul"*, mighty lances that struck wounds even at great distance. [93]

The combined effect of weight and percussive impact of this weapon might have been sufficient to crush a legionnaire's helmet and skull at medium range. Its

[93]Tacitus. Publius Cornelius. *Tacitus III: Histories IV-V, Annals I-III,* Cambridge, MA and London: Harvard UP, [1931] 1979; p. 353 (*Annals, liber 1, 64*) .

long, fire-hardened point would have been used for blunt impact on armored body parts as well as sharp, penetrating thrusts…without allowing the Roman to get into striking distance!

A weapon of these dimensions, used for cut and thrust, would have required enormous strength and skill to handle… and necessitated a two-handed, naginata-like technique[94]. Fighters would have needed wide berth to handle the hastas.

During the battle of Idistaviso in A.D. 15 , where the warriors were massed so densely that they could not handle their weapons to their fullest potential.[95] Germanicus advised his soldiers that the proper tactics for selecting the battle-grounds also would focus on woods and bushland, *"because the giant shields[96] of the barbarians and their enormous lances could not be handled as well among tree trunks and bush as the pila, gladii, and the close-fitting body armor."*[97]

The Germans fought without helmets, body armor, their shields were made of woven willow branches or thin boards.

Of course, if a warrior handling a 2.5 m-long weapon needed two hands, he would open himself up to enemy action. This problem could have been solved by a shield carrier, a team-up well documented among Germanic warriors of later periods.[98]

Revolutionary discovery

Before this backdrop, the importance of Pieper's discovery cannot be overstated. The existence of wooden, Dussack-shaped swords predating the Fechtmesser and Dussack proper by 1,300 years serves to establish the existence of specialized cut-and-thrust weapons (and the implied skill levels required to wield them) in an era that has thus far been considered a wasteland of edged-weapons fighting skills.

The morphological characteristics point at a deliberate, highly sophisticated approach to optimizing the respective functional qualities of the weapon—designed specifically to fulfill tasks its makers clearly grasped and applied consequently.

The easy and low-cost availability of these weapons also implies that a warrior could practice weapon-oriented sparring without consideration of the enormous cost represented by a bronze or iron blade.

Wood would allow defending and parrying *with* the weapon as in the later Dussack system, rather than avoiding the opponent's blows. This points at the possible existence of a sophisticated agonistic combat system—the roots of "fencing" with the Fechtmesser or Dussack in Northern Europe.

[94]It appears that Northern warriors appreciated the advantages of the two-handed approach to sword fighting. Demmin comments on the enormous tang lengths of certain German and Swiss scra-masaxes, which could measure between 15-25cm. (See Demmin, p. 329.)

[95]Tacitus; *Annals,* p. 413 (liber 2, 21).

[96]Demmin illustrates a Germanic shield 8 feet (!) high and 2 feet wide. (Demmin, p. 295)—then shows the figure of a warrior with a chest-high shield. Since an 8-foot shield would be useless in close combat, I assume he got his numbers mixed up or is using a measure that does not translate.

[97]*"nec enim immensa barbaro-rum scuta, enormis hastas inter truncos arborum et enata humo virgulta perinde haberi quam pila et gladios et haerentia cor-pore tegmina."* in *Annals,* p. 405 (liber 2, 14).

[98]Cf. the battle death of Teias in Procopius. *History of the Gothic Wars*, Cambridge, MA and London: Harvard UP [Loeb Classical Library], (1928) 1992; p. 413 f.

INTERLUDE

COMMENT COMBAT
Prize Fight with Sharp Weapons

Figg's trading card, ascribed to Hogarth (19th-century)

Trial of Skill, July 16, 1712[99]

Being a Person of insatiable Curiosity, I could not forbear going on Wednesday last to a Place of no small Renown for the Gallantry of the lower Order of Britons, namely, to the Beargarden at Hockley in the Hole; where (as a whitish brown Paper, put into my Hands in the Street, inform'd me) there was to be a Tryal of Skill to be exhibited between two Masters of the Noble Science of Defence, at two of the Clock precisely. I was not little charm'd with the Solemnity of the Challenge, which ran thus:

> *I, James Miller, Serjeant, (lately come from the Frontiers of Portugal), Master of the Noble Science of Defence, hearing in most Places where I have been of the great Fame of Timothy Buck of London, Master of the said Science, do invite him to meet me, and exercise at the several Weapons following, viz.*
>
> | | |
> |---|---|
> | *Back-Sword* | *Single Falchon* |
> | *Sword and Dagger* | *Case of Falchons* |
> | *Sword and Buckler* | *Quarter-Staff* |

If the generous Author in James Miller to dispute the Reputation of Timothy Buck, had nothing resembling the old Heroes of Romance, Timothy Buck return'd Answer in the same Paper with the like Spirit, adding a little Indignation at being challenged, and seeming to condescend to fight James Miller, not in regard to

[99] Steele, Sir Richard. *The Spectator*, No. 436, July 21, 1712 in Addison, Steele & others, Smith, Gregory (ed.) *The Spectator, In Four Volumes*, vol. iii, London: Dent [Everyman's Library], New York: Dutton (1907) 1967; p. 348f.

Miller himself, but in that, as the Fame went out, he had fought Parkes of Coventry. The acceptance of the Combat ran in these Words:

> *I, Timothy Buck of Clare-Market, Master of the Noble Science of Defence, hearing he did fight Mr. Parkes of Coventry, will not fail (God willing) to meet this fair inviter at the Time and Place appointed, desiring a clear Stage and no Favour.*

Vivat regina.

(...) It was carried with great Order. James Miller came out first; preceded by two disabled Drummers, to shew, I suppose, that the Prospect of maimed Bodies did not in the least deter him. There ascended with the daring Miller a Gentleman, whose Name I could not learn, with a dogged Air, as unsatisfied that he was not Principal. This Son of Anger lowred at the whole Assembly, and weighing himself as he march'd around from Side to Side with a stiff Knee and Shoulder, he gave Intimations of the Purpose he smothered till he saw the Issue of this Encounter.

Miller had a blue Ribbond tyed around the Sword Arm; which Ornament I conceive to be the Remain of that Custom of wearing a Mistress's Favour on such Occasions of Old. [100]

Miller is a Man of six Foot eight Inches Height, of a kind but bold aspect, well-fashioned, and ready of his Limbs; and such Readiness as spoke his Ease in them, was obtained from a Habit of Motion in Military Exercise.

The Expectations of the Spectators was now almost at its Height, and the Crowd pressing in, several active Persons thought they were placed rather according to their Fortune than their Merit, and took it in their heads to prefer themselves in the open Area, or Pit, to the Galleries. This Dispute between Desert and Property brought many to the Ground, and raised others in proportion to the highest Seats by Turns for the Space of ten Minutes, till Timothy Buck came on, and the whole Assembly giving up their Disputes, turned their Eyes upon the Champions. Then it was that every Man's Affection turned to one or the other irresistably. A judicious Gentleman near me said, "I could, methinks, be Miller's Second, but I had rather have Buck for mine."

Miller had an audacious Look that took the Eye; Buck a perfect Composure, that engaged the Judgment. Buck came on in a plain Coat, and kept all his Air till the Instant of Engaging; at which Time he undress'd to his Shirt, his Arm adorned with a Bandage of red Ribband. No one can describe the sudden Concern in the whole Assembly; the most tumultous Crowd in Nature was as still and as much engaged, as if all their Lives depended on the first Blow.

The Combatants met in the Middle of the Stage, and shaking Hands as removing all Malice, they retired with much Grace to the Extremities of it; from whence they immediately faced about, and approach'd each other, Miller with a Heart full of Resolution, Buck with a watchful untroubled Countenance; Buck regarding principally his own Defence, Miller chiefly thoughtful of annoying his Opponent. It is not easy to describe the many Escapes and imperceptible Defences [101] between the two Men of quick Eyes and ready Limbs; but Miller's Heat laid him open to the Rebuke of the calm Buck, by a large Cut on the

[100]Steele is romanticising. The different-colored ribbons are armigers—which still adorned the Great Figg and the other 18th-century prize fighters.

[101]This is a particularly interesting comment, considering that the techniques used by the Masters of Defence are usually ridiculed as clumsy and old-fashioned by most modern writers whose command of language is much less acute than that of Steele.

Forehead. Much Effusion of Blood covered his Eyes in a Moment and the Huzzas of the Crowd undoubtedly quickened the Anguish. The Assembly was divided into Parties upon their different ways of Fighting; while a poor Nymph in one of the Galleries apparently suffered for Miller, and burst into a Flood of Tears.

As soon as his Wound was wrapped up, he came on again with a little Rage, which disabled him still further. But what brave Man can be wounded into more Patience and Caution? The next was a warm, eager Onset which ended in a decisive Stroke on the left Leg of Miller. The Lady in the Gallery, during this second Strife, covered her Face; and for my Part, I could not keep my Thoughts from being mostly employed on the Consideration of her unhappy Circumstance that Moment, hearing the Clash of Swords, and apprehending Life or Victory concerned her Lover in every Blow, but not daring to satisfy herself on whom they fell.

The Wound was exposed to the View of all who could delight in it, and sowed up on the Stage. The surly Second of Miller declared at this Time, that he would that Day Fortnight fight Mr. Buck at the same Weapons, declaring himself the Master of the renowned Gorman; but Buck denied him the Honour of that courageous Disciple, and asserting that he himself had taught that Champion, accepted the Challenge.

There is something in Nature very unaccountable on such Occasions, when we see the People take a certain painful Gratification in beholding these Encounters. Is it Cruelty that administers this Sort of Delight? Or is it a Pleasure which is taken in the Exercise of Pity? It was methought pretty remarkable, that the Business of the Day being a Trial of Skill, the Popularity did not run so high as one would have expected on the Side of Buck. Is it that People's Passions have their Rise in Self-love, and thought themselves (in Spite of all the Courage they had) liable to the Fate of Miller, but could so easily think themselves qualified like Buck?

ADVENTURES IN
LOST COMBAT ARTS 6

Victorian impression of
a 14th-century battle

Carnage at Wisby

*"Hacon the Jarl and many of his men sat on a tree trunk and a bowstring twanged
on Bui's ship; the arrow fell on Gissur of Valders, a lord of the land, who sat nearest
the jarl, and was proudly clad. Some went on board the ship and found Howard the
Hewer standing on his knees by the ship's bulwark, for his legs were smitten from him:
He had the bow in his hand. And when they came out on the ship, Howard asked,
'Who fell from the tree trunk?' They said that he was called Gissur. 'Then was my luck
less than I would.' — 'That bad luck was great enough,' they said, 'and thou shalt not
do more', and they slew him."*[102]

By all standards, Howard the Hewer should have died right after receiving a
sword or ax stroke that took both his lower legs off at or below the knee.
He should have bled to death within minutes, or at least been knocked out
of commission by shock, to die a miserable ignominious death of exsanguination
and hypothermia sometime before the sun rose over the lead-gray depths of the
Northern Ocean again.

Yet he survives the horrible injury long enough to see the end of battle,
observe his enemies assemble on the beach, scrounge his devastated ship's deck for
a bow and arrow—and then shoot the man he mistakenly believed to be the leader
of his foe . . . all the while balancing on the bleeding stumps of his legs!

[102]Sturlason, Snorri.
***Heimskringla, or, The Lives
of the Norse Kings,*** New York:
Dover, 1990; p. 149; (first
published as Monsen, Erling
(ed.). ***Heimskringla, or The
Lives of the Norse Kings by
Snorri Sturlason,*** Cambridge:
W. Heffer, 1932.)

They've gotta be kidding...

The Nordic sagas—compilations of near-compulsive raids, battles, treachery, murder and mayhem—abound with descriptions of single and mass combat in which mortal enemies deal blows that make a Yukon lumberjack competition look like a tipsy gay pride parade on Halloween in San Francisco.

The modern mind, carefully screened from things truly ugly and gut-wrenching, cringes at the very thought of injuries like the one sustained by Howard.

In fact, questions may arise as to the veracity of the accounts contained in the old Norse sagas. Flesh wounds we might accept. But a stroke ferocious enough to shear off both legs at once as if they were straws must be the result of heroic bragging. (After all, how many modern fencers have managed to cut through a rolled-up newspaper with a sharp replica weapon...?)

Historians of the pre-Kegan school have traditionally cared very little about the lot of the individuals, their skills, lives, and deaths that provided the backdrop for the sandbox games of the strategists. Accordingly, vivid battle lore barely registered in the illustrious minds, discredited as the tall tales of impolite barbarians.

But since the 1930s, archaeological evidence has backed up the savage tall tales down to details.

Killing field

During large-scale excavations in the 1930s, Bengt Thordemann, in collaboration with Dahlberg and Sjövall, determined that the mass graves at Wisby contained the bodies of approximately 1,800 warriors. Only 64% of those killed were deemed fit for military service, whereas 22% are considered too young, and 14% too old to have been part of a professional fighting force. Thordemann thus believes that the entire male population of the area had been mustered to fight off the invaders that fateful July 27th, 1361.

Weapons used to dispatch the men of Wisby to Valhalla apparently were swords, axes, crossbows, morning stars, maces and lances, possibly even war hammers. The defending Gotlanders probably also used emergency weapons such as sticks, and clubs. Yet despite indications of a rain of arrows, Thordemann states:

"Injuries from cutting weapons (swords and axes) are by far the most numerous and occur in 456 cases."[103]

Of course, there are some difficulties attached to deduce fighting techniques from the nature of the wounds. For one, it is impossible to tell if a wound was caused by the blade of a sword or a battle-ax. Furthermore, the injuries recorded only represent a potentially

[103]Thordemann, Bengt. *Armor from the Battle of Wisby, 1361, Stockholm:* Kungl. Vitterhets Historie och Antikvitets Akademien, 1939; p. 160.

very small part of the actual number of injuries received, as only very powerful blows would be able to cut through armor, clothes, and flesh to leave marks—or even sever—bones:

Still, the number of bodies with evidence of powerful cut injuries is striking:

"Bearing in mind the remarkable toughness and strength which a live bone possesses, we are astonished at the enormous force with which some of the blows must have been struck."[104]

But back to Howard

Based on the forensic evidence of Wisby, Thordemann found that there are far more injuries to the lower extremities than to the upper ones. Cut injuries to the arms amount to only 15% of the total—a fact that can be attributed to the use of shields. (Even though the heroes of the sagas frequently make short shrift of shields...)

Among the lower extremities, injuries to the tibia amount to a whopping 65% of the total, with femur at 14.3% and fibula at 19.3%.

"The reason why the tibia has received so many injuries from blows is probably because this bone lies in a very superficial and exposed position and is only protected by a thin covering of flesh, and also that the armor did not reach to this part of the body."[105]

A cynic might add that hits against the shins hurt, no matter if they're dealt with a sharp or blunt object. That's because the deep peroneal nerve, a.k.a. anterior tibial nerve, lies exposed on the surface of the tibia from a point about seven inches below the knee all the way down to the front of the ankle:

"An unusually sharp pain results, which in addition to weakening the whole leg, also paralyzes the muscles which flex the foot and toes upward. (...) Severe trauma to this nerve will produce 'footdrop', a condition where the toes drag on the ground with every forward step, greatly reducing the opponent's mobility."[106]

Still, we are not talking about a whack against the shins. Howard's legs have both been cut off. While Thordemann adduces berserk battle frenzy for the vehemence of a cut like this, it must be noted that this injury that is not exactly rare in the sagas of the manly North.

Njal's Saga[107] records at least 11 cases of such drastic amputations of the lower extremities, ranging from a cut-off toe (chapter 145) and a ripped-open thigh (chapter 145) to legs "swept off", "sliced off", "severed above the knee" (chapters 17, 82, 129), and at the thigh (chapter 99), and "mid-thigh" (chapters 146, 151).

Egil's Saga[108] presents two cases of legs severed. One appears incidental, when Egil pursues one of King Eirik Bloodaxe's posse:

[104]Thordemann; p. 163.

[105]Thordemann; p. 167.

[106]Mashiro, N. *Black Medicine—The Dark Art of Death,* Boulder, CO: Paladin Press, 1978; p. 80.

[107]Magnusson, Magnus and Palsson, Hermann (transl. & edd.) *Njal's Saga,* London and NY: Penguin, 1960.

[108]Palsson, Hermann and Edwards, Paul (transl. & edd.) *Egil's Saga,* London and NY: Penguin, 1976.

"He was trying to climb a slope, but Egil hewed at him, slicing his leg off."[109]

Chapter 17[110] also illustrates one tactical approach a fighter would take against a superior opponent: When faced with a berserk in an *einvigi* (a formal variety of single combat), Egil strikes rapid blows against his opponent, keeping him from hitting back. After a brief rest, Egil again rushes against his opponent, getting *"so close that Ljot stepped back, and his shield didn't cover him. Then Egil smote him above the knee and cut off his leg. Ljot fell, and at once died."*

Thordemann's described one find, Reg.no. Db 7—which is the lower part of a right leg, which has been severed by a single blow that passed obliquely through the fibula, tibia, the upper part of the talus, and the medial part of the *tuber calcanei.*

Loss of limb

Sudden death[111] as a result of a cut-off leg frequently features in *Njal's Saga,* although it is not the rule. Sometimes, there was time for well-placed sarcasm:

> *"Kolskegg whirled round and lept at him, swung at his thigh with the short-sword, and cut off Kol's leg.*
> *'Did that one land or not?' asked Kolskegg.*
> *'That's my reward for not having my shield,' said Kol. He stood for a moment on one leg, looking down at the stump.*
> *'You don't need to look,' said Kolskegg. 'It's just as you think—the leg is off.'*
> *Then Kol fell dead on the ground."*[112].

There's even two men who suffer the same fate as Howard:

> *"Then Ogmund Tangle-Hair sprang at Gunnar from behind, but Kolskegg saw it and swept both his legs off, and then pushed him into the river, where he drowned at once."*[113]

And later *"Kari ran at Vebrand and drove his sword through him, and then hacked both legs from under Asbrand."*[114]

Thordemann backs up these accounts with the description of a skeleton found at Wisbyand depicted on page 192.

> *"...in situ, the lower extremities of a man who had both lower legs cut off, probably by a single blow which struck the right tibia from below on its ventral side and the left tibia on its inside. The cut penetrated almost to the medullary cavity of both tibiae..."*

Interestingly, the weapons used to cut off other people's legs in the sagas are usually not the heavy battle axes so popular with the Nordic he-men of the period. They are swords. The wound typically occurs as a result of one fighter losing his shield—either by having it chopped to bits, or his opponent cutting through the lower part of the shield or, as in Egil's case, forcing the attack so the shield is held too close to the body.

[109] *Egil's Saga;* Chapter 45; p. 103.

[110] quoted after Oakeshott, R. Ewart. *The Archaeology of Weapons—Arms and Armor from Prehistory to the Age of Chivalry,* New York and London: Frederick A. Praeger, 1960; p. 157.

[111] Of course, it is difficult to verify that death occurred instantly. The swoon and loss of consciousness as a result of shock and sudden drop in blood pressure may not have constituted death in the technical sense, but be taken for death by the survivor who had to report on the incident.

[112] *Njal's Saga,;* chapter 62; p. 149.

[113] *Njal's Saga,;* chapter 72; p. 162.

[114] *Njal's Saga,;* chapter 151; p. 337.

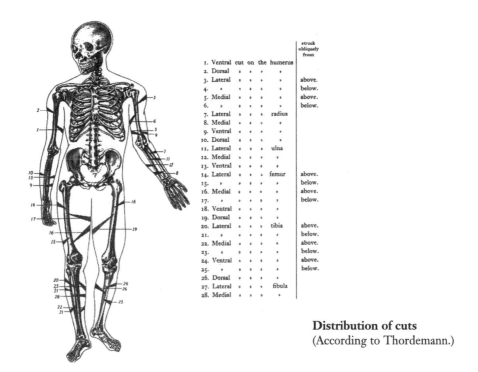

		struck obliquely from
1. Ventral cut on the humerus		
2. Dorsal " " " "		
3. Lateral " " " "		above.
4. " " " " "		below.
5. Medial " " " "		above.
6. " " " " "		below.
7. Lateral " " " radius		
8. Medial " " " "		
9. Ventral " " " "		
10. Dorsal " " " "		
11. Lateral " " " ulna		
12. Medial " " " "		
13. Ventral " " " "		
14. Lateral " " " femur		above.
15. " " " " "		below.
16. Medial " " " "		above.
17. " " " " "		below.
18. Ventral " " " "		
19. Dorsal " " " "		
20. Lateral " " " tibia		above.
21. " " " " "		below.
22. Medial " " " "		above.
23. " " " " "		below.
24. Ventral " " " "		above.
25. " " " " "		below.
26. Dorsal " " " "		
27. Lateral " " " fibula		
28. Medial " " " "		

Distribution of cuts
(According to Thordemann.)

It is therefore safe to assume that at least a large number of severe bone injuries documented at Wisby was caused by swords...

Making headway!

In the sagas, head injuries are frequently the result of ax blows rather than swords. The skulls of Wisby bear testimony to the devastating power of these weapons—illustrating that the larger-than-life accounts of the skalds and poets were firmly rooted in reality.

Here's a short sampler of cranial injuries discovered at Wisby:

- cranium with several cuts, the most severe of which, striking sagittally from above, cut off a large portion of the left part of the cranium.
- cranium with injuries caused by both arrows and blows, where a large part of the calotte has been detached. The most powerful blow was struck horizontally, obliquely from behind, and from the left.
- cranium bearing the marks of a powerful blow that was struck frontally from above, cutting off a portion of the parietal bone, and the occipital bone.
- cranium with several cuts which have caused a large part of the calotte to drop off.

To compare: In *Beowulf*, Ongentheow fights against Wulf and Hygelac:

"Wulf son of Wondred smote at him wrathfully with his weapon, so that the blood spurted out from the veins on his forehead at the stroke. Yet was the old Scylfing in no wise daunted, but quickly dealt out a worse return for that murderous blow, when the mighty king turned on his adversary. The brave

son of Wondred had no chance to deal a counter-blow at the Old man, for Ongenthiow cut through the helmet he wore, and he had to give way and fall to the earth covered in blood; yet he was not doomed and he survived, though the wound had touched him close. Then when his brother lay low, the valiant thane of Hygelac let his broad blade, his ancient sword of giants, strike against the wall of the shield, shattering the helmet which giants made; and then the king, the people's guardian, fell with a mortal wound."[115]

Chin up!

In the battle of Bravoll in Eastern Gotland between Harald Hilditonn and Sigurd Hring, Vebjorg, a shield maiden, attacked Soknarsoti, and with a blow at his cheek cut through his jaw and chin. He put his beard into his mouth and bit down on it to keep his lower face from dangling down and fought on.

Thordemann describes the cranium of an old, almost toothless man, partially remaining in the mail coif. He had received a very powerful cut on the lower maxilla, so that a large part of the alveolar process was gone.

At Wisby, *"only fifteen cuts are to be found on the lower maxilla (...) The blows were all very powerful and nine completely severed the lower maxilla; they are evenly distributed to the right and left sides. (...) Most of the cuts (10) strike vertico-horizontally from above. The horizontal ones (3) have all cut off a longer or shorter piece of the alveolar process.*"[116]

On the skulls, the cuts on the right side amount only to 31% of the total—whereas the corresponding figure for all the bones of the extremities is 42%. This difference is *"explained by the fact that many of the cuts were made by blows aimed for the left side, which, however, did not strike the left extremities but the right ones, which were therefore wounded on the inside.*"[117]

We may thus be able to deduce certain facts about the fighting style from the documentable wounds.

The case of Meister Hildebrand

Meister Hildebrand, the instructor and companion of Didrik von Bern, is said to have mastered the technique of a single sword cut against which there was no way of defense (much like the mysterious *Botte secreta* advertised by Italian fencing masters in the Renaissance).[118] Another of Didrik's fighters, Fasholt, also finishes most fights with one cut against the helmet.

Let us briefly consider how that would have worked. Hildebrand, armed with sword and shield and wearing a helmet, would be facing an equally equipped opponent who at the moment of Hildebrand's attack would have had the advantage of three defensive weapons: his sword, his shield, and his helmet.

Trying to cleave the shield was a risky undertaking: The sagas tell of swords and spears being damaged, or the blade wedged in the wood—and then wrested from the attacker's grasp by the defender's twisting of the shield![119] The shield could not only be used to block the blow, but to deflect it by adjusting the angle of impact.

[115]As quoted in Ellis Davidson, H.R. ***The Sword in Anglo-Saxon England***, Woodbridge: The Boydell Press, 1994; p. 195.

[116]Thordemann; p. 185.

[117]Thordemann; p. 166.

[118] *"Meister Hildebrand hatte das Ding voraus vor allen Kämpen, daß er den Hieb mit dem Schwert versteht, daß kein Mann dem mit dem Schild zuvorkommen konnte, wo er nur zum Kampf kommt. Und meistens erringt er den Sieg auf einen Hieb".* (Mb 187), quoted after Ritter-Schaumburg, Heinz. ***Die Nibelungen zogen nordwärts,*** München and Berlin: Herbig, 1980; p. 115.

[119]*Njal's Saga*; chapter 45; p. 117, and chapter 77; p. 170.

Fighters like *Njal's Saga's* Gunnar, Kari, and Skarp-Hedin were masters of time cuts against the blade or haft of the weapon, as well as the arm wielding it. Unless it was unavoidable, the sword's edge was not used for parrying:

"It was only when the shield had been so cut up that it was useless that one used one's sword to parry with, and then one would try only to use the flat of it, for if sword-edge clashed with edge much damage resulted. This is in fact what happened to Kormac, for he parried the stroke of Bersi's Hviting with Sköfnung's edge; Hviting's point broke off, and Sköfnung got a bad nick in the blade, which caused Kormac a deal of worry (because it was Skeggi's sword) and greatly annoyed Skeggi." [120]

Attacking, a man like Hildebrand therefore would have two options: aim at a target not covered by any defensive weapon. Or actively divert the main defensive weapon (the shield) by way of a feint, then cut into the opening. On the defense, Hildebrand would have had to evade or parry the opponent's attack, and then securely riposte into an opening. Both solutions would have required excellent control of the blade and body. In short, he would have to be a skilled swordsman.

Oakeshott comments:

"It was very important to be able to change the direction of your stroke at the instant you saw that it was going to miss its target, even if this meant turning a downward blow into an upward one, or a forehand to a backhand." [121]

Fasholt, on the other hand, preferred the direct cut against the opponent's helmet, which not only knocked out most enemies but usually killed them outright. Thordemann observes:

"As 80% of the blows struck vertically from above belong to the group 'not more than one cut', it indicates that these blows were difficult to strike. For [this group] the fronto-sagittal cuts predominate (57%) as was to be expected, and the sagittal ones include about a quarter of the single cuts, where as the transverse ones are not quite one fifth." [122]

We have to keep in mind that an opponent is not a post but tries to evade, parry or block with his shield. Being a skilled fighter, he would also have known where his opponent was going to strike. How comes a man like Fasholt could beat most warriors to the punch? There must have been more to it than brute strength.

In a warrior society where individual feats of arms were the cornerstone of a man's reputation, any botto secreta would have had limited shelf life. It is said that both Hildebrand and Fasholt not once felled a man using his technique, but as a rule succeeded in defeating any opponent with one cut.

This would only have been possible if they had been able to adapt their attack to the respective technique of the attacker, i.e. if they had mastered the elements of an Art of Defence.

[120] Oakeshott; p. 159.

[121] Oakeshott; p. 158.

[122] Thordemann; p. 184f.

Mobile combat

Thordemann enlists the help of Major Nils Hellsten of Stockholm to reconstruct the way of fighting:

> *"The warriors carried their shield on their left arm and held their sword (or ax) in their right hand. The left foot was placed a little in front of the right one. When attacking each other, the combatants took a step or a jump forward. The first blow was generally aimed straight down or from the attacked man's right-hand side. In nearly all cases, the attacked warrior was able to ward off this first blow by means of his shield and at the same time he generally brought the sword of the attacking warrior over to his left side.*
>
> *This was made use of by the latter in such a way that he aimed his second blow obliquely downwards to the left-hand side. If this blow was not warded off it struck the left half of the head and body, the lateral side of the left leg, and the medial side of the right leg, this last, however, being less probable as the left leg was in front of the right one. This second blow was considerably more difficult to parry, which is probably one of the most important reasons for the difference in percentage between right- and left-sided cuts. (...)"*[123]

In his otherwise excellent book *The Viking Art of War*[124], Paddy Griffith tries to characterize the Viking way of edged-weapons combat:

> *"The impression we get of Viking 'fencing' is therefore that they must have used their swords in rather the same way that they used their axes—in a series of heroic great swings with the full weight of the whole man and his weapon behind each. The weapons' edges were kept sharp, but they would probably not have had much less effect even if they had been blunt. They were for cleaving shields, or skulls, or arms, or legs rather than for any delicate finesse of rapier play. The tempo of the action would therefore have been slow and deliberate— a forester's 'chop...chop...chop' rather than a chef's rapid and fluid swish-wish-wish...' as he sharpens his carving knife."*[125]

Even without the unfortunate home-ec analogy and the over-used cliché of "finesse", Griffith's observations are valid only for the initial phases of combat. In mêlée and life-and-death scenarios, it is of course ludicrous to assume that each fighter paused after the cut to give his opponent the opportunity to pay him back in kind. (Apart from the fact that real-life fights with the rapier probably comprised more time of observant inactivity than the rapid-motion "finesse" of Errol Flynn may suggest.)

In pitched conflict, a fighter not only would watch out for his kinsmen as well as for himself, he would also be able to rapidly switch attack against one or several opponents, fight two-handed with sword and ax, spear and sword, or ax and spear, defend against multiple opponents in front of and behind him, as well as block, parry, and evade attacks by jumping, vaulting, and pivoting.

[123]Thordemann; p. 166.

[124]Griffith, Paddy. *The Viking Art of War*, London: Greenhill Books and Mechanicsburg, PA: Stackpole Books, 1995.

[125]Griffith; p. 174.

Oakeshott gives a clearer description:

"... as in modern wrestling and boxing, a good deal of preliminary maneu-
vering and feinting took place before one combatant or the other aw his
opportunity and smote. The other would then defend himself either by taking
the blow on his shield, or by evasive action such as ducking or dodging or
leaping aside—often he would leap right over the stroke, for it was always
a good idea to go for your opponent's leg below the shield."[126]

Backed up by the evidence at Wisby, the Norse and Icelandic sagas present
us with a very accurate picture of the state of Northern European martial arts in
the Middle Ages.

Cutting steel

There are a few modern parallels that could throw some light on how fighters
managed to shear through solid bone, even steel. Medieval samurai in Japan tested
the quality of a new blade by subjecting it to a—from a modern, Western perspective — gruseome rigmarole: A specialist would take condemned criminals, often
in groups of two, and systematically execute clearly defined cuts against their living
bodies, until there was not a piece of human flesh left larger than the size of a hand.
He then would sign the *nakago* (tang) in gold, complete with date, place, the number
and nature of cuts.[127]

In the West, one of the last writers to devote space to sword tricks is Professor
of Fencing J.M. Waite[128], "late of the Second Life Guards".

The purpose of one of his exercise is to ut a bar of lead in two at one stroke,
practicing how to apply force and edge and finishing the cut with speed. Key to
success are free delivery, true edge, and the precision required to strike an object
with the center of percussion at great velocity. Here's how it works:

"The best sized sword for a man of average strength is one weighing 3
1/4 lbs., with a blade 1 3/4" wide and 31" long (...) A weak man would
cut better with a smaller [weapon], and a very powerful man would find a
larger one more suitable.
The bar of lead (...) should be about 12" long and triangular (equilateral)
in shape with flat ends, so that you can stand it on one end. It may be either
suspended or stood on the top of a table or stool; I prefer the latter way, as it
is not so steady when suspended. (...)
Having taken your distance, throw your hand quickly back into the bend
of the left arm and on to the left shoulder to get an impetus, and keeping both
feet firm on the ground, deliver a horizontal cut from left to right as rapidly
as possible, using the elbow and forearm freely, and throwing the weight of
your body into the cut. Arm straight and point of the sword to your right
front at the finish of the cut.
In cutting, the wrist should be well sunk, the upper knuckles turned up,
and a firm grip of the sword maintained, particularly at the moment the
sword strikes the lead. The sword, with the edge leading, should not be

[126]Oakeshott; p. 158.

[127]See Craig, Darrell. *Iai:*
The Art of Drawing the
Sword, Rutland, VT and
Tokyo: Charles E. Tuttle Co.,
1981; p. 135 f.

[128]See Waite; pp. 125 ff.

turned in the slightest degree, but kept on a level line so that the cut will be perfectly horizontal. (...) A little tallow on your sword will show you what part of the blade you cut with, and will also slightly assist the cut.

The lead (...) may (...) also be cut with a downward chop: the way in which Coeur de Lion is said to have cut the handle of a steel mace."

Waite also wreaks havoc on sheep carcasses, and teaches how to cut an apple wrapped in a silk handkerchief... without damaging the latter.

The way of the staff

But even wooden weapons have horrendous effects. The martial tradition of quarterstaff fighting, popularized in ballads and songs, dates from these early days. But the merry cudgeling romanticized in the songs of Robin Hood tempts the historian to forget that the quarterstaff in fact was a terrible weapon. J.C. Holt produces some statistics from Robin Hood's home county to document the effect of the staff as a weapon:

"In the 103 cases of murder and manslaughter presented to the coroners of Nottinghamshire between 1485 and 1558 the staff figured in 53, usually as the sole fatal weapon. The sword, in contrast, accounted for only nine victims and one accidental death.[129]

He goes on to quote a particularly grisly passage from the *Calendar of Nottinghamshire's Coroners' Inquests 1485-1558*:

"On 4 September (1527) John Strynger (...) assaulted Henry Pereson (...) with a staff (...) which he held in both hands, striking him on the top of the head so that his brains flowed out and giving him a wound 1 inch deep, 2 inches wide, and 3 inches long of which he immediately died."[130]

Swetnam (1617)

[129]In Holt, J.C. **Robin Hood**, London and New York: Thames and Hudson, (1982) 1989; p. 170.

[130]In Hunnisett, R.F. (ed.). **Thoroton Society**, Record Series, xxv, 1969, no. 82.

[131]Aylward, J.D. **The English Master of Arms,** London: Routledge, 1956; p. 26.

The staff usually proved to be the superior weapon if pitched against the sword in direct combat. Aylward recounts how the quarterstaff-armed *"John Peeke of Travistock fought three Spanish rapier-and-dagger men at once in the presence of the Duke of Medina-Sidonia at Xeres, and defeated them all."*[131]

Terry Brown inlcudes what appears to be an updated period account of the episode in his English Martial Arts:

> *"Armed with the weapon of his choice Peeke stood ready to meet his nect challenger. However, the Spanish were clearly no longer so confident in the prowess of their soldiers for, to Peeke's consternation, two swordsmen stepped forward to fight him. Peeke sarcastically asked if more would join them. The Duke of Medina asked how many he desired to fight. 'Any number under sixe,' replied Peeke.*
>
> *The Duke smiled scornfully and beckoned a third man to join the original two. Peeke and the rapier men warily traversed each other, all the while thrusting and warding, till finally Peeke gambled on an all-out attack. His first blow left one of his adversaries dead, and his subsequent blows left the other two injured and disarmed. (. . .) Peeke's feat so impressed his Spanish captors that they released him and granted him safe conduct to England."*[132]

As late as the 1730s, Roderick Random and his friend Strap arm themselves "with a good cudgel each" before setting out on the dangerous trip to London, more than once offering satisfaction by boxing and cudgeling. Had fencing history indeed been one of linear Darwinist evolution, where the superior system survived, modern fencing tournaments would be fought with six-foot fiberglass staffs in a circular arena!

[132]Brown, Terry. *English Martial Arts,* Hockwold-cum-Wilton: Anglo-Saxon Books, 1997; p. 68.

INTERLUDE

COMBAT FOR SURVIVAL
Rencontre

Saviolo (1595)

Dead Poets Society
Rencontre in Hog Lane, A.D. 1589[133]

On the afternoon of September 28, 1589, between two and three o'clock, William Bradley and "Christoferus Morley" of London, gentleman, were fighting together in Hog Lane.[134]

Thus abruptly does the framer of the indictment at the coroner's inquest the next day begin his tale. He says nothing about how the combat began, whether it was Marlowe or Bradley who gave the provocation, or whether the two men were enemies who fought on sight. Leaving all such matters to the imagination, he plunges, as Marlowe's companion was to do, into the midst of the fray.

The people in the street, seeing swords flashing, raised a clamor. Shakespeare, in *Romeo and Juliet* (I.i.80), gives us the cry of the citizens at such a time: "Clubs, bills, and partisans! Strike! Beat them down!"

Thomas Watson[135] of London, gentleman, was evidently close at hand. He drew his sword, like Romeo, to separate the men and keep the Queen's peace. Such, at least, is the pacific motive with which the coroner's jury credits him. But Marlowe was more wary than Mercutio, or perhaps only more weary by now and ready to welcome a rest. Instead of risking a wound under his friend's arm, he drew back and ceased from fighting.

Bradley, however, was in no mood to stop. He saw Watson, with drawn sword, coming between him and his opponent, and instantly turned to meet his new enemy.

"Art thou now come?" he called out. "Then I will have a bout with thee."

[133] Eccles, Mark. **Christopher Marlowe in London,** Cambridge, MA: Harvard UP, 1934; p. 9f. Albeit scholarly to the core, this book is a highly readable piece of detective work with fascinating insights into both the origins of the incident, the personalities involved, and the legal system of Tudor London.

[134] According to the author's research, this particular road was in the vicinity of Finbury Fields, *"frequented by duelists as well as by archers."* Eccles reasons: *"Since Marlowe and Bradley met in a place so convenient for dueling, their coming together in Hog Lane may not have been entirely premeditated. (...) Since Bradley had already sought sureties of the peace against Watson and his friends, the chances are that he had either challenged or been challenged by Marlowe or Watson to settle their quarrel in the fields."* (p. 121).

[135] The poet of *A Passionate Century of Love* and friend of Marlowe's.

These, except for proper names, are the only English words in the record. They suggest that the quarrel was more than a moment's standing: that the new enemy was also an old one.

At once Bradley flung himself on Watson and attacked him not only with his sword in one hand, but also with a dagger in the other.[136] With these weapons Bradley succeeded in cutting and wounding Watson so severely that his life was despaired of. Watson protected himself as best as he could with his sword. To save himself, he even retreated as far as a certain ditch in Hog Lane; but beyond this limit he could not flee without the peril of his life.

Bradley, following up his advantage, pursued his adversary to continue the assault. Watson had no way of escape; and thereupon, for the saving of his own life, he struck Bradley a mortal blow. The sword entered the right breast near the nipple, making a wound an inch in breadth and six inches deep.

Of this mortal blow, at Finsbury in the county of Middlesex, William Bradley instantly died.

[136]Rapier and dagger are, of course, the weapons of choice used by fashionable gentleman in Elizabethan London. It is interesting to note, however, that Watson does not have a dagger—the lack thereof could shed some doubt on the author's insinuation that the incident was a premeditated albeit unregulated duel rather than an spontaneously combusting rencontre between two old enemies.

Coda: On September 28, 1589, Watson and Marlowe were arrested for the murder of William Bradley and committed to Newgate prison. The next day, the coroner held an inquest upon Bradley's death. The jury determined that Watson had acted in self-defense. Marlowe was admitted to bail on October 1 and freed on signing a recognizance in the sum of forty pounds. Watson was incarcerated to await the Queen's mercy. He was pardoned on February 12, 1590, and died two and a half years later. Marlowe was killed by Ingram Frizer at an inn at Deptford on May 30, 1593—yet another great Elizabethan murder mystery.

ADVENTURES IN
LOST COMBAT ARTS 7

Medieval Wacky Whackers

"Hercules initiating
the Olympic Games."
(Burrell Collection)

F ew modern fencing authors make do without paraphrasing Castle's
comments about the

"rough and untutored fighting of the Middle Ages [which] represented faith-
fully the reign of brute force in social life as well as in politics. The stoutest
arm and the weightiest sword won the day (...) Those were the days of
crushing blows with mace or glaive, when a knight's superiority in action
depended on his power of wearing heavier armor and dealing heavier blows
than his neighbor, when strength was lauded more than skill, and minstrels
sang of enchanted blades that naught could break."[137]

As we have seen in the past examples, some details just don't want to agree
with this hypothesis. Medieval society ruled by brute force? What about the

[137]Castle, Egerton. **Schools
and Masters of Fence from
the Middle Ages to the 18th
Century.** London: George Bell
& Sons, (1884) 1892 (revised
ed.); p. 6.

Church's international diplomacy and power politics? The weightiest sword? Why, then, would it take a practitioner of the Noble Science of Defence 14 years of hard, relentless practice to achieve the status of Master?

Or what about the old Franco-Burgundian tapestry in the Burrell collection at Glasgow, Scotland? In my opinion, this work of art, entitled *Hercules Initiating the Olympic Games*, could be as important to the history of fencing as the Bayeux Tapestry is for arms and armor.

The tapestry dates from the mid-1400s and shows Hercules, Theseus, three Amazon queens, and a number of baton-armed combatants against the backdrop of what the medieval mind imagined Mt. Olympus to look like.

Hercules is not actively involved in the competition. He carries the staff of the magister ludi or umpire (still represented in the *director's épée* in 19th-century duels), and, in contrast to all other figures, appears to be wearing metal arm defences.

Of course, the artist did not attempt to produce an authentic image of a mythological Greek event. (The concern about "authenticity" is a modern, and, if you believe Heine, thouroughly bourgeois phenomenon.) Hercules occupied a high place in the esteem of the Burgundian dukes who probably commissioned this tapestry. Accordingly, it should be regarded as a contemporary interpretation of a classical subject, reflecting the artist's immediate experience and environment, as far as costume, armaments—and in all probability the system of baton combat itself are concerned.

The background and arms and armor context of this tapestry have been discussed before.[138] However, little attention has been paid to the actual analysis of the fighting style itself. This is surprising considering that this could be the earliest depiction of the first genuine sports fencing system in human history—about a century younger than that of the Central European Dussack, which even Karl Lochner grudgingly accepts as the first true sports-oriented combat system.[139]

The weapons used are batons, considerably less than three feet long. They vary in quality from crudely smoothed cudgels to elaborately decorated staffs that may have been painted, maybe even wrapped with colored cloth. Some are tipped with spherical knobs, perhaps made of metal. Two have additional decorations in the middle of the baton, maybe encrusted with precious stones. All batons have a circular hand guard reminiscent of the "Wacky Whacker" foils that have recently become popular in the United States.

What sets apart this system from other images of contemporary combat systems, however, is the use of the left hand for passive and active defense. This circumstance makes it possible to arrive at reasonable conclusions regarding target area and striking techniques.

The use of the left hand

The classical literature of the art of fencing includes the use of the unarmed left hand from the earliest printed volume. In Sainct Didier's *Traicté contenant les secrets du premier livre sur l'espée seule* (1573,)[140] the left hand was used to deflect and grab the opponent's blade. It was kept near the opponent's point, or close to the fencer's own body to protect vital points of one's anatomy, either on the torso or the lower face. One of Sutor's illustration, a poorly reproduced engraving he

[138]Wells, William and Norman, A.V.B. — "An Unknown Hercules in the Burrell Collection," in *The Scottish Art Review*, vol. 8; No. 3, (1962); p. 11f.

[139]Lochner, Karl E. *Waffenkunde für Sportfechter und Waffenliebhaber*, Wien: self-published, 1960; p. 31 and *Die Entwicklungsphasen der europäischen Fechtkunst*, Wien: self-published, 1953; p. 20.

[140]cf. Dubois, Georges. *Essai sur le traité d'escrime de Saint-Didier publie en 1573*, Paris, 1918.

had copied from Meyer, illustrates a shaolin-like hand and foot position. While the raised foot can be blamed on an error in perspective, the position of the empty hand still is characteristic for the general style of single rapier practised before the Thirty Years' War.

Later on, fencers faced the opponent with the right side of the body turned toward him. In this position, the role of the (averted) left hand greatly diminished, atrophying into a means of maintaining balance and providing additional impetus to forward body movements like the lunge. The same is evident in Chinese shaolin styles, where the empty left hand is considered the "secret sword." [141]

Deflect and defend

Sir William Hope recommends *"in playing with sharps, have always your left hand in readiness to put by your Adversaries scattering, or contretemps thrusts; if you make use of your left hand with Judgement, you will also find a great advantage in it, but trust not all to it, for it is only to be used as a help to your sword."* [142]

Labat, Danet and Angelo still occasionally lapse into active defense with the left hand or lower arm. In addition, both Danet and Angelo describe ethnospecific guards such as the Spanish or German guards, where the left hand is used to cover target area in the guard position. In England, the left arm and elbow are used as passive protection of the lower face in late 18th century singlestick play. And in 1892, the *Deutsche Stoßfechtschule*, compiled and published by the association of German fencing masters, advises épée fencers to maintain *"the left hand extended, fingers closed, with their outer or inner side flat on the left side of the chest. The hand can thus be used for defense if appropriate."* [143]

Of course, for all practical reasons, there was no reason to even teach this technique because it simply was inappropriate in most scenarios: In 1912, Ristow stipulates explicitly that the use of the left hand for defense in épée duels is prohibited, but that the use of the unarmed hand or arm for parrying is admissable for saber duels. [144]

Club and baton

The use of the club (Kolben) is documented not only in the tournament, but also in judicial combat,[145] where it was supplemented by shield and *cuir bouillon* armor (leaving the fighters barefoot and bare handed.) This tradition dates back to Louis the Pious, who ordered that *"a man (. . .) charged with theft for the first time can clear himself by oath but thereafter if two or three accuse him, he can defend only by combat and shield, the device then recently introduced where doubt as to credibility existed."* [146]

Hutton helps out with his account of "How Two Tailors Fought to the Death with Shield and Cudgel," commenting that

[141] See Yang, Dr. Jwing-Ming and Bolt, Jeffery A. ***Northern Shaolin Sword***, Boston: Yang's Martial Arts Academy, 1985; p.23: *"Mastering the sword requires learning to project power into the weapon, but if a person generated power only on one side of the body, disorders would result. To avoid this, sword practitioners hold the empty hand with the index and middle fingers extended and the thumb folded over the other two fingers. When power is projected into the sword, it is also projected from the extended fingers of the empty hand to balance the energy. This is known as the secret sword."*

[142] Hope; p. 144.

[143] Verein Deutscher Fechtmeister. ***Deutsche Stoßfechtschule nach Kreußler'schen Grundsätzen,*** Leipzig: Verlag von J.J. Weber, 1892; p. 11.

[144] Ristow, Gustav. ***Ehrenkodex,*** Wien: Verlag von L. W. Seidel & Sohn, 1912 (2nd ed.); p. 157. Barbasetti's ***Ehrenkodex*** (Wien: Verlag der Allgemeinen Sportzeitung, 1898), translated by Ristow, also includes this option (p. 97).

[145] In England, the club survived as a tool of judicial process for property disputes until the end of the 16th century.

[146] Goebel, Julius. ***Felony and Misdemeanor: A Study in the History of Criminal Law,*** vol 1, (1937) Philadelphia: University of Pennsylvania Press, 1976; p. 79.

> *"any person, gentle or simple, who might have the misfortune to take the life of another in self-defence could claim sanctuary on declaring that the fight had been a fair one, and that he was ready to maintain the same with his body in the lists; and this done, all process of law against him had to cease, nor was any person allowed to molest him except by taking up his challenge. The weapons, too, were curious. They consisted of a stout wooden club and a shield of wood."*[147]

But the clubs used at tournaments and the ordeal had little in common with those depicted in the tapestry.

Where they hit

Out of the 15 figures depicted as wielding batons in the Glasgow Tapestry, seven are using the left arm in a defensive or passive offensive function. Two (figures 2 and 3) protect their lower necks by positioning the left hand either on or above the endangered area. The intention is to protect not only the clavicula but the *nervus vagus* and the carotid sinus, a traditional karate striking point. A shock to the baroreceptors in the carotid artery forces the nervous system to respond with a drastic drop in blood pressure, which cuts off the blood supply to the brain almost immediately:

> *"Fainting is immediate and unavoidable, and yet the helpless victim has actually no more than a slightly bruised neck."*[148]

Figure 1 appears to protect against this by covering target area. Figure 2, however, will use his left in a sweeping motion, maybe grasping the attacker's baton. Both cover heart and solar plexus with the upper arm and elbow. A similar possibility is implied in the left hand position of figure 5, where the left arm covers the heart, solar plexus, and the "floating ribs". These can be broken by a relatively light blow and damage both liver and stomach:

> *"Such a blow is commonly delivered from the side, traveling toward the center of the body. This is a favorite nightstick target."*[149]

Face and neck are protected by a steep lateral hanging guard, which can be turned into a whipping, Schläger-like slash by a combined motion of arm and wrist, as well as shifted into wider head guards similar to those used in figures 1, 3, 4, 9, 10 and 11. Figures 4 and 8 protect the heart (or solar plexus), both actively and by covering target. A similar stance can be found in the Ready Position (*Tindig Serrada*) and Lock and Block Position (*Laban tayong*) of Escrima.[150]

The face is protected by both the baton and the empty left hand (figures 6 and 7). Figure 7 also provides a hit at a possible striking technique: It is the spitting image of the transitional stance of the *abaniko*, a fanning strike executed horizontally, diagonally, or vertically. Body and arms provide a powerfull whipping motion.[151] In Escrima, this manoeuvre is used to set up an opponent, feint, and pick the target area. Figures 4, 7 and 5 could represent successive stages of this action

[147]Hutton; p. 16.

[148]Mashiro, N. *Black Medicine: The Dark Art of Death,* Boulder, CO: Paladin Press, 1978; p. 32.

[149]Mashiro; p.50.

[150]See Wiley, Mark V. *Filipino Martial Arts: Cables Serrada Escrima*, Rutland, VT and Tokyo: Charles E. Tuttle Co., 1994.

[151]Wiley; p. 69.

Unfortunately, these static illustrations only provide tantalizing bait for speculation if it comes to reconstructing the actual motions and actions of this system. But there are some inevitable conclusions you can arrive at:

The target area obviously includes head and torso. Both arms are used for offense and defense. Hits, maybe even thrusts, were aimed at the head, face, neck, belly, and torso and caught or parried with the ulna of the left arm (as in Victorian singlestick) and with the protective angle of both weapon and baton arm (as in modern Schlägerplay).

Unisex pastime

It is safe to assume that this system was not used as a practice or warm-up exercise: Practice systems tend to focus on the actual target area used in serious competition. In the *Kolbenturnier*, all parts of the body would have been covered by armor. Moreover, in the tapestry the thumb of the left hand tends to be separated from the closed body of the hand, making it a sensitive and highly fragile appendage if the full force of club blows had been brought to bear. This speaks for controlled, low-impact strikes unpracticable at either the mortal combat of the ordeal or the tournament.

Another argument is that the three female figures are also equipped with batons. Figure 13 is in an at-ease position. Figure 12 appears to at least protect her arm with the baton (if she isn't actually lashing out), while figure 16 could be in the process of an overhanded angled thrust. There are cases of women fighting in club ordeals, but women were only spectators at tournaments. (Here, however, the classical allusion to the Amazon queens may have gotten the better of the artist.)

Even a superficial analysis of the historical evidence has to arrive at an undisputable conclusion. The modern judgment of the quality of classical and medieval fencing systems is overly simpistic if not downright patronizing. The Glasgow tapestry all by itself indicates that there may have been well-developed sports fencing traditions in a period we have come to regard as the Dark Ages.

Hercules and his gang appear to prove that even back in the 15th century, it was not that important what size a man's weapon was. It mattered how he used it.

INTERLUDE

ANTAGONISTIC COMMENT COMBAT
Saber Mensur

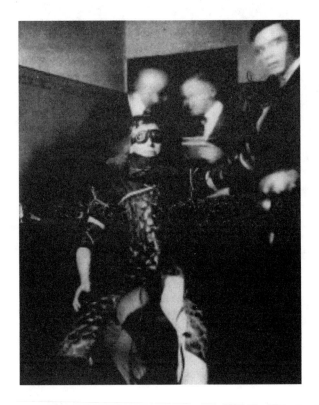

"Mit Binden und Bandagen"...
The safest way to fight with sabers.

Tramps Abroad:
On the Use of the Basket-hilt Saber

While Schläger Mensuren were widely tolerated or at least not persecuted outright in Germany, the duel with the viciously curved basket-hilt saber has always been regarded as illegal combat with lethal weapons by German authorities. This is why accounts from outsiders are exceedingly scarce.

These heavy weapons are comparatively cumbersome to handle—the sword arm was extended nearly horizontally while cuts were generated from lower arm and wrist.

While most experts these days assume they posed little threat to fencers, it should be noted that practised fencers were able to wield the Korbsäbel with amazing speed and force. In official encounters, the bandages and other protective devices worn by fencers varied according to the degree of the insult. During encounters at the Säbelmensur, there was ample opportunity for serious, even life-threatening injuries. Depending on the reason for and the nature of the challenge, the degree of gravity applied to the execution of the duel could vary. The most serious challenge was *sine sine* (Latin: "without, without")—fought without goggles, left axillaris knot and heart iron, and greatly reduced arm bandages.

Ready for Combat.
(c.1920)

Sine duels (fought wearing either goggles or heart iron and limited arm protection), to *cum* (Latin: "with") — wearing goggles, high-reaching pants, heart iron, both axillares knots, a steel-enforced fencing glove, arm bandages that covered all joints, a braided silk scarf that protected the outside of the arm and, optionally, a crease-free shirt.

Matter of honor

An *Ehrengericht* (court of honor), consisting of respected members of neutral fraternities, had the final say in determining the validity of the challenge and settle on the degree of protection allowed.

The causes for saber duels appear trivial enough from a modern perspective. A sarcastic remark sufficed for individuals. Among student fraternities, arguments about who had precedence on official occasions could result in challenges of entire groups.

One example has been recorded in the annals of the Corps Normannia Berlin:[152] In the early 1870s, the Normannia and the Berlin Corps Borussia had a difference of opinion with the Corps Guestphalia. They argued that by suspending Corps activities for a certain period, the Guestphalia had lost its status and precedence as one of the older Corps in Berlin, along with its seat farther up on the table arrangement during official banquets.

Each member of the Normannia and the Borussia challenged each member of the Guestphalia to a duel with heavy sabers, adding up to a total of 36 duels. During the 14 duels that actually were fought, one man lost an eye, and a member of the Berlin Borussia received a cut across the chest that split his ribcage open and sliced dangerously close to the heart. (He survived.) After three semesters of fighting, and gallons of blood shed, the quarrel was finally put aside.

[152]Eule, Andreas Peter (ed.)
***Materialien zur Geschichte
des Corps Normannia Berlin***,
Berlin: Simon Druck, 1992;
Part II, p.23 f.

Road to extinction

Barbasetti, who was introduced to the Schläger and basket-hilt saber Mensur during the time he was teaching at the St. Annahof in Vienna in the late 1890s, comments on Schläger and saber in his *The Art of the Foil* (1932):

> *"These forms of combat appear barbarous, or at least ridiculous, to Anglo-Saxons and Latins. The first because of the futility of its cause, and the second because of its implacable ritualistic severity. But one should not express an opinion on these matters without first having thought of the individualistic character and the peculiar psychology of the Teutonic race.*
>
> *The duel between students cannot be taken seriously. It is not in the least dangerous; it is really only a fictitious battle with the object of exercising the nerves and preparing the student for a more serious conception of social relationships.*
>
> *The slightest breach of etiquette and of tradition on the part of the student brings about this duel, which is surrounded with all the chivalrous proceedings. It is an excellent experimental system to teach the art of knowing how to behave among men. (. . .) The saber Mensur for affairs of honor is a very serious matter and requires boldness to handle as well as military discipline."*[153]

Today, the basket-hilt saber is all but extinct even in Germany and Austria. The odd duel is rumored to take place once in a decade in utmost secrecy, partly because of the severe legal consequences for everyone involved and partly because of the lack of interest in fighting any more than the required number of Schläger bouts among most contemporary Corps students.

One of the rare English-language descriptions of a German basket-hilt saber duel can be found in the diaries of Gordon Bolitho, a New Zealander who studied in Heidelberg in 1930:

> *"The duelers were already in their places. Their clothes were as bloody, from old fights, as the strip of material on which they were to meet.*
>
> *Their long, thickly padded trousers reached to their armpits, leaving the chest and shoulders bare. Thick black cloths were wound around their throats: their eyes were protected by iron tubes, about a quarter of an inch in thickness. They looked like absurd goggles. The fighting arms were padded. Of course I could not understand what the umpires said. But the one word "Silentium!" cast a spell upon the room. We were frozen into silence.*
>
> *The names of the two dueling associations and the reason for the duel were announced and then the fighters and their seconds took their places. The duelers faced each other, the length of a sword apart, and the seconders crouched to the left of their men. The seconds, too, were heavily padded and they wore gauze frames [154] over their heads and faces. The air in the room was thick and heavy: too many breathed in the low attic to allow the cold outside to penetrate to us.*
>
> *The fighting was quick, dangerous and bloody. The curved sabers cut the air with a swish: they met with a sharp clang—sometimes there were sparks. As in boxing, the saber duel was made up in rounds. In each round, four slashes were made by each man.*

[153] Barbasetti, Cav. Luigi. *The Art of the Foil*, New York: Dutton, 1932; p. 271

[154] Bolitho probably means fencing masks, which usually are equipped with leather bibs and neck flaps and have the principal or hat color of the Corps sown to the padded top.

I had wondered, on the way up the stairs, if the sight of the blood would affect me. I watched it flow with equanimity. The slashing sabers were so exciting that I never thought about the element of butchery.

The reason for the duel was an insult... I did not understand how much of an insult, when the announcement was made. The man who was insulted had to give up, with gashes on his face and chest which were terrible. The results depend upon whether both members can last out the space of time. The victor was not badly damaged, but the poor wretch who had tried to avenge his insult was horrible to see. His chest and face were gory. The blood ran down in thick, dark rivulets. His face was cut from the left eye to the upper lip: I saw the gash open and show the gums and teeth inside. The doctors came in. Fifty-three stitches were necessary to sew up the gashes. This was an unusually gory fight and my friends were delighted, for my sake."[155]

Announcing a "Bloody One"
(Early 20th-century postcard)

Fighting chancellor

Germany's Iron Chancellor, Otto von Bismarck (1815-98) came to Göttingen in 1832, where he joined the Corps Hannovera. He fought 32 documented Mensuren with the basket-hilt Schläger which at that time was being taught by Meister Christian Kastrop.

The following Mensur [156], however, was fought with curved bladed basket-hilt sabers, and up until the Weimar Republic, was one of the best-known student duels ever to have taken place in Germany:

"At the Kaiser, near Rheinhausen Gate, they were preparing for a Mensur. Down on the country road, in the melted snow, the lookout walked back and forth. Ludolf Fromme of the Hannoverians, Ludolf Fromme from Hardegsen. He ate an apple and occasionally looked up to the windows of the second floor, where metal rang suspiciously. Bismarck had wrought a mocking verse about him that now hung from his collar like text scrolls from the little people you find on the illuminated parchments of the middle ages. (...)

[155]Bolitho, Gordon *The Other Germany*, London, New York: Appleton-Century, 1934; p. 14f.

[156]from Strobl, Karl Hans. *Der wilde Bismarck*, Leipzig: L. Staackmann Verlag, 1915; p 141f. Strobl (1877-1946) studied in Prague, Brünn and Vienna and was a member of four fighting Corps. While even the archive of the Hannovera in Göttingen des not have an exact description of the Bismarck-Röder Mensur, we can assume that the account reflects Strobl's own experiences.

Now Ludolf Fromme was thinking about revenge while walking up and down in the slush. A verse, a mocking verse about Bismarck, when he returned from the fencing grounds as a Mensur corpse. That was as certain as the multiplication table: Bismarck would be defeated by Herr von Röder. It was just a matter of finding a rhyme. But he just couldn't find something that rhymed with Bismarck, no matter how much braingrease he applied.

Upstairs, too, the mood wasn't optimistic. This one Mensur really was to be regarded as the extract of six; five Westphalians had declared to have spoken, in the eye of God, while being completely intoxicated. Only Herr von Röder stubbornly insisted that he had been completely sober and now was ready to take responsibility.

'He plays the revolutionary but really only wants the fight,' said Wuthmann. 'Our Baribal may be pretty good, but Röder will hack him in pieces We'll be able to carry him in a handkerchief.'

Gustav Scharlach, defender of the French Principle, Gustav Scharlach, connoisseur of women, secretly hinted that the King of Prussia had nothing to do with it, but some Queen of Hearts from Göttingen. Only a case like this could excite people enough to measure skills with each other.

The great hall, where the Cow Dance took place every Sunday, was so crowded that it was hard to see how one could make space for a Mensur at all. All the corps were there, everyone smoked long pipes, and the pledges carried the fencing equipment from its hiding place.

'Coming through,' Wehner yelled and pushed through with a basin of hot water. Doctor Gans, the medic, stood and polished the rust off his utensils with glass paper. 'What pig messed up the medical kit. Some idiot must have put it into the eaves.'

In a corner sat Groomsman Thomas, the Mensur oracle. He had witnessed so many Mensuren that higher arithmetic had run out of numbers. When asked, 'Thomas, what round, he lifted the right hand with the palm forward to the ear, hit into the air and said 'Eh!' There were no surprises for him on the fencing loft any more, and if Archangel Michael had squared off against Archangel Gabriel, even their heavenly feints wouldn't have been anything new to him. . .

Now a few young Bremensians were standing in his accustomed corned and listened to him oracle. Thomas said 'Eh!' and only because his apprentice Bornemann was with him, he added 'Abgestochen,[157] of course.'

Wuthmann fixed the curved blade in the broad basket-hilt. It was a last service of love that he did for his Leibfuchs.[158] The pommel nut was tightened with infinite care. Then he held the saber in front of him: the blade stood firm and straight. 'Space please, gentlemen!' The weapon whistled thin and sharp.

'Prost to the Hildesheimers,' a Red Mecklenburgian called. Beer mugs rattled. The sound was thirst-inspiring.

Bismarck was already being strapped into the plastron. 'I want something like that, too!' (. . .)

'Beer for the Kindskopf,[159]' Dammers roared.

Bandaging was finished. The heavy wraps were not being used today, neck and pulse were only protected by thinly lined silk straps. Umpire

[157] *abgestochen* literally means "stuck" (as in "stuck pig".) It is the fighting students' term for "termination of the Mensur because of disabling injury."

[158] *Leibfuchs* roughly compares with the American "Little Brother," *Leibbursch* corresponds to the "Big Brother."

[159] lit.: "child's head," yet another of Bismarck's nicknames at the Hannovera. This one he owed to his bright voice.

215

Bornemann of the Hildesheimers emerged. 'Are the gentlemen ready?'

'If my Cassubian gets stuck, I'll take on this Röder myself later on,' Wuthmann whispered.

A trail opened up before Bismarck. He saw the field of battle, and beyond his opponent—who stuck in his badages like a fat, muscular mastiff in a harness. The neck bandage pushed his chin into the fleshy abundance of his red face. And his right fist in the dirty glove was lying like a field stone on the arm of his Witness.

Creating room for the Mensur meant that what receded from the middle of the room had to rise along its walls. Thus the place of battle was surrounded by a steep wall of men like a real arena. There were two, three layers of people, first those standing on the floorboards; then those standing on chairs, then those standing on tables. Doctor Gans at his table just barely could avoid having his painstakingly assembled collection of instruments stepped on. Everyone was smoking from long pipes, as if they had to fill the room with clouds so both fighters battled in a realm of fog, Northern battlekings on a mythical island. It was amazing: Some where hanging with one hand from the windowsill and yet they puffed as if their life depended on it.

'Leibfuchs, stand firm,' said Wuthmann. 'He likes to run over his opponents.[160] If you sit on your behind, I'll disown you. Take on a wide guard position. And if you see an opening, hit into it like Blücher.'

'Of course, Leibbursch.'

'Okay, then let's get to it.' Wuthmann spat behind him, that was his Mensur blessing. He slipped into the cuff and apron, tore the cap over his head by the large visor and grabbed his iron.

'Mister Umpire, sir!'

'Mister Umpire, sir!'

The lifting of caps on both sides; weapons dipping: warlike courtesy.

Small swarthy Bornemann of the Hildesheimers climbed on a chair. What he lacked in length he made up by his sharp eyes. Amidst the whirring blades, he was able to watch each single cut. there were no doubts, everything was captured precisely in the moment. Bornemann, the disciple of Menur oracle Thomas, could have become the professor of Mensur sciences, had the Georgia Augusta had a chair for this kind of thing.

[160]Of course, this is not to be taken literally. "Running over" here means a rapid, forceful, and unexpected lunge against the unprepared oppoent, probably right at the beginning of the round.

"Slices" in quarte against low tierce. L.C. Roux (1885)

216

He also had the right, cutting voice of the referee:

'Silentium for the settlement of a matter of honor between Herr von Bismarck, Hannoverae, and Herr von Röder, Guestphaliae as the challenged party. Twenty-four rounds with small caps. The seconds now take the command.'

Bismarck and Röder rattled up from their chairs. The withered blood crusts on the fencing pants crackled, and creaking, the stiff leather straps shifted into position. Now only, one could see how tall that pledge of the Corps Hannovera really was. But his childlike face showed oddly from between the cap's visor and the neck bandages.

With one step he went into position. Nails in the floor indicated the fighters' range of movement. Opposite him Bulldog Röder crouched for the lunge. The extended blades touched for the first time: with a bright, joyful sound, the edges jerked into each other.

In this moment Bismarck's left hand reached up and tore the red Hannoverian cap from his head. The gaudy thing flew into the crowd, followed by the cap from Röder's head.

There was a whispering and muttering. 'What a nut.'

—'What an idea! I guess he has a metal head'[161]

Wuthmann looked at his protege from underneath the visor.

'The seconds have the command,' Bornemann twanged from his chair.

No time for introspection. 'Bind the blades,' cried Wuthmann.

'They are bound!'

'Sie hauen aus!'

There the Westphalian lunged, with a cut as if he wanted to split his opponent in two. Bismarck's parry was barely perceptible, but it must have been succesful, because Röder already moved back and Bismarck's riposte whirred after him, humming along his blade, booming into his basket.

At the door in the back the Mensur oracle said: 'Forget about sticking pigs today...' The word went around, all along the crowd, immediately changed the entire atmosphere. This Bismarck was no sacrificial lamb. He had good sharp teeth!

The opponents were on guard. Bismarck had stretched forward a bit: Body, arm and blade formed a flat curve toward the opponent's right eye. He saw nothing but this enemy eye and the sacred red-blue-gold of the basket, from which the curved blade grew, thirty-three inches long. Now there was a flash toward him, double, left and right, he caught the sparkles in his basket, swung, but did't make the heavy dragoon's cut against the angled cover, but just a small, innocuous, harmless little cut to the other side. It slapped the arm bandages, tender and comfortable.

A deep breathing and snorting all around: Scandalous! This pledge didn't take the affiar seriously enough.

On the other side the Mensur prophets stepped up to the Westphalian. Each whispered some piece of advice: Röder snarled at them like a vicious mutt.

Wuthmann threatened his people with his second's sword. 'Shut up!'

The next round. Now the opponent stood withdrawn into himself. After some light skirmishing the seconds' halt intervened.

[161] Caps worn during a Mensur in this period were made of thin silk and had a wide rim to protect the eyes against descending cuts. While they did nothing to buffer the percussive impact of the blade, the could only by cut if the edge hit at a perfect angle.

Now even the most untalented pledge had grasped that a decision was imminent. Necks were extending, in the back a chair collapsed onto which a fourth spectator was about to climb.

Bismarck began with a straight, firm quarte that was steeply measured at Röder's temple. Then there was a horrible crash, blades screaming, four, five cuts humming onto each other and into each other, lunge and guard collided, and from the center of this confusion something glorious separated itself, an iron-cold cut that everybody saw and that seemed to execute what Bismarck had pointed at at the opening of the round.

A fine, red line showed on Röder's temple. Now its edges pulled apart, and liquid welled out of it in slow strokes as if driven by a pump. Red, bright red on face and shirt, the cloth drank blood. Over the old rusty brown crusts wine-colored cascades sank, and big drops splashed onto the dusty ground. A lump of humans closed around the Westphalian.

Bornemann's bright voice was heard: 'Herr Röder, Guestphaliae, has declared himself hit. Mensur ex.'

Wuthmann had already started to unwrap Bismarck. He squeezed his shoulders, pressed his thumbs into his upper arms, boxed him on the back. 'Leibfuchs! Churl!... Cassubian! I've got to have this blade. I'll hang it over my bed. If your king is worth anything, he'll thank you and send you two bottles of French red.'

Bismarck had to press a lot of hands. Honest pride was glowing from his babyface. When he had slipped out of his armor, his right shot into his pocket. He felt for that small piece of velvet ribbon that softly slipped through his fingers..."

ADVENTURES IN
LOST COMBAT ARTS 8

Fechtschule
(15th century)

Pride and Prejudice

One of the most important influences shaping fencing techniques was the status consciousness of the social groups engaging in sword-play.

Throughout the Middle Ages, we find a curious stratification taking place in the social status and the practice of martial arts. In the earliest Teutonic sources, the instructors at arms count among the most esteemed and honored members of a noble's retinue: Old Hildebrand, tutor and instructor to Didrik, is a nobleman in his own right. His son Hadubrand is as eager as any hot-blooded young aristocrat to meet the suspected impostor at arms.

But later on, we find the *kemphen, campiones, pugiles,* and *gladiatores* of the 1300s and 1400s who were leading marginal existences, hiring themselves out to substitute for free citizens and noblemen in ordeals and wagers of battle. But even in this shadowy stratum, there are pronounced differences. Fencers such as the German *Lohnkämpfer* (hired fighters used in public ordeals in land disputes etc.) could be both rightless, traveling people but also respected members of urban fighting guilds.[162]

Born of the people

The Noble Science of Defence was a tradition deeply rooted in the class of craftsmen. Unlike the seven *artes liberales,*[163] the *artes mechanicae* were practiced by people who needed to actively earn a living. Like the liberal arts, they were organized into seven spheres: the trades, warfare, seamanship (with geography and business,) agriculture (including home economics), forestry and animal husbandry (including veterinary medicine) as well as the courtly arts. The latter not only comprised dance, horsemanship and painting, but also games and sports.

[162]The best modern account on the social distinctions between the Central European fencing masters can be found in Hils, Hans-Peter. ***Meister Johann Liechtenauers Kunst des langen Schwertes,*** Frankfurt: Peter Lang (Europäische Hochschulschriften vol. 257), 1985; p. 207f.

[163]i.e., grammar, rhetoric, dialectics, music, arithmetic, geometry, and astronomy.

Fencing masters therefore had two pronouncedly different planes to ply their trade. They taught as weapon masters in the military and among the warring nobility. And they catered to the active and passive entertainment needs of the courts and the guilds and merchants—whose prosperity provided sufficient resources for large-scale social occasions.

This already indicates that the social background of the European fighting masters is all but clear cut. Historians tend to either associate them with the dishonest trades like jugglers or actors, or to elevate them into the sphere of nobility.

Indeed, recorded history documents a close link between showmanship and swordplay: The earliest manuscript illustrations of fencers have been interpreted as depicting entertainers performing sword dances. (Considering how ritualized combat "forms"—like the *kata* of Oriental arts—were transmitted in non-European countries, the connection between martial arts and sword dancing actually makes sense[164].)

Needless to say, the traveling "skirmishers" were esteemed as entertainers but overall despised as *fahrendes Volk*—traveling folk or drifters. (The interrelation between fencers and actors, albeit on a moe acceptable social level, remains traceable throughout Shakespeare's career, revived in modern times by the silver screen involvement of masters such as Aldo Nadi and Ralph Faulkner.)

Grappling for life

The most prominent guilds of central Europe were those of the Marxbrüder and the Federfechter. These privileged schools were formed mainly by urban craftsmen whose professional training and accreditation system closely mirrored that of the fencing companies, not only in central Europe, but in England and France as well.

Although the company of the fighters of St. Mark ("Marx" in some German dialects) was older than that of the Free Fencers of the Feather, both companies had similar fencing traditions, as well as similar fighting (including fencing and wrestling) rules, prohibiting the breaking of legs and arms, as well as thrusts into the eyes and reproductive organs. In fact, they related so closely to each other that each group's candidates for Master status and accreditation not only had to pass before a board of his own association—but also before the other organization.[165]

Like in the days of Njal, Gunnar, Kari, and Egil, grappling, wrestling, and other close combat elements were integral part of the guilds' system as far back as the 1400s. (A tendency to connect fencing and wrestling practice not exclusively with antagonistic [i.e., combat] training, but to practice it agonistically in social surroundings, and to frame it in certain rules for that purpose, becomes very obvious in Auerswald's *Ringerkunst*.) But despite the regulatory framework that regulated the active and passive entertainment of wrestling, the techniques used appear to have been applicable in life-and-death situations.

Among the Federfechter listed by name and city of origin in the Nuremberg Fechtschul Rhymes of 1579,[166] we find carpenters, shoemakers and cobblers, turners, goldsmiths, and dyers. The Marxbrüder are furriers, potters, cobblers, dyers. I have pointed out previously that in Grimmelshausen's *Simplicissimus*, we find the young picaro (in his temporary incarnation as "Jäger von Soest") being trained by a furrier, who "because of that fact" (*"dahero"*) not only was a Meistersänger, but also an excellent fencer in all weapons.[167]

[164]e.g., the martial art of Kali's preservation in native Filipino dances, or the Pyrrhic Dance.

[165]Many fencing historians today tend to separate Marxbrüder and Federfechter according to their supposed "weapon of choice": The Federfechter, being the younger organization, are widely identified with the "progressive" rapier, the poor Marxbrüder as being incorrigible reactionaries in their supposed preference of the two-handed sword. Both groups, however, practiced all edged and staff weapons with equal zeal.

[166]Wassmannsdorff, Karl. *Sechs Fechtschulen der Marxbrüder und Federfechter aus den Jahren 1573 to 1614,* Heidelberg: Buchhandlung von Karl Groos, 1870; p. 32f.

[167]Grimmelshausen; p.191-2.

This furrier indeed may have been a late Marxbruder, considering that this was the furriers' association of choice.[168] As becomes clear in subsequent chapters, this honest craftsman-turned-musketeer not only taught Simplicius how to fence with edged and pole arms, but also turned him into an expert wrestler.

Grimmelshausen presents a (fictitious) encounter of Simplicius[169], which demonstrates the usefulness of grappling techniques in antagonistic fight scenarios:

"About a week or four before Christmas I marched out of camp with a good gun, down the Breisgau. (...) But after I had passed Endingen and came to a single house, someone shot at me so that the bullet tore a piece from the rim of my hat. And immediately, a strong, burly churl launched himself at me from the house, shouting that I should drop my gun.

I replied, 'By god, compatriot, not to please you,' and cocked my weapon.

He, however, drew a thing from his belt that looked more like an executioner's sword than a broadsword[170], and rushed at me. As I sensed his serious intent, I aimed and hit him in the forehead that he spun around and finally dropped to the ground.[171]

To take advantage of this, I wrested the sword from his fist and wanted to run it through his body.

But as it didn't want to go through,[172] he jumped back to his feet unexpectedly, grabbed me by the hair, and I him, too. His sword I already had thrown aside.

Then we began such a serious came that each man realized the bitter strength of his opponent, and yet no-one was able to become master of the other. At some point I was on top, at some point he was, and then we rapidly were back on our feet, which didn't last long as each sought the other's death.

The blood that ran out of my nose and mouth I spat into my enemy's face since he appeared to desire it so fervently—that helped me because it hindered his seeing. Thus we dragged each other through the snow for one and a half hours. And we became so exhausted that it appeared that the one's weakness could not fully conquer the other man's exhaustion with fists alone, nor that one could kill the other's by his own strength and without weapons.

The art of wrestling, in which I had practiced myself back at L., served me well back then, otherwise I would have lost without doubt, because my enemy was much stronger than I, and eisenfest[173] as well. And as we finally had tired out each other nearly to death, he said, 'Brother, hold it. I give myself up to you.'"

The Ladybug Trick: Some grappling techniques illustrated by Grimmelshausen's contemporary Jakob Sutor appear again in late 19th-century manuals, such as Charlemont, J. ***L'Art de La Boxe Française***, Brussels: self-published, 1878 (2nd ed.); p. 117: *"Coup de tête et remassement des jambes"* and Sutor, Jakob. ***Neu Künstliches***

Charlemont (1878)

[168] In his foreword to Roux, W. *Anweisung zum Hiebfechten* (Jena, 1840), Dr. K.H. Scheidler ruminates that Marxbrüder and Federfechter attracted different trades (p. 11). It indeed seems that the furriers had a predilection to fight in the Brotherhood of the Golden Lion of St. Mark: Both professional and fencing guild affiliation were matters of family tradition in this day and age.

[169] von Grimmelshausen, Hans Jakob Christoffel. *Der Abenteuerliche Simplicissimus Teutsch.* (1668) München: dtv, 1975; p. 348 f.

[170] Much like the English term "sword", the German word *Degen* historically is used liberally to describe straight-bladed military and civilian weapons as diverse as smallsword and basket-hilt broadsword. In this context, it normally would denote a rapier or cut-and-thrust sword.

[171] Although hit squarely in the forehead, the bullet does little more than raise a bump and momentarily stun the man. Simplicius ascribes this to a semi-magical *Schelmenhaut* (lit. scoundrel's skin)—but does not appear to be overly surprized. Magic notwithstanding, this (fictional) event may serve to illustrate the comparatively variable effects firearms could have had even in the mid-17th century. (Most theories still credit the penetration power of early fire arms with the abandonment of plate armor as well as the development of the art of fencing.)

[172] Early on, this sword is compared to an executioner's sword, a pure cutting tool which apart from its size, weigh, and handle construction was characterized by a blunt, often near square point. Of course, it would be useless for thrusting or running through.

[173] lit. "iron-proof"

Fechtbuch, (Frankfurt: Johann Bringern, 1612) Frankfurt: Johann Scheible, 1848; p. 18. The aim is to throw the opponent on his back.

Sutor (1612)

Guarding the monopoly

These fighting tradesmen were proud and fierce enough to back up their integrity with fist and weapons whenever necessary. The Federfechter Augustin Staidt, a knifesmith by trade, in his rhyme boldly states:

"Wer mich und mein löblich' Handwerk veracht' / den schlag ich auf den Kopf, dass es ihm im Herzen kracht."[174]

Considering this martial spirit among the German masters, the wrath incited among their English cousins, the London Masters of Defence, by the bold usurpation of teaching privileges by Saviolo and Bonnetti suddenly becomes very understandable. Had the Italians attempted the same in Frankfurt, where the Marxbrüder played on home turf, they would have been forced to square off against their Hauptmann and four other masters. Usually, the results of these encounters—organized or "improvised"—convinced the respective pretender either to join their school or abandon the weapons trade for another honest way of making a living.

Both guilds were sticklers for law and order and personal integrity. If a member used his skills to commit murder, went into frivolous debt, or committed an act or crime against secular or clerical law, he was eliminated from the company, his name erased from the membership rolls.

The Days of the Dussack

The traditions, ethics, and, of course, the weapon play of the Marxbrüder and Federfechter not only were popular at home. They also had international appeal, or at least close analogs abroad. A brief hint at the Dussack's international appeal is given in Grimmelshausen: Simplicius, at one point of his arduous journeys through the Orient, is traded to the king of Korea by tartars. He briefly comments:

"There they valued me because no-one was my equal with the Dusecke."[175]

Egerton Castle, the 19th-century patron saint of fencing history, derives the term Dussack or Dusägge—the old Germans were rather liberal in their orthography, not to mention the dozens of dialects they wrote in—from the Bohemian word tesák, pointing at a potential Czech rather than Germanic origin of the weapon.

Karl Lochner,[176] however, rejects this approach, pointing out that the term already appears around 1500 in many different regions of Germany, whereas the

[174]"Who despises me and my praiseworthy craft / I'll hit on the head that it resounds in his heart."

[175]Grimmelshausen; p. 473.

[176]Lochner, Karl E. *Waffenkunde für Sportfechter und Waffenliebhaber,* Wien: Eigenverlag, 1960; p. 32.

Prague fencing guild, to whose influence the Dussack is usually ascribed, became notably active only in the 1570s. Lochner cites two other etymological interpretations that link the Dussack with the oldest European edged weapon, the slashing or fighting knife or sax. According to him, the term could be derived from "two-sax"—double knife or long knife—or "tusik sax"—blunt knife or fencing knife.

Should the etymological tie-in to the ancient sax be correct, the Dussack's earliest ancestor is the short, single-edged sword-knife found at Vimose and Thorsbjerg, which is thought to have originated between A.D. 100 and 300. Much like the modern Filipino bolo (a sword type still used as an all-purpose tool by Filipino farmers, which also is the main weapon of the martial art Escrima), the European Fechtmesser or fighting knife was both weapon and tool at once.

The weapon appears mainly in fencing manuals of the early 16th century. But even before, we find many codified references pointing at a systematic approach to fighting with the long knife in Johann Lichtenauer's fragments of *"8 stend im dussek"* (which is thought to have originated in the 1380s), as well as in the Second Gotha Codex of Hans Talhoffer (1467) which contains 8 plates on the long knife.

The Fechtmesser of the Old Masters was a metal weapon with a 60 cm long and 4.5- 5cm wide one-edged, wedge-shaped blade, nearly straight or with little curvature. In early versions, the point lies within the blade's axis, only later do we find raised points.

When exactly the change from the fighting knife to the Dussack proper took place is uncertain. (A rare iron Dussack, dated to have been made at the beginning of the 16th century, was found at Nymburg. This weapon, including elegantly curved knuckleguard was forged from one piece of metal, with a prolonged and curved blade c. 60 cm long and weighing 600 g. It is the only specimen of its kind in the Czech Republic.)

The weapon commonly referred to as Dussack today, however, was made exclusively of wood [177], its handle being little more than an oval aperture in the wood. In 1570, Joachim Meyer speaks of 10 *Leger* or *Huten* (guards), four main cuts, 16 secondary cuts, executed with broad sweeping motions. It remains unclear what rules were followed for competitive bouts.

An illustration in Sutor's *Neu künstliches Fechtbuch* [178] depicts a Dussack fencer drawing blood from his opponent's head, "killing his lice."

As the rapier became a symbol of the Renaissance courtier, the Dussack is most closely associated with the guilds and burghers of the German and other central European cities that thrived as commercial and trade centers.

Apprentices of craftsmen and merchants frequently learned their trades in cities as distant form the German heartland as Milan or Warsaw and probably played a major role in spreading the practice of this most civilian and *bürgerlich* of all fencing weapons throughout Europe.

In civilian life, the Fechtmesser, a close relative of the falchion, remained a standard weapon for trials of skill until the early 18th century. Its late derivative is the infantry hanger. (In Russian, the term tesak still denotes a rather short, heavy, and slightly curved saber.) Hanger and falchion were able to survive the changes in edged weapons fashions for several centuries. Falchions still appear on the trading card of Master Figg by Hogarth (now regarded as an early 19th-century fake). The hanger could be found as a standard infantry sidearm until the early 1900s.

[177] Some accounts mention Dussacks made from leather that are used like truncheons by guardsmen. See also p. 125f.

[178] Sutor, Jakob. *New Künstliches Fechtbuch*, (Frankfurt: Wilhelm Hoffman, 1612) Stuttgart: Verlag v. J. Scheible, 1849; p. 35. The most recent edition of this book was published in 1994 by San Casciano Verlag.

Fencers, beggars, and mendicants

Some historians hold that there was a third guild, the so-called Luxbrüder. In his *Turnkunst*, Friedrich Jahn claims that the term Luxbruder was derived from *Luchs* (lynx), for the guile and cruelty ascribed to the feline. According to him, the term was synonymous with the French *naturalist*, denoting a fighter who did not adhere to the principles of the art and the rules of honor and used forbidden thrusts and hits.

Scheible, however, believes that they were the fighters of St. Luke, a minor and subordinate guild, whose members could not join any of the other guilds or teach their craft for money. However, the two other guilds allowed them to fight and spar with their members.

The Luxbrüder appear to be the predecessors of the Klopffechter (lit.: "knock-fencers"), who really were traveling entertainers exhibiting their skills for money at country fairs, weddings, and banquets throughout the 17th century. (In England, we find an analog development that culminates with the Prize Fighters of the 17th and 18th centuries, whose most famous proponent was Master Figg.)

It was these predecessors of Douglas Fairbanks and the World Wrestling Federation whose antics gave fencing a bad name. In the *Fugger News-Letters* (private communications to Eduard Phillip Fugger of Augsburg who headed the immense Fugger trade empire) we find a curious note on "A Joust in Vienna," dating March 12, 1603:

> *"Last Sunday we had here a magnificent tournament and tilting at the ring, accompanied by wonderful pageants. Among others there came one von Tiefenbach with one hundred fencers, poor, blind, crooked and lame mendicants in rags and tatters, just as they sit in the streets and beg for charity."*[179]

Fencers counted among beggars and vagabonds—this was the lowest level of public esteem fencing would ever hold!

Scholars of the sword

Yet even at a time when these professional fencers were regarded with distrust by the authorities and the establishment, their swagger and trademark habits found imitators among the rebellious young: The Klopffechter of the late 16th century appear to have carried their weapons unsheathed. Consequently, European universities had to admonish students to carry their swords at their side like respectable citizens, not tucked under their armpits or over their arms *(non sub axillaris et super brachia, sed appensos corporis)*.[180]

It is interesting to note in this context that most universities and higher schools did not allow their students to attend the fencing schools. Of course, students did anyway. After all, the sword was a status symbol. And not just any sword would do. In 1629, a student at Altdorf, Germany, wrote home:

> *"Since I must have a sword, I wanted first to ask Mother to buy it for me. Brother has sent me a sword, but it is a child's sword, not a student's, and I am often made fun of because of it."*[181]

[179]von Klarwill, Victor (ed.). *The Fugger News-Letters* (transl. by de Chary, Pauline), New York and London: G.P. Putnam's Sons, 1924; p. 244.

[180]Bonjour, Edgar. *Die Universität Basel von den Anfängen bis zur Gegenwart 1460-1960*, Basel: Helbing & Lichtenhahn, 1960; p. 140f.

[181]Ozment, Steven (ed.). *Three Behaim Boys—Growing Up in Early Modern Germany*, New Haven, CT and London: Yale University Press, 1990; p. 184. The letter writer, Stephan Carl Behaim, was a notorious ne'er-do-well, cheater, and embezzler who died like a dog of sepsis in Brazil in 1638.

Of course, at that time the bearing of arms was explicitly prohibited in the Altdorf School Ordinance—which reads pretty much like modern U.S. high school regulations:

"Item 9: Bearing weapons is forbidden.
Item 10: Weapons brought to school are to be given to teachers or to those running the boarding houses.
Item 11: He who wounds a fellow student with a weapon will be thrown into the city prison and expelled from school."

In the late 15th century, prohibited weapons not only included swords. The Ingolstadt Bursengesetz (college/dormitory law) of 1472 explicitly states that the term weapons means not only swords, rapiers, lances, daggers, sticks, clubs and rocks, but also armor, cuirass and all sorts of head-, arm- and leg-protection; in short, everything that can be used for attack and defense, even knives longer than 6 inches.[182] All of the listed weapons appear to have been used effectively by students.

Academic freedom

The rhetoric of the administrators aside, students in the 15th and 16th centuries were living in a legal vacuum. They were subject to the strict letter of the university laws that often claimed precedence over the secular, even clerical law.

The enforcement of these rules, however, was left to the administrators who, as in the case of the University of Basel, needed to make sure that attendance and recruitment of new students was not overly taxed by all-too-severe punishments. As a result, students often lived and fought in utter lawlessness.

In Basel, a student killed a young clerk of the bishop's after a fight. Claiming priority over the secular authorities, the rector of the university screened the culprit from legal persecution, incensing the bishop, who in turn made use of his right as chancellor of the university to deny academic promotions. As a result, disgruntled candidates for the master of arts degree wined and dined a group of soldiers, who had just returned from Nancy. They incited them to roam the streets of Basel in full armor, brandishing weapons and torches, threatening to attack and ransack church property and churches. The bishop, understandably, quickly gave in . . . [183]

Fights among students and trade apprentices were commonplace, severe, and often lethal. Nightly drinking banquets culminated in wild brawls with the city night guards and militiamen, many of whom were tradesmen and guild fencers themselves. These conflicts continued, first along the class lines of urban society, and later among the upper class of central Europe, until well into this century.

Many universities found that the only possible way to keep students away from the fencing and wrestling schools, as well as the parks and meadows where they practiced running, ball games, and target throwing, was by threatening to withdraw the university's legal protection and making offending students subject to the local authorities.

[182]Scheidler; p. 17.

[183]Bonjour; p. 77.

Hogarth (1735)

The politics of caste

In William Hogarth's 1735 painting *The Rake's Levée* (scene II of the *Rake's Progress* series) the youthful spendthrift is surrounded by the representatives of the parasitic industries catering to the whims and distractions of aristocrats with too much time and money on their hands.

Of interest to fencing historians are two characters in the background. One is a dandified fencing master who carries off his fashionable wig elegantly as he poses in tierce with a button-tipped foil. This is Maitre Dubois, who according to Samuel Ireland was a man *"memorable for his high opinion of the Science of Defence, which he declared superior to all other arts and sciences united."*[184]

Scowling down at him is a stout man of the people in a modest brown coat. His wig is simple and as conspicuously out of place as the quarterstaffs he holds close to his body. Master Figg, the most famous English prize fighter in history, obviously holds little respect for the foppish fencing master.[185]

Hogarth's vignette poignantly illustrates the social rift between the practicians of the art of fencing and the age-old Noble Science of Defence. James Figg—Hogarth also immortalized him in his "Southwark Fair," where the frowning fighter parades on horseback with a basket-hilt backsword—is the personification of the plebeian martial artist, the gladiator proficient in a large variety of edged weapons and pole arms.

But he is the greatest if not the last of his breed, his art slated to be degraded to a sideshow attraction on country fairs in the course of two centuries. And as the fighting arts became a spectacle for the lower orders, caste-conscious aristocrats and patricians opted for the more elegant fencing masters practicing the Italian and French schools of the rapier and smallsword.

By the middle of the 17th century, these weapons already had become status symbols. (In fact, some men of fashion reportedly replaced the blades with wooden lathes—to reduce the weight of the weapon without compromising the show-off splendor of the imported hilt.)

Keeping up with the Joneses

For people not born or elevated into the gentlemanly class, the censure they incurred for misappropriating these symbols could be damaging. Enemies of the philosopher Benedict de Spinoza, for example, spread an evil rumor that Spinoza in his youth had been living it up and was seen wearing a sword in the company of ill-reputed gentlemen.[186] But even the most hostile of his biographers—and he had many of those—had to concede that Spinoza's virtuous way of living made such a pretentious action highly unlikely.

[184] Quoted after Aylward, J.; p. 190.

[185] The difference between these two masters also was reflected in their deaths. They died within 7 months of each other in 1734, Dubois of a lingering wound received in a duel with an Irish fencing master. Figg, on the other hand, passed on four years after his last public battle—the most honored and respected of his gladiatorial profession.

[186] Gebhardt, Carl (ed.). *Spinoza—Lebensbeschreibungen und Gespräche,* Leipzig: Verlag Felix Meiner, 1914; p. 100.

In China, the Way of the Sword was a widely respected art, not only because the skills and techniques were hard to master, but because moral and spiritual qualities were required to attain the highest state of perfection. As in Renaissance Europe, a scholar of the fighting arts would have to master a variety of other short weapons. The *jen ker* (sword master) had to prove his will power, perseverance, and discipline throughout the long years of training required.

In his book *Northern Shaolin Sword*, Dr. Jwing-Ming Yang writes:

"Because the sword is mainly a defensive weapon, it requires a strategy of calmness in action, and to achieve this, one needs patience, calmness, and bravery,"[187] as well as loyalty and humbleness, righteousness and justice. These were the key characteristics of martial arts Masters in general, not only in Asia but in Western and Northern Europe as well.

A matter of class

The straight-bladed cut-and-thrust broadsword and the quarterstaff had dominated weapon play throughout the middle ages. The Italian-style rapier found favor mostly with courtiers and their urban entourage and imitators. We get an inkling of the interconnection of gentlemanly pastimes and the popularity of the rapier in the *Second Fruites* of the Italian expatriate Giovanni "John" Florio, whose Italian-English conversation books were popular among the literate Tudor gentry.

Florio's book, published in London by Thomas Woodcock in 1591, contains the first example of "product placement" and advertising in fencing history. In the seventh chapter, "Of civill, familiar, and pleasant entertainements betweene two Gentlemen,"[188] the conversation between the foppish young cavaliers jumps from "sweete waters" (perfumes) to glove fashions to rapier play.

Florio "plugs" his compatriot V.S.—no other than fencing master Vincentio Saviolo—who had his quarters *"at the signe of the red Lyon."* Apart from his fencing prowess, *"hee hath good skill in every kinde of weapon, hee shootes well in a peece, he shootes well in great ordinance, and besides he is a verie excellent great souldier."* But what sets Saviolo apart from the "manie honest and proper men" among the native masters of arms was that *"hee is a good dancer, hee dances verie well, both galiards, and pavins, hee vaultes most nimblie, and capers verie loftilie."*

Grace in motion

It was the appeal of Saviolo's gentlemanly bearing and the grace of his "lofty capers" that sold many Elizabethan city dwellers with higher social pretensions on his rather costly establishment. Vincentio Saviolo, member of a long-established family of Padua, belonged to the gentlemanly caste. (In Italian, the word *armageri*—lit.: "the ones bearing arms"—is synonymous with the English word "gentlemen".) English fencing masters as a rule were plebeians and craftsmen.

Saviolo's appeal to the upper crust of Tudor London becomes even more obvious if you consider the emphasis he puts on defining when a gentleman should assume his honor violated and how to proceed in a socially acceptable fashion.

[187]Yang, Dr. Jwing-Ming. *Northern Shaolin Sword*, Boston: YMAA, 1985; p. 20.

[188]Florio, John (Giovanni) *Second Fruites,* (London: Th. Woodcock, 1591) Delmar, New York: Scholar's Facsimiles and Reprints, 1977; p. 117f.

Saviolo manages to deal with the technical aspects of the single rapier and rapier and dagger in just 99 pages of *His Practice* (1595). Itt takes him 178 pages to explore the intricacies of the code of honor in *Of Honor and Honorable Quarrels* (1594).[189]

In his two volumes, Saviolo addresses the specific needs and requirements of gentlemen and courtiers who had adopted the fashionable rapier with lavishly decorated and often imported hilts as a fashion accessory, and who on occasion solved their "honorable quarrels" within the narrowly defined, *comment* combat scenario of the duel.

Upwardly mobile

This specialization on one target group becomes especially visible if Saviolo's work is compared to that of his compatriot Giacomo di Grassi, whose *True Arte of Defense* was published in London concurrently with Saviolo's books.[190] Di Grassi covers the correct handling of more than a dozen contemporary weapons, including the staff and edged polearms such as the partisan, bill, halberd and pike. Di Grassi's target audience, however, is the soldier and fighting man, not the foppish courtier. And the warrior differs fundamentally from the duellist:

> *"The soldier differeth from other men, not because he is more skilful in handling the sword or iavelyn, but for that he is expert in everie occasion to know the best advantage & with iudgement both to defend himself with anie thing whatsoever, and therewithal safely to offend the enemy: In which & no other thing consisteth true skirmishing."*[191]

Di Grassi's philosophy is not at all different from that of George Silver, whose *Paradoxes of Defence* (1599) today are frequently discounted by historians as anachronistic, reactionary, and opposed to "progress".

Turner and Soper[192] argue that Silver's treatise was outdated because military combat had adopted other weapons, mainly firearms, that had made the sword obsolete. This is only partly correct. In the military, the sword itself had always been a secondary weapon. Lacking the important medium- and long-range potential of polearms and missiles (such as bolts, arrows, javelins or bullets), the sword was a weapon of last resort for in-fighting, to be used only when long- and medium-range weapons could not be applied effectively.[193]

Again, the authors confuse the spheres of practice. Military combat or extempore fights with bandits on the crime-ridden highways were fundamentally different from swordplay at the salle or duelling ground.

This is Silver's main argument: A courtier's rapier was as misplaced on a 16th-century battlefield or highway as a red Mustang convertible would have been among the Bradley fighting vehicles of Desert Storm:

> *"in battels, and where the variety of weapons be, amongst multitudes of men and horses, the sword and target, the two hand sword, the battel-axe, the blacke-bill, and halbard, are better weapons, and more dangerous in their offence and forces, than is the sword and buckler, short staffe, long staffe, or*

[189]Saviolo, Vincentio. *Of Honor and Honorable Quarrels,* London: John Wolfe, 1594 and *His Practice,* London: John Wolfe, 1595, both contained in Jackson.

[190]Grassi, Giacomo di. *His True Arte of Defence*, London, 1594, also contained in Jackson.

[191]di Grassi, p.43.

[192]Turner, Craig & Soper, Tony. *Methods and Practice of Elizabethan Swordplay*, Carbon & Edwardsville; Southern Illinois UP, 1990.

[193]"Targetiers," highly specialized soldiers armed with heavy shields and broadswords, were used in sieges to enter a breach first under the cover of their shields until the beginning of the 17th century. They operated not only in backward regions such as Scotland, Ireland and Eastern Europe, but even in progressive Holland. Turner's assumption that Silver's armory was antiquated is valid only for fashion-conscious urban environments.

forrest bill. The sword and target leadeth upon shot, and in troupes defendeth thrusts and blowes (. . .) far better than can the sword and buckler. (. . .)

For the single rapier, or rapier and poiniard, they are imperfect and insufficient weapons: and especially in the service of the Prince, when men shall ioyne together, what service can a souldier do with a rapier, a childish toy wherwith a man can do nothing but thrust, nor that neither, by reason of the length, and in everie moving when blowes are a dealing, for lacke of a hilt is in danger to have his hand or arme cut off, or his head cloven."[194]

Silver's criticism of the fashionable Italian establishments focused on their limited repertoire of skills. In fact, he appears to echo Miyamoto Musashi, the great Japanese strategist and author of the *Book of Five Rings*, who wrote:

"If the school is primarily interested in building up a clientele and displays the trophies won at tournaments (. . .), it gives the student the wrong idea about the Way of the warrior. Essentially, such a school is trying to sell its wares to the public by using the long sword [in Tudor London: the rapier] as a means to accumulate wealth. This is absolutely not the way of the warrior."[195]

(As to the rivalry between sword and rapier, the conciliatory conclusion of Dagger in the 1615 A Worke for Cutlers sums up the spheres of combat each weapon was intended for and used in:

"Then in briefe it shall bee thus: Sworde, you shall beare Chiefe force ith [in the] Campe, and be made Generall of the Field, to beare sway every where. As for you, Rapier, since Duels are put downe, you shall live quietly and peacablie heere 'ith Court, and goe every day in Velvet: You shall be Frendes with everie one, and bee on everiy ones side, that if occasion serve, and Sworde be absent, so that matters are driven to a push, Rapier shall be the onely man to perform a combate."[196])

The Italian fencing masters who set up shop in Elizabethan London and their French successors were vintage "lifestyle" entrepreneurs. They provided a specialized service and catered to the comfort and whims of their customers. By providing printed codices of honor, they also created an artificial and self-sustaining need among courtiers and upwardly mobile citizenry to adapt to the new fashion and get acquainted with the courtly weaponry.

Taking advantage of peer pressure and the *nouveaux riches'* characteristic of imitating even the most asinine fad, they were so successful that they practically eradicated the native martial arts, which lingered on for two hundred years but finally dissolved, split up into different "sports" or were completely overcome by the more fashionable weaponry and its techniques. As professor Kiernan puts it in his recent book:

"Newcomers to a class (. . .) are apt to pick up and exaggerate its hallmarks, and intransigent behavior in the aristocracy might be worsened by an influx of new members, eager for acceptance. (. . .) Because in England social mobility made more room for climbers, such snobbery was exceptionally prevalent there; but everywhere duelling must have owed it a heavy debt."[197]

[194]Silver. *Paradoxes;* p. 32, Jackson. p. 530.

[195]Musashi, Myiamoto. *The Martial Artist's Book of Five Rings* (transl. Steve Kaufman), Boston, Rutland, VT, and Tokyo: Charles E. Tuttle Co., 1994; p. 83.

[196]Sieveking, Alfred Forbes (ed.). *Worke for Cutlers, or, A Merry Dialogue betweene Sword, Rapier, and Dagger. Acted in a Shew in the famous Universitie of Cambridge A.D. 1615*, London: C.J. Clay & Sons, 1904; P. 47.

[197]Kiernan, V.G. *The Duel in European History: Honour and Reign of Aristocracy,* Oxford: Oxford UP, 1989; p. 91.

198A similar dispute was to arise two centuries later between Domenico Malevolti Angelo and the French Masters of Defence when the great French encyclopedist Denis Diderot opted to reprint Angelo's *L'École des Armes, avec l'explication générale des principales attitudes et positions concernant l'Escrime* (London: R. & S. Dodsley, 1763), better known as *The School of Fencing.* verbatim under the heading "Escrime" (Fencing) in his *Encyclopédie* (Paris, 1751-65). The choice of the English Italian incensed the French *Compagnie des Maîtres en fait d'Armes.* After all, during his brief stint in Paris, Angelo had indeed taken lessons from the famous Monsieur Teillagory, but had never presented himself for the public trial demanded by the *Compagnie's* statutes.

As in Elizabethan England, the status of Master as well as the concurrent (and very lucrative) teaching privileges were only conferred on candidates who had submitted to the decade-long training process and passed rigorous practical exams at public trials. Their protests irked Angelo. When Guillaume Danet, syndic of the *Compagnie* and the best known French master of his time, published his *L'Art des Armes* (Paris: Herissant Fils, 1766-67) Angelo denounced it as being a poorly disguised plagiarism of his own *École.* Danet countered that Angelo's book was outdated, as it still included recommendations on the arcane cloak-and-sword and lantern-and-sword techniques no man would encounter anywhere in civilized Europe. The quarrel escalated into trading professional insults for several years, one side attempting to denigrate the other's achievements much like modern-day politicians.

Like today, however, publicity sold books. Angelo's lavishly illustrated book (47 colorized copper plates) saw two further editions within less than five years (in 1765 and 1767). And it didn't stop at that. In

(note continued on p. 243)

"Base mechanicks"

In the 1400s, English Masters of Defence, particularly those in urban London, for the most part were members of the trades and guilds. The Treher clan of London, famous fighters for several generations, were fishmongers by trade, thus members of the five great victualling mysteries that represented a civic nobility of sorts. Others were wire drawers, glovers, tailors, gunners, even watermen, and butchers.

It remains unclear if the English masters were actually practicing artisans and tradesmen, or if their membership in the respective professional associations was more or less a paper front. By 1540, however, the uphill battle of the native fencing masters had resulted in professional recognition through Henry VIII.

Until James I revoked the privileges of guilds and companies in the Monopolies Act of 1623-24, fencers aspiring to the teaching privileges of Master of Defence had to pass through a rigorous apprenticeship that usually lasted 14 years. For each promotion, they had to challenge the masters at a certain number of weapons.

For the Free Scholar's prize, the applicant had to face off against any challengers at three weapons: long sword, back sword and sword and buckler. Provosts had to prove their skills in the same weapons, plus one pole arm. When John Blinkinsopps played his Free Scholar's prize, he met 10 answerers to his challenge at the long sword, 12 at the back sword, and 18 at the sword and buckler, with more than 80 (!) bouts fought.

Merchants of Defence

In 1576, an Italian going by the name of Rocco Bonnetti set up shop as a fencing master in London. He considered himself a gentleman, having been a captain in the service of the Venetian Republic and an emissary and secret agent of Catharina dei' Medici.

Rocco target-marketed his services and establishment to noblemen and gentlemen, providing suitable surroundings for men of fashion and leisure in his school. His school could be considered the first upscale health club.

There were gold-fringed carpets, writing stands with gilded paper, even— an unheard-of luxury for his time—a clock with a large dial. His students paid dearly, between £20 and £100 per year. But where the plebeian masters had only wooden benches and ash sticks to offer, Rocco flattered his clients' vanity by prominently displaying their coats of arms where they could hang their garments and fencing equipment.

The establishment of his school, of course, was a blatant infringement on the Masters' privileges that had been renewed by Elizabeth only a few years before. Fully aware of Rocco's powerful connections among his students and sponsors, they offered him a compromise:

They would cut the Red Tape and waive the required 14-year apprenticeship if Rocco agreed to play the prize for the Masters license, according to the rules. In characteristic arrogance, Rocco refused to even recognize the "base mechanicks" who had dared to challenge him.[198] (His setting up shop in London could be compared to a foreign doctor opening a medical clinic in New York City without approval of the medical board, simply because of his connections to local politicians.)

Angry young men

As several angered Provosts continued to harass him into putting his skills to the test, Rocco chose a rather modern way of handling the situation: Instead of laying the issue to rest once and for all by fighting it out like a Master would have, he complained to the Lord Mayor of London. There are no official records of any punitive actions being taken against these angry young men by the magistrate. Although the Masters appear to have calmed down the most rambunctious Provosts, the deep resentment against the Italian impostor continued to smolder for years.

Only once did Rocco face off against a native fighter, a man named Austen Bagger, who made a nuisance of himself outside Rocco's house. Silver describes Bagger as a *"verie tall gentleman of his handes, not standing much upon his skill, but carying the valiant heart of an Englishman."* [199] That means he was a tradesman more courageous than skilled in the trade of arms... a mere amateur!

Enraged by Bagger's taunts, the Italian seized up the situation. Seeing Bagger stand in the street with his sword and buckler, he grabbed his two-handed sword and rushed outside.

The deliberate choice of weapon on Rocco's side illustrates that this man was no fool. Silver categorizes the two-handed sword as superior to the sword and target, the sword and buckler, the sword and dagger and, of course, the rapier and poniard. [200] Obviously, there should have been no reason for Rocco to lose this fight: After all, he was a professional with superior hardware pitched against an amateur.

But lose he did. In the ensuing fight, Rocco was wounded in the leg, *"over the breech"* and *"under his feet"*. [201] Bagger, *"in his good nature, gave him his life."*

Another time, when he drew his rapier on an (unarmed) waterman, he was soundly thrashed with an oar. But even Silver concedes that in this encounter, the "vantage" was with the improvised pole arm.

Despite the outrageous fees for his classes, Rocco—like many other men of fashion—never escaped pecuniary dire straits and was later forced to re-enter his career as a secret agent. He died in 1587. [202]

Risk and reward

By the 1590s, Italian fencing entrepreneurs were putting their lives at stake. Challenges by native fighters, whose versatility in multiple weapons and their more efficient use actually made them superior in fights to the death, cost more than one Italian master his life. Saviolo only survived because he prudently avoided putting his professed skills to the test by ignoring George and Toby Silver's challenge for a public trial of arms—earning Silver's ironic praise that he was a much better Christian than fighter. [203] His patrician arrogance, the haughty disregard for the plebeian masters, and a clear intuitive assessment of potentially life-threatening situations prevented him from getting in trouble...

Ieronimo, on the other hand, did earn Silver's (posthumous) respect as a valiant man. A native Englishman named Cheese challenged him with sword and dagger, to which Ieronimo

(continued from p. 243)

1787, Domenico's son Henry decided that a smaller format would sell even more copies and subsequently had Diderot's plates re-engraved to fill an oblong octavo, *The School of Fencing* (London, 1787). A second edition of this version followed in 1799.

[199] Silver. *Paradoxes;* p. 66.

[200] Silver. *ibid.* p. 31.

[201] Anglin links Rocco's death to the wounds received in the fight against Bagger, whereas Hutton only blames Bagger for "relegating Rocco to private life".

[202] See Silver. *Paradoxes;* p. 66. Plus, Anglin, Jay P. "The Schools of Defense in Elizabethan London," in *Renaissance Quarterly,* vol. xxxvii, #3, Fall 1984; p. 393-410; Aylward, J.D. *The English Master of Arms;* Hutton, Sir Alfred. *The Sword and the Centuries;* p. 150f.

[203] Silver. *Paradoxes;* p. 70.

"drew his Rapier and dagger, put himself into his best ward or stocata (sic) which ward was taught by himselfe and Vincentio [Saviolo], and by them best allowed of, to be the best ward to stand upon in fight for life, either to assault the enemie, or stand and watch his comming, which ward it should seeme he ventured his life upon, but howsoever with all the fine Italienated skill Ieronimo had, Cheese with his Sword within two thrustes ran him into the bodie and slue him."[204]

Modern fencing historians tend to reduce the conflict between the Italian and English traditions to one of cut ("reactionary") vs. thrust ("progressive"). For some reason, the general assumption is that the Masters did not know how to thrust.

Oddly, no-one seems to have bothered to take a gander at this (or any?) passage in Silver: Cheese beats (and kills) Ieronimo fair and square *with a thrust, on his second attack!*

But the Italian systems' lack of versatility was more than made up by the artificial demand their popular masters created. When the popularity of the Italian schools began to translate into political clout, the fate of the martial artists was sealed. Fencing, once part of a free man's survival training, declined to become a part of class-conscious socialization— *"frecher Stolz des Herrn geword'nen Bürgers",* catering to the status symbolism of young aristocrats and bourgeois.

Young English provincials whose parents had high-flying pretensions for them—like Roderick Random's old schoolmate, 'squire Gawky—would be sent to town, for their *"improvement in writing, dancing, fencing"*[205], obtaining a superficial mastery of the art, never, however, being able to reach the balance and spiritual center of the true fighter.

(Thus, the Italian entrepreneurs could be regarded the Renaissance equivalent of the 1950s "Coca Cola imperialists," a mercantile force powerful enough to eradicate an entire substratum of a millennia-old native combat culture.)

But even in the early 17th century, marketing your services to rich kids was not all roses. Swetnam gives us a taste of the scattered, fad-driven interest a master might run into when teaching the promising offspring of the upper crust and those who felt they should be:

"Most youth, for example, are willing to goe to Schoole at the first, but within a weeke or lesse, away must the booke be laid, for feare lest much learning make them madde, as Festus said to Paul, for they will waxe dull and weary with a little paines taken. And next, they must to the Fence Schoole, but there I am perswaded they neede not learne offence, and I thinke a little defence is enough for them; for many will be wearie of well doing quickly, saying as the Porters of Bristow, a new Maister, a new, and hang up the old; even so, from the Fence schoole they must goe to the Dauncing schoole, thinking that to be the onely exercise in the world, but with a little practise they waxe weary of dancing likewise: then they say, Oh that heere were one to teach Musicke!..."[206]

And to think they didn't have "Attention Deficit Disorders" and other responsibility-deferring pseudo-clinical illnesses to blame back then![207] Yet it is these young gentlemen of class, means, leisure, and scattered attention spans that we owe the birth

[204]Silver. *ibid.*; p. 72.

[205]Smollett, Tobias. *The Adventures of Roderick Random,* (1748), Oxford & New York: Oxford University Press, (1979) 1981; p. 24.

[206]Swetnam; p. 48.

[207]Coach Richard Oles of Salle Pallasz in Baltimore, where I fenced for the short period between graduate school and children, recently appeared in a newspaper interview with an observation that curiously echoes Swetnam: *"Then came television.* Oles says with resignation. *'People with short attention spans and low thresholds of concentration cannot succeed in this sport.'* All this, Oles asserts, is why in 100 years of Olympics and international competition, the United States has medaled only four times—all in the bronze category. *'We always come back with our tails between our legs.'"* in Duffy, John. — "Touche! For fencing pro Oles, thrust never sleeps," in "Lifetimes" section of *Towson Times* (Towson, MD: Patuxent Publishing), Dec. 17, 1997; p.16.

of the art of fencing to:

> *"The moderns having adopted the small sword in preference to the ancient*
> *arms, it gave rise to a new species of defence, distinguished by the appellation*
> *of Fencing, which justly forms part of the education of persons of rank; giving*
> *them additional strength of body, proper confidence, grace, activity, and address;*
> *enabling them, likewise, to pursue other exercises with greater facility."*[208]

Learning the use of the rapier and smallsword still involved at least the notion that the skills gained by the exercise might come in handy in a duel—much like some suburban mothers today believe an hour or two at Kim's Karate will build up Junior's self-esteem on the schoolyard. But Martelli already prioritizes what the true focus of contemporary fencing was:

> *"In short, the exercise of arms, unites two inseparable qualities, the agreeable*
> *and useful: the former, as it affords gentlemen a noble and distinguished*
> *amusement; the latter, as it contributes to the formation of their gait, and*
> *furnishes them with the means of defence, either of their honour or their*
> *life, if one or the other should be called in question by disagreeable accident,*
> *or attacked by turbulent and quarrelsome persons, whose correction tends to*
> *the good of society in general."*[209]

Right...

In the decades that followed, the smallsword disappeared from daily life. Still, fencing was taught with a vague sense of its martial usefulness and character-building qualities:

> *"The art of fencing, taken in a military sense, is, undoubtedly, of immense*
> *value; but I can further, with safety, say that it is also a part of a good*
> *education."*[210]

High society

When the assorted specters of Marx, Engels, and Lenin began to haunt Europe, fencing's snobbish image as a pastime of the rich and useless was fully established. A tell-tale characterization is included in an (otherwise excellent) East German fencing book:

> *"The class character of the sport of fencing is reflected in pre-WWII*
> *Germany. Before 1933 [Hitler's assumption of power], there were two roof*
> *organizations in which fencing was practiced, the DFB and the Fencing*
> *Association of the German Athletic League. The DFB, where circles of the*
> *military and the upper bourgeoisie had established themselves, had about*
> *2,000 members in 1930. In the Fencing Association of the German Athletic*
> *League, 12,000 members were registered at that time, during which fencing*
> *experienced great expansion.*

[208]Angelo, Henry. — "Preface"; in Angelo, Domenico. *The School of Fencing with a General Explanation of the Principal Attitudes and Positions Peculiar to the Art,* (London, 1787) New York: Land's End Press, 1971; p. v.
[209]Martelli; p. iv.
[210]Corbesier, Antoine J.. *Theory of Fencing; with the Small-Sword Exercise,* Washington: Government Printing Ofiice, 1873; Preface.

Since the Workers' Gymnastics and Sports Association, whose leadership belonged to the right-wing Social Democrats, rejected sports such as fencing or tennis as 'bourgeois', a worker interested in fencing had practically no opportunity to practice this sport. Only after 1930, until the fascist assumption of power, groups were founded within the Fighting Association of the Red Sports Unit, in which the working class could exercise the sport of fencing."[211]

Apart from the *realsozialist* jargon, the "authors' collective" signing off on this book is actually quite on target. Take the case of Luigi Barbasetti and the genesis of the prominent Viennese Union Fencing Club[212]:

High pretensions

Barbasetti is one of the most important figures in Central Europe, considered as one of the most instrumental men to spread the new Radaelli method of saber fencing beyond Italy, and into one of the last bastions of traditional broadsword fencing.

Born at Cividale (Friaul), Italy, in 1859, he taught fencing at the renowned Scuola Magistrale at Rome from 1885 to 1891. He then became instructor at a fencing club in Trieste, where he was invited to participate in a tournament by Count Sordina in 1894. Viennese fencers at that tournament were so impressed by his abilities that they invited him to come to Vienna to head a spanking new fencing establishment.

On January 1, 1895, Barbasetti opened his salle St. Annahof in Vienna. Like Bonnetti 300 years before, his digs boasted revolutionary luxuries... electric light—and a bathroom! On January 18, the statutes of the Union Club were approved. Barbasetti became the accredited fencing master of the club, at the handsome salary of 1,200 guilders.

The Union Club was not just any club. An initiation fee of 20 guilders and annual fees of 100 guilders made sure the riffraff stayed out. When in March of 1895, the club's leadership decided to change the name to Union Fencing Club (UFC), they also voted a true blue blood into the presidency: Alexander Prince von Thurn and Taxis, who was to remain in office until 1938.

Out of the 45 members registered by 1896, the majority belonged to the Austrian, Hungarian, and German high nobility, and included court functionaries and foreign ambassadors... a membership exclusive and influential enough to make Emperor Franz Joseph himself granted the distinguishing acronym k.u.k.[213] in its name in 1912, and allowed the club to add the Imperial eagle to its coat of arms in 1913.

Much like his compatriot Saviolo in Elizabethan London, Barbasetti made good use of his connections, publishing his *Das Säbelfechten* (1899), *Das Stoßfechten* (1900) and his *Ehrenkodex* (1901) to add both to his revenues and reputation, while creating a continuing demand for his services. In 1904, he founded the Akademie der Fechtkunst in Wien, modeled on the Academia nazionale di scherma in Rome. He became president, systematically expanding his influence internationally until he retired from this office in 1910. When World War I broke out—which pitched the Austro-Hungarian Empire against Italy—Barbasetti returned to Italy.

[211] *"Deutlich spiegelte sich der Klassencharakter des Fechtsports in Deutschland vor dem zweiten Weltkrieg wider. Vor 1933 gab es mit dem Deutschen Fechterbund und dem Fechtverband der Deutschen Turnerschaft zwei Verbände, in denen der Fechtsport betrieben wurde. Der Deutsche Fechterbund, in dem sich vorwiegend Kreise des Militärs und der Großbourgeoisie etablierten, hatte 1930 etwa 2000 Mitglieder. Im Fechtverband der Deutschen Turnerschaft waren zu dieser Zeit, in welcher der Fechtsport große Verbreitung fand, rund 12000 Mitglieder erfaßt. Da der Arbeiter-Turn-und-Sportbund, dessen Führung der rechten Sozialdemokratie angehörte, Sportarten wie zum Beispiel Fechten und Tennis als "bürgerlich" ablehnte, bestand für den am Fechtsport interessierten Arbeiter im Prinzip keine Möglichkeit, diese Sportart zu betreiben. Erst nach 1930 entstanden bis zur faschistischen Machtübergreifung in Halle und Berlin in der Kampfgemeinschaft für Rote Sporteinheit Gruppen, in denen die Arbeiterklasse den Fechtsport ausüben konnte."* Barth, Berndt et al.. **Fechten: Ein Lehrbuch für die Grundausbildung im Florett-, Säbel- und Degenfechten**, Berlin (East Germany): Sportverlag Berlin, 1979 (2nd ed.); p.12.

[212] Wenusch, Michael. **Engarde, Parade, Touché: Die Entwicklung des Wiener Fechtsports**, Wien: Wiener Stadt- und Landesarchiv, 1998.

[213] i.e., *kaiserlich und königlich*, "imperial and royal"

By then, most of civilized Central Europe was fencing according to the Radaelli method...

Nazi pastimes

Fencing's social history is full of ironies. Particularly in Germany.

For a short period, a simplified system of Meyer's two-handed sword system was practiced by the Hitler Youth.[214] It was heavily promoted by the historian of the Corps students, Wilhelm Fabricius[215] in a rather blatant attempt at currying favor with the brown *"Kameraden des großen Bundes."*

The Nazis, driven by the fencing enthusiasm of individual functionaries such as Reinhard Heydrich[216], who focused heavily on competitive fencing during the 1936 Olympic Games.

Ironically, it was the weapon popularized by the most reactionary layers of pre-WWI high society that became the favorite toy with the genocidal maniacs of the National Socialist Workers Party... Heydrich himself favored the modern saber, recruiting German fencing clubs to *"build up an SS team of the best fencers in Germany, or to make it look as if such men were best off in the SS."*[217] All SS officers and NCOs at some point were instructed to take saber lessons.

On the other hand, the honest old Schläger[218] of the student fraternities was vilified as bourgeois and anti-social:

Despite lifting the Weimar Republic's prohibition of the Mensur in 1933 to maintain support for the still shaky power structure, the youth and student organizations of the Nazi Party prohibited dual membership in a Nazi organization and a duelling Corps on July 8, 1935, replacing the latter with Nazi-controlled *Kameradschaften* who were to practice fencing with the sports saber.

Rudolf Hess himself followed suit on May 14, 1936 by prohibiting Party Members from belonging to any old-style fraternity. This included the tradition-carrying alumni organizations. By then, however, the different roof organizations had either joined up with the Nazis (like the Deutsche Burschenschaft) or dissolved (like the roof organizations of the Corps).[219]

But the Nazis had not counted on the old fencing instructors. Fencing masters like the Göttingen master Christian Seemann-Kahne catered to the *Kameradschaften* much like they did before to the Corps—only that they now taught the light Italian saber rather than the Schläger and basket-hilt saber. Seemann-Kahne turned out to be a living archive of fencing anecdotes and secrets. As soon as 1940, the interest among the students had shifted back toward the old traditions.

[214]Amberger, J. Christoph. —"Bruises and bumps: The short-lived revival of the two-handed sword as a Hitler Youth camp sport," in *Hammerterz Forum*, vol. 2, #4 / vol. 3, #1; p. 22f.

[215]see Fabricius, Wilhelm. *Ritterliche Waffenspiele: Schwert- und Stockfechten, Bogenschießen, Armbrustschießen, Bau von Übungswaffen*, Stuttgart (Germany): Franckh'sche Verlagsbuchhandlung, 1935.

[216]Amberger, J. Christoph. —"Sabers and Swastika: Heydrich's Grab for the FIE Presidency," in *Hammerterz Forum*, vol. 2, #1 (Summer 1995); p. 8f.

[217]Deschner, Günter. *Reinhard Heydrich—A Biography of the Man behind the "Final Solution"*, New York: Stein and Day, 1981; p. 121.

[218]The Schläger or Hieber is a variety of the military backsword systems practiced until the 1850s. Heck's American encyclopedia (Heck, Johann Georg. *Iconographic Encyclopedia of Science, Literature, and Art*, vol. III, New York: Rudolph Garrigue, 1851) is based on an 1840s edition of the German Brockhaus encyclopedia, and depicts a system that closely resembles that of contemporary Schlägerplay. In fact, weapons and practice were so similar that German university bureaucrats were able to sell hilts and weapons confiscated during raids on fencing students to the military. (See Assmann, Rainer. —"Studentische Waffen 1840— 'Acten betreffend...konfiscierter Gegenstände'," in *Einst und Jetzt*, vol. 42 (1997); p. 87. The Schläger replaced the aristocratic smallsword after the French Revolution, when Republican, anti-aristocratic sentiment ran high among students in the German states.

[219]Like with any aspect of public life in Germany, who did and who didn't do what in

(note continued on p. 236)

Some *Kameradschaften* actually turned back into clandestine Corps, who even contracted to have Seemann-Kahne teach Schläger again:

> *"The light saber was dropped soon in favor of Schläger fencing. One wanted to focus on the Schläger because the foremost aim was that every member of the Kameradschaft was to be prepared to step up to the first opportunity that arose to take up sharp weapons without long preparations. Thus it was kept throughout the war. When the older ones were ready, they began to practice the heavy saber again (. . .) also with Seemann-Kahne, while the pledges studied the Schläger first."*[220]

German during the Nazi period can trigger the most poisonous discussions. Some of the more worthwhile contributions regarding the convoluted and controversial history of the Corps in the early years of the Third Reich can be found in the following articles: Wippermann, Wolfgang. — "Wie war es wirklich? Wichtige Daten zum Thema Corps und Nationalsozialismus" in **Der Corpsstudent**, Nr. 1/96, 3. Jahrgang; p. 17.
—"Zu: Wie war es wirklich? Wichtige Daten zum Thema Corps und Nationalsozialismus, in *Der Corpsstudent*, 1/96" in **Der Corpsstudent**, Nr. 3, 3. Jahrgang (3/1996); p. 126.
Heither, Dietrich. —"Zu: *Der Corpsstudent*, 1/96" (Letter to the Editor), in **Der Corpsstudent**, Nr. 2/96, 3. Jahrgang (3/1996); p. 92.
Knorre, Erik von. —"Zu: 'Wie war es wirklich?', in *Der Corpsstudent*, 1/96", in **Der Corpsstudent,** Nr. 3, 3. Jahrgang (3/1996); p. 126.
    The best monograph on the subject is Weber, R.G.S. **The German Student Corps in the Third Reich**, New York: St. Martin's Press, 1986.

[220] Stadtmüller, Franz et al.. **Geschichte des Corps Hannovera zu Göttingen 1809-1959**, Göttingen: Corps Hannovera, 1963; p. 286.

INTERLUDE

ANTAGONISTIC COMBAT
Combat for survival

Kraut Control: How American GIs Were to Fight Sword-Wielding Axis Officers in World War II

U.S. Field Manual 21-150[221] is the last original military manual to seriously include unarmed defence against an opponent wielding European-style swords—a remote possibility even back in 1942!

They are built around the assumption that the GI would encounter an opponent trained in classic western swordsmanship:

• **Your best defense against a lunge with the sword**

"An individual trained in the use of the foil or épée will approach you in the manner illustrated in Figure A. (...) As your opponent lunges with the sword, with the point aimed at your midsection, you execute [a] sideward movement of the body (...) to the right, at the same time tapping the blade of the attacking weapon smartly with either your forearm or wrist—the weapon should not be grasped with the hand. (Figure B.)

Figure A

Immediately [after] you have tapped the sword aside, you will take a short step with your left foot, and immediately raise your right leg, kicking your opponent behind the knee joint forcibly, at the same time that you bring the heel of your right hand against your opponent's chin. (Figure C.)

Figure B

• **Defense against a straight saber cut**

"The average saberman will attempt the downward cut illustrated in Figure D.

Your immediate reaction is to step as close to your opponent as possible, bringing your left forearm against his striking arm. (Figure E.)

Figure C

[221]War Department.
Basic Field Manual 21-150: Unarmed Defense for the American Soldier,
Washington, DC: Government Printing Office, June 30, 1942.

Figure D

Figure E

Immediately [after] you have broken the force of the blow, raise your right knee and your right hand simultaneously. The fingers of your right hand, palm uppermost, will be brought with great force into your opponent's solar plexus while your knww is simultaneously brought into his groin. (Figure F.)

Figure F

Figure G

• **Defense against a cross-cut with the saber:**

"It is unusual for a trained inividual to attempt a cut illustrated in Figure G. But if the attempt is made, you will step with your right leg and present your right fore-arm against your opponent's striking arm.

You will make no attmpt to stop the blow directly, but [let it] continue its momentum in the direction in which it is moving, stepping to your opponent's right rear with your left leg, and reaching over his left shoulder with your left hand. (Figure H.)

You will now be in a position behind your opponent, grasping his wrist with the palm turned away from your body. Grasp his right lapelwith your left hand, crossing over the front of your opponent's throat.

Figure H

Figure I

Simultaneously, raise your right leg and, placing the sole of your foot against the right knee joint, push strongly. This action will topple your opponent backward and place you in a position to break his right elbow over your thigh or hip. (Figure I.)"

Fencing School
Commenius (1658)

Glory Days of the Foil

When it comes to recreating historical fencing styles, the foil these days sure takes the cake for being the least respected—because least "realistic"—weapon of 'em all. Maybe there's too many "girls" doing foil... maybe the modern right-of-way rules are a tad to rarefied to appeal to us tough guys out for the quick kill. Or maybe it's just because each true swordsman at heart has to be a contrarian... and there are just too many people fencing foil these days.

Among the small but growing number of historians and re-enactors devoted to reconstructing historic fencing systems, the foil has become a symbol of decadence—a weapon instrumental in turning "real" swordsmanship into pretentious aristocratic calisthenics... or worse, the subject of endless newsgroup discussions with the subject header "The Flick".

Le flic, c'est chic

The foil, the argument goes, created the sport of fencing sometime in the last decades of the 1600s, when foreign interlopers (Italian, French, Spanish) established a strain of swordplay that was far removed and outside the traditional schools of defence—who used rapiers and swords, or at least sturdy ash sticks to acquaint their acolytes with how painful a slip-up in your ward could be.

And it is true. Masters like the German Hundt show the odd rapier player wielding a swept-hilt rapier with a ridiculous grapefruit-sized ball at the point. Also, fencing masters depicted in 17th- and 18th-century prints are a tad on the scrawny side... without the brawn and bulk of Meyer's, Sutor's, even Roworth's muscle-bound masters.

But like so many other aspects of fencing history, the story of the foil is far less linear than most experts have come to accept. For one, there's more to the terminology than meets the eye...

"Fencers' foiles, which hit but hurt not," as Shakespeare called them in *Much Ado About Nothing*—weapons used for practice play—are mentioned as far back as Elizabethan drama. Hamlet's famous duel, for one, is fought with foils, not rapiers.

Shakespearean usage of the word "foile" refers to any rebated weapon, *"i.e., a weapon equipped with a buttoned tip. Accordingly, in the 16th and first half of the 17th century, this would have been a practice rapier with a rectangular blade that had little in common with its modern counterparts."*[222]

Egerton Castle derives the word foil from the Old French *fouler* or *refouler*, to turn back, applying *"to all rebated weapons, whether a sword for practice, a lance, or any other weapon."*[223]

Wilson points out that he *"can see nothing in Shakespeare to show that he knew of buttons. Had he done so, they would undoubtedly have been referred to in Hamlet, where on the contrary it is perfectly obvious that the word 'foil' means a sword or rapier with bated edge and blunted point, and where indeed the treacherous scheme of Laertes would have been impossible had buttoned fleurets been intended."*[224]

English terminology, however, plays a subordinate role if it come to fencing history. Civrny comments:

"It is commonly assumed that the fioretti *or* fleurets *were named for their protective leather buttons, the so-called* mouches, *which were attached to the points of the weapons for practice and were similar to flower (fleur) buds. Si non e vero, e bene trovato: Even if it ain't true, it's a good story."*[225]

[222]Fare, Malcolm. —"Fencers' foiles, which hit but hurt not," in *Hammerterz Forum*, vol. 3, # 4/vol. 4, #1 (Spring/Summer 1997), p. 5f.

[223]Castle, Egerton. *Schools and Masters of Fence from the Middle Ages to the 18th Century*. London: George Bell & Sons, (1884) 1892 (revised ed.); p. 197.

[224]Wilson, J. Dover. —"Introduction (Including some speculations on thefencing-match in Hamlet)." in Silver, George. *Paradoxes of Defence*, London: Oxford UP (The Shakespeare Association Facsimiles No. 6), 1933; p. vii.

[225]Civrny, Dr. Cestmir. *Florett*, München: self-published, 1993; p. 3.

[226]Fare; ibid.

The first depiction of this weapon has commonly been attributed to de la Touche's *Les Vrays Principes de l'Épée* (1697). It *"had a guard composed of a series of iron bars curving up from the handle to form a crown or basket. A square, cord-bound handle connected the guard to a globular or egg-shaped iron pommel. (...) Toward the end of the 17th century, the guard was simplified to a figure-of-8 design with a short crossbar and four bars extending from this to meet about 1.5" down the blade."*[226] (De la Touche's hilt is illustrated in a fine print of a fencing master in the Bibliotheque Nationale in Paris.)

The de la Touche-type foil's morphology, of course, has little in common with that of the classic figure-eight foil, which probably was used in the 18th century, but only appears in 1787 in the portrait of the Chevalier de Saint George, and about two decades later in La Boëssiere's *Traité de l'Art des Armes* (1818). This simple design dominated the French foil school and its offspring in Britain and America.

The situation was different in Spain and Germany, where rapier-type weapons with flat or diamond-shaped blades were used. Fare comments:

"After some experimenting with open hilts during the 17th century, this weapon branched off into four distinct forms, all based on an enclosed guard with ricasso, arms, and crossbar. (. . .)

Neapolitan and Sicilian fencers used what has come to be regarded as the traditional Italian foil. It had a deep bell guard about 4 inches in diameter, a 3-inch deep ricasso, and a crossbar joined to the guard by straight arms 1 1/4 inches long that allowed two fingers to be hooked round the bar. Following the Napoleonic era, another, lighter type of foil became popular in northern Italy. (. . .) With a shallow dish guard about 3 1/2 inches in diameter, a 2-inch deep ricasso, and a crossbar joined to the guard by curved arms, the fencer would hook his index finger round the bar.

In a curious variation used in Germany and the Netherlands, the crossbar touched the shell with no connecting arms, making it necessary for the forefinger to lie along the bar. (. . .) In Spain, a cup-hilt rapier foil distinguished by a diamond-shaped blade and a knuckle guard was used into the early 20th century. Large rings through which two fingers could be placed met inside a broad shell about 5 inches in diameter by 2 inches deep."[227]

Steel baskets, dish hilts, cup hilts, ricassos, no ricassos, rings, pas d'anes, quillons, bars, attached bars, unattached bars, diamond-shaped blades, rectangular cross-cut blades—all labeled as predecessors or close relatives of the modern fencing foil... seems like when it comes to establishing morphological criteria for defining what is a foil, we're just one dog-faced boy short of a freak show!

The proof's in the pudding

I recently happened upon a source which illustrates that the foil indeed might be older than the accepted beginning of iconographic evidence. A woodcut from Johann Amos Commenius' *Orbis sensualium pictus* (Nuremberg, 1658)[228] presents an interesting view of a 17th-century fencing school. Students are grappling, wrestling, and fencing with the two-handed sword—and what could be a foil! Commenius' work was a Latin primer for children. It contained about 150 engravings with text in both Latin and German. The German version was translated

[227]ibid.

[228]This print is included in Bauer, Max. *Sittengeschichte des deutschen Studententums,* (Dresden: Paul Aretz Verlag, n.d.) Schernfeld: SH Verlag, 1991.

into many languages, including English versions in 1659 and in 1672. The English translation[229] of plate 32 "The Fencing School" reads:

> *"Fencers meet in a Duel in a Fencing-place, fighting with swords (1), or Pikes (2), and Halberds (3) or Short-swords (4), or Rapiers (5), having Bals at the point (lest they would one another mortally), or with two-edged swords and a Daggar (6) together. Wrastlers (7)… take hold of one another, and strive whether can throw the other, especially by tripping up his heels (8)."*

The weapon in question is equipped with a small, circular cup hilt, as well as a golf ball-sized ball at the point. The fencers use the left hand as active and passive defence.

Equally interesting is the assortment of weapons on the floor. Ordered in sequence "from the smallest to the tallest" like in the Fechtschul fights of the Marxbrüder and Federfechter a century before, they include Dussacks, short sword (or dagger), staff, and halberd.

(The English translation obviously needs to be approached with a grain of salt. After all, the wooden Dussack is identified as a "short sword", the obviously friendly encounter at "Rapiers" is called a "Duel.")

When I first suggested that the weapons depicted in Commenius could be foils (in the modern sense of being practice weapons specifically designed for agonistic combat, rather than blunted or "rebated" weapons), many authorities disagreed. Malcolm Fare, editor of the British fencing magazine *The Sword* and by far the most knowledgeable person on foils I have ever had the pleasure to correspond with, wrote to me:

> *"Your piece on the 'Glory Days of the Foil'[230], based on that intriguing woodcut of 1658, was certainly entertaining, although I disagree with your conclusion. The interesting thrusting weapons shown in the woodcut, and the weapons used in Hamlet's duel, I would call practice rapiers.*
> *They are only foils in the sense of being rebated weapons, just as the long swords in the Swiss National Museum in Zurich and the Metropolitan Museum of Art in New York, and the practice rapier in the Victoria and Albert Museum in London, are described. But in the modern sense of a weapon made purely for sport or exercise with its own rules and conventions, the foil has its origin in mid-17th-century France, and is shown for the first time by de la Touche in 1670. This is very different from those rebated weapons used in practice for duels with their sharp equivalents."[231]*

While far from trying to re-write accepted fencing history based on a single and generic iconographic source, I believe this comment points at the main problem: Very different weapons are being referred to as foils.

The main usages of the word foil in the English language appear to describe the following types:

Type I (old usage): blunt(ed)/rebated/ball- or button-tipped weapon for thrust, or cut and thrust, used to prepare for antagonistic combat

[229]This was taken from a reprint of the 1672 English version, found in *The Tudor-Stuart Sourcebook*, edited by Jeff Singman, and pointed out to me by *Hammerterz Forum* reader Scott Crawford.

[230]Amberger, J. Christoph. — "Glory Days of the Foil," in *Hammerterz Forum* vol. 4, ##3 and 4, (July 15, 1998); p. 22.

[231]Fare, Malcolm, in a fax to the author dating from Aug. 17, 1998.

Type II   (modern usage): a) blunt(ed)/rebated/ball- or button-tipped thrust weapon specifically designed and made for use in a closely defined and regulated competitive agonistic combat
b) blunt, button-tipped, standardized thrust weapon designed for a specialized, closely defined and regulated competitive agonistic combat scenarios, whose length, weight, dimensions are dictated by central regulatory authorities and whose target is restricted to the torso of the opponent.

The classification of Type II b) covers the modern sports weapon and its immediate predecessors (distinguishing them from sports épées, for example). But unless we specify clear weight limits and blade dimensions, Types I and II a) still defy clear classification when applied to the gray area of the period characterized by the different styles of foils.

The crucial difference, it would appear, boils down to the weapon's intended use and the intent underlying its construction:

Where does foil fencing begin?

You will notice that I do not differentiate between the two combat scenarios in my Grid of Steel: Unless the assertion of superior skill levels is the predominant motivation of the exercise (which would classify the encounter as "Olympic"), I label both of them as "Olympian", characterized by the motivation to *"competitively assert superiority of skill ('winning') by scoring a predetermined number a clearly defined objectives (e.g., hits on 'targets') while adhering to a clearly defined, enforced, or implied code of behavior."*

The objective of scoring a "hit" on the target, i.e., bringing the point of the blade in contact with the opponent's body, or a specific part of the opponent's body without injuring him underlies both scenarios. The target definition is arrived at by either abstractly/implicitly (modern fencing) or empirically (duelling practice) equating successful target contact with inflicting an incapacitating injury.

Civrny again makes an important observation:

"[The foil] *was simply a practice weapon, a practice sword*[232], *with a lighter, shorter, and, most importantly, blunted blade, with which thrusts could be executed with less risk. (. . .) It is interesting that the word* Florett, fleuret, fioretto *is found rarely in works dealing with its mastery and theory. It was frequently replaced by the word* l'épée, spada, Degen, *perhaps because one has always regarded the foil as a practice weapon for the Degen, thus a subordinate weapon."*[233]

(It might also be worth noting that the 18th-, 19th-, and early 20th-century usages of the German word "Rapier" or "Rappi(e)r" by fencers (as opposed to collectors), with the qualifiers of *"Hau-"* (cut) and *"Stoß-"* (thrust), denotes a blunt practice weapon!)

[232]Here again, he uses the German Degen, which covers any kind of thrust and cut-and-thrust weapon and duelling sword, as well as the modern épée.

[233]Civrny; ibid.

Martelli, while elaborating on the (classic figure-8) foil, still indicates that in the early 1800s, fencing combined the aspects of gentlemanly amusement and overall athletic fitness with at least the notion of being able translate the skills learned with the foil to the duelling ground and the smallsword.[234] (In fact, his illustration of the carte thrust is a mirror image of Angelo's technique, the only difference being that Angelo depicts practice for agonistic combat with the smallsword, whereas Martelli illustrates agonistic competitive foil practice:

Angelo (1763/1787)   Martelli (1819)

Thus, underlying intent appears not to be not sufficient enough to tell the difference. As Malcolm Fare correctly pointed out above, an important characteristic of the foil is that it is *"made purely for sport or exercise with its own rules and conventions."* This means for a foil to be a foil, it has to be used in a systematic, regulated environment specific to the weapon.

Competitive spirit

What differentiated the regulatory framework between foil Types I and II a)? In *Hamlet*, Shakespeare provides a hint that Type I was indeed used in an explicitly agonistic Olympian (if not Olympic!) context. Wilson quotes his research:

> *"The phases of the match are called 'passes' or 'bouts' in the Folio and Second Quarto but 'venies' in the First Quarto (...) 'The King, sir,' declares Osric to Hamlet, 'hath laid, sir, that in a dozen passes between yourself and him, he shall not exceed you three hits; he hath laid on twelve for nine.' (...) 'This wager,' writes Dr. Johnson 'I do not understand. In a dozen passes one must exceed the other more or less than three hits. Nor can I comprehend how, in a dozen there can be twelve to nine.' (...)*
>
> *The first part of Osric's wager I interpret as follow: The King stipulates that Laertes must win three up in the match. But what of the rest, 'he hath laid on twelve for nine? Here, I think ... the 'he' in this clause is identical with the 'he' in the clause that immediately precedes it., viz. Laertes; and that 'laid on' means (...) laid down conditions. In other words, Laertes on his side makes stipulations for a match of twelve passes instead of the usual nine."*[235]

Silver, Saviolo, and the English translators of di Grassi do not bother with regulatory frameworks. But Wilson believes to recognize the 9-hit system in Silver's challenge to the Italianate masters when he *"proposes a series of matches of nine bouts each: 'three bouts apeece with three of the best English Maisters of Defence, & three bouts apeece with three unskilful valiant men, and three bouts apeece with three res-*

[234] See Martelli's full quote on page 233. I remember being told as a beginner that the foil was the practice weapon for the duelling sword or épée— in the 1980s...

[235] Wilson; p. xif.

[236] Wilson; p. xiii.

olute men half drunke' (p.3); and he would hardly have cast his mock challenge in this form if nine bouts had not been customary in playing for a prize."[236]

(We find Laertes' 12-touch system alive and kicking both in Martelli and in Henry Angelo's *Reminiscences*—specifically tailored to the use of the foil! [237])

What makes a foil a foil?

The intent of not injuring the opponent while achieving the combative objective translates into common physical characteristics of both Type I and Type II a) foils: The point is blunted or rebated, and frequently covered with a button or ball-shaped buffer that reduces the blunt impact by dissemination of pressure.

Considering that replacing a broken or damaged blade was greatly facilitated only after Wilkinson's introduction of the screw pommel and threaded tang in 1867, we have to keep in mind that the previous practice of riveting blades made the blade-hilt assembly far more permanent than modern fencers are accustomed to.

That means once a (rebated) blade had been fixed in a foil of Type I (remember, the "practice rapier"), it was likely to remain there until it broke. Meanwhile, the *piece de resistance* of the weapon, the hilt, was undergoing the same rough treatment modern fencers subject their weapons to.

I pointed out earlier that an important part of the rapier's and smallsword's appeal and effect was its status symbolism and qualities as an accessory of the man of fashion. Gentlemen of leisure plowed considerable sums of money into their sidearms—most of which went into the artistic and representative decoration and design of the hilt. Thus, I consider it somewhat unlikely that these men would intentionally put their investment at risk of being permanently marred in fencing practice. Cheaper hilts would probably have been fitted with rebated blades...

Wilson again adduces *Hamlet* when he hints at an early standardization of foils:

"'These foils have all a length?' asks the unsuspicious Hamlet as he takes his choice; and rapier blades at that time of day might be of almost any length from 3 ft 8 in. to 5 ft. 5 in., the longer ones being recommended by some as giving their possessors a great advantage in thrusting."[238]

These considerations would lead me to assume that Shakespeare's foiles (Type I) were weapons specifically designed and manufactured with standardized blade lengths (at least in the traditional set of two) for fencing practice. They can be classified as foils of Type I or II a) by virtue of their rebated blade and a cheaper, more simple hilt—even though their design and dimensions were oriented closely along the lines of the fashionable antagonistic weaponry of the day.

A la mode

The assumed analogies of practice and combat weapons could be an important factor in determining the character of the weapons depicted in Commenius. If one of the distinguishing characteristics between foils of Type I and Type II a) is that the latter were *not* cheaper, blunted copies of "sharps", then the following observations could be made:

[237] See also our next Adventure in Lost Combat Arts.

[238] Wilson; p. viif.

247

The weapons depicted on page 241, as far as one can make out, have comparatively deep cup hilts, very much like modern épées. Cup-hilt rapiers were indeed fashionable sidearms in Europe... but by the 1650s, their attraction as everyday accessories was limited mainly to Spain and the Spanish Empire.

Furthermore, the classic cup hilt combines the protective cup with long cross-bars, and a knuckle-guard[239]. While Commenius' image may indeed be an incorrect rendition of the originals, the lack of ferrous extensions, curved or straight, reaching out from the guard is noticeable. Furthermore, the fencer on the right appears to be in the process of delivering a thrust in pronation, with the round pommel of his weapon resting against the root of his thumb. Many (but not all) cup-hilt rapiers tended to have smaller, flatter pommels.

Even though several contemporary Italian authors still depict cup-hilt weapons—such as Martelli's 1686 *Regole della scherma*—these weapons maintain very pronounced crossbars. And a decade after the end of the Thirty-Years War (1618-48), the swords popular in Germany tended to have swept hilts...

Money talks

This overlaying and intersecting of criteria that would help us to clearly define what weapons we are looking at, points at the possibility that the traditional segregation of "modern" foil and "bated rapiers" is insuffient to explain certain continuities in both the usage and morphology of the weapons in question.

From a historical perspective, it is important to note that the presence of foils or rebated rapiers (used for thrust fencing in competitive agonistic scenarios) against the backdrop of the traditional weaponry of the medieval and Renaissance Master of Defence establishes that the foil had been fully incorporated into the repertoire of the fighting guilds by the 1650s.

And why not? There were lucent and lucrative arguments to support integrating the smallsword and foil into the curriculum... the least of which was that chronically cash-strapped masters had to pay their creditors: The most attractive prospects for lessons were young noblemen and fashion-conscious burghers and students itching to put their expensive fashion accessory to manly use. Once crossed with silver, the gnarled palms of even the grumpiest old Meisters would happily close around the handle of a foil.

The Devil and Mr. Kreußler

This convergence of weaponry is evident in the biographies of the masters teaching them. Take Wilhelm Kreußler, for example, the founder of the most influential German fencing dynasty. Born in 1597, Wilhelm was a member of the Marxbrüder when he came to Jena in 1619, where he—in accordance with his teaching privileges—opened a fencing academy.[240]

Apart from the traditional weapons repertoire of the fighting guilds, Kreußler taught the thrusting system of the Rappier. He personally taught his sons Wilhelm and Gottfried, who in 1669 were granted the exclusive privilege to serve as official fencing masters at Jena university.

[239]This kind of weapon, with a slightly shallower dish and greatly reduced crossbars, and shorter blade, is referred to as a *Raufdegen* (lit. "brawling sword") by German historians, and used to constitute the weapon of choice of German students.

[240]See also Lölke, Jörg. — "Studieren mit flotter Klinge: Jenaer Fechttraditionen," in *Uni-Zeitung Jena*, May 28, 1996.

Johann Wilhelm Kreußler, grandson of Wilhelm, was probably the most flamboyant of the clan. His following encounter with the Saxon king August is the stuff legends are made of:

Der Schwarze (The Black[241] One)

by Georg Bötticher

In Dresden's royal palace / fences the corps of squires,
and there's many a brave one / who excels in thrust and jump.
The foils are ringing, / it resounds: "En avant!"
Ho! How it rings, stomps! / And bout follows bout!

All around, fine gents and ladies / and—everyone's allowed—
lots of folk, and among them / a little schoolmaster,
a puny fellow, / in blackish garb,
but bright enthusiasm / sparks from dark eyes.

To rattle the Black One, / one in fencing clothes calls
"Now, do you want to try once, / Uncle Spanking Rod?"
And laughter rings out all around. / But—like the dickens—
he jumps in, takes the sword / and quickly puts himself on guard.

Then fast as lightning, / he binds the other's steel,
and then he momentarily / disarms another three,
and so the fifth, the sixth / and now the seventh, too.
From all sides now the fighters / jump to square with him.

He knows how to take them, / huzzah!—depending on the man,
to thrust and also parry, / he beats, disarms them all.
The news about the Black One / who faces all the blades,
reaches the Old Master, / the teacher of defence.

He closes in with naked blade, / and everyone makes room,
watching, compassionate and gloating / at the black-dressed shrimp.
But that one returns quite friendly / and without malice
"Now let's rock," and sticks / the sword under his left arm.

The Old One waves the blade. / "You mock me—Thunderbolt!"
A flash! And in the corner / his foil flies rattling.
"Another!" Like a tempest / the Old One's blade alights…
Again, the other one beats / from the fist his blade.

Thunderstruck, the Old One stares— / Has the world turned upside down?
Then a shout: "The King![242]" / The sovereign stands before him.
A guest reported to him what / a schoolmaster could do.
Now he himself came down to see / the black-dressed wonderman.

[241] Not, of course, referring to epidermal pigmentation but to predominant color of dress.

[242] August der Starke (the Strong) King in Saxony and Poland.

249

Kreußler kneeling before King August – after disarming the Saxon monarch six times in a row. German masters taught "Kreußlerian" principles of thrust fencing until World War I. Unlike the poet, Kreußler did not limit himself to disarmament techniques.

He watched the last bouts / and takes, as it's known
himself a master of the art, / a rapier [243] up without delay.
And forcefully with thrusts / he falls upon the Black One
that even the super-nimble one / can hardly fend him off.

Only a few seconds, / then the king's steel flies
with hollow rattle ceiling-ward. / And yet—and yet again!
The king stomps the ground, / and draws a blade again,
And six time does the Black One / render him weaponless.

He, barely master of himself, / insists of him
"Churl! If you aren't the Devil / you must be Kreußler!"
Brightly laughing, the other / salutes and bends the knee.
"At your service I'm the latter, / the latter, in person."

The Kreußler method, codified by Kahn in the early 1700s, was practiced without interruption throughout Germany until the beginning of the 20th century.

This means that the foil and its techniques had been adopted, assimilated, and fully incorporated in the curriculum of the privileged urban fighting guilds, and were taught by masters fully immersed in the medieval traditions, not only by specialists. The roots of the modern sport thus were shaped and modified by the same masters responsible for teaching the classic weapons such as the Dussack, the great sword, and the rapier. Thus, it is the masters who provide the element of continuity in rapier, smallsword, and foil practice from the early 16th century to the late 1800s.

[243] Here it is, the German use of "Rapier" as "foil".

INTERLUDE

AGONISTIC COMBAT

The Strenuous Life in the White House

Teddy Roosevelt (U.S. president from 1901-09), for one, liked to groom his public image as a warrior by working out to a different tune:

"At a White House reception the other day, the president appeared with his arm bandaged, and it then developed that he and General Leonhard Wood, during rainy days, were getting their exercise by having bouts at singles-stick in the upper rooms of the Executive Mansion. In these days of vigorous Americanism it pleases the people to think that the head of the nation plays as hard as it works."
(*Harper's Weekly*, c. 1905)

– Leonard Wood, by the way, is the general staff officer who signed off on Patton's saber manual

[244]Castle, Egerton *Schools and Masters of Fence*, London & New York: G. Bell & Sons, 1910; p.293.

[245]in Ward, Edward. *A Vade Mecum for Malt-Worms,* London, n.y. (c. 1712) II, 8

[246]This is a corruption of the real duel's "first blood" rule, which allowed a duel to be ended after one of the parties had been injured. It also corresponds to the *"Anschiss"* of the early German Schläger regulations: A Mensur could be ended after one of the fighters had received a bleeding cut one inch long or deep. It is preserved in the modern Mensur's criteria for announcing a *"Blutiger,"* which allows a second to stop the ongoing round of the bout.

[247]Hutton, however, recounts an instance in which two combatants almost beat each other to death, *"their shirts (to say nothing of the skin underneath them) are torn to tatters, but nothing of it counts until one of them gets a 'broken head'".* See Hutton, Alfred. *The Sword and the Centuries,* (London: Grant Richards, 1901), Rutland, VT: Charles E. Tuttle Co., 1973; p. 354.

A Singlestick Match in Victorian England

Since quality steel blades were still prohibitively expensive at the end of the 18th century, many fencing systems centered around the wooden practice weapons. For the broadsword (double-edged), the backsword (single-edged), and the spadoon, the practice weapon was the singlestick, wielded particularly *"by those whose social position did not admit of their wearing 'the sword' (i.e., the small-sword.)"*[244]

In the 1700s, singlestick and cudgelling were popular pastime, not only *"in Moor's most pleasant Field, where Northern Lads / With Western Youths, contend for broken Heads"*[245] but all over Britain.

By the mid-1850s, however, when Thomas Hughes wrote his famous *Tom Brown's Schooldays,* singlestick had become a neglected art even in the rural areas of Southern England. Hughes himself recalls singlestick competitions as a rustic amusement in the 1820s, where every country fair boasted singlestick or backswording tournaments in which local and regional players competed for prizes. His account of this sport ranks among the best in English literature:

"The weapon is a good stout ash-stick with a large basket-handle (...) The players are called "old gamesters," — why, I can't tell you, — and their object is simply to break one another's heads: for the moment that blood runs an inch anywhere above the eyebrow, the old gamester to whom it belongs is beaten, and has to stop [246]. *A very slight blow with the sticks will fetch blood, so that it is by no means a punishing pastime, if the men don't play on purpose, and savagely, at the body and arms of their adversaries* [247].

The old gamester going into action only takes off his hat and coat, and arms himself with a stick: he then loops the fingers of his left hand in a handkerchief or strap which he fastens around his left leg, measuring the length, so that when he draws it tight with his left elbow in the air, the elbow shall just reach as high as his crown. Thus you see, as long as chooses to keep up his left elbow, regardless of cuts, he has a perfect guard for the left side of his head [248].

Then he advances his right hand above and in front of his head, holding his stick across so that its point projects an inch or two over his left elbow, and thus his head is completely guarded, and he faces his man armed in like manner, and they stand some three feet apart, often nearer, and feint, and strike, and return at one another's heads, until one cries 'hold,' or blood flows: in the first case they are allowed a minute's time, and go on again; in the latter, another pair of gamesters are called on. If good men are playing, the quickness of returns is marvelous; you hear a rattle like that a boy makes drawing his stick along palings, only heavier, and the closeness of the men in action to one another gives it a strange interest, and makes a spell at backswording a very noble sight." [249]

But while the broadsword and spadoon are cut-and-thrust weapons, single-stick fencers were not allowed to thrust. Cuts were executed from a hanging guard by a flipping, whip-like action of the wrist. Parries were always taken in pronation.

The weapon typically consisted of an inch-wide, yard-long ash-wood stick that tapered toward the tip. Eighteenth-century singlesticks had a basket-like guard ("pot") made of reed, later versions were outfitted with triangular guards of stiff cow or buffalo hide. Fencers stood with their legs straight and fought without lunging or advancing. There was, however, considerable movement of the feet, *"as in the fencing of the rapier period."* [250]

Singlestick continued to exist in urban English salles and was still practiced in the 1920s, mainly by British public schools and by American Navy cadets, who used it for cutlass practice. At that point, however, it had dropped its unique double-armed hanging guard and had been adapted to the rules of modern sabre fencing.

The use of the point was re-introduced and cuts at the legs were allowed (although they were considered foul play by many salles.) Hutton recounts an incident at Henry Angelo's St. James's Street School of Arms in the late 1850s, when a Mr. Rolland squared off against a notorious bully, non-commissioned officer in the Royal Artillery Segeant T—y, who had unfairly beaten Rolland in a previous encounter by cutting "inside the leg," even though both combatants had agreed on regarding this action as foul play.

[248] It seems that the tying down of the left arm varied according to region: *"In Glouchestershire it was evidently fastened to the thigh, the arm being at full length; in Wiltshire it appears to have been fastened to the belt in such a way that the man could raise his elbow to protect his eyes, but nothing higher."* See Hutton; p. 348

[249] Hughes, Thomas. *Tom Brown's Schooldays* (London: Macmillan, 1857), Oxford: Oxford UP, 1989; p. 35 f.

[250] Hutton; p. 348.

"The pair engaged; the sergeant led off in his customary violent fashion, but Mr. Rolland played in a manner that had never been seen before. This time he was serious. Usually he would lead off with a frank attack; now he was strangely quiet. He parried the furious blows, and only now and then replied with a riposte. T——y, fancying that this man was afraid of him, redoubled his energy, and gradually tired himself, which was exactly what his opponent intended he should do. At least the supreme moment arrived. Rolland all of a sudden crouched like a tiger, like a tiger sprang forward, and with all the force of his spring and the weight of his mighty arm landed a fearful blow exactly on the point of the inside of his adversary's knee. The biter was bit. Sergeant T——y uttered a shriek of agony, and fell fainting on the floor. He was carried to the dressing-room, where they fomented his leg with hot water and did the best they could for him at the moment. He was taken in a cab to the hospital, where he remained over a month, and it was three months before he was able to mount a horse again."[251]

The hit didn't improve the Sergeant's salle manners. In a later incident, an opponent's singlestick broke off at the buffalo-hide hilt. T——y took advantage of the situation to land several vicious hits on his unarmed opponent. Seeing himself abused in this unfair and ungentlemanly fashion, his victim used the basket the way many soldiers used their hilts in close combat, namely to land a tremendous punch against the face of T——y that sent him sprawling to the floor. Angelo, who had been watching the encounter, added a kick for good measure and told T——y to pack and never show his face again at his school.

Cane fencing

Cane fencing was popular throughout the 19th century, when no gentleman would have been caught dead on the street without his walking stick. Cane fencing and singlestick became synonymous toward the end of the 19th century, and many military manuals treat canes as training weapons for the saber and broadsword. Combat with the walking stick closely resembles 19th-century saber schools, with their characteristically wide moulinets that were aimed at confusing the opponent. Thrusts were as important as cuts, and often executed with both hands.

Cane fencing flourished in Germany, Switzerland and France, while it never became popular in Britain and the United States. As cuts against the legs and the lower body were allowed and very severe blows were exchanged, fencers were attired with masks, padded gloves and vests, as well as shin guards.

A variety of cane fencing was the combat with sword-canes, which became fashionable in the second half of the 19th century and enjoyed only brief popularity. This system remotely resembled Renaissance rapier and dagger play, the shaft of the cane being used in the right hand, the sword or dagger part held in the left. Only French-made trifoil-blades (resembling short modern épée blades) were used with the right hand like short foils. Frequently cane fencers were ambidexterous and able to defend themselves even against entire gangs of assailants. On other occasions, they got their heads perforated by thugs with a gun.

[251] Hutton; p. 359.

253

H. Angelo's Fencing
Academy (c. 1795)

How to Defend a Monopoly:
Strategic Planning in Running a Salle

Any way you cut it, the London Masters of Defence took it on the chin between 1585 and 1625.

First, the ordeals and wagers of battle that not only offered handsome fees but free publicity, had become so rare that the venerable John Stow, in his *Summarye of the Chronicle of England* (London, 1573) and Lord Chief Justice Dyer (writing in 1585) can't help but chronicle one and the same non-event from 1571 in their respective tomes.[252]

Then, Italianate interlopers such as Rocco Bonnetti and Vincentio Saviolo thumbed their noses at the Masters' official letters of privilege: They short-circuited the accreditation process (necessary to legally teach the Noble Art) by networking directly among the most influential and prosperous clients.

(Sure, they usually ended up with three feet of "Running foxe" through the belly when called upon to back up gentlemanly and commercial pretension by skill at arms in life-and-death scenarios. But that did little to diminish their appeal to young aristocrats more interested in strutting that imported rapier hilt daddy's allowance had paid for in polite society than getting their ivory hides tanned by an untouchable fishmonger-provost during the 14-year training period it took to become a Master...)

[252]See page 147.

And adding insult to injury, James I revoked the Masters' privileges in the Monopolies Act of 1623/24—opening the doors to any Sean, Jacques, and Antonio who wanted to peddle fencing lessons for the cold, hard coin of the realm in the City.

Give me your brash, your brazen

Among those to enter London in search of fame and fortune during the following century and a half was Domenico Angiolo Malevolti Tremamondo. Born in 1716 at Leghorn, Italy, he was a riding instructor by avocation who during his brief stint in Paris, had taken lessons from the famous Monsieur Teillagory—who also trained the great Chevalier d'Eon...

But even without having himself presented himself for the public trial demanded by the statutes of the Compagnie'des Maîtres en fait d'Armes (the cousins of the English Masters), he managed to score several impressive victories in public matches against English and Irish social fencers, quickly gaining access to key clients at court and in the royal family.

Angelo's key fight took place against a Dr. Keyes:

> "On his return to London with his patron and friend, the Earl of Pembroke, he received a card, inviting him to a public trial of skill with Dr. Keyes, reputed to be the most expert fencer in Ireland. The challenge being accepted, the Thatched House Tavern was appointed for the scene of action, where my father [i.e., Domenico] attended at the time prescribed, two o'clock, though he had been riding the whole morning at Lord Pembroke's. His lordship, with his accustomed condescension, walked into the apartment arm in arm with his friend and protégé. My father was not prepared, however, for such an assemblage, many ladies of rank and fashion, as well as noblemen and gentlemen, being present, and he, expecting only to meet with gentlemen, was in his riding dress and in boots.
>
> My father, who had never seen his antagonist until this moment, was rather surprised at the doctor's appearance, he being a tall and athletic figure, wearing a huge wig, without his coat and waistcoat, his shirt sleeves tucked up, exposing a pair of brawny arms, sufficient to cope in the ring with Broughton or Slack; and thus equipped, with foil in hand, he was pacing the apartment.
>
> The spectators being all assembled, after the first salutation from the doctor, which was sufficiently open and frank, previous to the assault he took a bumper of cogniac, and offered another to my father, which he politely refused, not being accustomed to so ardent a provocative.
>
> The doctor having thus spirited himself to the attack, began with that violence and determined method which soon discovered to those who were skilled in the science, that, in the true sense of the term used by the French, he was no better than a tirailleur, jeu de soldat—Anglicized, a poker.
>
> My father, to indulge him in his mode of assault, for some time solely defended himself against his repeated attacks without receiving one hit; for, as the brandy operated, a coup d'hasard in the doctor's favor would only

have encouraged him the more. Hence, allowing his opponent to exhaust himself, and my father having sufficiently manifested his superior skill in the science by thus acting on the defensive, with all the elegance and grace of attitude for which he was renowned, after having planted a dozen palpable hits on the breast of his enraged antagonist, he made his bow to the ladies, and retired amongst the plaudits of the spectators."[253]

Anglicizing his name to Domenico Malevolti Angelo, he ran a tight ship: Within a few years, he dominated London's upscale fencing market, turning his Haymarket establishment into a fashionable meeting place of the British aristocracy and international crack fencers such as Le Brun, Saint-Georges, d'Eon, Léger, and Fabien.

But nature abhors a vacuum. And a free market despises a monopoly. Accordingly, the Angelos were in for a lesson straight out of the book of the old Masters. But unlike the Masters, they appear to have been as good in strategic thinking as they were on the fencing loft.

Domenico's son Henry—who got his final polish at the hands of Motet at the Académie d'Armes de Paris—took over the family business. This included the task of fending off foreign competitors.

A passage from his *Reminiscences* gives a tantalizing glimpse into the thinking of a high-carat business man:

In 1785, Monsieur Le Brun, a celebrated fencing master (and father of Le Brun fils, one of the co-founders of the Paris Societé), visited London. The Angelo place at Haymarket was a central rendezvous for all the foreigners who were either masters or amateurs of the science. Henry was his first antagonist:

"I soon found out, as the pugilists called it, that he was a 'good customer' (a queer one to deal with), so much so, that, however I might have distinguished myself before my scholars, with the number of fencing-masters, &c. whom I have opposed, here I had nothing to boast of. I should observe that he was a left-handed fencer, and in full exercise at Paris; and of course he must have been daily in the habit of fencing with many, while in the course of years I might not meet with six of superior force.

Finding such an excellent competitor, and as I thought that it would be beneficial to my scholars to accustom themselves to practise against a left-handed fencer, I told him he would be welcome to us all. His next visit was to Lapiere, a Frenchman, who had his academy in Piccadilly, where they fenced together.

A few days afterwards, in the Orange coffee-house, some one said that Le Brun had been to Lapiere, and boasted that he had hit him twelve to one. This came to the ears of Lapiere, and though LeBrun denied that he had ever said so, he did not hesitate to affirm that he could do it.

This threat exasperated Lapiere; and considered as he was, by all, not only an excellent master, but a superior antagonist, and as he had often shown his abilities when opposed to the most skillful, independent of his fine manners and conduct, he was a general favorite, and well established in his profession. Inconsiderately, for he had nothing to gain, he publicly challenged Le Brun, which the latter accepted.

The day was fixed to meet at my room in the Haymarket, which at the hour was crowded with all the first amateurs of the science. Each adversary

[253]Angelo. *Reminiscences;* p. 76.

257

was dressed in a white jacket, the buttons of their foils were dipped in liquid; that of Lapiere's red, Le Brun's black.

The latter made the first attack, and but a few seconds after they had placed themselves on guard, to the astonishment of the beholders, three black spots appeared within the circle (a certain space to receive hits only) on Lapiere's jacket (a straight thrust, cut over the point, the reprise in low carte.)

This, like the first knock-down blow in a pugilistic contest, so very much disheartened Lapiere, that he was afterwards a lost man. The other, elevated with his premature success, soon after gave nine hits more, when on receiving only one, he made his bow to the company, and declined continuing any longer the assault.

Every one was glad to leave the room, as they were almost suffocated with heat. Poor Lapiere remained deserted by his friends, disconsolate, and covered over with black spots (many that he had received out of the circle). When he had left the room, Mr. John Trotter, my worthy patron at that time, and who was one of the spectators, and myself, examined the jackets; we counted twelve 'palpable' hits within the given place (breast), whilst the other had received only one. "[254]

But let's recap

Henry Angelo not only was an excellent fencer in his time, he also managed to run a high-class service business—at a time when the sword was declining in popularity, in what was a provincial backwater in the fencing world, against popular foreign competitors. He cleverly avoids a public match with the superior opponent, which could have damaged his reputation in case of a dramatic loss.

According to Aylward, Lapiere had arrived in London from Lille in 1782. Henry Angelo *"often fenced with him, and therefore knew his powers."*[255] The subsequent annihilation of Lapiere at the hands of Le Brun—and particularly the vivid image of the defeated, deserted Lapiere—could imply that the rumors that drove Lapiere into the coffee-house in the first place might have been strategically placed by someone close to Angelo.

Professional honor

The question that remains is why Lapiere reacts so strongly to the "rumors". After all, it doesn't seem to matter much by what margin a master would lose or win against another. We have to call on a contemporary of the protagonists to fully understand Lapiere's outrage at the insinuation that Le Brun's could be him 12:1.

A passage in Martelli explains the enormity of such claim:

"Now if one hits twelve before the other hits eight, the conqueror may assuredly (even between good fencers) consider himself superior to his adversary, who can never (upon an average) hit him more than eight. And if a man can hit, at all times, twelve to six, he surely may consider himself, in the same proportion, as possessing double the dexterity of the adversary.

[254]Angelo; p. 260f.

[255]Aylward, J.D. *The House of Angelo; A Dynasty of Scientific Swordsmen,* London: The Batchworth Press, 1953; p. 150.

At the same rate, therefore, is one superior to the other, according to the number of hits made by the respective person.

Hence we may naturally conclude, that if a man hits another, upon an average, two-to-one, the inferior party must pay great attention, and practise much, to arrive to even two-thirds of the other's ability, (if both parties are of equal courage, and under the same kind of instructions.)

A man, therefore, cannot be called a capital fencer, that is among the first class of amateurs, if he cannot upon an average, hit nine to twelve with any one that he engages.

When this subject is properly considered, how very inferior a man must be looked upon if he cannot hit three or four in twelve. Such a fencer cannot surely be compared to one who can be sure of hitting at the rat of three or four to one. (...) No one, even the best fencer in the world, can be sure to prevent a chance hit (for one or two hits in twelve can only be looked upon as such.)"[256]

Damned if you do...

This explains both Lapiere's reaction to the rumors, and his response in ultimate defeat: The former could be interpreted as a predictable, well-crafted and downright Byzantine provocation which in itself posed a hands-on threat to the status and livelihood of a fencing master. (This is on par with "giving the lie" to an Elizabethan gentleman: Lapiere has to respond—or incur ridicule and loss of business.)

But the defeat at the hands of Le Brun is worse than any negative publicity he could have garnered by avoiding the fight, or not responding to the rumors. It not only means the loss of a bout to a fellow master. It means he was outfought, outdone—and even more importantly, hopelessly outclassed!

Even his one palpable hit, according to Martelli, no longer is attributable to skill but only to mere chance!

His clients' response is immediate. There's no consolation, no "attaboy". They leave him a broken man, deserted by his retainers. Lapiere is finished—and he knows it.

Aylward mentions that Lapiere was so despondent about his humiliation that he committed suicide.[257] Angelo not only had the elimination of a competitor take place in his establishment, and thus must have received a considerable boost in publicity.

[256]Martelli, C. *An Improved System of Fencing, wherein the Use of the Small Sword is Rendered Perfectly Plain and Familiar, Being a Clear Description and Explanation of the Various Thrusts Used with the Safest and Best Methods of Parrying, as Practised in the Present Age. To which is Added a Treatise on the Art of Attack and Defence,* London: J. Bailey, 1819; p. 34.

[257]Aylward, J.D. *The English Master of Arms,* London: Routledge, 1956; p. 211.

EPILOG

When I first wrote and published the *Secret History of the Sword* in 1996, it was a 40-page booklet intended as a subscription premium for *Hammerterz Forum*. This collection of some of the essays you've encountered in this greatly enlarged and revised edition was reviewed in *Renaissance*, a re-enactment magazine.

Among other undoubtedly very well-intended things, the reviewer wrote: *"Amberger's scholarly methods have not generally been utilized by the modern fencing masters, and while the works of modern masters are based on practical experience, the historic background tendered by many of them should often be dismissed (e.g., Olympic Champion Aldo Nadi boasted that he had never read more than a single line from any book on fencing, yet still put spurious historical notions about swordplay into his written works. (. . .) While it is unlikely Amberger could defeat a champion in a by-the-rules fencing match, it is much more likely that he could hold his own if the rules went out the window, and a certainty that he could crush Nadi in a historical dicussion on swordplay."*[262]

Since you have read this far, you will not be taken by surprise if I tell you that I am not a modest person. In fact, I have made a career of not being modest. Still, I have never felt comfortable using this quote in any way to promote either myself or *Hammerterz Forum*.

I have deep respect for the modern masters and coaches of fencing... and an even deeper respect for Aldo Nadi and his students who, like William Gaugler, are preserving the art of fencing in its most pure and competitive incarnation.

It would never occur to me to speculate what would happen if I or another Schläger fencer were to square off with Nadi, rules or no rules. Because the outcome would be clear: We would be beaten fast, resoundingly—*and deservedly*.

When I was reading over the manuscript of this edition with the *Renaissance* comments in mind, I noticed that I indeed do frequently call up Nadi to illustrate discrepancies or difference of opinion. But this is not because I believe Nadi's views are "spurious" or "should be dismissed." I chose Nadi because his style, articulateness, and firmness of opinion provided an ideal wall to bounce my own ideas off.

And even though peace in the Middle East is an easier thing to achieve than arriving at a consensus among fencers about the history of the art, I would like to point out that the basis of combat with edged weapons is indeed mutual respect:

Two parties meeting with a piece of honed steel in hand, and engaging in artful combat, consciously accept the implicit and explicit rules dictated by weapon and convention. And if you are willing to go to these lengths, no difference of opinion can possibly be serious enough that it could not be put aside over a glass of beer.

[262] See Varhola, Michael. — "The Secret History of the Sword," in *Renaissance*, vol. 2, #2 (Issue #6), 1997; p. 50.

ABOUT THE AUTHOR

Born in 1963, J. Christoph Amberger grew up in what used to be West Berlin, Germany.

He studied Latin, English, history, dentistry, Gaelic, English and American Literature, journalism, philosophy, and economics with varying degrees of devotion and perseverance at the Freie Universität Berlin, the University of Aberdeen in Scotland, and the Georg-August-Universität Göttingen before obtaining his Master of Arts at St. John's Graduate Institute in Annapolis, Maryland.

He has been living in the United States since 1989, is married and has two children. Amberger today is Executive Publisher of Agora Financial Publishing in Baltimore.

A regular contributor to *American Fencing*, the magazine of the United States Fencing Association, and to the British fencing magazine *The Sword*, as well as the German *Einst und Jetzt*, he founded *Hammerterz Forum* in 1994. He has been featured in the Discovery Channel's 1997 documentary series *Deadly Duels*, has been a consultant to the Metropolitan Museum of Art in New York for the exhibition The Academy of the Sword, and is considered one of the foremost experts on historical edged-weapons combat in the United States.

After becoming a member of the Corps Normannia Berlin and the Corps Hannovera Göttingen, two of the most respected duelling fraternities in Germany, he fought seven Mensuren with the bell-guard and basket-hilt Schläger between 1985 and 1987 and acted as a second in 25 more. His weapon of choice on the sports fencing strip is the saber.

SELECT BIBLIOGRAPHY

Alessandri, A. and André, Émile. *L'Escrime du Sabre a Cheval*, Paris: Ernest Flammarion, n.y. (c. 1880)

Altenstein, Axel von. *Der Fechtsport*, Leipzig: Grethlein, c. 1911

Amberger, J. Christoph. *The Secret History of the Sword: Adventures in Ancient Martial Arts*, Baltimore: Hammerterz Verlag, 1996 (1st ed.)
  — 1997 (2nd enlarged ed.)

—"Below the Belt—A Brief History of Sabre Taboos," in *American Fencing*, vol. 43 #2; p. 10f
—"Below the Belt—A Brief History of Sabre Taboos," in *The Sword*, New Series #41, January 1995; p. 28f
—"Sabers and Swastika: Heydrich's Grab for the FIE Presidency," in *Hammerterz Forum*, vol. 2, #1 (Summer 1995); p. 8f
—"Bruises and bumps: The short-lived revival of the two-handed sword as a Hitler Youth camp sport," in *Hammerterz Forum*, vol. 2, #4 / vol. 3, #1 (Spring/Summer 1996); p. 22f
—"Ultimate Male Bonding—A Schläger Mensur at Göttingen, A.D. 1987" in *Hammerterz Forum*, vol. 3, # 3 (Winter 1997); p. 8f
—"Glory Days of the Foil," in *Hammerterz Forum* vol. 4, ##3 and 4, (July 15, 1998); p. 22

American Fencing, Boulder, CO: USFA, vol. 42, #4 (April, May, June 1992); p. 19
  — vol. 43 (July, August, September 1992); p. 6

Angelo, Domenico Malevolti Tremamondo. *L'Ecole des Armes, avec l'explication générale des principales attitudes et positions concernant l'Escrime (The School of Fencing)*, London: R. & S. Dodsley, 1763
  — London: S. Hooper, 1765 (2nd ed.)
  — 1767 (3rd ed.)
  — Lausanne: Edita S.A., 1968

—*The School of Fencing, with a general explanation of the principal attitudes and positions peculiar to the Art. Translated by Thomas Rowlandson.*, London, 1787
  — 1799 (2nd ed.)
  — New York: Land's End Press, 1971
  (see also Diderot)

Angelo, Henry [and Rowlandson, Thomas]. *Hungarian and Highland Broadsword*, London: H. Angelo, 1799
— *Angelo's Pic Nic; Table Talk including Numerous Recollections of Public Characters*, London: John Ebers, 1834
— *Reminiscences of Henry Angelo*, London: Kegan Paul, Trench, Trübner & Co., 1904

Angelo, Col. Edward Anthony. *Observations on Angelo's Military Exercises formed by (the late) Henry Angelo, Esq., Superintendent of Sword Exercise to the Army*, London: Parker, Furnivall, and Parker, 1853

Anglin, Jay P. —"The Schools of Defense in Elizabethan London," in *Renaissance Quarterly*, vol. xxxvii, #3 (Fall 1984); p. 393f

Angolia, John R. *Swords of Germany 1900/1945*, San Jose, CA: R. James Bender Publishing, 1988

Applegate, Col. Rex. *Combat Use of the Double-Edged Fighting Knife*, Boulder, CO: Paladin Press, 1993

Armstrong, Hunter B. —"The Way of the Gladius," in *Hoplos*, vol. iv, #4 (August 1985)
—"The Way of the Gladius," in *Hammerterz Forum*, vol. 3, #2, (Fall 1996); p. 9f

Assmann, Rainer. —"Studentische Waffen 1840—'Acten betreffend...konfiscierter Gegenstände'," in *Einst und Jetzt*, vol. 42 (1997); p. 87

Aylward, J.D. *The House of Angelo; A Dynasty of Scientific Swordsmen,* London: The Batchworth Press, 1953
— *The English Master of Arms,* London: Routledge, 1956

Barbasetti, Cav. Luigi. *Das Säbelfechten,* Wien: Verlag der Allgemeinen Sportzeitung (Victor Silberer), 1899
— *The Art of the Foil,* New York: Dutton, 1932
— *Ehrenkodex,* Wien: Verlag der Allgemeinen Sportzeitung, 1898

Barth, Berndt et al. *Fechten: Ein Lehrbuch für die Grundausbildung im Florett-, Säbel- und Degenfechten,* Berlin (East Germany): Sportverlag Berlin, 1979 (2nd ed.)

Bartunek, Josef. *Ratgeber für den Offizier zur Sicherung des Erfolges im Zweikampf mit dem Säbel,* Esztergom (Hungary): self-published, 1904

Bataillard, Ch. *Du duel, considéré sous le rapport de la morale, de l'histoire, de la législation et de l'opportunité d'une loi répressive. Suivi de combat et duel de la Chasteneraye et de Iarnac,* Paris, 1829

Bauer, Max. *Sittengeschichte des deutschen Studententums,* (Dresden: Paul Aretz Verlag, n.d.) Schernfeld: SH Verlag, 1991

de Beaumont, C. L. *Fencing: Ancient Art and Modern Sport,* London: Nicholas Kaye and South Brunswick and New York: A.S. Barnes & Co., 1971

de Becker, Gavin. *The Gift of Fear,* New York: Little, Brown & Co., 1997

Berriman, Capt. M. W. *The Militiaman's Manual and Sword-Play without a Master. Rapier and Broad-Sword Exercises copiously explained and illustrated; (. . .),* New York: D. Van Nostrand, 1861 (2nd ed.)

Berry, Herbert. *The Noble Science: A Study and Transcription of Sloane Ms. 2530, Papers of the Masters of Defence of London, Temp. Henry VIII to 1590,* Newark, DE: University of Delaware Press, 1991

Bierbaum, Otto Julius. —"Gamasche, der Pommernfuchs," in Conrad, Heinrich (ed.) *Das Duellbuch,* München: Georg Müller, 1918

Bingener, F. Dieter. *Die Klingen der Sportfechtwaffen: Florett, Säbel, Degen,* n.p. [Germany]: Akademie der Fechtkunst Deutschlands (Schriftenreihe Fechtkunst Band 1), 1997

Boehm, Christopher. *Blood Revenge: The Enactment and Management of Conflict in Montenegro and other Tribal Societies,* Philadelphia, PA: University of Pennsylvania Press, (1984, 1987) 1991

Bolitho, Gordon. *The Other Germany,* London, New York: Appleton-Century, 1934

Bonjour, Edgar. *Die Universität Basel von den Anfängen bis zur Gegenwart 1460-1960,* Basel: Helbing & Lichtenhahn, 1960

Breck, Edward. *Fencing,* New York: American Sports Publishing Co., (1894) 1902

Brown, Terry. *English Martial Arts,* Hockwold-cum-Wilton (England): Anglo-Saxon Books, 1997

Burton, Sir Richard. *The Book of the Sword,* London: Chatto & Windus, 1884

Butler, Samuel. *Hudibras, in Three Parts, Written in the Time of the Late Wars. Corrected and Amended with Additions,* London: T.W., 1726

Cass, Eleanor. *The Book of Fencing*, Boston: Lothrop, Lee, and Shepard Co., 1930

Castello, Julio Martinez. *The Theory and Practice of Fencing*, New York: self-published, 1931
— New York and London: Charles Scribner's Sons, 1933
(Due to the prevalence of the latter, it is usually quoted as the first edition of this work.)

Castle, Egerton. *Schools and Masters of Fence from the Middle Ages to the 18th Century.* London: George Bell & Sons, (1884) 1892 (revised ed.)

Chandler, David. *The Art of War in the Age of Marlborough*, New York, 1976

Civrny, Dr. Cestmir. *Florett,* München: self-published, 1993

Clements, John. *Renaissance Swordsmanship: The Illustrated Use of Rapiers and Cut-and-Thrust Swords*, Boulder, CO: Paladin Press, 1997

Commenius see Bauer

Conwell, Charles. —"Was Patton Right?," in *American Fencing*, vol. 42, #2; p. 16

Corbesier, Antoine J. *Principles of Squad Instruction for the Broadsword*, Philadelphia: J. B. Lippincott, 1869
— *Theory of Fencing; with the Small-Sword Exercise*, Washington: Government Printing Office, 1873

Cowen, J.D.. —"Das Schwert von Krautergersheim (Elsaß)," in *Germania*, vol. 30, #3/4 (1952), p.381

Craig, Darrell. *Iai: The Art of Drawing the Sword*, Rutland, VT and Tokyo: Charles E. Tuttle Co., 1981

Craig, Robert H.. *Rules and Regulations for the Sword Exercise of the Cavalry, to which is added The Rules for Drill and the Evolutions of the Light Cavalry*, Baltimore: self-published, 1812

Crosnier, Roger. *Fencing with the Saber*, London: Faber & Faber, (1954) 1965 (2nd ed.)
— *Fencing with the Electric Foil*, London: Faber & Faber, 1961

Czarnetzki, Alfred (ed.). *Stumme Zeugen ihrer Leiden: Paläopatholgische Befunde*, Tübingen: Attempto Verlag, 1996
— (et al.). *Menschen des frühen Mittelalters im Spiegel der Anthropologie und Medizin*, Münster, Bonn, Liestal: Württembergisches Landesmusem, 1983

Danet, Guillaume. *L'Art des Armes*, Paris: Herissant Fils, 1766-67

Daeves, Dr. ?. —"Die Untersuchung altdeutscher Eisenteile," in *Rundschau deutscher Technik*, vol. 20, no. 26, June 27, 1940

de Camp, Sprague (et al.). *Dark Valley Destiny: The Life of Robert E. Howard, The Creator of Conan*, New York: Bluejay Books, (1961) 1983

Dean, Bashford. *Handbook of Arms and Armor, European and Oriental, including the William H. Riggs Collection*, New York: The Metropolitan Museum of Art, 1915

Demmin, August. *Die Kriegswaffen in ihrer geschichtlichen Entwicklung von den ältesten Zeiten bis auf die Gegenwart*, Gera-Untermhaus: Eugen Köhler, 1891

Deschner, Günter. *Reinhard Heydrich—A Biography of the Man behind the "Final Solution"*, New York: Stein and Day, 1981

Diderot, Denis and d'Alambert, J. de R. (edd.). —"L'escrime" and —"Fourbisseur" in *Encyclopédie méthodique ou dictionnaire raisonné des sciences, des arts, et des métiers*, Paris and Amsterdam, 1751-75
— Paris: Inter-Livres, c. 1985

Dresdner Paukkomment: Bestimmungen zur Regelung schwerer Ehrenhändel, Dresden: A. Dressel, 1912

Dubois, Georges. *Essai sur le traité d'escrime de Saint-Didier publié en 1573,* Paris, 1918

Duffy, John. —"Touche! For fencing pro Oles, thrust never sleeps," in "Lifetimes" section of *Towson Times* (Towson, MD: Patuxent Publishing), Dec. 17, 1997; p. 16

Dumézil, Georges. *Loki,* Darmstadt: Wissenschaftliche Buchgesellschaft, 1959

Durova, Nadezhda and Zirin, Mary Fleming (transl). *The Cavalry Maiden—Journals of a female Russian Officer in the Napoleonic Wars,* London, Glasgow, Toronto, Sydney, Auckland: Paladin Grafton Books, 1988

Eccles, Mark. *Christopher Marlowe in London,* Cambridge, MA: Harvard University Press, 1934

Egil's Saga (see Palsson)

Ellis Davidson, H.R.. *The Sword in Anglo-Saxon England,* Woodbridge: The Boydell Press, 1994

Elton, Hugh. *Warfare in Roman Europe A.D. 350-425,* Oxford: Clarendon Press, 1996

Eule, Andreas Peter (ed.). *Materialien zur Geschichte des Corps Normannia Berlin,* Berlin: Simon Druck, 1992

Evangelista, Nick. *The Encyclopedia of the Sword,* Westport, CT and London, 1995
— *The Art and Science of Fencing,* Indianapolis, IN: Masters Press, 1997
— *Fighting with Sticks,* Port Townsend, WA: Loompanics, 1998

Ewers, Hanns Heinz. —"Armer Freddy" in *Ameisen,* München: Georg Müller Verlag, 1925

Fabricius, Wilhelm. *Ritterliche Waffenspiele: Schwert- und Stockfechten, Bogenschießen, Armbrustschießen, Bau von Übungswaffen,* Stuttgart (Germany): Franckh'sche Verlagsbuchhandlung, 1935

Fare, Malcolm. —"Fencers' foiles, which hit but hurt not," in *Hammerterz Forum,* vol. 3, # 4/vol. 4, #1 (Spring/Summer 1997), p. 5f

Faucitt, William (ed.). *Regulations for the Prussian Cavalry* (London, 1757) New York: Greenwood, 1968

Ferguson, Diane. *USFA Program Book 1992 World Cup Sabre,* Denver, CO: USFA, 1992

Ffoulkes, Charles. *Arms and Armament—An Historical Survey of the Weapons of the British Army,* London: George G. Harrap & Co., 1945

Fiore di Liberi. *Il Fior Battaglia, Duellatorum in armis, sine armis, equester, pedester,* Milano, 1410
— facsimile by Francesco Norvati, 1902

Florio, John (Giovanni). *Second Fruites,* (London: Th. Woodcock, 1591) Delmar, NY: Scholar's Facsimiles and Reprints, 1977

Frevert, Ute. *Ehrenmänner: Das Duell in der bürgerlichen Gesellschaft,* München: C.H. Beck, 1991

Gajkowski, Matthew. *German Squad Tactics in WWII,* n.p.[West Chester, OH?]: privately published, 1995

Galas, S. Matthew. —"The Flower of Battle, An Introduction to Fiore dei Liberi's Sword Techniques," in *Hammerterz Forum,* vol. 2, #3 (Winter 1995/96); p. 18 f
— "Kindred Spirits: The Art of the Sword in Germany and Japan," in *Journal of Asian Martial Arts,* vol. 6, # 3, (1997); p. 20f
— "Johannes Liechtenauer: The Father of German Swordsmanship," in *The Fight Master,*(Las Vegas, NV) Spring/Summer 1998; p. 7f

Garmonsway, G.N. (ed.). *The Anglo-Saxon Chronicle,* London: J.M. Dent & Sons (Everyman's Library), (1953) 1990

Garrett, Maxwell R. and Heinecke, Mary F.. *Fencing*, Boston: Allyn and Bacon, 1971

Gaugler, William. *The History of Fencing: Foundations of Modern European Swordplay*, Bangor, ME: Laureate Press, 1998

Gebhardt, Carl (ed.) *Spinoza—Lebensbeschreibungen und Gespräche*, Leipzig: Verlag Felix Meiner, 1914

Gilbey, John F. *Secret Fighting Arts of the World*, Rutland, VT & Tokyo: Charles E. Tuttle Co., (1963) 1989

Goebel, Julius. *Felony and Misdemeanor: A Study in the History of Criminal Law*, vol 1, (1937) Philadelphia: University of Pennsylvania Press, 1976

Goldsworthy, Adrian Keith. *The Roman Army at War, 100 BC—AD200*, Oxford: Clarendon Press, 1996

Graham, Col. H.. *History of the 16th Light Dragoons (Lancers)*, n.p. (London?), 1912

di Grassi, Giacomo. *His True Arte of Defence*, London, 1594, (see also Jackson)

Griffith, Paddy. *The Viking Art of War*, London: Greenhill Books and Mechanicsburg, PA: Stackpole Books, 1995

Grimmelshausen, Hans Jakob Chrisstoffel. *Der Abenteuerliche Simplicissimus Teutsch*, (1669) München: dtv, 1975

Halliburton, Richard. *Seven League Boots*, Indianapolis: Bobbs-Merrill Co., 1935

Hamilton, John. *The Only Approved Guide Through All the Stages of a Quarrel Containing the Royal Code of Honor; Reflections on Duelling; and the Outline for a Court for the Adjustment of Disputes*, London: Hatchard & Sons; Liverpool: Bentham & Co., and Dublin: Millikin, 1829.

Hammerterz Forum, Baltimore: Hammerterz Verlag, (1994-)

Hanson, Victor David. *The Western Way of War: Infantry Battle in Classical Greece*, New York: Alfred Knopf, 1989

Heck, Johann Georg. *Iconographic Encyclopedia of Science, Literature, and Art*, vol. III, New York: Rudolph Garrigue, 1851

Heither, Dietrich. —"Zu: *Der Corpsstudent*, 1/96" (Letter to the Editor), in *Der Corpsstudent*, Nr. 2/96, 3. Jahrgang (3/1996); p. 92

Hergsell, Gustav. *Die Fechtkunst*, Wien, Pest, Leipzig: A. Hartleben's Verlag, 1881
— *Talhoffers Fechtbuch as dem Jahre 1467*, Prague: self-published, 1887
— Herne (Germany): VS Books, 1998
(This is a simplified reprint of Hergsell's work, incorporating the plates with modern German translation of the text.)
— *Duell-Codex*, Wien, Pest, Leipzig: A. Hartleben's Verlag, 1891

Herodotus and de Sélincourt, Aubrey (transl.). *The Histories*, Harmondsworth, Middlesex and New York: Penguin Books, (1954) 1984

Hewes, Robert. *Rules and Regulations for the Sword Exercise for the Cavalry, to which is added the Review Exercise*, Boston: William Norman, 1802.
— *An Elucidation of Regulations for the Formations and Movements of Cavalry*, Salem, 1804

Hewitt, John. *Ancient Armor and Weapons in Europe*, (Oxford: John Henry & James Parker, 1855) London: Random House, 1996

History of the Highland Regiments, Highland Clans, etc. from Official and other Authentic Sources, Ediburgh: Thomas C. Jack, 1887

Hils, Hans-Peter. *Meister Johann Liechtenauers Kunst des langen Schwertes*, Frankfurt: Peter Lang (Europäische Hochschulschriften, vol. 257), 1985

Hobbes, Thomas. *Leviathan,* (1651), Indianapolis: Bobbs-Merril Educational Publishing, 1958.

Holt, J.C. *Robin Hood,* London and New York: Thames and Hudson, (1982) 1989

Homer and Fitzgerald, Robert (transl). *The Odyssey,* Book xviii, ln. 80-120, New York: Random House Vintage Classics, (1960) 1990

H[ope], Sir W[illiam]. *The Scots Fencing Master,* Edinburgh: John Reid, 1687

Huber, Ted. *Fundamental Swordplay—A Practical Manual for the Foil, Epee, and Sabre,* Ann Arbor, MI: Edwards Brothers, Inc., 1939

Hughes, Thomas. *Tom Brown's Schooldays* (London: Macmillan, 1857), Oxford: Oxford University Press, 1989

Hunnisett, R.F. (ed.). *Thoroton Society,* Record Series, xxv, 1969, #82

Hutton, Sir Alfred. *The Sword and the Centuries,* (London: Grant Richards, 1901) Rutland, VT and Tokyo: Charles E. Tuttle Co., 1973
   — New York: Barnes & Noble, 1995

Jackson, James L. (ed.). *Three Elizabethan Fencing Manuals,* Delmar, NY: Scholar's Facsimiles and Reprints, 1972

Jaques, Darrin W.. —"Thrust vs. Cut: A biomechanical analysis of forces," in *Hammerterz Forum,* vol. 2, #4/vol. 3, #1 (Spring/Summer 1996); p. 6

Jones, Archer. *The Art of War in the Western World,* Urbana, IL & Chicago: University of Illinois Press, 1987

Juvenal and Ramsay, G.G. (transl.). *Juvenal and Persius,* Cambridge, MA & London: Harvard University Press [Loeb Classical Library], (1918) 1990

Kegan, John. *The Face of Battle—A Study of Agincourt, Waterloo, and the Somme,* (London: Jonathan Cape Ltd., 1976) London: Penguin, 1978

Kennet, Basil. *Romae Antiquae Notitia: or, the Antiquities of Rome. In two parts,* London, 1737 (10th ed.)

Kenoyer, Jonathan Mark. —"Thangkairol: Manipuri Sword Fighting of Eastern India," in Kiyota, Minoru and Lee, Jordan (edd.). *Personal Growth through Martial Arts: Studies in Kendo, Fencing, and Indian Swordsmanship,* Madison, WI: Center for South Asia Publications, 1997

Kiernan, V.G.. *The Duel in European History: Honour and Reign of Aristocracy,* Oxford: Oxford University Press, 1989

Klarwill, Victor (ed.) and de Chary, Pauline (transl.). *The Fugger News-Letters,* New York and London: G.P. Putnam's Sons, 1924

Klusmann, Otto Günther. —"Begegnungen im Kriege 1939/45," in *Mitteilungen Hannovera Göttingen,* Göttingen: Corps Hannovera; #83 (August 20, 1990)

Knorre, Erik von. —"Zu: 'Wie war es wirklich?', in *Der Corpsstudent,* 1/96", in *Der Corpsstudent,* Nr. 3, 3. Jahrgang (3/1996); p. 126

Kufahl, Hans see Schmied-Kowarzik

Latham, John Wilkinson. *British Military Swords from 1800 to the Present Day,* New York: Crown, 1966

LeGoff, Jacques. *The Medieval Imagination,* Chicago and London: University of Chicago Press, 1988

Leiber, Fritz. —"Fafhrd and Me," in de Camp, Sprague (ed.). *The Spell of Conan,* New York: Ace, 1980; p. 130

Lochner, Karl E.. *Die Entwicklungsphasen der europäischen Fechtkunst*, Wien: self-published, 1953
— *Waffenkunde für Sportfechter und Waffenliebhaber*, Wien: self-published, 1960

Lonnergan, A.. *The Fencer's Guide*, London: self-published, 1771

Lucian and Harmon, A.M.(transl.). —"Toxaris, or Friendship," in *Works in 8 Volumes*, (vol. v,) Cambridge, MA: Harvard University Press and London: William Heinemann Ltd., [Loeb Classical Library], (1936), 1972

Lurz, Frank. *Duelling: Swordplay and the Wounded Adversary, A Thesis Presented to the Faculty of the Military Fencing Masters Program*, San José, CA: San José State University, 1996

Maclaren, Archibald. *A System of Fencing for the Use of Instructors in the Army*, London: Adjutant-General's Office, Horse Guards, 1864

Magnusson, Magnus and Palsson, Hermann (transl. & edd.). *Njal's Saga*, London and NY: Penguin, 1960

Malory, Sir Thomas. *Morte Darthur*, (London: Caxton, 1485) in Kermode, Frank et al. (edd.). *The Oxford Anthology of English Literature*, (vol. 1,) New York, London, Toronto: Oxford University Press, 1973

Marey-Monge, Guillaume. *Memoire sur les armes blanches*, Strasbourg., 1841
— and Maxwell, Henry Hamilton (transl.). *Memoir on Swords* etc., London: John Weale, 1860

Marshall, S.L.A.. *Men Against Fire*, New York: William Morrow, 1947

Martelli, C. *An Improved System of Fencing, wherein the Use of the Small Sword is Rendered Perfectly Plain and Familiar, Being a Clear Description and Explanation of the Various Thrusts Used with the Safest and Best Methods of Parrying, as Practised in the Present Age. To which is Added a Treatise on the Art of Attack and Defence*, London: J. Bailey, 1819

Martincic, Albert. *Kevey und seine Fechtschule*, Graz (Austria): self-published, 1983

Mashiro, N. *Black Medicine—The Dark Art of Death: The Vital Points of the Human Body in Close Combat*, Boulder, CO: Paladin Press, 1978

Mathewson, Thomas. *Fencing Familiarized; or, a New Treatise on the Art of the Scotch Broad Sword*, Edinburgh?: W. Cowdroy, 1805

Maxwell, Henry Hamilton see Marey-Monge

Megerle, Ulrich (Abraham a Santa Clara). *Centi Folium Stultorum in Quarto, oder Hundert Ausbündige Narren*, Wien: Megerle and Nürnberg: Lercher für Weigel, 1709

Meienreis, Walther. *Säbelfechten*, Leipzig: Grethlein, c. 1913

Musashi, Myiamoto and Kaufman, Steve (transl.). *The Martial Artist's Book of Five Rings*, Boston, Routland, VT, and Tokyo: Charles E. Tuttle Co., 1994

Nadi, Aldo. *On Fencing*, New York: Putnam, 1943
— Sunrise, FL: Laureate Press, 1994
— *The Living Sword*, Bangor, ME: Laureate Press, 1995

Nagy, Laszlo. *Bibliographie des Fechtens*, Graz (Austria): Akademie der Fechtkunst Österreichs, 1987

Nicholson, Lewis E. —"Hunlafing and the Point of the Sword," in Nicholson, Lewis E. and Frese, Dolores Warwick (edd.). *Anglo-Saxon Poetry: Essays in Appreciation*, Notre Dame, IN and London: University of Notre Dame Press, 1975

Nickel, Helmut. —"About the Sword of the Huns and the 'Urepos' of the Steppes," in *Metropolitan Museum Journal*, vol. 7, 1973; p. 131

Njal's Saga see Magnusson

Nolan, Capt. L.E.. *Cavalry: Its History and Tactics,* London, 1854 (2nd ed.)

Oakeshott, R. Ewart. *The Archaeology of Weapons—Arms and Armor from Prehistory to the Age of Chivalry,* New York and London: Frederick A. Praeger, 1960
     — New York: Barnes & Noble, 1995

O'Rourke, Matthew J. *A New System of Sword Exercise, with a Manual of the Sword for Officers, Mounted and Dismounted,* New York: Geo. R. Lockwood, 1873

Ozment, Steven. *Three Behaim Boys—Growing Up in Early Modern Germany,* New Haven, CT and London: Yale University Press, 1990

Pall Mall Gazette, May 25, 1891.

Palsson, Hermann and Edwards, Paul (transl. & edd.). *Egil's Saga,* London and New York: Penguin, 1976

Pardoel, Henk. *The Complete Bibliography of the Art and Sport of Fencing,* Kingston, Ontario: School of Physical and Health Education, Queen's University, 1996

Patton, Lieutenant George. S., Jr. —"Mounted Swordsmanship," in *The Rasp,* 1914
     — Copyright 1996-97, The Patton Society
     (see also *Saber Exercise)*

Pavese, Generoso. *Foil and Sabre Fencing,* Baltimore: Kings Bros., 1905

Pennick, Nigel. *Practical Magic in the Northern Tradition,* Guildford (England): The Aquarian Press, 1989

Perrin, Noel. *Giving Up the Gun: Japan's Reversion to the Sword, 1543-1879,* Boulder, CO: Shambala, 1980

du Picq, Ardant. *Battle Studies,* New York: Macmillan, 1921

Pieper, Peter (Pit). —"Runen," in *Symbole und Zeichen,* Bremerhaven (Germany): Landkreis Cuxhaven, 1991; p. 84f

Plato and Jowett, B. (transl.). *Apology, Crito, Phaedo, Symposium, Republic ,* New York: Walter J. Black, 1942
     — and Fowler, Harold North (transl.). *Euthyphro, Apology, Crito, Phaedo, Phaedrus ,* Cambridge, MA and London: Harvard University Press [Loeb Classical Library], (1917) 1995
     — and Burnet, John (transl.). *Euthyphro, Apology of Socrates and Crito,* Oxford: Oxford University Press, (1924) 1974
     — and Lamb, W.R.M. (transl.). *Lysis, Symposium, Gorgias ,* Cambridge, MA and London: Harvard UP [Loeb Classical Library], (1925) 1991

Pleiner, Radomir. *The Celtic Sword,* Oxford and New York: Oxford University Press [Clarendon Press], 1993

Poliakoff, Michael B. *Combat Sports in the Ancient World: Competition, Violence, and Culture,* New Haven, CT: Yale University Press, 1987

Pollington, Stephen. *The English Warrior from earliest times to 1066,* Hockwold-cum-Wilton (England): Anglo-Saxon Books, 1996

Pothmann, Alfred (ed.). *Das Zeremonialschwert in der Essener Domschatzkammer,* Münster (Germany): Aschendorff, 1995

Procopius and Dewing, H.B. (transl.). *History of the Gothic Wars* Cambridge, MA and London: Harvard University Press [Loeb Classical Library], (1928) 1992

Provisional Regulations for Saber Exercise, United States Army, Washington: Government Printing Office, 1907

Randall-MacIver, David. *The Iron Age in Italy: A Study of these Aspects of the Early Civilization which are neither Villanovian nor Etruscan,* Oxford: Clarendon Press, 1927 Westport, CT: Greenwood Press, 1974

Regan, Geoffrey (ed.). *The Guinness Book of Military Anecdotes,* New York: Canopy Books, 1992

Reinhardt, Hank. —"Hype—As Ancient an Art as Swordmaking," in *Knives '87,* n.p.: DBI Books, 1987
    — special reprint Conyers, GA: Museum Replicas Ltd., n.y. (1987?)

Richardson, Thom. —"China and Central Asia," in Coe, Michael D. (ed.). *Swords and Hilt Weapons,* New York: Weidenfeld & Nicholson, 1989; p. 176f

Ristow, Gustav. *Ehrenkodex,* Wien: Verlag von L. W. Seidel & Sohn, 1912 (2nd ed.)

Ritter-Schaumburg, Heinz. *Die Nibelungen zogen nordwärts,* München and Berlin: F.A. Herbig, 1980
    — *Dietrich von Bern—König zu Bonn,* München and Berlin: F.A. Herbig, 1982

Rondelle, Louis. *Foil and Sabre,* Boston: Dana Estes & Co., 1892

Roux, W. *Anweisung zum Hiebfechten mit geraden und krummen Klingen,* Jena: Verlag von Friedrich Mauke, 1840

Roux, Friedrich August Wilhelm. *Deutsches Paukbuch,* Jena: Mauke, 1867

[Roworth,C.] *The Art of Defence on Foot with the Broad Sword and Sabre Uniting the Scotch and Austrian Methods into one Regular System, to which is added Remarks on the Spadroon,* London: Printed for T. Egerton at the Military Library near Whitehall, 1798

Saber Exercise [by Patton, George S., Jr.], Washington: Government Printing Office, 1914

Santa Clara, Abraham a. see Megerle

Saviolo, Vincentio. *Of Honor and Honorable Quarrels,* London: John Wolfe, 1594
    — *His Practice,* London: John Wolfe, 1595
    — see Jackson

Setter, Jürgen (ed.). *Paukkomments: Eine Materialsammlung,* Erlangen? (Germany): Schriftenreihe der studentengeschichtlichen Vereinigung des CC (# 25), 1986

Schmied-Kowarzik, Josef and Kufahl, Hans. *Fechtbüchlein,* Leipzig: Reclam, 1894
    — *Duellbuch,* Leipzig: J.J. Weber, 1896

Scott, B.G.. *Early Irish Ironworking,* Belfast, 1990

Seitz, Herbert. *Blankwaffen II,* Braunschweig: Klinkhardt & Biermann, 1968

Sieveking, Alfred Forbes (ed.). *Worke for Cutlers, or, A Merry Dialogue betweene Sword, Rapier, and Dagger. Acted in a Shew in the famous Universitie of Cambridge A.D. 1615,* London: C.J. Clay & Sons, 1904

Silver, George. *Paradoxes of Defence,* London: Edward Blount, 1599.
    — London: Oxford University Press (The Shakespeare Association Facsimiles No. 6), 1933.
    — Amsterdam and New York: DaCapo Press, 1968
    — see Jackson.

Smollett, Tobias. *The Adventures of Roderick Random,* (1748), Oxford & New York: Oxford University Press, (1979) 1981

Stadtmüller, Franz et al. *Geschichte des Corps Hannovera zu Göttingen 1809-1959,* Göttingen: Corps Hannovera, 1963

Steele, Sir Richard. *The Spectator,* No. 436, July 21, 1712 in Addison, Steele & others, Smith, Gregory (ed.) *The Spectator, In Four Volumes,* (vol. iii,) London: Dent [Everyman's Library] and New York: Dutton (1907) 1967; p. 348f

Stoqueler, J.H.. *The British Soldier,* n.p. (London?): 1857 (see also Regan)

Stow, John. *The Summarye of the Chronicles of Englande (…)* abridged, London, 1573.
  (see also Berry)

Strobl, Karl Hans. *Der wilde Bismarck,* Leipzig: L. Staackmann Verlag, 1915

Sturlason, Snorri. *Heimskringla, or, The Lives of the Norse Kings,* New York: Dover, 1990.
(First published as Monsen, Erling (ed.). *Heimskringla, or The Lives of the Norse Kings by Snorri Sturlason,* Cambridge: W. Heffer, 1932.)

Sullivan, James E. *Official Sporting Rules Containing the Official Rules for Miscellaneous Games and Contests Not Scheduled in Other Numbers of Spalding's Athletic Library,* New York: American Sports Publishing Co. (A.G. Spalding), 1909

Sutor, Jakob. *Neu Künstliches Fechtbuch,* Frankfurt: Wilhelm Hoffman, 1612
  — Stuttgart (Germany): Verlag v. J. Scheible, 1849
  — Limburg a.d. Lahn (Germany): San Casciano Verlag, 1994

Swetnam, Joseph. *The Schoole of the Noble and Worthy Science of Defence,* London: Nicholas Okes, 1617

Tacitus, Publius Cornelius
— and Hutton, M. (ed. and transl.). *Tacitus, in Five Volumes,* (vol. I,) Cambridge, MA: Harvard UP and London: William Heinemann Ltd., (1914) 1980
— and Goold, G. P. (ed. and transl.). *Tacitus, in Five Volumes,* (vol. III,), Cambridge, MA: Harvard UP and London: William Heinemann Ltd., (1931) 1979

Talhoffer (see Hergsell)

Taylor, John. *The Art of Defence on Foot with the Broad Sword and Sabre: adapted also to the Spadroon, or Cut-and-Thrust Sword,* London: T. Egerton, 1804

Tegner, Bruce. *Self-Defense Nerve Centers and Pressure Points for Karate, Jujitsu and Atemi-Waza,* Ventura, California: Thor Publishing Co., (1968) 1990

Terrone, Leonardo F.. *Right and Left Hand Fencing,* New York: Dodd, Mead, & Co., 1959

Textor, Horst-Ulrich. —"Die Bergakademie Freiberg und das Brauchtum ihrer Studenten (1765-1845)", in *Einst und Jetzt,* vol. 41, München: Verein für corpsstudentische Geschichtsforschung, 1996; p. 234f

Thimm, Carl A.. *A Complete Bibliography of Fencing and Duelling, as Practised by All European Nations from the Middle Ages to the Present Day,* London & New York: John Lane, 1896
— New York: James B. Cummins Bookseller, 1992

Thordemann, Bengt. *Armour from the Battle of Wisby, 1361,* (vol. 1,) Stockholm and Uppsala: Kungl. Vitterhets Historie och Antikvitets Akademien, 1939

Tilmont, R.L., Breed, Geoffrey H., O'Connor, W. Scott (edd. and transl.). *Fencing: Foil, Epee, Sabre, Theory, Methods, and Regulations practiced at the Military School of Joinville le Pont,* New York: The Amateur Fencers League of America, 1915

Turner, Craig and Soper, Tony. *Methods and Practice of Elizabethan Swordplay,* Carbon & Edwardsville: Southern Illinois University Press, 1990

Turner, Sir James. *Pallas Armata. Military Essayes of the Ancient Grecian, Roman, and Modern Art of War*, (London: Richard Chiswell, 1683) New York: Greenwood Press, 1968

Varhola, Michael. —"The Secret History of the Sword," in *Renaissance*, vol. 2, #2 (Issue #6), 1997; p. 50

Veaux, Baron de. *Les duels célebres*, Paris: Éd. Ronveyre, 1884

[Vebell, Edward.] *Sports Illustrated's Book of Fencing*, Philadelphia and New York: J.B. Lippincott Co., 1962

Vegetius Renatus, Flavius and Clark, John (transl.) *On the Military Institutions of the Romans*, Harrisburg, PA: The Military Service Publishing Co., 1944

Verein Alter Corpsstudenten (VAC). *Ehren- and Waffenordnung*, 1937.

Verein Deutscher Fechtmeister. *Deutsche Stoßfechtschule nach Kreußler'schen Grundsätzen*, Leipzig: Verlag von J.J. Weber, 1892

P. Virgilius Maro, *Aeneid*, in Hart, Levi and Osborn, V.R. (edd. and transl.) *The Works of P. Virgilius Maro*, Philadelphia, David MacKay Co. [Classic Interlinear Translations], 1882

Waite, J.M. *Lessons in Sabre, Singlestick, Sabre & Bayonet, and Sword Feats; or, How to use a cut-and-thust sword*, London: Weldon & Co., 1880

Wallechinsky, David. *The Complete Book of the Olympics*, New York: Penguin, 1984

War Department. *Basic Field Manual 21-150: Unarmed Defense for the American Soldier*, Washington, DC: Government Printing Office, June 30, 1942

Ward, Edward. *A Vade Mecum for Malt-Worms*, London, n.y. (c. 1712)

Ward, Geoffrey C., Burns, Ric and Burns, Ken. *The Civil War, An Illustrated History*, New York: Alfred A Knopf, 1990

Wassmannsdorff, Karl. *Aufschlüsse über Fechthandschriften und gedruckte Fechtbücher des 16. und 17. Jahrhunderts*, Berlin: R. Gaertners Verlagsbuchhandlung, 1888
— *Sechs Fechtschulen der Marxbrüder und Federfechter aus den Jahren 1573 to 1614*, Heidelberg: Buchhandlung von Karl Groos, 1870

Wayne, H.C.. *Exercise for the Broad Sword, Sabre, Cut and Thrust, and Stick*, Washington: Gideon & Co., 1849

Weber, R.G.S.. *The German Student Corps in the Third Reich*, New York: St. Martin's Press, 1986

Weinmann, Dr. Wolfgang (ed.). *Chronik alter Kampfkünste*, Berlin: Weinmann (1979), 1990 (4th ed.)

Welle, Rainer. *"...und wisse das alle höbischeit kompt von deme Ringen"—Der Ringkampf als adelige Kunst im 15. und 16. Jahrhundert*, Pfaffenweiler: Centaur, 1993

Wells, William and Norman, A.V.B.. —"An Unknown Hercules in the Burrell Collection," in *The Scottish Art Review*, vol. 8; No. 3, (1962); p. 11 f.

Wenusch, Michael. *Engarde, Parade, Touché: Die Entwicklung des Wiener Fechtsports*, Wien: Wiener Stadt- und Landesarchiv, 1998

Wilberforce, R.G. *An Unrecorded Chapter of the Indian Mutiny*, 1894 (see also Regan)

Wilcox, M. —"Dueling at a German University," unattributable, post-1882; p. 599f, in the author's collection. (Could be identical with "Dueling at Jena University," in *The Hawk*, Feb.2, 1892, as listed in Thimm.)

Wiley, Mark V. *Filipino Martial Arts: Cables Serrada Escrima*, Rutland, VT and Tokyo: Charles E. Tuttle Co., 1994
— *Filipino Martial Culture*, Rutland, VT and Tokyo: Charles E. Tuttle & Co., 1998

Willcock, M.M. *The Iliad of Homer*, London: Macmillan, 1978

Wilson, J. Dover. —"Introduction (Including some speculations on the fencing-match in Hamlet)." in Silver, George. *Paradoxes of Defence*, London: Oxford UP (The Shakespeare Association Facsimiles No. 6), 1933

Wippermann, Wolfgang. —"Wie war es wirklich? Wichtige Daten zum Thema Corps und Nationalsozialismus" in *Der Corpsstudent*, Nr. 1/96, 3. Jahrgang; p. 17
—"Zu: Wie war es wirklich? Wichtige Daten zum Thema Corps und Nationalsozialismus, in *Der Corpsstudent*, 1/96" in *Der Corpsstudent*, Nr. 3, 3. Jahrgang (3/1996); p. 126

Würzburger S.C.-Paukcomment, Würzburg: Universitätsdruckerei von H. Stürtz, 1891

Xenophon.and Brownson, Carleton L. (transl.) *Anabasis*, Cambridge, MA and London: Harvard University Press [Loeb Classical Library], (1922) 1992

Yang, Dr. Jwing-Ming. *Northern Shaolin Sword*, Boston: YMAA, 1985

Bibliographies

Thimm, Carl A.. *A Complete Bibliography of Fencing and Duelling, as Practised by All European Nations from the Middle Ages to the Present Day*, London & New York: John Lane, 1896
— New York: James B. Cummins Bookseller, 1992

Bar none, this is the best, most useful bibliography available. Its only drawback: In ends in 1896.

Nagy, Laszlo. *Bibliographie des Fechtens*, Graz (Austria): Akademie der Fechtkunst Österreichs, 1987

A thorough and hard-to-get kitchen-table production of the Austrian Fencing Academy… produced in extremely poor quality.

Pardoel, Henk. *The Complete Bibliography of the Art and Sport of Fencing*, Kingston, Ontario: School of Physical and Health Education, Queen's University, 1996

Currently the most complete catalog of fencing and swordfighting books, particularly modern editions. Available from Henk Pardoel, School of Physical and Health Education, Queen's University, Kingston, ON K7L 3N6; Canada; e-mail: 3hwmp@qlink.queensu.ca

APPENDIX A

Journals

Hammerterz Forum, *P.O. Box 13448, Baltimore, MD 21203, USA; zoergiebel@aol.com.; 4 issues (1 year) US$35.*

What can I say: I started it, and I still run it. *HF* tries to present the most cutting-edge articles on fencing history, by the Gen-Xers of historical swordfighting research.

The Sword, *1 Baron's Gate, 33 Rothchild Road, London, W4 5HT; England, U.K.; tel. (44-181)742-3032; fax (44-181)742-3033.* Edited by Malcolm Fare, one of the best authorities on fencing literature and the history of modern fencing, this quarterly is the official magazine of British Fencing. Overseas subscriptions (that's us) are £20. Excellent articles on historical systems are more frequently found than in its Yankee cousin.

The Fight Master, *c/o Society of American Fight Directors, Paul Denhardt (SAFD Secretary), 320 South Ward Street, Macomb, IL 61455, USA.*

Published twice a year, you frequently find excellent articles on historical issues, as well as the latest scoop on stage and silver screen fencing. Well worth the US$35 membership fee.

Journal of Japanese Sword Arts, *c/o Kim Taylor, Dept. of Animal and Poultry Science, University of Guelph, Ontario, Canada N1G 2W1; fax (519)836-9873.*

One of our small but growing number of self-motivated, independent little swordfighting publications, Kim Taylor has a broad horizon when it comes to include aspects of Western sword arts. Highly recommended!

Hoplos and Hop-Lite, *c/o International Hoplology Society, 315 Foothills Dr., Sedona, AZ 86336, USA; fax. (520)204-2394; hoplos@aol.com.*

The official letter of the IHS, this is one of the most venerable resources on palaeo-hoplology since its inception by the late Donn Draeger. A bargain at US$25.

Veteran Fencers Quarterly, *3075 Overlook Place, Clearwater, FL 34620, USA; tel.(813)535-3404; fax (813)531-5766.*

The seniors of modern fencing have enough backbone to take refreshingly controversial positions on fencing, with a more pronounced perspective. At US$8, it doesn't get any better.

American Fencing, *c/o United States Fencing Association, Inc., 10 Olympic Plaza, Colorado Springs, CO 80909, USA; http://www.usfa.org.*

Apart from the party line and pages and pages of ranking schedules, *AF* frequently contains extremely worthwhile articles on all aspects of fencing.

Subscriptions for non-members of the USFA are US$12 in the U.S. and US$18 elsewhere. (Subscription is included in US$35 annual USFA membership fee subscribe.

Historic Manuals

Apart from hunting down costly originals, there's just one way to get a wide range of historical fencing and swordfighting manuals: **Patri Jones Pugliese**, *39 Capen St., Medford, MA 02155 USA* has become an institution among sword enthusiasts with Donald Trump research ambitions and a Donald Duck budget. Patri makes dozens of hard-to-get manuals from the 15th to the 20th century available an photocopies...at just about cost!

Weapons and Equipment

Museum Replicas, *2143 Gees Mill Road, Box 840 Conyers, GA 30012, USA; tel.(800)883-8838 or (770)922-7500; musrep@mindspring.com.*

American Fencers Supply, *1180 Folsom Street, San Francisco, CA 94103, USA; tel.(415)863-7911.*

George Santelli, Inc., *465 South Dean Street, Englewood, N.J. 07631, USA; tel. (201)871-3105.*

Triplette Competitions Arms, *162 West Pine Street, Mount Airy, NC 27030, USA; tel.(910)786-5294.*

Blade, *212 West 15th Street, New York. NY 10011, USA; tel.(800)828-5661.*

Sports fencing

The most popular form of fencing today. To find out if there's a club near you, contact the **USFA**, *One Olympic Plaza, Colorado Springs, CO 80909, USA; tel. (719)578-4511, fax (719)632-5737; http://www.usfa.org.*

The best coaches are the toughest. Soft constitutions probably won't be able to stand no-nonsense instructors—but then soft constitutions don't tend to achieve much anyway.

The USFA is as good and as bad as any bureaucracy who's made itself dependent on one major contributor of revenues. If you're not likely to turn into a top-tier fencer, the subscription to *American Fencing* and the ability to participate in tournaments are US$35 well spent.

"Classical Fencing"

There's a sub-stratum of fencing enthusiast who a) don't like the USFA, b) reject modern sports fencing as frivolous, c) have given up on pursuing the athletic challenges of sports fencing, or d) all of the preceding.

They call themselves Classic Fencers, are a scattered bunch, and often appear more interested in getting a credit card with a picture from Domenico Angelo's manual than in anything else.

But there are exceptions: Adam A. Crown's In Ferro Veritas considers itself an association of fencers studying fencing as a martial art rather than a sport. For more information on his program, contact **IFV**, *c/o Adrian A. Crown, 1045 Coddington Road, Ithaca, NY 14850, USA; tel.(607)277-3262; ifv@clarityconnect.com; http://www.clarityconnect.com/webpages/ifv/default.html.*

At its best, Classic Fencing aims at combining proper form and combative elegance with athletic ability—but the true classic fencers don't call themselves such. Here's the cream of the crop.

The San Jose State University Fencing Masters Program was established in 1979 to meet the need in the United States for professionally-trained and certified fencing teachers comparable to Italian and French masters.

There are three levels of certification: Instructor at Arms (6 semester units), Provost at Arms (12 semester units), and Master at Arms (18 semester units). The candidate for the Master at Arms certificate must hold a bachelors degree from an accredited college, as well as a provost's diploma or proof of equivalent professional experience. The written examination for certification is generally held each year in March and the oral and practical examinations in May.

Contact: Dr. William M. Gaugler, *c/o Department of Theater Arts, San Jose State University, One Washington Square, San Jose, CA 95192-0098 USA.*

Nick Evangelista takes a cerebral approach to fencing: "If you don't use your brain, you're only fencing a shadow game, a parody of swordplay. Whichever school you follow—French or Italian—real fencing goes on between your head and your sword hand. If you pay attention to the art of fencing (which is gaining control over your own actions), and the science of fencing (which is learning to interact efficiently and effectively with your opponent), then the sport of fencing (which is getting five touches before the other guy) will take care of itself. Touches, rather than being a product of force and aggression, will simply be a natural by-product of good fencing."

Contact Nick Evangelista, c/o **Evangelista School of Fencing**, *6751 County Road 3850, Peace Valley, MO 565788, USA; tel. (417) 256-0432; ale@townsqr.com; homepage: mail.townsqr.com/ale*

Literature

Gaugler, William M. *The Science of Fencing: A Comprehensive Training Manual for Master and Student; incl. Lesson Plans for Foil, Sabre, and Épée Instruction,* Bangor, ME: Laureate Press, 1997.

– A Dictionary of Universally Used Fencing Terminology, Bangor, ME: Laureate Press, 1997. (Available from Laureate Press, tel.(800)946-2727.)

Evangelista, Nick. *The Art and Science of Fencing*, Indianapolis, IN: Masters Press, 1997. (Available from Masters Press, tel.(800)9SPORTS)

(Nick also recently published an excellent little book on singlestick fighting, combining historical and self-defense techniques: Evangelista, Nick. *Fighting with Sticks*, Port Townsend: Loompanics, 1998. Available from Loompanics, tel. (800)380-2230.)

Rapier fencing

Master Ramón Martinez, (c/o Martinez Classical Fencing and Historical Swordsmanship; tel.(201)330-8670; VKGS28F@prodigy.com) is one of the last masters to teach Spanish rapier, along with Italian rapier, smallsword, saber and épée, in the United States.

Classes are held every Monday and Wednesday from 6-9:30 P.M. in downtown Manhattan, New York City, at Studio KHDT, 330 Brome Street. Also, contact him through his website at http://pages.prodigy.com/kmoser/fencing.htm

Historical armed combat

If historical fencing is all about difference of strong opinion, opinion doesn't get any stronger than at John Clements's **Historical Armed Combat Association**. Check out their website at *www.thehaca.com*.

Schläger fencing

The ancient art of the Haurapier, Hieber, or Schläger is still taught in Germany and Austria, only among all-male duelling student fraternities (*schlagende Verbindungen*). Of all the organizations, the Weinheimer and Kösener Corps are the most accessible to foreigners. The only condition: Active members have to be enrolled at the local university.

Schläger fencing is not taught as a martial art, but as integral part of a collective experience lasting for at least 3 semesters. Corps consider themselves life-long associations of friends. Thus, most Corps will reject people who're just into learning how to fence.

But there are ways. In 1993, my friend Didier Pallanca, a French national living in New York City, managed to negotiate a 6-week stint at the Corps Hannovera in Göttingen, during which he learned the basics of the Schläger and fought his first Mensur. He assures me he's a changed person!

There are two organizations teaching the ancient German weapons: The Akademie der Fechtkunst Deutschlands (AdFD) and the Verband der

Fechtmeister (VdF):

AdFD, c/o *Mike Bunke, Schulstr. 12, D-24867 Dannewerk, Germany; tel.(49-4621)31201; fax(49-4621)31584.*

VdF, *c/o Kurt-Joachim Betz, Meischterstr. 18, D-35043 Marburg, Germany; tel.(49-6421)46600.*

Should you ever feel like trying it, contact me at **Hammerterz Verlag**, *P.O. Box 13448, Baltimore, MD 21203, USA; zoergiebel@aol.com,* before you hop on a plane.